D0926475

Advising Ike

◆ ◆ ◆ ◆ ◆ ◆ ◆ ◆ ◆ ◆ ◆ ◆ ◆ ◆

Advising Ike

The Memoirs of Attorney General

Herbert Brownell

Herbert Brownell

with John P. Burke

Foreword by John Chancellor

University Press of Kansas

© 1993 by Herbert Brownell

All rights reserved

Published by the University Press of Kansas (Lawrence, Kansas
66049), which was organized by the Kansas Board of Regents and is
operated and funded by Emporia State University, Fort Hays State
University, Kansas State University, Pittsburg State University,
the University of Kansas, and Wichita State University

Library of Congress Cataloging-in-Publication Data

Brownell, Herbert, 1904–

Advising Ike : the memoirs of Attorney General Herbert Brownell /
by Herbert Brownell with John P. Burke ; foreword by John Chancellor.

p. ; cm.

Includes index.

ISBN 0-7006-0590-8

1. Eisenhower, Dwight D. (Dwight David), 1890–1969—Friends and
associates.   2. United States—Politics and government—1953–1961.
3. Brownell, Herbert, 1904–   . 4. Attorneys general—United
States—Biography.   I. Burke, John P., 1953–   . II. Title.

E836.B755   1993

973.921'092 — dc20

[B]   92-37584

British Library Cataloguing in Publication Data is available.

Printed in the United States of America

10 9 8 7 6 5 4 3 2 1

The paper used in this publication meets the minimum requirements of the
American National Standard for Permanence of Paper for Printed
Library Materials Z39.48-1984.

To Doris and our children

Joan, Ann, Tom, and Jim

Contents

❖ ❖ ❖ ❖ ❖ ❖ ❖

Contents

Photographs follow page 86

Foreword

The trouble with people like Herbert Brownell is that there are never enough of them to go around. They are always in short supply, these men and women of high intelligence, great common sense, and an almost extrasensory ability to see straight to the heart of a problem. They are indispensable. Organizations cannot run without them; governments depend upon them. There are not enough of them.

They are often reticent to the point of near-invisibility. Such a man is Herbert Brownell, who resigned as a senior official of the U.S. government in 1957. At his final press conference he said he was going home to New York City to be a private citizen, to resume the practice of law. He would not write a book about his colorful experiences as President Eisenhower's attorney general. He would not go on the lecture circuit or appear on television programs. This lack of pretense won the hearts of the reporters, and Brownell's stylish departure from the Department of Justice is remembered by the Washington press corps today. Few cabinet members have ever left town with such unassuming elegance.

We must be thankful now, more than three decades later, that he has set down the story of his life and times. He has much to tell. Brownell was witness to events that changed the lives of all Americans in the last half of the twentieth century, events that changed America's role in the world as well as changing its domestic politics, race relations, law, and ultimately, quality of life.

The United States was mainly a country of two-lane roads and cities centered around railroad stations when the Eisenhower administration came to power. There was no interstate highway system as we know it today, and therefore no shopping malls, extended suburbs, or edge cities. There was no rock and roll, no credit cards, no diet drinks, and no computers. Four out of five homes had no television sets.

American politics in 1952 was still an old-fashioned, handshaking enterprise of face-to-face campaigning, rallies, motorcades, and torchlight parades. Presidential campaigns had not yet become duels of television advertising. The Democratic party was still supremely powerful in the states of the old Confederacy, and the moderate wing of the Republican party, headed by Thomas E. Dewey, was still the dominant force in the party, although it was under growing attack from Senator Robert Taft and the conservative wing.

Black Americans were still forced to live under the "separate but equal" conditions of racial segregation upheld in the *Plessy v. Ferguson* Supreme Court decision of 1896. In the five decades of the twentieth century there had been no civil rights law passed by Congress, and the United States was becoming a place of increasing racial tension.

All these factors would change during Dwight Eisenhower's presidency, as would the country's position in world affairs. And for five of the Eisenhower years, Herbert Brownell was one of the president's most important advisers.

When he was a young lawyer in Manhattan, Brownell had already developed the skills that would make him a grand master among political operatives. He had a sharp memory for names and faces, skill in argument, a sense of humor, and a fundamental love of the intricacies of politics. In 1932, he was elected to the New York State Assembly, representing a district in Greenwich Village. He was only twenty-eight years old, and a Republican, but he prevailed despite the nationwide Democratic landslide that swept Franklin Roosevelt into the White House that year. Brownell served in Albany until 1937, and one wonders how far this intelligent and attractive young fellow might have gone had he decided to stay in politics and run for higher office.

Instead, he became a master of the organizational complexities of presidential politics. His friend Thomas E. Dewey, elected governor of New York in 1942, made him a member of his "kitchen cabinet," and Brownell became Dewey's ambassador to politicians and political reporters across the United States. When Dewey became the Republican candidate for president in 1944, he asked Brownell to become chairman of the Republican National Committee.

The Republican nominee in 1944 was stiff and formal, a short man who favored dark suits and large Homburg hats. Brownell writes: "Dewey at this point in his career had not developed the geniality in public appearances that characterized his later years. His physical appearance was also a little off-putting." It seems that the famous Dewey mustache was a problem. Mrs. Dewey insisted that it remain, but in the newsreels of that pretelevision era, according to Brownell, "the black mustache loomed out of proportion and made Dewey look like a villain." The candidate's appearance led to the celebrated remark by Alice Roosevelt Longworth that Dewey looked "like the groom on the wedding cake." (Mrs. Longworth later denied making that comparison, declaring, "I never said it. I wish I had.")

There was a grim side to the 1944 Dewey-Roosevelt campaign, and it involved the president's health. Brownell gives us details, from inside the Dewey campaign, on the Republican view of President Roosevelt's health—they all believed it was very bad. Brownell says the campaign had information that the president had made numerous secret trips to Bethesda Naval Hospital under an assumed name. A dispute arose within Dewey headquarters over whether or not the candidate should make Roosevelt's health a public issue, and Dewey said he would not. There were some dramatic moments in the 1944 election, but it was in no way as suspenseful as the 1948 Dewey-Truman struggle, in which the manager of the Republican campaign was, again, Herbert Brownell.

Brownell's memoir is haunted by the growing civil war in the Republican party between the moderates, led by Dewey, and the conservatives, led by Senator Taft, the latter the son of President William Howard Taft, who had lost a savage fight to Theodore Roosevelt's Republican moderates in 1912. Of Robert Taft, his enemies said he had the best mind in Washington "until he made it up." He was called "Mr. Republican," had presidential ambitions, and was the leader of the party's conservatives. Brownell says, "Dewey was not the kind of Republican they wanted at the head of the party when it regained the White House." The last Republican president had left the Oval Office in 1933. This was 1948.

There were many reasons for Harry Truman's microscopic margin of victory that year, but the main reason, according to Brownell, was "the short-sighted actions of the Republicans in Congress." The Republicans who controlled the Eightieth Congress had been stingy with money for grain-storage facilities in farm states, and when agricultural prices fell by nearly 50 percent in the fall of 1948, there were not enough silos to store the excess supply. Farmers had to unload their crops at disastrously low prices. Truman blamed the problem on the Republicans, and Dewey had no response because Truman's charge was true. The farmers voted Democratic, and several key states went for Truman. Thus, Brownell argues, the congressional wing of the Republican party, dominated by conservatives, lost the 1948 presidential election. The popular view of that election is that "Give 'em hell" Harry Truman came from behind and, with grit and pluck, won it for the Democrats. Brownell says the Republicans lost it.

Four years later, Brownell was one of many moderate Republicans who wanted Dwight Eisenhower to run for president. Eisenhower was then supreme commander of NATO and was scrupulously avoiding politics, even though Henry Cabot Lodge, Thomas E. Dewey, and Ike's old battle-field comrade, Lucius D. Clay, were actively organizing on his behalf. Brownell, who had manged two presidential campaigns and had served as Republican national chairman, was the most experienced politician in this group. He was sent on a secret mission to Paris in early 1952, under an assumed name, to meet with the general—the name Brownell did not appear on Eisenhower's official appointment list.

Eisenhower told him he had offered a deal to Senator Taft: Support the views of the internationalist wing of the party and I will not challenge you for the presidential nomination. Eisenhower said Taft had declined. Brownell told the general that Taft already had the support of 40 percent of the delegates to the Republican convention and if Eisenhower wanted the nomination, he would have to fight for it. Eisenhower seemed surprised. The two men talked alone, without interruption, for ten hours. Eighteen days later, Eisenhower resigned as supreme commander and came home to start his political career.

I was one of the reporters covering the Republican National Convention in Chicago in 1952. It was in many ways the last of the classic conventions, with flair and color, parades and demonstrations, and an outcome that was by no means certain. Senator Taft controlled the machinery of the convention. Herbert Hoover and General Douglas MacArthur, both speakers at the convention, supported Taft. Most of the state delegations from the South were for Taft.

Standing against this array of power were the popularity of Eisenhower and the experience of Herbert Brownell. Brownell was not the campaign manager; his association with two Dewey defeats ruled that out. He was, however, the commander in chief of the Eisenhower forces. A long battle was fought between the Taft and Eisenhower armies at that convention. There was savage backwoods warfare about party rules and the seating of the rival delegates. One by one, the Taft strong points fell. There were fistfights on the convention floor. In the end, the way was cleared for Eisenhower's nomination on the first ballot. General Brownell had won the battle. It is worth wondering if General Eisenhower understood how it had been won. I have covered twenty national party conventions and hardly any were as politically complicated as the Republican one in 1952.

When the two men dined alone the night of their victory, Eisenhower was surprised, again, when Brownell told him he had the power to choose his running mate. The following morning, a meeting of party elders met to help Ike pick a vice-presidential candidate. Tom Dewey forcefully proposed one man who was accepted by the group and by Eisenhower: a thirty-nine-year-old, first-term senator from California, Richard M. Nixon. When the convention ended, Brownell went back to New York and the practice of law.

Two months later, Nixon was in deep trouble because of his "secret fund." His California supporters had privately contributed $18,000, ostensibly to pay his incidental expenses, and Nixon, who was in the middle of a presidential campaign, hadn't told anyone about it. According to Brownell, Eisenhower was close to throwing Nixon off the ticket; Dewey, his sponsor, told Nixon to resign; General Clay seemed to want him shot at dawn. But Nixon made his famous "Checkers" speech on national television, one of the classic mea culpa performances of all time, and he wasn't fired. Instead, Brownell was hired—again. He had been brought in to advise on the Nixon mess, and Eisenhower asked him to stay on as his personal representative at campaign headquarters. When the votes were counted, Eisenhower had won 442 votes in the electoral college to Adlai Stevenson's 89.

Eisenhower asked Brownell to be his chief of staff. Brownell said he'd spent twenty-five years as a lawyer and wanted to spend another twenty-five years practicing law. The president-elect responded, "Well, how about being attorney general?" And it was done.

It is tempting to wonder if Brownell's intelligence and great common sense could have been put to use in other causes. He has been so good at most of the things he has done in his life that it is easy to think of him as a risk-free genius automaton. But I think this view misses the character of the man and the lesson of his career. Herbert Brownell believes that some things are decisively important. He believes in political moderation, in a constructive role for the United States in the world, in the uses of the law to protect human rights, and in the value of government as a positive force in life. He expresses those beliefs in this book. He is a partisan man and a quintessential Republican, but he doesn't believe that extremism in the pursuit of liberty is no vice. He would not have leased his high IQ to Robert Taft or Barry Goldwater, a fact that makes Herbert Brownell different from many of the high-IQ advisers in American politics today. Too many of them are able to work different sides of the street for fun and profit, political androgynes with no fixed beliefs. Not Herbert Brownell.

That is why he was an ideal colleague for Eisenhower, who was another moderate. My favorite Eisenhower story, told in this memoir by Brownell, is about the choice of a justice of the Supreme Court. One day Ike told Brownell that the next nominee to the Court should be a Democrat, because his previous nominees had been Republicans. The president said the Supreme Court belonged to all the people and that Democrats ought to know they've got a friend on it. Brownell went out and found a qualified judge on the New Jersey Supreme Court named William J. Brennan, and as a justice of the Supreme Court, Brennan served with great distinction for more than thirty years—because Eisenhower believed the Court belonged to all the people. That kind of comity has been drained out of our national government, but its existence earlier makes it a pleasure to read these memoirs.

Brownell had a distinguished career as attorney general, and a front-row seat at some famous dramas. He watched the downfall of Senator Joe McCarthy, and he makes the case for Eisenhower's hands-off public attitude in that affair. Ike was not always above the battle with McCarthy. When McCarthy attacked the U.S. Army a year after the 1952 election, Eisenhower moved against McCarthy in public and in private. Millions of people watched the Army-McCarthy hearings on television, and the senator looked like an unshaven monster. The Republican Senate leadership wanted the cameras shut off, but the White House suggested they be kept on. At one famous moment, Joseph Welch, the lawyer representing the army said: "Until this moment, Senator, I think I had never gauged your cruelty or your recklessness. . . . Have you no sense of decency sir, at long last? Have you left no sense of decency?" Welch became an instant national celebrity. He had gotten his assignment as counsel for the army through the White House, having been recommended by Tom Dewey. Six months after this episode, McCarthy was "condemned" by a Senate vote of 67 to 22. Eisenhower has been widely criticized for not moving in a more public way against McCarthy, but Brownell argues that any other strategy would only have built McCarthy up.

There were, in my view, several Eisenhowers in the Oval Office at the same time. There was "the general," who told Brownell, "If you have to use force, use overwhelming force and save lives." The General Eisenhower accepted an armistice in the Korean War, sent federal troops into Little Rock and U.S. Marines into Lebanon. The General Eisenhower warned the country, in his farewell address, about the military-industrial complex. There was the international statesman Eisenhower, who acted swiftly against old allies in the Suez Crisis and made sweeping disarmament proposals in the United Nations.

And there was the timid Eisenhower, who moved with glacial caution on civil rights, always seeking to placate the conservatives, always seeking a safe middle way on contentious domestic issues. Journalists tended to criticize the timid Eisenhower, but another theory of his presidency is emerging in the work of historians who show that he exercised a powerful unseen influence on government. I have read persuasive evidence of that theory.

Still, the great man was so innocent in the ways of American politics that he once suggested his brother Milton might be a suitable running mate in the 1956 presidential election. This proposal was received by a stupefied party leader and instantly dropped.

Brownell deals with all of those things, and many more, in this panoramic memoir. There were more adventures after he went home to New York from Washington., He lived an exciting life, and he practiced law for sixty-two years before starting to wind down.

His discretion and his good manners are legendary, but I think he sometimes carries modesty too far. One of the best things ever said about Herbert Brownell was written by Dwight Eisenhower in his diary on May 14, 1953, when he was president and Brownell was attorney general. Here it is, in full.

"Herb Brownell. Here is a man with long experience in politics, especially in the conduct of political campaigns. It would be natural to suppose that he would become hardboiled, and that the code by which he lives could hardly be classified as one of high moral quality. The contrary seems to be true—certainly he has never suggested or proposed to me any action which could be considered in the slightest degree dishonest or unethical. His reputation with others seems to match my own high opinion of his capabilities as a lawyer, his qualities as a leader, and his character as a man. I am devoted to him and am perfectly confident that he would make an outstanding president of the United States."

Herbert Brownell did not include this extraordinary tribute in his memoir, so I thought I'd put it here.

John Chancellor
Nantucket Island
September 30, 1992

Acknowledgments

I wish to express, first and foremost, my admiration for the scholarship and literary skill of my coauthor, John P. Burke. He has made the writing of these memoirs a most enjoyable joint enterprise.

My children, to whom this volume is dedicated, have encouraged me to write this account and have furnished many constructive suggestions for its content; I am indebted also to J. Lee Rankin, to David Brownell, and to Professor Thomas Greene of the University of Michigan Law School, as well as to my brother Philip C. Brownell, for their helpful editorial critiques.

My longtime secretary, Margaret Callaghan, spent many hours on the manuscript, and I appreciate her diligence and loyalty through the years. I also wish to express my deep appreciation to my literary agents, Fifi Oscard and Kevin McShane; to my editor, Michael Briggs; and to my copy editor, Claire Sutton, for their guidance and interest in the preparation of this book.

Finally, these memoirs do not purport to be a documented history. They represent my recollection of events in which I participated together with some background to illuminate those events. I realize (and trust that the reader will understand) that these memoirs, centered as they are on my personal experiences and perceptions, minimize the contributions of others—parents, teachers, family, and colleagues—to the events described.

Herbert Brownell
New York City
August 1992

1

Early Years

❖ ❖ ❖ ❖ ❖ ❖ ❖ ❖ ❖ ❖ ❖ ❖ ❖ ❖ ❖ ❖

The summer of 1924 marked an important—and in some ways prescient—point of transition in my life. Yale had accepted me for admission to its school of law, and with my brother Samuel Brownell, then in the midst of graduate study at Yale, I bought a thirdhand Model T Ford and made my first trip across the country as we journeyed from our home in Nebraska to New Haven. We were on a tight budget as we traveled eastward, staying in fraternity houses for free lodging along the way and taking our meals at the cheapest establishments we could find. Our old Model T was often no match for the unpaved roads travelers then encountered in many places, but our youthful excitement more than made up for any difficulties we experienced en route.

As I reflect on that journey, I recall not only the lively memories of travel with my brother but also the curious way it was to anticipate the course of my life. Our deliberately circuitous route took us through Washington, D.C., and New York City, places that would figure prominently in my life in the years to come. We arrived in Washington on Armed Services Preparedness Day, and after locating cheap accommodations—a dollar a night—at an old hotel near Union Station, my brother and I strolled down Pennsylvania Avenue to see the usual sights. Near the White House we came across a large but empty reviewing stand that President Coolidge and his cabinet would soon occupy to review the Armed Services Preparedness Day parade. We stood on the curbstone across the street to catch a glimpse of the president and his party, and after several hours they arrived. I recall in particular noting the presence of Coolidge's attorney general, who was seated almost directly opposite from where I stood.

Little did I realize that one day I would occupy the great office that he then held.

Nor, as we drove through New York City, did I sense that this great metropolis would become the center of my political and legal career. When our car broke down in the middle of Times Square—a harrowing experience even then—I could not have foreseen that nearby were many places that would loom large in my life: Wall Street, where my law practice would be located for many years; Greenwich Village, which would mark my entrance into the electoral arena; Gramercy Park, where I would spend many happy years with my wife and family; the Roosevelt Hotel, where I would plan political strategy with Gov. Thomas E. Dewey; the Commodore Hotel, where a group of us would later convene to draft General Eisenhower for the presidency and where the president-elect would hold his first cabinet meeting; and Columbia University, where, to my astonishment, Eisenhower would one day ask me to become his attorney general.

Times Square and the curbstone on Pennsylvania Avenue were a long way from the little Nebraska community of Peru, on the banks of the Missouri River, where I was born in 1904. My mother and father had settled there after coming from upstate New York in 1891. My father, originally from Little Compton, Rhode Island, grew up in Madison County, not far from Utica, New York, and my mother was from Chenango County, in the southern tier of the state near Binghamton. My father attended Oswego Normal School, a teachers college now part of the State University of New York system, and Colgate Academy. My mother often recounted that she had greatly desired to go to college but that whatever funds were available for higher education went to send her brother to college and law school. Her father instructed her at home—after a year or so at Houghton Seminary—in the Greek and Roman classics and the Bible. Her family had strong connections to Hamilton College: My great uncle who served as U.S. attorney general went there, and my mother's family was reputed to have produced graduates of Hamilton in almost every generation in the college's early history. I later received an honorary degree from Hamilton, so I, too, can count myself an alumnus of that institution.

My father first taught high school at a place called Deansboro, near Utica, but he was soon offered a position as a professor of science at the Nebraska State Normal School, a teachers college in Peru. He specialized in training teachers of high school rank to teach the physical sciences such as physics, chemistry, and astronomy. The campus, known as the Campus of 1,000 Oaks, lay in the country abutting the river, and from the hilltops one could see Iowa, Missouri, and Kansas on a clear day. And there were many clear days in that dry country adjacent to the long flat plains of central and western Nebraska.

One of my chief recollections of early childhood in Peru is the wonderment of looking through the telescope in the astronomy observatory as my father described the stars and constellations in the evening sky. Later, through my high school and college years, he taught at home and in the classroom the importance of respecting "the scientific method" (experiment, observation, deduction, hypothesis, and verification) when pursuing the mysteries of life and of the universe in the laboratory and observatory.

In 1910 the family moved to the state capital at Lincoln, where my father became a professor at the Teachers College of the University of Nebraska, a land-grant state university. He was a popular professor among the aspiring teachers as well as the author of a number of textbooks and manuals on the teaching of science. Somehow, he and my mother managed to put their seven children through the university on a salary that, though larger than the one in Peru, did not permit much beyond the necessities of life, especially during the Great Depression of the early 1930s.

Despite these limits, our home had a well-stocked library of the classics, a luxury of sorts on which my parents insisted. There were a few books, mysterious to me, in Latin and Greek, which had come from my grandfather, the Reverend Samuel Miller, a Civil War veteran who could speak and write in both those languages. On the living room table were the *Springfield* [Mass.] *Republican*, *Harper's*, *Century*, and *Scribner's* magazines (with mysteries by S. S. Van Dyne), the *World's Work*, the *Literary Digest*, and the *Youth's Companion*, the last a religious magazine for young people. Lytton Strachey was the favorite current biographer, and I remember my mother reading aloud to my father from his biographies as well as from the writings of the early New England poets and authors.

The home I remember best was a frame house my parents rented during my teens on a spacious corner lot in east Lincoln. I say spacious because, although the house itself was not large by any means, I remember helping my father and older brother in subzero weather shovel the deep winter snows off seemingly endless sidewalks. Father was an avid gardener and tended the flowers, the rose arbor, and the vegetable garden.

He trimmed the spreading maple trees and cleaned the debris from a walnut tree that produced choice nuts, which we children cracked with a hammer and devoured. We had no family car in those days and walked a mile or so each way to school and college. Our entertainment was centered in the home. With so many brothers and sisters, someone was always available for a game of cards, although we never could play on Sunday—at least with my parents' knowledge—since it was a day reserved for church meetings and Sunday school.

My father saw to it that we did household chores and had part-time jobs that kept us busy. When we moved from the largely rural area of Peru to Lincoln we took along the family cow, Peggy, and for some years I earned my allowance by milking the cow and selling the extra milk to neighbors. We also had a large garden, and my parents let me sell the extra produce to our neighbors. Later I supplemented these sources of spending money by delivering newspapers for the *Nebraska State Journal*.

My mother was an especially important inspiration for my later involvement in the affairs of the community and the nation. She was active in the University Faculty Club, the Congregational church (which we attended regularly), the YWCA, and various literary societies. She was an ardent "dry" and wore the white ribbon of the Women's Christian Temperance Union, so there was never any liquor in our house. Nor was tobacco permitted; she was ahead of her time in pointing out the dangers in smoking cigarettes. She had a beautiful voice and sang in an amateur light-opera group. She often took me to hear the best singing in town, the choir at the local black church. The family piano was stocked with sheet music that my mother and sisters played, mostly vocal accompaniments, college songs, Civil War melodies, and classical pieces. Even now, while shaving and without forethought, I often find myself humming tunes I picked up in those early days.

My parents' conversation in our home oftentimes centered on their families, friends, and acquaintances in upstate New York and on political affairs there. My mother had been courted, before she met my father, by one of the Republican state leaders, and she had spent a year living with relatives in New York City, where her uncle was a judge in the New York City courts. As an adolescent, I was aware of figures in New York politics such as Roscoe Conkling and Harvey Hinman as well as of the battles that raged among the various political factions in the state. Thus, as I grew up, I felt that upstate New York was a part of my life. This background would stand me in good stead later in life: when I went to the New York legislature I had more of a background than I would otherwise have had in understanding how politics, especially Republican party politics, operated in New York State.

My rather precocious interest in politics was furthered by a hobby I developed as a child of collecting the pictorial calling cards that candidates then used to hand out; I once had hundreds of them. I learned about the offices they were running for, their party affiliation, their stands on the issues, and what they looked like. I recall even telling my parents at times whom they should vote for, although I doubt if they ever followed my advice.

World War I was also at the center of our interests in those years. I read the war news aloud to my father every morning while he drank his coffee. He kept a large map of Europe at hand and had the battle lines marked on it with colored pins. Every day he changed the pins to show the advances and reverses of the British, French, and U.S. forces.

I also remember that President Woodrow Wilson's director of propaganda, George Creel, was attempting at the time to arouse hatred for the kaiser and his army. As a result, the Nebraska legislature launched an investigation into alleged pro-German influence by certain members of the faculty of the state university. It was conducted in a Joe McCarthy style, employing demeaning and irresponsible tactics with which I became all too familiar in later years. We were outraged when our landlord, a professor of German at the university, was interrogated by the committee and found to be "tainted" because he had been born in Germany and taught the German language to American students. His house was smeared with yellow paint by unknown persons during the course of the "hearings."

This early revelation about the fragile nature of individual liberty was powerfully reinforced during a trip to Europe in 1932. By chance one day I was in Darmstadt, Germany, and outside the hotel where I was staying a large crowd had gathered to hear Hitler speak. For several hours he shouted and screamed at the top of his voice yet somehow established a magnetic bond with the crowd. As I walked about among the audience, I found this performance, especially its effect on those assembled, quite chilling. Later, in Rome, I heard Mussolini make one of his speeches (and during the 1950s I had a chance to hear a radio address by Nasser). Those dramatic demagogues helped me formulate my ideas about the differences between our government and dictatorships, even dictatorships that seem to have some measure of popular support, and about the dangers that certain types of leaders can pose even within democracies. The ability to tap latent prejudices and appeal to hate is the common link among them.

We have had great orators in the course of our own history. I can remember going to hear the celebrated speeches of Nebraska's three-time presidential candidate, William Jennings Bryan. A magnetic personality, he drew big crowds, but he had a different kind of appeal. He would denounce Wall Street, the bankers, and the railroad interests—powerful, populist concerns. But unlike the Hitlers or the Mussolinis, he never played on people's hatred or prejudice.

The Lincoln, Nebraska, of my boyhood taught me enduring lessons about the kind of healthy political debate that is a vital and necessary component of a democracy, and it also offered a unique setting for a young man who was attracted to the world of politics. Not only did we have William Jennings Bryan, but we also had his brother, Charles W. Bryan, who was the mayor of Lincoln and later a candidate for vice-president. Charles Dawes, who became Coolidge's vice-president, lived there for some years as did Gen. John J. Pershing, the American commander in World War I. George Norris, an outspoken progressive, was a prominent Nebraska politician and later its U.S. senator. Although Lincoln was a fairly conservative community, Norris enjoyed strong support among the university faculty. Many of my father's friends and colleagues on the faculty who came into our home were ardent Norris supporters, and the ideas of the Progressive movement were frequently the central topic of dinner-table conversations and other social occasions. The parents of Ted Sorensen (later President Kennedy's legal counsel and speech writer) were also active on the local political scene and supporters of Norris.

Lincoln was also a popular stopping point for politicians from out of state. The politics of the day presented numerous opportunities to see candidates and other political notables firsthand and to experience the challenge of different political ideas and the thrill of political competition—activities we have largely lost in the media-dominated politics of today. I would always go down to the railroad station and listen to William Borah, Idaho's powerful senator, when he came to town. The whistle-stop campaigns of the presidential candidates would regularly visit Lincoln. I don't know where I got the yen to do it—it was that early in my life—but I recall Woodrow Wilson and Charles Evans Hughes coming through in the

1916 campaign as well as Wilson's later tour to garner support for the League of Nations. I also developed an interest in the local candidates, and in college I was given my first real political job—and made a bit of spending money doing it—preparing advertising blurbs for a Republican candidate for governor, Adam McMullen. Political involvement had become an avocation by the time I left Nebraska for the East, and when I came to New York to begin my legal career, I quickly became involved in a civic movement to oust Tammany Hall from control of the city government. I got right into it, and I guess I thought everyone did!

The student population at the University of Nebraska revealed that Nebraska was a melting pot of many nationalities. The majority were from families who had lived in the United States for many years, families who had moved from Illinois, Ohio, Minnesota, and from farther east. Almost no one, however, came from the southern states. But there were many newly arrived Scandinavians, a sizable community of German farmers, and some Russians and Armenians. And Czechs—then called Bohemians—furnished most of the tackles and guards on the famous Cornhusker football teams.

Gone from the state itself, of course, were the pioneers; the Native Americans had been placed on reservations by the U.S. Army. The Mormons, after a brief stop in the state, had moved farther west. But there were a few small bands of dissidents: itinerant hoboes who traveled from town to town by freight trains and the unemployed members of the radical IWW (International Workers of the World).

I lived at home until graduation from the university. In those days the tuition at the state university for in-state students was practically free—the only out-of-pocket expenses were the cost of textbooks and a student-activities fee of ten to twenty dollars a semester. To pay for my education and other expenses, I held part-time jobs. I was employed for a while as a janitor in a Lincoln Congregational church. I also worked for the University Publishing Company selling school supplies. Also, the firm took promissory notes from school districts in payment for the supplies the districts would purchase—usually the districts were short of cash—and my job was to peddle these notes to private investors in the Lincoln community. I not only made money but also learned a lot of Nebraska geography.

Through high school and college I took part in many extracurricular activities in journalism and debate. Outstanding in my recollection was the year I was editor-in-chief of the *Daily Nebraskan,* the university's student newspaper popularly called "the Rag." I also was a member of Sigma Delta Chi, the national journalistic honor society. During my senior year, I taught journalism at Doane College at Crete, Nebraska. Then, too, I enjoyed membership in the Innocents, the men's senior honorary society at the university, and in Phi Beta Kappa, the national scholastic honor society. Years later when I returned to the campus as attorney general of the United States to give the commencement address, I was awarded an honorary Ph.D. degree from the university. The governor of Nebraska also honored me in later life by bestowing membership in the mythical "Nebraska Navy."

During my second year in college, I joined a Greek-letter fraternity, Delta Upsilon, and my undergraduate social life centered on the fraternity. I became president of the local chapter and many years later served as president of Delta Upsilon International and of its affiliate DU Educational Foundation.

Because I wasn't much of an athlete I settled for very amateurish tennis. I wasn't much of a soldier either but did end up with the rank of acting sergeant at the end of a compulsory course in the Reserve Officers Training Corps (ROTC). My first major trip outside of Nebraska, except for visits to relatives in upstate New York, came during my college years when I was a guest of the Edgar A. Burnett family at their cottage in Estes Park, Colorado. Burnett was chancellor of the university and made a lasting impression there by starting the University Foundation for donations from graduates and friends—now immensely successful. His son Knox Burnett and I were classmates, and together we climbed Longs Peak and adjacent summits in the Rocky Mountains.

It was a toss-up between a legal career and journalism when I graduated from the University of Nebraska at age twenty. The decision was made when I received a much-needed scholarship grant from Yale Law School that together with a loan from my father (repaid with 6 percent interest) financed my law school years. Yale's generosity marked an important turn in my life: Without the scholarship I might have pursued a career in journalism.

Life at Yale was relatively spartan; my finances did not allow much in the way of extravagance. I could not afford to live in the subsidized dormitories near Hendrie Hall, finding quarters instead in cheaper boarding houses near the campus. I took most of my meals at the university commons, where I was relieved to find I could get by on one dollar a day.

I must confess that I really didn't know what I was getting into when I went to law school. I had no idea whether I would like it, but I took to it like the proverbial duck to water and never had any second thoughts after I got started. My favorite subject was constitutional law taught by Prof. Edwin M. Borchard. Unlike other legal subjects, constitutional law meshed with my interests in history and government (so too with my other favorite courses: administrative law and international law), and Borchard emphasized precisely these themes in understanding the development of constitutional interpretation. He would challenge us especially to think about the interrelationship between personality and constitutional issues, inviting us to ask, for example, to what extent the development of constitutional law can be traced to the personalities of the presidents and the justices involved in the great disputes that mark its history. Later on, when I was a member of the New York legislature, I collaborated with Professor Borchard in obtaining the passage of a trail-blazing law that provided for government compensation to persons wrongfully convicted of a crime. I also helped another faculty member—Karl Llewellyn—in the passage of a uniform commercial code for the state.

My association with other members of the Yale faculty also continued over the years. Dean Thomas W. Swan became a judge of the U.S. Court of Appeals, Second Circuit, and introduced me at the time of my first appearance as attorney general before the Judicial Conference of the United States. One of his successors as dean, Charles E. Clark, invited me to join the Yale Law School faculty in 1929. Clark had written a book on code pleading, and I wrote one of the chapters, on the joinder of parties, for him. His son, Elias Clark, later became the master at Silliman College at Yale and selected me to become one of the college's fellows, a position I still enjoy.

During my second year in law school I was named editor- in-chief of the *Yale Law Journal*, a post that was the culmination of my formal legal education. I wrote notes for the journal as well as editing it, which enabled me to develop skills in legal research under the close supervision of a faculty member. As editor-in-chief I canvassed the field in search of topics that were of current interest in the law, giving me a broader perspective than I would ordinarily have had just from my classwork. I also developed lifelong friendships with my coeditors on the journal: Homer Surbeck, Frederick Sheffield, and James P. Hendrick.

Two other individuals who would later rise to prominence in public life were members of my law school class: Estes Kefauver and Brian McMahon. Both men would later become Democratic members of the United States Senate, Kefauver from Tennessee and McMahon from Connecticut. My earlier law school association with Kefauver, however, did not leave me immune from his senatorial criticism when we both were later serving in Washington. On one occasion, he accused me of not prosecuting a conflict-of-interest case involving the controversial Dixon-Yates project, a matter related to the Tennessee Valley Authority in his home state. He tried to turn the baseless charges into a new Teapot Dome scandal, but I refused to testify before his committee as long as his allegation was unsubstantiated. Kefauver could not produce the evidence; the committee then voted that the charge was baseless, and I proceeded to testify.

Robert Hutchins was an especially interesting figure on the faculty during my law school years. When I was leaving Yale to begin law practice in New York, he introduced me at the annual law school banquet as the "iron hand in the velvet glove," and in 1930 he offered me a position on the University of Chicago Law School faculty, where he had just become president. At Yale, Hutchins was regarded as a dynamic but cynical fellow. He was amusing to the law students, many of them only a few years younger than he was; they laughed at his jokes. He was boyish in appearance, almost one of us. His relative youth, however, was a bit deceiving. Born in 1899, only five years my senior, Hutchins had joined the law faculty in 1925, immediately following his own graduation. Within three years he had risen from instructor to dean, achieving that post at the age of twenty-eight, a feat matched only by his appointment as president of the University of Chicago in 1929 at the ripe old age of thirty.

I got to know Hutchins well during my year as editor of the law review since he was a faculty adviser. An iconoclast in many ways, he was challenging; he didn't accept anything just because it was orthodoxy, a view new to me. I started in law school with a conventional view of life: I didn't go to Yale to change the world; I went to see how the world worked and how I could fit into it "as it was," an important distinction. Thus, as I entered law school, I didn't have any of the interests for political reform that I would develop later in life. Like Borchard, Hutchins challenged this cast of mind and encouraged me to think that things could be changed and for the better. And, if one didn't act, things would change for the worse. This was a new concept to me. As I look back, I thank him for that, despite the different course our political views and conceptions of reform would subsequently take.

Yale Law School was an exciting place to be during this period. The approach of many faculty members differed from the standard fare of legal education: the case-study method that had originated at Harvard. At Yale, the faculty were developing a different philosophy of law now known as "legal realism." While using the case method as a starter, they expanded the teaching of law by dipping into political science, psychology, medicine, and other areas of learning. These experiments were valuable to me. The emphasis was on finding out not only what the judges said but why they said it. In my view, that is the right way to understand court opinions: to look behind the words of an opinion, see why it was made, and ask if making it served any useful function. The case-study method, by itself, was more static: The law was laid down with no attention to how the judge came to his decision, the task being to try and fit everything into what he said. This approach was really an artificial way of understanding the law, but generations of law students were taught this way. It was in a sense a "hornbook" approach to the law: You looked for the principle and then tried to fit your case into it instead of fitting your case into what is a good thing to do from a constitutional standpoint and the place of the Constitution in an evolving polity and society. More generally, my legal education again caused me to realize that I had to learn something more than how to operate the existing machinery of life. It opened up new vistas and gave me the idea I could change a few things on my own. It hit me at the right time of my life; I became much more open to new ideas than I had been before. It was a first-class legal education, and when I began to practice law I found that out; I could fit right into a leading law office, knowing I had the right training.

Our heroes in law school shared in this conception of the law that Yale pioneered: Justices Oliver Wendell Holmes and Louis Brandeis of the Supreme Court and Benjamin Cardozo of the New York Court of Appeals (who would later serve on the Supreme Court) and Learned Hand of the federal bench in New York. During my editorship of the law review, I invited some rather unorthodox jurists to Yale to address us as well as other thought-provoking speakers such as Arthur Garfield Hayes of the American Civil Liberties Union and Rabbi Stephen Wise, a leader in the New

York reform movement. By the time I left law school, I had an easy transition to the New York political scene and, most important, association with individuals whose approach to the law I admired and tried to emulate.

My political views, I should add, were those of a moderate Republican. My views about the law and about politics were not, however, inconsistent, at least to my mind. Cardozo's *Nature of the Judicial Process* remained my bible on the role of the law, yet as a rock-ribbed Nebraskan I understood the need for fiscal restraint on the government's part. I was disturbed by the expenditures of Roosevelt's New Deal, although not always its aims. I favored the creation of the Securities and Exchange Commission, for example, and the efforts in criminal-law and court reform, which were taking shape during this period.

But basically I was anti–New Deal and opposed two of its far-reaching doctrines. One was the National Recovery Act (NRA), which sought to substitute for our tradition of a free-enterprise system an economic policy of allowing industry-wide cartels composed of big government, big business, and organized labor to fix prices and otherwise dominate the domestic economic scene. I believed in strong antitrust enforcement to curb combinations that were in restraint of trade. The NRA was later declared unconstitutional by the Supreme Court. The other New Deal policy I opposed was President Roosevelt's 1937 "court packing" plan, which would have destroyed the independence of the judiciary but was later defeated by the Senate. These controversies made a deep impression on me and illustrate the importance of the doctrine of separation of powers among the three branches—executive, legislative, and judicial—to prevent development of a dictatorship.

This blend, on the one hand, of interest in legal reform and an awareness that the Constitution and public policy need to be understood according to changing societal needs and, on the other, a recognition that fiscal caution and healthy skepticism about whether government is the best means to respond to social ills is the foundation of the moderate Republicanism I was to embrace and champion. Later it led me to admire Tom Dewey and then Eisenhower. They were both fiscal conservatives, but each had a social agenda that could be fitted into it; they were not Tories by any stretch of the imagination.

At the end of my second year in law school I clerked during the summer for the firm of Hall, Cline & Williams back in Lincoln. I fully intended to set up practice in Lincoln after law school but at the last moment decided to follow many of my classmates to New York City. Emory Buckner, a former Nebraskan, put a good word in for me at his firm—then known as Root, Clark, Buckner, Howland & Ballantine (now Dewey, Ballantine). I was hired and spent two exhilarating years there.

During those two years at Root Clark, I became acquainted with John Marshall Harlan, whom I was to recommend in later years to President Eisenhower for appointment to the United States Supreme Court. I vividly remember Harlan at an office dinner, rendering in cockney accent with great pathos a ditty he had learned at Oxford where he had been a Rhodes scholar:

> 'E was just a tender law clark
> Pure and unstyned was his nyme,
> But the partner made an "herror"
> and the poor clark got the blyme.

Then in 1929 I transferred to a smaller firm: Lord, Day & Lord, where I spent the rest of my sixty-two years of law practice (except for my days in public office). The Lord, Day & Lord firm was founded in the early 1800s and has had a prominent and distinguished history in the New York community. It gave me many years of enjoyable and rewarding professional experience. The firm has recently expanded by merger and diversified and is known as Lord Day & Lord, Barrett Smith.

When I first came to New York I teamed up with two other young lawyers from the Root, Clark office, and we established rather spartan bachelor quarters at 7 East Eighth Street, next to the famous old Brevoort Hotel at the corner of Fifth Avenue and Eighth Street. One of my roommates was Robert G. Page, who later became the president of Phelps, Dodge Copper Company. The other was John A. Dunlop, a Canadian-born Rhodes scholar who later became counsel for American Cyanamid Corporation. He and I traveled to Europe in 1929 (just before the stock-market crash on Black Monday) for my first adventure outside the United States.

My roommates and I were new to New York and together we explored its cultural treasures. We bought cut-rate tickets to the theater—one hour before curtain time—at Gray's drugstore. We were standees at the opera. We attended the Goldman band concerts in Central Park. And I saved enough money to pay off my debt from law school days.

I was fortunate to have relatives in New York when I arrived from New Haven. My father had written his cousin George, who was general counsel for the Erie Railroad, to watch out for me. I spent every Christmas Eve—later with my wife and family—in the George Brownell home, and the tradition carried on to the next generation, George A. and Katherine Dodge (Khaki) Brownell, both of whom were prominent in the professional life of the New York community. During these years I was fortunate in that my younger brother Phil and his wife Leola and my sisters Louise Trow and Gertrude Randol were living in New York at various times, and we explored the cultural life of New York together.

The change to the small firm in 1929 gave me an immediate opening to plunge into corporate-securities work at a higher level of responsibility and at the same time to participate in extracurricular activities without the regimen required in a larger firm. I liked the informality of a smaller office where we called lawyers and staff by their first names and where we met senior partners socially as well as professionally.

Illustrative of these congenial surroundings in the new firm was my experience with Allen B. A. Bradley, a senior partner. When he discovered that I had lost my meager savings in buying stocks on margin just before the 1929 crash, he asked me if I wanted to make an investment that was not only sound but would give me lifetime satisfaction. He then introduced me to the world of antique furniture. I studied auction catalogs and visited dealers with Mr. Bradley, who was himself a noted antique-furniture collector. The purchases I made have, over the years, validated the advice he gave me.

Another partner, Henry deForest Baldwin, called me to his office one day to say he thought that by now I was settled enough in the New York community and that I should consider joining a club. He pointed out I could perhaps join a golf club or a city athletic club or a college club or a socially elite club. But he concluded that if I looked forward to lifelong friendships from persons in the arts, education, and other professions, his recommendation would be the Century Association. He himself had been a member for such a long period that he was accorded the honor of sitting at the head of the "long table." He sponsored my membership, and now that I rank as one of the oldest members I can look back with great appreciation to his friendly interest and on the associations in the Century that have so enriched my life.

The way firms operated in those days was of course quite different from the typical law firm today. Although some firms could be quite authoritarian, they were also less ruthless in hiring and then firing their younger

members. The small size of the firm in the 1930s and 1940s allowed an atmosphere of informality. If a young associate wanted to get married or
take a European trip, he would check with a senior partner, who would
decide on a purely ad hoc basis. During Christmas week he would be
called into a senior partner's office to learn the amount of his annual bo-
nus—entirely dependent on the firm's income for the year and the partners' decision of the associate's contribution to the success of the firm.
Perhaps the associate had experienced extraordinary expenses during the
year due, say, to illness in the family; allowance was made for this in figur-
ing his compensation for the year. The associate was not grouped with
others but judged individually. One might not get ahead as fast as today,
but one became an integral part of the life of the firm at an early stage with
correspondingly heightened interest in its success and reputation. One's
loyalty to the firm, resulting from this system of personalized association,
was a lifelong loyalty, and one's social life and friendships were built
around the firm.

Developments of one's talents as a lawyer and a sense of camaraderie
among members of the firm were the guiding norms then, rather than
achieving the maximum amount of "billable hours." The system under
which I matured as an attorney may not have produced any better results
for clients, but it did foster a more balanced life. I thrived within this more
informal atmosphere; my senior partners especially encouraged my interest in political service. I was not financially disadvantaged for it, as might
be the case today. The lesser emphasis on legal specialization that existed
at that time also enabled me to develop the broad skills that would prove
useful later in life, especially as I began to be active in politics and to associate with leading political figures.

2

Entering Politics

❖ ❖ ❖ ❖ ❖ ❖ ❖ ❖ ❖ ❖ ❖ ❖ ❖ ❖ ❖

My entry into politics and public life occurred in 1931 when I had been practicing law in New York City for only four years. The voters in the city were ready to rebel against the local Democratic party, dominated by a political organization known as Tammany Hall. The matter came to a head when major scandals involving Mayor James J. (Jimmy) Walker and members of his administration were exposed by a legislative investigating committee whose chief counsel was the distinguished and respected Judge Samuel Seabury. Seabury uncovered a tangle of bribery and corruption, such as brokerage accounts in Walker's name totaling more than $1 million, which the mayor could not explain. Other evidence revealed that Walker had been given money from businessmen to further their interests with the city, including letters of credit from a group that wanted to obtain a bus franchise from the city and a payment of $246,693 from a man who hoped to sell tiles to the city for its subway stations.

My involvement in the reform movement began when a call was sent out for young lawyers to watch the polls for signs of corruption. Many of the young lawyers I knew participated, and it led several of us to become involved in the New York Young Republican Club.

In 1931 a group of Young Republicans,[1] rebelling against the moribund city Republican organization, decided to support the Seabury investigations by selecting one of their members to run for the New York State Assembly in order to sponsor legislation needed by the investigating committee. I was chosen to be the candidate, and Thomas E. Dewey, the future governor of New York, was named as my campaign manager.

The assembly district where I lived at the time was controlled by Tammany Hall, as was almost all of New York City. A large number of Republican contributors, although supporting the party every four years in the national election, went along with Tammany's control of city and local politics; in fact, they considered the Tammany boss-system convenient. Because Tammany selected candidates who almost invariably won and who thereby became beholden to it once in office, Republican business leaders could get the legislation and other favors they wanted by dealing directly with the Tammany bosses rather than with individual city officials or a hundred members of the legislature in Albany.

The local Republican party organization in those years was almost an appendage of Tammany Hall, and its reputation was hardly much better. It survived off the patronage appointments it would receive from Tammany, and the holders of these jobs made up a rather skeletal and barely functioning party organization.

At the county level, the party leader was Sam Koenig. Koenig would get a certain number of jobs each year from Tammany, which he would then dole out to district leaders in return for their continued support of him as county chairman. He thus had little interest in challenging Tammany's control or in winning more election victories for Republicans. And on those occasions when Tammany needed Republican support, Koenig made sure that Republican officeholders, who usually owed their nomination to him, "cooperated" with the Democratic machine.

In my own assembly district, the party organization was even more of a rag-tag, bob-tail group. Tammany won almost all the elections there and the Republican leader, Clarence Fay, posed little threat to their control. Fay would receive one or two patronage jobs a year from Koenig, and the local municipal court district also provided some patronage, a half-dozen or so jobs such as court messengers and doorkeepers. The persons who held these positions, in turn, were usually the precinct captains who got out the vote on election day and kept Fay in power. Fay, like Koenig, would get a few other patronage crumbs from Tammany, such as assignments to appraise post office sites and the like. Such was the system that we set out to eliminate.

One of the reasons why the Young Republicans were able to be active in the district and promote me as a candidate for the assembly was that the party organization had not won an election in the district for a number of years and did not think the nomination was worth anything. Still, they wanted to get some new manpower in there, and by encouraging us they did. Indeed, they got a bit more than they bargained for: We revitalized the local organization and promoted candidates for office, myself included, who would wage more active campaigns.

We also ended their control of the party. Once we became active in the district, some of my supporters were able to replace Fay's cronies as neighborhood election-district captains. One by one, we soon controlled a majority of the districts, which enabled us to throw Fay out as district leader. The Young Republicans and other reformers who were active in other assembly districts achieved similar success so that eventually, at a raucous and tumultuous county committee meeting, we were able to throw out Koenig as county leader and replace him with Chase Mellon. And, at the state level, the increasing number of reform-minded legislators enabled us to end the Old Guard's control of the assembly by electing a new majority leader who subsequently became speaker of the assembly when the Republicans took control. These events occurred in a period of less than four years, and it led to the creation of a strong, reform-minded Republican party in the state and paved the way for Tom Dewey's eventual election as governor. The ability of reform-minded citizens to effect such changes against an essentially moribund but entrenched party organization was one of my first lessons in practical politics.

I had no intention at the time of making politics a career. None of us involved in the movement had any personal political ambitions, above and beyond doing what we believed was necessary to secure the kind of legislation needed to fight corruption, a goal we saw as the duty of any ordinary citizen. There was a bit of a prejudice among the reformers against going into organizational politics—it smacked of the kind of Tammany Hall system we were fighting. But we recognized the strength that organization could bring: Involvement in party politics could lead to the selection of better candidates, and with better candidates political standards would quite likely improve. Furthermore, if the political reformers knew something about the fundamentals of party organization, we believed that more effective results would come about. Subsequent political experience has borne this out: in observing reform movements over the years, I have seen well-intentioned individuals rush in without proper preparation and knowledge, with disastrous results. They don't know how to run a political campaign sensibly, for example, so they think it is necessary to make deals with rather shady political characters; the outcome can be worse than the situation was at the start.

One of my goals after I became involved in politics was to try to make organizational politics more respectable as an avenue for political participation and to try to narrow the gap between rank-and-file voters and the party organization. Party organization, in my mind, is a tool for effective democratic politics, not an end in itself. This is true for elected representatives as well: They are there to represent their constituents and the views and programs they have articulated in their campaigns, not just to serve at the bid and call of party leaders. Indeed, for my part, I was sometimes regarded by the party organization as a bit too independent since county leaders thought it their prerogative to tell assembly members how to vote; I never went along with that. Fortunately, my constituents never did either, and my district always stood behind me.

Two older friends, James R. Sheffield and Henry deForest Baldwin, especially encouraged me to run for office and take part in government. Sheffield had been the U.S. ambassador to Mexico under President Calvin Coolidge. His son Frederick was one of my classmates at Yale Law School, who with his father and mother made my entry into New York as a bachelor much happier at their home on the upper East Side, at the Metropolitan Opera and the New York Philharmonic, and at their camp on Saranac Lake in the Adirondacks. Baldwin, a Democrat, was my senior law partner and had had experience in city government under a reform administration. He and his son Sherman, also a law partner, helped make the decisions that later eased my way in and out of public life.

The Tenth Assembly district in Manhattan was to be the testing ground for the Young Republican reform movement. It included Greenwich Village where Fiorello LaGuardia had started his political career. LaGuardia's first political manager, Louis Espresso, was a local Republican boss, and he taught me how to ring doorbells as an election-district captain on Eighth Street and to get out the voters on election day.

With no money but with an enthusiastic volunteer group of young men and women, we combed the district. I had the nerve to call upon Alfred E. Smith, former governor of New York and Democratic candidate for president, to ask for his vote. Years later, at a dinner of the Friendly Sons of St. Patrick, he told me I was the first Republican he had ever voted for.

The garment district of Manhattan, Times Square, the Grand Central region, Murray Hill, Gramercy Park and Union Square, and most of Greenwich Village were all in the assembly district. I spoke on street corners off the back of a truck bearing the American flag and did house-to-house canvassing among all the polyglot nationalities that made up the voting population of the district. Faced with the realities of New York City's melting-pot electoral politics, I came to realize I represented a minority within a minority—I was a Republican, born outside the city, and a white, Anglo-Saxon Protestant to boot.

The Tenth Assembly district headquarters were located on the third floor of a walk-up loft building at 8 West Twenty-eighth Street. The diversity of its members could hardly have been greater. In addition to the party hacks around Fay, the nucleus consisted of a few aging holders of Republican patronage from prior national Republican administrations, such as custom house clerks or post office employees and some patronage holders from the federal courts. One or two survivors from the suffragettes' fight for the right of women to vote were loyal party members as were some upstate New Yorkers from traditional Republican families. There were local tradesmen who received business from the organization, such as florists, grocers, and real estate agents. There was a large contingent of Italian voters who had their own social club and who always invited me to march in the annual Columbus Day parade up Fifth Avenue. There was the artistic crowd from Greenwich Village and the theater district. Into this melange the Young Republican Club introduced several dozen "reformers"—young men and women generally originating from outside New York City who were crusaders against municipal corruption. It is worth noting that at this same time my law school classmate, Richardson Dilworth, was mobilizing a group of young people to fight municipal corruption in Philadelphia—in his case against a corrupt Republican municipal government.

Our annual fund-raising event was the Tenth Assembly District Ball held at the old Astor Hotel in Times Square. After the speeches by local candidates and dancing to the music of a name band, the evening closed with a grand march around the ballroom floor—first by twos, then fours, eights, sixteens, and thirty-twos, ending with the final sweep across the dance floor in rows of sixty-four. If we netted enough to pay the year's rent of the club headquarters, the affair was considered a success.

The Young Republicans enjoyed mixing with the old-timers and soon learned how to canvass for votes from apartment to apartment, gather nominating petitions, watch the polls for fraud, and get out the vote on election day. In those days our young canvassers—men and women—experienced no threat of danger in the streets at night. Gradually we molded our diverse elements into a fighting team. Part of our success in this effort came from our shared political goals, but part also developed as a result of working in such a diverse district. The individuals assigned as captains to a city block or two, for example, came to know and enjoy contact with voters of very different cultures and nationalities; the people they dealt with politically were quite different from those they encountered in their law offices and businesses. Social activity and personal attachments thus reinforced shared political values as a means for keeping individuals interested and committed.

Fighting Tammany Hall, of course, always remained our biggest concern, and our campaign song emphasized it:

> Tammany Hall's a patriotic order
> Tammany Hall's a great society
> Fourth of July they always wave the flag, boys
> But never will they waive immunity
> Tammany Hall, like Robin Hood, professes
> To take it from the rich and for the poor
> Tammany Hall becomes a bit confused at times
> And takes from all to give to Tammany Hall.

During my first campaign I made my first political "deal." My opponent, Langdon Post, started attacking me as a carpetbagger from Nebraska; among the voters in Greenwich Village that attack had teeth. So my campaign manager and I met with our opponent and told him if he persisted in calling me a carpetbagger I would retaliate by pointing out that he lived on swanky upper Park Avenue. I knew that to many Greenwich Villagers that was a worse sin than being from Nebraska. Thus we made a deal that neither would mention the subject of residence again.

Most of the voters in those days had phonographs in their homes. We prepared and distributed by mail a phonographic plastic disc. I spoke on the issues, introduced by the mellifluous voice of my manager, Thomas E. Dewey. It caught the attention of the press. We narrowly lost that first race, but defeat only encouraged us. It showed us that by organizing, to the point of being able to canvass the district, we could eventually win.

On the personal side the race was a great success, for during the campaign I met the woman who was to become my wife and the mother of our four wonderful children. Doris McCarter was a Texan living in New

York at the time. We were married in Christ Church (Methodist), on Sixtieth and Park Avenue, by Rev. Ralph Sockman and became active members there. We spent our honeymoon traveling by ocean liner from New York to Glasgow—just the reverse of the honeymoon trip taken years before by her parents from Glasgow to New York. Her family tolerated the fact that I had only one-quarter Scottish ancestry.

From the beginning until her death in 1979, Doris was an enthusiastic partner in all my political ventures and in my public life. Throughout our many shifts from private to public life and back again, she accepted the economic risks and the ensuing disruptions to family and school life and friendships with good cheer and ingenious planning. She was a vivacious and popular hostess and engendered a happy environment for our family circle. In addition, she maintained an active interest in the theater and in advances in the field of nutrition and engaged in Republican party affairs in New York and Washington.[2]

Our Young Republican efforts in 1931 encouraged me to run for the assembly the next year (the terms of assembly members were then for only one year). I was assisted in my efforts by another able campaign manager, Thomas E. Stephens, who later served as appointments secretary to President Eisenhower. My previous opponent, Langdon Post, had broken with Tammany Hall and was running as an independent. With two other candidates in the field I was able to win the race by 300 votes. But the forces of political corruption were still at work: I was elected despite the invasion of the district by a group of "floaters" who came by ferry to New York City from New Jersey under the aegis of Jimmy Hines, a notorious Tammany district leader, who was later sent to jail by Dewey. The floaters went from one polling place to another, voting in each place under the name of a local voter who had not yet appeared. Our volunteer organization followed one of those floaters, who was wearing a bright red tie and thus was easily identifiable. He was prosecuted and convicted by a young assistant U.S. attorney, J. Edward Lumbard, who later became a distinguished judge of the U.S. Court of Appeals, Second Circuit. The practice of floater voting quickly came to an end.

In several of my reelection campaigns, the Democratic party nominated to run against me a young lawyer in my own office (Lord, Day & Lord). We each waged a vigorous campaign in the evenings but associated in the firm's library during office hours. As the *World-Telegram* newspaper put it, regardless of the outcome Lord, Day & Lord was a sure winner of the assembly contest. In later years, my opponent in the political campaign, Thomas F. Daly, successfully tried all the court cases that arose out of the New York World's Fair of 1939–1940, and I handled its corporate matters.

The composition of my district, with its mix of immigrant groups from southern, central, and eastern Europe, also forced me to become familiar with the Socialist point of view; usually the Socialist party put up a candidate against me, and sometimes even a Communist would run. Never having dealt with such a fundamentally different political philosophy, I had to learn to answer their arguments in the frequent debates we would have in schools, churches, and on street corners. I could not be too complacent just because I was running against a Democratic opponent where both parties agreed on our constitutional form of government and a free-enterprise economy. The Socialist and Communist candidates were sophisticated in their knowledge of political philosophy, economics, and politics, and I had to stand up and debate them on the issues they raised.

My entry into the assembly—the first of five terms—was newsworthy not only because of a Tammany upset but also because I was one of only a very few Republicans statewide to defeat an incumbent Democrat in the 1932 Roosevelt landslide. Even the popular congressman Fiorello LaGuardia was defeated. But I had focused my campaign entirely on the winning issue of municipal reform.

In those days the New York State legislature was still a part-time job. Sessions ran from January through March, and the legislature convened for business only from Monday evening through Wednesday. Since the salary was low—$1,500—I continued to practice law part-time. But my involvement in politics increased, and I began to assume greater responsibilities as a legislator. Starting the following year, with the election of LaGuardia as New York City's mayor on a Fusion (anti-Tammany) ticket, I sponsored the mayor's reform legislation in Albany along with Abbott Lowe Moffatt, the only other Republican member of the assembly from the greater city. This included a bill to establish a citywide park department headed by Robert Moses. I served as chairman of the newly created New York City Committee, which involved me intimately in the effort to reorganize city government, especially through passage of a new, reformed city charter. I also was a member of the Judiciary Committee. On the political side, I campaigned in upstate counties to help reelect my fellow assemblymen, including the counties where my father and mother had lived. I learned to speak over the radio when I gave weekly reports to my constituents over the municipal station, WNYC, then in its infancy. I learned about the intrusion of politics into one's private life when, because of a controversial vote I had cast in the assembly, I was hung in effigy by members of the left-wing American Labor party in front of our apartment on normally quiet West Twelfth Street.

I learned especially about the nitty-gritty side of legislative politics: compromise, bargaining, and occasional logrolling as well as the almost tribal system of personal and political ties and allegiances. I quickly determined that in politics one's enemies today could become one's allies tomorrow, and vice versa, so one did not denounce one's opponents too strongly or too personally. I also discovered that legislative politics could take some unexpected turns. Once when I was advocating passage of a bill to create a new New York City charter, I faced strong opposition from Tammany Hall since this was a major piece of reform legislation. The bill was so hotly debated that I almost got into a fistfight in the well of the assembly with a Democratic member—we had to be pulled apart; it was quite exciting. The bill was called and roll call was taken, and it looked as if the bill would be narrowly defeated. The speaker of the House held up announcing the outcome and told me I was one vote short. I knew the one vote had to come from the Democratic side, and I had almost given up when suddenly a Brooklyn machine Democrat with a rather unsavory reputation stood up and switched his vote, allowing the bill to pass. I later learned that he had had a feud with the Democratic leader of the assembly that morning over patronage and had decided to teach the leader a lesson. Thus he became a "one-day reformer."

Since the Democrats controlled both the governorship and the state senate (and in 1935 the assembly as well), I had to deal with the Democrats over every piece of legislation I sponsored. The leader of the Democratic-controlled state senate was John Dunnigan and the assembly Democratic leader was Irwin Steingut. To get my bills through I had to negotiate with these two politically wily and astute men. My strength resulted from my position as one of the two Republican members of the assembly from the city; I was handling Mayor LaGuardia's legislative program. LaGuardia, of course, had great clout as mayor of New York City. The Democratic leaders felt they had to deal with me even though I was a relatively new member of the assembly. Steingut was smart but a bit slippery; I could generally trust Dunnigan to carry out his word. As a particular type of politician, they were foreign to my experience; but I was fascinated by them and quickly acquired in my dealings with them certain skills in the art of legislative politics. I also got along well with the rank-and-file Democratic members. Since most of them were from the New York City area, we would travel on the train together to Albany, often playing bridge en route. I developed a good personal relationship with many of them, and if one of my bills didn't hurt them politically, they would support it. By an odd quirk of fate, one of the Democratic members later became commissioner of internal revenue and was caught up in the scandals of the Truman administration. It was my obligation as attorney general to prosecute him, and he was convicted and served a term in federal prison.

Among the Republicans, I had the problem of being a representative from a New York City district in a party that was dominated by members from upstate. Still, I was accepted by those leaders partly because both my father and mother had been born in upstate New York. They knew I couldn't be all bad, despite the suspicions generated by ties to New York City. The Republican leader in the assembly was Joe McGinnies, an elderly man—at least I thought of him then as such—from western New York State; he ruled with an iron hand. He did a lot of favors for me, however, because one of my senior partners, Franklin B. Lord, had been counsel to Charles Whitman when he was governor. McGinnies liked and respected Lord, so he gave me good committee assignments. Also, many Republican members lived at the Ten Eyck Hotel when the legislature was in session, and the leading Republican members had formed a little club there—we paid small dues and even had a slot machine, which was illegal but not unknown in Albany at the time. I was admitted to the club during my first year, which enabled me to sit in on rump meetings with the legislative leaders. At breakfast I would sit with the Republican leaders, and we would go over the legislative calendar for the day, deciding which bills would be brought up for consideration. Thus I learned the inside machinery and saw how the leaders organized the day-to-day workings of the legislature. In my second term, I was appointed to the Rules Committee, which, like the Rules Committee in Congress, had tremendous power in determining how legislation would proceed through the assembly; I served on that committee for the rest of my four terms in Albany. Here too was an important political lesson: How something is considered by the legislature could often be as important as the substance of what is considered.

I was also a member of a congenial group of younger Republican legislators, many of whom had attended Ivy League colleges. The group included Jerry Wadsworth, the son of former U.S. Senator James J. Wadsworth, Laurens Hamilton of the Alexander Hamilton family, and Pritch Strong from Rochester. We and our wives had a circle of our own that served our social as well as political needs within the Republican caucus. I also organized a group of Young Republican lawyers from New York City, who developed legislation for me; I had my own legislative program instead of having bills handed to me by some organized interest as was common at the time.

The association that had developed among the younger, reform-minded members enabled us to gain control of the assembly from the more conservative, upstate members, who often were just spokesmen for local interests and political machines. They believed that social legislation and other aspects of the reform movement were the governor's concern, not theirs, and Gov. Al Smith had capitalized on that view and dominated the legislature in this area. Smith would give them what they wanted on the local level, and they would passively allow him to take the lead on statewide issues. It was not until Tom Dewey became governor in 1942—long after I had left the assembly—that the more progressive elements among Republican legislators achieved ascendancy; Dewey was able to build a political coalition among members from the growing suburban areas of Westchester, Nassau, Suffolk, and Erie counties. But the seeds for that were sown when I was still serving in Albany in 1935. The Democrats had gained a majority in the assembly that year, so instead of reelecting the old speaker as our leader we elected Irving Ives (later a United States senator). Our support came largely from the suburban areas that would eventually give Dewey his political base and that also enabled us to gain control of the state Republican party. We also began to build support within the state Republican party for Dewey's run for governor in 1938 and his eventual victory in 1942. Our work was cut out for us because the upstate Republicans really had little interest in electing a governor; their emphasis was on local politics and control of the assembly. It was even difficult to get them to hand out literature for the gubernatorial campaigns or to think about a political strategy that would link the various statewide and local offices into a semblance of a party ticket instead of running personal campaigns for each office.

The most powerful lobbyist in Albany in those days was George Meany, representing the State Federation of Labor, who later became a national figure as head of the AFL-CIO. Every legislative day he would enter the assembly chamber early in the morning and distribute to the desk of each Democratic member from New York City a copy of the calendar for the day, marked with a "Yes" or "No" alongside each bill that was to be considered, representing the recommendations of the State Federation of Labor. I later observed that those assemblymen who slavishly followed Meany's recommendations often ended up by being rewarded with a judgeship on a New York City lower court.

Years later I again met George Meany when I was United States attorney general and he was a member of an advisory commission to the U.S. prison system. He opposed and I favored a program to give all inmates in the federal-prison system an opportunity to engage in productive labor for pay during their incarceration; he expressed the traditional viewpoint of organized labor, which didn't want competition from "prison-made goods." Meany won that fight. But I still think that a failure to develop a productive life for those people who are incarcerated remains one of the chief problems in our criminal-justice system today.

Although during my assembly years I did not have many direct dealings with Meany—he regarded me as just another hopeless Republican—I did strike up a friendship with Mike Quill, who headed the transit workers' union. I helped secure passage through the Republican-controlled assembly of an eight-hour day for subway workers, so he always had a soft spot in his heart for me. On the other hand, I was always opposed by the teachers' union because I tried to reform the teachers' pension system by putting it on a sound actuarial basis.

At the time, a controversial issue arose in financial circles over whether the securities issued by public utility companies should be open to public bidding by prospective underwriters. The system traditionally had been that each utility had a "relationship" with a particular investment-banking house and did not offer the marketing of its securities to other prospective underwriters. I sided with the reformers and sponsored legislation to require public bidding, with the objective of lowering the financing costs of the utilities and consequently lowering utility rates to consumers. As I look back at the incident it was my first ideological choice in public life. In effect, that is when I decided to be a moderate Republican rather than a member of the conservative Old Guard, reserving my independence to judge each issue on its merits. The legislature passed my bill and it became law, with personal consequences I could not foresee.

Twenty years later, I was called upon by Robert R. Young—at that time a stranger—who asked my firm to become counsel to his syndicate, which was organizing a hostile takeover of the New York Central Railroad in opposition to the management. Management was backed by the banks and investment houses then dominant in Wall Street. I asked Mr. Young why he had come to us. He replied that he remembered my action as a youthful legislator in sponsoring a bill, generally opposed by Wall Street interests, to require public bidding for public utility-company securities and he thought I would be independent enough to support his challenge to the New York Central management. In any event, he succeeded in his challenge when we won the hard-fought proxy contest. Young's chief financial backer was Sid Richardson, an independent oil tycoon from Texas, whom I was later to know as a strong backer of the movement to elect Eisenhower as president. The story goes that Bob Young telephoned Richardson to gain his financial backing for the New York Central proxy fight. Richardson was called away from the poker table to take the call. When he returned to the game, his buddy asked, "What's up, Sid?" "I just bought a railroad," the free-wheeling Texan replied. "Which one?" asked his buddy. "Dammit, I forgot to ask," said Richardson, quietly upping his poker bid.

Working with Thomas E. Dewey, who by that time had been appointed by the governor as special prosecutor of organized crime, I sponsored anticrime bills and election-law reforms. One of these reforms, which has served well over the years, required that the voting machines in New York City be impounded on election night and later reopened in the presence of bipartisan observers. This has served to eliminate the old practice whereby election clerks paid no attention to the actual results shown on the machine when they transcribed the tallies onto paper for their official report to police headquarters on election night—a modern method of stuffing the ballot box.

Working with Robert Moses, I sponsored legislation to create the World's Fair Corporation and to build the Aquacade building at Flushing Meadow Park and the marina at Flushing Bay. I made many friends by sponsoring legislation to authorize sidewalk cafes in Manhattan, working with Alderman Thomas J. Curran and a citizens' committee headed by Tony Sarg, the puppeteer.

Favors for constituents were part of the life of an assemblyman. When the city government proposed to cut Gramercy Park in two in order to run a bus line down Lexington Avenue to Fourteenth Street, my constituents were rightly up in arms. My law partner, Parker McCollester, was president of the Gramercy Park Association, and together we researched the history of the terms by which Samuel Ruggles deeded the park to the city. We discovered that Ruggles's deed stipulated that the land be used only for park purposes; the deed in hand, we successfully blocked the city's plan.

On another occasion, some constituents complained that they were awakened unnecessarily at an early hour by the bells ringing atop the Metropolitan Life Insurance Company building. A friend of mine, Frederick Tanner—who was himself a former assemblyman and as a Republican leader had given Fiorello LaGuardia his first chance to run for Congress—was legal counsel to the company. Tanner listened sympathetically to my plea and acted to postpone the ringing of the bells till a later hour.

During my years in the assembly, Al Smith—though he had left the governor's chair in 1929—was still the great hero in political circles. Even the Republicans liked him. Although they had opposed some of his efforts, they regarded him as a good governor. Herbert Lehman was governor during my assembly years. He came from the great Lehman banking family, and many people in Albany joked that the family had sent him into politics because he wasn't a very good banker. Lehman was a plodder but an honest man and a hard worker. People trusted him, and I admired his reliability despite our political differences. Franklin Roosevelt, by contrast, was still considered somewhat of a patrician dilettante when I served in the assembly, especially by the old-time politicians. They often told snide jokes about him and treated him as a passing fancy. Al Smith had the common touch, but FDR was regarded as an aristocrat who looked down on politicians. In fact, they thought he would be an awful flop as president; that he would come to be regarded as a "great president" never entered their minds—and these opinions were held by many of the Democrats in Albany.

During my years in the assembly I entered into community service in the district. I was a trustee of the Northern Dispensary, an old institution that specialized in giving medical (especially dental) service to the poor. I served as a director of the Children's Village, a charity that provided educational and vocational services to boys from broken homes. And I was a trustee of the New York School of Social Work, which trained social service workers and later became affiliated with Columbia University.

But five strenuous political campaigns and time-consuming assembly duties were enough.[3] I had accomplished the goal I had set at the beginning: active participation in the reform movement in the city to oust Tammany Hall and to bring in the new type of municipal government exemplified by Fiorello LaGuardia and Robert Moses. At the end of the 1937 session, I announced my decision not to run for reelection and returned full-time to my law office.

Although I would not return to elected political office in New York State, my experience in Albany and the lessons I drew from it proved helpful when I went to Washington. First, when I was presented to the United States Senate at my confirmation hearings, I was introduced by Sen. Irving Ives, who had been our successful reform candidate for Republican leader as well as my seatmate in the assembly. Ives introduced me to the members of the Senate Judiciary Committee: "This fellow is all right because he is really a legislator at heart." That was a big plus for me because it indicated to them that I was a fellow they could deal with: Here was someone familiar with the legislative process and the give-and-take of practical politics.

The other lessons that proved useful guided me in my recognition of the need to present Congress with my own legislative program, my ability to craft one, and my awareness of the strategies and tactics that were needed to gain their approval. After taking office as attorney general, I saw the need for various reforms and changes. Yet it was unusual for an attorney general to have his own legislative agenda; Congress was not accustomed to it. But I knew that Congress might be amenable to my suggestions if I developed good personal relationships with them, as I had done with the New York Democrats, thus allowing the less politically controversial issues easier passage, and if I was willing to let them claim the credit for my proposals, a strategy that is effective whether the legislator is a member of the New York State Assembly or the United States Senate.

If I had done nothing more in politics or government after my five years in the New York legislature, I still would have enjoyed my first taste of public life; it broadened my outlook on life and created many lasting friendships. It also made me a charter member of the "I Love New York" enthusiasts. Without that experience I would never have learned firsthand about the diversity of life in a great metropolitan center or of the importance of recognizing the viewpoints of persons and groups in order to make our system of government work. So many examples come to mind.

As a legislator I was taken on a tour of the lower East Side of Manhattan where tenements with only outdoor toilets still existed. I visited the outstanding community center in my district—Greenwich House—which furnished social services to immigrants. In my district, too, was a jail where husbands were incarcerated for failure to pay alimony. They had to stay there, under the old law, until they paid. If they had no assets, that meant life imprisonment because they couldn't earn while in jail. I obtained legislation to change that. Robert Moses educated me on the importance of more city parks, and under his guidance, I was instrumental in establishing a "vest-pocket park" in my district. I visited the old Ruppert Brewery on the upper East Side and learned from Colonel Ruppert, of Yankee baseball fame, about the place of organized sports in our society. When the National Recovery Act (the Blue Eagle) became a significant (although short-lived) New Deal component of the economic life of New York, as a public official I got acquainted with David Dubinsky and the needle trade, located in my district. In the media, I rubbed up against Arthur Krock and James Hagerty, Sr., of the *New York Times*, Harry Luce of Time-Life, Ben Sonnenberg and Ted Husing in public relations. I visited P.S. 41 in my district and learned about the inadequacies of our metropolitan school system. My education as an assemblyman combined the elements of two autobiographies that I relished: *The Education of Jacob Riis*, the New York reformer, and *The Education of Henry Adams*, the New England reformer. My time as a member of the New York State Assembly still retains a fascination for me.

This political experience, too, was a valuable adjunct in my private law practice, aside from learning New York statutory law. It is elementary that a lawyer must know a client's case and its strengths and weaknesses. But to be a good legal adviser, a lawyer should research the opponent's case too—its strengths and weaknesses. In nine cases out of ten, in my experience, a realistic compromise settlement results. And life in the legislature was a constant series of realistic compromises.

After deciding not to seek reelection to the assembly, I was almost at once asked to be general counsel for the World's Fair of 1939–1940, a three-year, full-time retainer for which I established a branch law office of my firm on the fairgrounds in Flushing Meadow Park. Our family moved to Port Washington (and later to Plandome) on Long Island for the duration of the fair.

Grover A. Whalen became president of the Fair Corporation, and I was privileged to work with him on a daily basis during the fair. He was one of New York's most colorful citizens and had been widely known as the city's official "greeter." Then and in later years he organized the city's official receptions for distinguished visitors; he originated the tickertape parades. Charles Lindbergh, returning from his history-making solo flight across the Atlantic, Gertrude Ederle, fresh from her triumphant swim across the English Channel, Dwight Eisenhower, returning from his victories over Hitler, were among the celebrities who rode up lower Broadway in open cars to be received at City Hall. Whalen always dressed immaculately and formally and sported a gardenia in the buttonhole of his jacket.

Whalen had been born on New York's lower East Side and rose to be general manager of the Wanamaker department store. Rodman Wanamaker "loaned" him to head a businessmen's committee to support "Red Mike" Hylan for mayor, and he became Hylan's secretary, then a commissioner of plants and structures. Later he became police commissioner under Mayor Jimmy Walker and was a much publicized and popular figure as he rode his black horse to personally direct theater traffic. He was a natural to head the World's Fair because of his flair for public relations and his administrative ability. He traveled to foreign countries to persuade their governments to exhibit at the fair in lavish pavilions. His breakthrough in selling the fair occurred when he succeeded in getting the USSR to participate, after which Britain, France, Italy, Belgium, Japan, and many other nations followed.

The biggest U.S. corporations then were eager to enter and build giant pavilions. The high point in industrial exhibits was the introduction of television to the American public. Facsimile broadcasting and radiotype short-wave transmission of electrical writing were likewise featured. DuPont demonstrated the miracle of making nylon. General Electric and Westinghouse featured fluorescent tube lighting. AT&T gave free long-distance calls to thousands of visitors. Borden presented Elsie the cow and electrical milking machines. Innovations in science and the latest trends in the arts were portrayed dramatically, rivaling the industrial exhibits.

I nearly lost my assignment as legal counsel when the first industrial exhibitor was signed up—the Lucky Strike cigarette company. The closing of the transaction was scheduled in my office in front of cameras and reporters. Unfortunately, my secretary was not familiar with the rivalry of tobacco companies, and when she laid out the cigarettes and ashtrays for the assembled dignitaries she displayed Chesterfield cigarettes—no Lucky Strikes.

One of the great promotional events to publicize the fair included sponsoring the round-the-world flight by Howard Hughes. Whalen arranged to have the plane christened the "New York World's Fair," and Hughes delivered invitations to visit the fair to the heads of foreign governments wherever he touched down. The worldwide publicity for the flight was tremendous. All of us in the fair's organization followed the progress of the flight hour by hour. When I was rushing to join the welcoming crowd on Hughes's triumphal return to Floyd Bennett Field, I was stopped by a traffic cop for speeding and never reached the field; fortunately, the arrest of the fair's legal counsel for speeding did not make the papers. At the reception for Mr. Hughes at the Whalen home in Washington Mews, the famous but even then publicity-shy aviator saw the crowd of VIPs waiting to shake his hand and unceremoniously ducked out the back door, leaving Mr. and Mrs. Whalen and Mayor LaGuardia to explain as best they could why the guest of honor did not appear.

The Fair Corporation was set up by legislation as an autonomous enclave within New York City. We were empowered by the legislation to enter into a lease from the City of New York to use Flushing Meadow Park to hold the fair. The city was a tough landlord. The city commissioner of parks was Robert Moses, and he insisted that all buildings at the fair be temporary except for the New York State and City pavilions, so that the area would eventually be used again exclusively for park purposes. Thus, despite public outcry, the magical Trylon and Perisphere and the fantastic color fountains, which symbolized "the World of Tomorrow" all around the world, had to be torn down at the conclusion of the second year of the fair. Today the Flushing Meadow Park region is known as the home of Shea baseball stadium and the National Open Tennis Center.

To turn the rubble and garbage-infested site at Flushing Meadow into the beautiful and exciting park that it became involved many novel legal problems. We established our own police force, fire department, sanitation department, and building code. There were hundreds of contracts to be drawn—with foreign governments, state governments, and giant industrial companies and with many famous architects, artisans, and artists. Among the contracts for the amusement section at the fairgrounds were agreements with the well-known theatrical producers Billy Rose and Mike Todd, both of whom later became my clients in private practice.

One of the liveliest legal disputes at the fair resulted in my having a temporary falling out with Robert Moses, for whom I had worked in his luckless gubernatorial campaign in 1934. Long Island's Grand Central Parkway, which was under Moses's jurisdiction as park commissioner, ran through the fairgrounds. Our plans called for the erection of temporary industrial pavilions on either side of the parkway—General Motors, Ford, General Electric, and AT&T among others. Moses challenged the fair management under a law that prohibited electric advertising signs within 200 feet of a parkway. Financial disaster loomed if the law was enforced against the fair because the big corporations would not enter the fair if they could not display advertising signs on the exterior of their pavilions. Drawing on my legislative experience I persuaded my friend Leonard W. Hall, then an assemblyman who was later to be Republican national chairman, to sponsor a two-year exemption for the fair. The exemption bill passed and was sent to the governor. Moses, who prided himself on his iron-clad domination of the legislature on matters affecting parks and parkways, denounced me in the press and urged Governor Lehman to veto the bill. The governor, however, was a great supporter of the fair and signed the bill. The only casualty was Bob Moses's friendship—and that was restored in his later, more mellow years.

Moses was a fighter. He was honest. He had great organizational ability and built up a corps of young architects, engineers, and landscape architects who were intensely loyal to him. He developed political skills under the tutelage of Gov. Alfred E. Smith and learned to manipulate public officials. This combination of assets made him invaluable to Governor Smith and later to Franklin D. Roosevelt and Fiorello LaGuardia. He built highways, bridges, parks, and playgrounds with a ruthless efficiency, finishing these projects on time and within the budget. He fought the vested interests opposed to his projects with sarcasm and venomous public assaults. Everybody admired the results, but many people were embittered by his tactics. He was a conservative Republican serving in New Deal governments, and when he ran for governor his platform was entirely too conservative for the liberal electorate of New York State. I enjoyed his company and admired his independence in public life. He was restless even in his advanced years—always seeking power. He had contempt for small minds in public life. At a cocktail party he would say, "See those big-shot politicos over in the corner whispering to each other—that's a sure sign that nothing important is going on."

Confrontation with the USSR came next in organizing the fair. The So- viets had built a huge pavilion, capped by the Red Star, which was a major attraction. As part of its entertainment program, the fair management booked folk-dancing programs sponsored by groups of nationalists from Latvia and Lithuania. The USSR claimed sovereignty over those countries and threatened to withdraw if the dances—very popular—were contin- ued. (As I write these memoirs over fifty years later, these same Baltic states have finally been freed from Soviet domination.) I negotiated with the USSR commissioner, Constantine Oumansky, and the dances finally were allowed to continue. But later, at the outbreak of World War II, the Russians dismantled and packed up their pavilion, Red Star and all, and withdrew from the second year of the fair.

An incident occurred during the fair that heightened my insight into New York City politics. The fair's president, Grover Whalen, was desig- nated by Democratic party leaders as their candidate for mayor. The in- cumbent, Mayor LaGuardia, was planning to run for reelection as the Re- publican-Fusion candidate, as was City Comptroller Joseph McGoldrick. Both LaGuardia and McGoldrick were members of the Executive Commit- tee of the Fair Corporation. They demanded that Whalen resign his post if he accepted the Democratic party offer. Whalen called a meeting of the five Democratic county leaders of New York City in his office at the fair- grounds and asked me to attend as his lawyer. The leaders disclosed many political secrets of their methods of dealing with the nationalities and religious groups that make up the New York City electorate. Whalen withdrew from the mayoralty race, and LaGuardia and McGoldrick were reelected. Since then I have sat in many a high-powered council of leaders of the Republican party, but never again was I invited to a Democratic powwow.

Recently while driving into the city from Long Island I noticed that a highway leading to the old World's Fair grounds had been named the Harry Van Arsdale, Jr., Highway. That really is ironic, I thought, as I re- membered that Van Arsdale had been head of Electricians Union Local No. 3 at the time that the fair was being constructed. He had called a strike of electricians about a month or so before the scheduled opening date of the fair. To settle the dispute the fair and the exhibitors with pavilions on the fairgrounds had to pay overtime wages for weeks, and the resulting extra costs were threatening the solvency of the Fair Corporation. But the extra costs were paid—the fair opened on time—and Van Arsdale's union members were the financial winners. I'm not sure that Grover Whalen would have approved the naming of the Van Arsdale highway.

At the conclusion of the fair, I received a call from Thomas E. Dewey. He said his friend Edgar Nathan, Jr., was to run for borough president of Manhattan in 1941 on the Republican ticket and asked me to manage the campaign. I agreed. We called upon a hastily organized band of volunteers—Mrs. Nathan was by far the most energetic campaigner and she drew in the actress June Allyson. Our campaign was successful and Nathan (afterwards Judge Nathan) became borough president of Manhattan. I soon learned that Dewey's request to me was to test my ability as a campaign manager. He then asked me to manage his gubernatorial campaign of 1942, and our fast friendship over the years was sealed.

NOTES

1. A number of the more active members of the group, with the name "Mallards," have met regularly throughout the ensuing years on a social basis. Among the original members were Governor Dewey and Judge David W. Peck (a Dewey judicial appointee). J. Edward Lumbard and Paul W. Williams were members and both served during the Eisenhower years as U.S. attorney for the Southern District of New York. Others of the group also attained high public and judicial office.

2. Her obituary appeared in the *New York Times* on June 14, 1979:

Doris McCarter Brownell, the wife of former Attorney General Herbert Brownell, Jr., and a leader in cultural and civic affairs, died on Tuesday at her home at 635 Park Avenue.

Mrs. Brownell, whose husband served as Attorney General in the Cabinet of President Dwight D. Eisenhower from 1953 to 1957, cheerfully accepted the demanding duties of her position, from serving as an official United States representative at a series of international conferences to modeling Turkish garments at a benefit fashion show.

She also took to the campaign trail and was active in numerous organizations, including the U.S.O., the Women's National Republican Club and the American Stanislovski Theater.

She was born in Dublin, Tex., and graduated from Texas Woman's University in Denton. She was a social worker in New York City in the early 1930's when she met her future husband, a Nebraska-born lawyer who was serving in the New York State Assembly.

The couple married in 1934, and Mrs. Brownell soon found herself in the thick of Republican politics. As her husband moved from chairman of the Republican National Committee to the first Republican Cabinet in 20 years, Mrs. Brownell honed her own political skills as campaigner, speech writer and organizer.

Despite her devotion to politics, Mrs. Brownell was not above deflating the hyperbole that often surrounds political campaigning.

After Republican boosters made much of the fact that Mr. Brownell had met his wife in church, Mrs. Brownell set an interviewer straight about his presumed piety: "It was the church basement, at a political meeting," she said. "He was a young member of the New York Legislature and he came seeking votes."

A believer in proper diet and physical fitness, Mrs. Brownell once touched off a Washington cocktail party fad when she confided that she spent much of her time at such functions standing on tiptoes to improve body tone.

She also contributed to several culinary books and in 1975 published her own cookbook, "Star Performances in the Kitchen," a charitable venture.

In addition to her husband, Mrs. Brownell is survived by two daughters, Joan Brownell and Ann Sloane; two sons, Thomas M. and James B. Brownell; four sisters, a brother and three grandchildren.

A memorial service will take place at 4 P.M. Monday at Christ United Methodist Church, Park Avenue and 60th Street.

3. The voting results when I ran for the New York State Assembly were as follows:

1931	Langdon Post, Democrat	7,323
	Herbert Brownell, Republican	5,640
	William Cohn, Socialist	559
1932	Herbert Brownell, Republican	9,018
	Silva LaChapell, Democrat	8,647
	Langdon Post, Independent	5,728
	Jesse Hughes, Socialist	814
1933	Herbert Brownell, Republican	11,121
	Augustin Powers, Democrat	7,131
	Jesse Hughes, Socialist	714
	Frank Dorlo, Communist	362
1934	Herbert Brownell, Republican	8,593
	Herbert Brownell, Fusion	1,076
	Thomas F. Daly, Democrat	7,861
	William Farrell, Socialist	615

1935	Herbert Brownell, Republican	8,629
	Herbert Brownell, Fusion	1,104
	Thomas F. Daly, Democrat	8,382
	William Farrell, Socialist	417
	Dora Zucker, Communist	705
1936	Herbert Brownell, Republican	16,101
	Thomas F. Daly, Democrat	14,816
	Joseph P. Lash, Socialist	750
	George Powers, Communist	1,389

The above figures are from the *New York State Red Book* (Albany, N.Y.: J. B. Lyon Co.) for each of the years involved.

3

Working with Tom Dewey

❖ ❖ ❖ ❖ ❖ ❖ ❖ ❖ ❖ ❖ ❖ ❖ ❖ ❖ ❖

Thomas E. Dewey and I both came from the Middle West to New York City in the 1920s. He came from Owasso, Michigan, to attend Columbia Law School and to practice law and, on the side, to continue his voice-training lessons. I came to New York City from Lincoln, Nebraska, by way of Yale, to practice law and, on the side, to become active in reform politics. Our paths crossed many times in the years ahead, and we became political associates and close personal friends.

I first met Dewey in the Young Republican Club and got to know him well when he served as my campaign manager in the 1931 assembly race. At age twenty-eight, he went on to serve as chief assistant U.S. attorney under George Medalie and then succeeded Medalie (who ran unsuccessfully for the Senate in 1932) as acting U.S. attorney. With the change in presidential administrations in 1933, Dewey returned to private law practice. In 1935 Gov. Herbert Lehman appointed him as special prosecutor to clean up corruption in New York City, and I sponsored legislation in Albany that was useful for his work. Dewey successfully ran for district attorney of New York County (Manhattan) in 1937, and I campaigned on street corners for him. Throughout this period our personal association deepened, and I got to know his wife and their sons, Tom, Jr., and John, well. I was not involved in his 1938 gubernatorial race, however, which he lost to Lehman by only 60,000 votes. By 1942, when he ran for governor again, I had known him for over ten years.

I found Dewey attractive as a political figure because of our shared concerns about the kinds of political reforms needed in New York City and in the state during this period. He fought the Tammany political machine, corrupt labor officials, and organized crime. Dewey sent them all to jail.

The Tom Dewey I knew was also quite different from the popular perception of him as a rather wooden political figure, formally attired and with a mustache, who assumed he would be elected president only to find he had been beaten by a feisty Harry Truman. Dewey was aggressive, but he wasn't the kind of political fighter who lashed out at his opponents; he carefully and meticulously armed himself with the facts. At times this could prove a bit of a problem for him. When he was first running for governor he challenged Governor Lehman in the rather prosecutorial style he had successfully used against Lucky Luciano and others. This worked well in the courtroom but proved to be less effective in the political world. His attitude was that he should send his Democratic opponent to jail—political jail, that is. But the media, and certainly his opponents, regarded him as a rather tough and merciless prosecutor, qualities that may have been a defect politically.

Dewey was also smarter than most of the people around him and didn't suffer fools gladly. In the 1942 race, I would occasionally bring around a potential campaign contributor to meet with him and, as frequently happens in politics, the contributor had an idea or two—most of them screwy—that he wanted to press on the candidate. Dewey would tell him directly that it was a bad idea. Instead of the usual politician's practice of telling the person, "Thank you, I'm glad to get acquainted with you, and I'll take your ideas under advisement," Dewey would analyze the hell out of the proposal and show why it was worthless. Of course Dewey was right in his assessment, but his response sometimes made it a bit difficult for his campaign manager.

Dewey was always serious-minded, but unlike a seasoned backroom politician such as Al Smith, he was often impatient in listening to someone else and sometimes lacked an ability to laugh at himself and his mistakes. Yet for all these faults—which are only political faults really—I admired Dewey because he got things done. He assembled a first-rate staff about him and always had a practical goal: getting someone convicted or a bill passed through the legislature. Although I would not describe him as a political visionary, he knew what needed to be done. He was a true reformer and not a self-interested politician, and he had the zeal and ability to surmount opposition to his reform efforts. This didn't make him popular with those people he had to deal with, but it did make him effective.

Although his political style differed greatly from Al Smith's, both men came from modest backgrounds, both were reformers, and both rank as the most successful of New York's governors in this century.

During the time preceding Dewey's election as governor in 1942, the three most powerful Republican leaders in New York were strong Dewey supporters: J. Russel Sprague of Nassau County, Edwin F. Jaeckle of Erie County (Buffalo), and William Bleakley of Westchester County. They had known me as a result of my activities in the assembly and my subsequent involvement in the campaigns of various Republican candidates. In 1932 I had supported "Wild Bill" Donovan for governor and attended breakfast strategy meetings at his New York City home at 1 Beekman Place. In 1934 I had worked in Robert Moses's campaign for governor, becoming a member of the (Trubee) Davison committee for Moses, and I had helped write some of the candidate's speeches, along with Nicholas Roosevelt. Then in 1936 I was elected as a delegate to my first Republican National Convention, and I went to Cleveland to cast my vote for the "Sunflower" candidate: Gov. Alf Landon of Kansas. By 1940 I had been appointed by Ed Jaeckle, then the state party chairman, as legal counsel to the Republican State Committee, an unpaid, part- time position. The three leaders— Sprague, Jaeckle, and Bleakley—now supported Dewey's selection of me to be campaign manager of the statewide ticket and gave me their backing in party circles and in the campaign.

Dewey recognized that control of the party machinery would be critical to his political success. He built on the attempts we had begun in the assembly to curb the power of the rural, upstate Republican leaders, and by the early 1940s political power in the state Republican party had shifted to the cities and the rapidly growing suburban counties, like Westchester, Nassau, and Suffolk, where Dewey was popular and his associates were in control. In preparation for the 1942 campaign, Dewey also consolidated his power in New York City, replacing the county leader, Ken Simpson (who had backed Wendell Willkie for the Republican presidential nomination in 1940) with a strong pro-Dewey organization under the leadership of Thomas J. Curran.

Dewey's control of the state machinery enabled him to thwart the attempts of Wendell Willkie to secure the Republican gubernatorial nomination for himself. Willkie had tried to embarrass Dewey early in 1942 when, at a dinner with reporters, he had ticked off a list of names who would make acceptable candidates for governor, conspicuously omitting Dewey.

Various "Draft Willkie" clubs began to form—shades of 1940. Dewey quickly moved to lock up as many delegates to the state nominating convention as he could, an effort that proved successful due to his attention to and understanding of the workings of the state party machinery. For good measure, Ed Jaeckle moved the site of the state convention from a large auditorium in Buffalo to a smaller hall in Saratoga Springs; the ostensible reason for the shift was "wartime conditions," but we really wanted to prevent an opportunity for Willkie to repeat his strategy of stampeding a convention, as he had done at the national convention in 1940 when his supporters packed the galleries. Willkie finally realized he had no chance for the nomination and told reporters he was not a candidate. Dewey easily won the Republican nomination, although he probably could have beaten Willkie handily in a head-on fight.

Our prospects greatly improved when the New Deal coalition in New York State fell apart and separate candidates for governor were nominated by the Democratic and American Labor parties, making it a three-way race. The Democrats selected state Attorney General John Bennett, who was a Catholic, fairly conservative, and had strong links to the American Legion. Bennett was the choice of Jim Farley, the Democratic state party boss who had split with Roosevelt over the latter's bid for a third term. Evidently in an attempt to show Roosevelt who was boss of the Democratic party in New York, Farley strong-armed the Democratic state convention and secured Bennett's nomination over Sen. James Mead, who was more liberal and pro–New Deal. Bennett might have become a strong opponent, but to our relief liberals in the Democratic party defected from him. The American Labor party, which usually endorsed the Democratic candidates and was sometimes the source of votes that could provide the margin of victory (which had happened in the 1938 race), capitalized on the Democrats' disarray by nominating Dean Alfange as the "liberal alternative," hoping for support from President Roosevelt.

Dewey's close race for the governorship in 1938 aided our efforts greatly, and he had been an active candidate for the Republican nomination for president in 1940. I was not, however, closely involved in that effort; my only assignment was to try to garner some Dewey votes among the delegates from Nebraska. Although Dewey lost the nomination to Willkie, he had had a respectable showing so that by 1942 he had gained wide recognition both in New York State and nationally.

The state Republican party had no money. It had been out of power in the state for so long that it attracted few contributors. The only Republican funds in sight consisted of about $250,000 left over from Willkie's state campaign in the 1940 presidential election. I took the legal position that these funds belonged to the Republican party of New York State and hence were available for the Dewey campaign. Dewey was, of course, the official candidate of the party. The money was held in a separate fund by two distinguished Wall Street lawyers, Walter Hope and Arthur Ballantine. Neither was a Dewey supporter at the time (although, years later, Ballantine became Dewey's law partner). They were uncertain as to their legal responsibility under the circumstances. My negotiations to obtain the money were bogged down, so I drew up a complaint demanding that the fund be paid over to the official Republican party of the state. With the complaint in hand I had my final negotiation with the two senior lawyers, of whom I was very much in awe, and won them over.

With funds now available, the campaign was off to an auspicious start. The old pros were more respectful of the newcomer as a result of my obtaining the moneys. When I see the huge sums that are spent in political campaigns these days, I marvel that in 1942 we ran a winning race on a total budget of about $400,000—no expensive television advertising in those days![1]

The major political problem within the Republican ranks was to unite the upstate and downstate party leaders—traditionally suspicious of each other. Here I called upon my former assembly associates for help. Organization was a major factor—a statewide effort had to be created, not just reliance on the individual efforts of county leaders. And the campaign had to emphasize the entire Republican ticket; in the past, local party organizations had been content to concentrate their efforts on the local offices and the state senate and assembly races, often with little effort even to distribute literature for the candidate for governor. Therefore we formed a single campaign organization for the two downstaters on the ticket, Dewey and Nathaniel Goldstein, and the two upstaters, Tom Wallace and Frank Moore; their efforts were directed by the Dewey campaign staff that I headed. I should add that our work was aided by our control over the campaign war chest. We collected funds statewide and then distributed them to county leaders, thus encouraging allegiance to our campaign plans. The goal of party and candidate unity was attained and prevailed through the campaign.

Dewey campaigned hard, traveling throughout the state, even into areas such as Harlem that Republicans normally neglected. He made a number of radio appeals during the campaign, which I scheduled after popular programs. Dewey's speeches were the high point of the campaign; he was more at ease campaigning in 1942 than he had been in his maiden effort in 1938.

Dewey's campaign, too, had the benefit of an experienced group of loyal, hardworking volunteers who had been attracted to him in his early years in public service as special prosecutor and district attorney. They were idealistic but not starry-eyed. Dewey encouraged them to participate in political campaigns and to become knowledgeable about the practical workings of our political system. They worked in harmony with regular Republican-organization "pols," and I could not have managed a successful campaign without them.

On the last weekend of the campaign, a story was spread by our opponents of an alleged Republican scandal: A picture appeared in the press of Republican State Chairman Edwin Jaeckle supposedly reviewing a pro-Nazi German-American Bund parade of robed participants in Buffalo. The implication was clear, especially to Jewish voters, that the Republican party in the state, if victorious, would be led by a chairman sympathetic to Hitler. Mr. Jaeckle immediately denied that he had ever been associated in any way with the Bund, much less ever reviewed a Bund parade. He rushed back to Buffalo, went to the public library to review old newspaper files and finally identified the published picture as one of himself as a local public official attending the ceremonies of a highly respectable fraternal organization. He publicized the explanation and got the true story out. The "roorback" of 1942 had failed.[2] I can still remember the sighs of relief from George Medalie and Roger W. Straus, Sr., political mentors to Dewey, when the true story emerged.

Dewey's victory was smashing—a plurality of almost 650,000 votes. He made great inroads on the Democratic strongholds in New York City—inroads that he repeated in later campaigns—and he came within 12,000 votes of taking Manhattan, a remarkable feat for a Republican. His strong pro–civil rights stand led to lasting support from black voters in his subsequent presidential and gubernatorial campaigns. The entire Dewey statewide ticket was elected along with him, and Republican majorities in the state senate and assembly were increased. At the election-night victory rally, there was a portent of things to come as the crowd shouted "Dewey for President!"

After Dewey's election as governor, he and I discussed whether I would join his administration but I chose not to accompany him to Albany and instead to continue in private law practice. One day, one of the judges on the Court of Appeals, New York's highest court, decided to retire, and he came to me and said, "Now, I want you to be my successor on the court. You managed Dewey's campaign, you're a bright attorney, and obviously you can be appointed." Without any encouragement from me, he told a lot of people I should be his successor. It reached Dewey's ears, and I found out afterward that Dewey was shocked by the suggestion. So was I: I wasn't qualified to go on the court; I was only in my thirties at the time. When I found out about it, I went to Dewey and told him there was nothing to it; I was neither interested nor qualified for the position. Dewey was relieved. He then told me that he would offer me a position on the New York Supreme Court—the trial court in the state system—and then elevate me to the intermediate appellate division, where I could probably become the presiding judge after a year. I again refused. But the incident is revealing of Dewey's character. Despite my political service to him and our longstanding friendship, he knew I wasn't qualified to serve on the highest court and knew he could not appoint me, quite different from what most other politicians might have done under similar circumstances.

Later on Dewey appointed me as one of the two public members of the New York State Judicial Council, which was an unsalaried group of state judges plus the public members, headed by the chief judge of the Court of Appeals. Its purpose was to recommend to the governor and the legislature, from time to time, measures to improve the administration of the court system in New York State. I served until my nomination as U.S. attorney general.

I did agree to be part of Dewey's informal kitchen cabinet. As governor, Dewey kept a suite at the Roosevelt Hotel to serve as his living quarters and working office while in the city. He would come down from Albany at least once a month, more often occasionally, and meet with party leaders such as Sprague and Jaeckle and with advisers such as Medalie, Roger Straus, Bill Bleakley, John Foster Dulles, and me and solicit political advice from us. He would refer national Republican party leaders to me when they would come to visit, and I essentially became his liaison to the national party and other political groups. On occasion I served as his intermediary to Mayors LaGuardia and O'Dwyer on New York City legislation.

I would also suggest legislation to him when I thought his program needed a little humanizing, bills that would show the public he had broader concerns than just balancing the state budget. On one occasion, for example, I proposed that families be given tax credits for some of the funds spent on their children's education; Dewey adopted the proposal and it proved to be quite popular.

The men around him both in Albany and in New York City were smart and able. His cabinet was especially top-rate. Dewey could get good people to work for him, although he kept a watchful eye over their activities. If he had a failing it was in measuring the political skills of the individuals he appointed to his cabinet. They were good workmen, skilled in their particular area of expertise—good lawyers, good bankers, and good tax and budget analysts. But he didn't pay much attention to whether they could get along with the politicians in Albany. They, like Dewey, often acted as though they knew more than the legislators they were dealing with; it's hard to accommodate that attitude into a smoothly working political machine. I accepted that as Dewey's way: Because his system was producing good results, one couldn't change it, and if one couldn't adjust to it, there was no point in staying around. He knew that and so did we.

Unlike my later experience with Eisenhower, I found that Dewey would deal more directly and forcefully with political leaders. Following the 1942 victory, for the first time in decades, the Republican party controlled not only both houses of the state legislature but the governor's mansion as well. Dewey capitalized on this—plus his personal popularity, landslide victory, and control of state party machinery—to bring the Republican leaders in the legislature, normally at odds with a Democratic governor, in line. He looked on the Republican bosses as the ones who would round up the votes for him in the legislature, and he held Sunday evening sessions with them to map out strategy for the coming week's session. To the amazement of everyone, Dewey prevailed and the Republican leaders usually followed his lead.

Dewey could at times be confrontational in his dealings with legislators, but paradoxically this strengthened his hand: Few leaders were able to make much headway in direct discussion with him, and his reputation as an effective but dogged and ruthless prosecutor might have made some of them even a bit afraid of him. Dewey would express his own point of view and political demands in a direct, affirmative if not prosecutorial way. In many instances this proved quite effective, and people would knuckle under. The stronger leaders would argue with him, which Dewey liked. Eisenhower, by contrast, was more indirect; he would find out what the other fellow's point of view was, then go home and figure out what to do. Dewey would always take on a face-to-face political fight. He didn't care if it ended up in a shouting match; he would usually dominate the scene. Surprisingly, strong leaders didn't mind that. Dewey's confrontational style was not based on personal animosity or a need for emotional display but was grounded in his assessment of the facts and in his own considerable personal intelligence. He did his homework and could usually win on an intellectual basis. The leaders of the legislature came to know this and to respect him, and they accepted his leadership as a result. He was able to command the state Republican party apparatus much more than Eisenhower did on the national level. Dewey was a difficult fellow to manage a campaign for because he wanted to manage the campaign too. Yet I never had a confrontational relationship with him; we knew our respective roles.

For me the victory in 1942 was the beginning of a decade of managing political campaigns. No sooner was Dewey installed in the governor's mansion in Albany than the press began speaking of him as a likely candidate for the presidency in 1944. Soon reporters and party leaders from around the country began dropping by Albany. The governor was of course swamped with cabinet selection and development of his legislative program. He had no time for politics and declared he was not a candidate for the presidency. He referred many of these visitors to me in New York City, and I saw them, as a courtesy. Before I knew it, I was in the thick of national Republican party politics even though my base (and my bread and butter) was in my private law practice. By late 1943 Dewey had to face political reality. He was leading in the polls for the Republican presidential nomination. He chose a triumvirate—Sprague, Jaeckle, and me—to manage his political fortunes in 1944.

Jaeckle and Sprague were experienced Republican party leaders in New York State with many contacts in Republican circles in other states. In a sense the two men were rivals for Dewey's ear. Dewey could hardly afford politically to lose either one by preferring one over the other. Because I got along famously with both men and had Dewey's confidence as a political organizer as a result of his 1942 election as governor, I was thrown onto the national political scene as a member of the triumvirate. My major job was to act as liaison between Dewey and the national Republican organization and the party organizations in other states.

With World War II in full swing, attention to politics at home was understandably at a low pitch. But there was no way to postpone (as the British had done under their system) the regular, four-year cycle of presidential elections mandated by the Constitution. Despite low public interest, the campaign proceeded. Against the background of daily casualty reports, the campaign at times seemed unreal. The basic thrust of Dewey's efforts had to be to convince the voters that a Republican postwar administration would be better for the country than a resumption of the New Deal policies, which had failed to remedy unemployment before the war.

My first task was to build a new, Dewey-oriented national team. Dewey had run for president in 1940, but I did not know the leaders he had worked with throughout the country. I did realize that some of them were isolationists and did not approve of Dewey's increasingly internationalist approach to foreign affairs. Two of the ablest of these leaders were Ruth Hanna McCormick Simms of Illinois and E. G. Bennett of Utah. Mrs. Simms had served in Congress and showed the political skills of Mark Hanna (President McKinley's campaign manager and her father) and of Col. Robert McCormick (the controversial publisher of the *Chicago Tribune* and her brother-in-law). Bennett was a Mormon businessman with wide acquaintances in the Mountain and Far West states. They were superb organizers but grew steadily more dispirited as Dewey relied more and more for advice from John Foster Dulles, Eisenhower's future secretary of state, Dulles's brother Allen, and Elliott Bell, Dewey's chief speech writer, formerly business editor of *Business Week*. Years before, John Foster Dulles had offered Dewey a partnership in his prestigious law firm, Sullivan and Cromwell. The Dulles brothers and Bell were strong internationalists and favored a bipartisan foreign policy, a position that Dewey began to emphasize in speeches in 1943 and early 1944 in order to offset lingering suspicions of his isolationism. I managed to harness the organizing talents of Simms and Bennett for the duration of the 1944 campaign. Other Republican rivals such as Wendell Willkie never ceased to criticize Dewey for some of the speeches early in his career that had originally attracted Mrs. Simms and others of like mind to Dewey.

The campaign for the Republican nomination was comparatively dull. Dewey and Sen. Arthur Vandenberg of Michigan had tried to nudge the party toward an internationalist point of view at a conference of Republican leaders at Mackinac Island, Michigan, in fall 1943. Sen. Robert A. Taft and Gov. John W. Bricker of Ohio represented the isolationist sentiment still powerfully present within the Republican party. Willkie, the party's 1940 nominee, Bricker, Gov. Earl Warren of California, and Harold Stassen, the former governor of Minnesota, were active candidates for the Republican nomination. But the media tacitly assumed that the Republicans had no chance against FDR and paid little attention to Republican maneuverings.

Dewey remained in Albany, but his fortunes rose in the polls, largely as a result of his success as governor. In the short period since his election, Dewey had reorganized state government to eliminate waste and duplication, developed a healthy budget surplus and earmarked it for postwar reconstruction, established a state unemployment program for returning veterans, created an Emergency Food Council to ensure adequate supplies for farmers and consumers, eliminated "no-work" state patronage jobs and increased the number of state appointments based on merit, investigated the inhuman conditions and inadequate care at state mental hospitals, forced private power companies to reimburse the state for water diversions, and reapportioned the state legislature on the basis of "one man, one vote." Since much of the national news media was centered in New York, Dewey's remarkable achievements received wide attention.

Although Dewey had made up his mind to seek the presidency by the end of 1943, he could not wage an active campaign for the nomination. During the 1942 campaign for governor, he had pledged to devote himself "exclusively" to the affairs of New York State, and to announce an active drive for the presidency would have resulted in a charge that he was breaking his promise to the voters of New York. The question of making such a pledge had divided Dewey's top advisers at the time: Sprague believed it might hamper any efforts to secure the nomination in 1944, but Jaeckle thought it was necessary to defuse a possible charge by the Democrats that Dewey regarded the governorship as a mere stepping-stone to the White House. Jaeckle won the argument; thus in 1944 Dewey had to be a bit coy about publicly announcing a presidential bid, although privately his top political advisers set about to secure it for him.

Fortunately, no strong competition for the nomination developed. Willkie waged an active campaign but his florid style, his penchant for saying whatever was on his mind at the moment, and his distrust—mutual—of party leaders resulted in his making little headway. Dewey led him in the polls, and the more Willkie campaigned, the greater Dewey's lead grew. The only primary contest of note that year was in Wisconsin. Dewey initially sought to avoid a contest there because it might jeopardize his claims to be a noncandidate or weaken his chances if one of the other candidates beat him in a head-on race. He sent his cousin, Leonard Reid, to Wisconsin to plead with the delegates running under his name there to withdraw, but to no avail. Ruth Simms, based on her contacts in the state, thought Dewey would do well, perhaps fatally damaging Willkie. She proved correct in her assessment. Although Dewey neither campaigned nor ran as an announced candidate, he garnered the lion's share of the delegates at stake, gaining seventeen out of Wisconsin's twenty-four seats, with the remainder divided between Stassen and Gen. Douglas MacArthur. The Wisconsin primary not only knocked Willkie out of the race—he withdrew from active campaigning the next day—it ruined Stassen's efforts because he came from a neighboring state and ought to have done better. The primary also forestalled any boomlet on MacArthur's behalf.

By the time of the Republican National Convention in Chicago, Dewey was clearly the favorite among Republican delegates. Governor Warren of California remained a favorite-son candidate but did not generate much support outside his home state. Governor Bricker of Ohio remained in the race; although amiable and photogenic, he could not muster much support among rank-and-file Republicans. He was a superb old-fashioned political orator—I could imagine him delivering the Fourth of July speech in the square of some Ohio town on the topic of "God, Flag, and Country"— but he lacked a substantive political program. He trailed Dewey badly in the polls even though he was the candidate of the Taft wing of the party.

Thus, without really participating in a preconvention struggle, Dewey had the nomination in hand. Before and at the convention, Sprague, Jaeckle, and I met with delegates to assure them that Dewey would run if nominated. Dewey had authorized us to say that it was "our opinion" that he would accept the nomination; coming from individuals so close to him, the message was clear and prevented other candidates from locking up delegate support while Dewey kept his pledge and waited until his legislature had adjourned for the year.

I also prevailed on Gov. Dwight Griswold of Nebraska to deliver the nominating speech for Dewey. A young and popular governor, he was the leader of the moderate wing of the party in Nebraska and pro-Dewey. I felt that by having Griswold deliver the speech, we would signal that

Dewey had support in the midwestern farm states, normally Taft-Bricker country. Nebraska'a senator, Kenneth Wherry, was a prominent member of the Old Guard Taft wing of the party. A nominating speech by Griswold would show some weakness in their own backyard as well as strengthening the moderate group, led by Griswold, in the state party. Moreover, it would show that the Dewey campaign took the farm vote seriously, which would be important in the general election campaign against FDR.

Our strategy worked. On the third day of the convention, the names of candidates such as Stassen and Bricker and of favorite sons such as Illinois' Everett Dirksen and California's Warren were placed in nomination, but before the roll call began, each man withdrew. The vote was nearly unanimous, with only one delegate casting a lone vote for General Mac-Arthur.

Dewey asked me to sound out Governor Bricker on accepting the vice-presidential nomination, and Bricker agreed to run. Governor Warren was another vice-presidential possibility, but he spurned several feelers we sent out to him on his availability for the second spot on the ticket.

Although Bricker was not Dewey's first choice, he was to work out better as a vice-presidential candidate than Warren did four years later, particularly because of Bricker's ability to draw larger crowds than Warren did. As a fellow midwesterner, I had good rapport with Bricker and his staff, which was to last even during the fight in the Eisenhower years over his attempts to curb the president's treaty-making powers—the Bricker amendment. We never had a sharp word and always got along personally despite our political differences. Although he did not contribute much to a national program for the party, he restrained his conservative and isolationist views during the campaign. In party affairs, Bricker always seemed to be Taft's shadow, but he was a more commanding public presence. He knew how to make friends and charm the voters, and he understood the workings of the party organization. Years later, when both of us were out of politics, my legal practice occasionally took me out to Columbus, Ohio, and I would have lunch with Bricker; our personal friendship lasted until his death.

Nomination in hand and ticket firmed up, Dewey turned his attention, as ever, to the organization of his campaign. Control of the national party apparatus is a prerogative of the recently nominated presidential candidate in American politics, and Dewey asked me to be chairman of the Republican National Committee, in effect the chairman of the Republican party, and I was elected. Sprague and Jaeckle were the other likely candidates—out of our triumvirate—for the position, and I suspect that Dewey chose me because my selection would be least objectionable to the other two. Jaeckle was the leader of the western part of New York, Sprague the eastern part; if he had selected either he would have lost the other. Jaeckle had ambitions to be national leader, Sprague did not, and I suspect that my selection for the post hit him hard; however, I had worked closely with Jaeckle in the past and maintained—even to this day—a good relationship with him, even after he broke with Dewey.

James S. Kemper of Chicago was chosen as finance chairman of the Republican party at this time. Working closely together we managed to complete the campaign without incurring a deficit. At one point, without my prior knowledge, one of my law partners was retained by Eleanor Roosevelt, FDR's wife, to represent her in a tax case. When my factional opponents in the Taft wing of the party heard of this they demanded my resignation. The matter came before the Finance Committee of the party, and Kemper, with the complete support of Silas Strawn, a member of the Finance Committee and head of a distinguished Chicago law firm, quelled the revolt.

Jim Kemper later became ambassador to Brazil, appointed by President Eisenhower. He was one of the first leaders to alert our government to the ties between Fidel Castro of Cuba and the USSR. When I left Washington, Ambassador Kemper offered me the presidency of his great insurance empire. Our friendship with him and his family, starting in the 1944 presidential campaign, lasted until his death at an advanced age. He was a rugged individualist, famous for a black patch over one eye and his ever-present Havana cigar—he chewed them with the cellophane wrapping still intact and then discarded them.

Years later I became acquainted with his son, James S. Kemper, Jr., a fine amateur golfer. He was the sponsor of the Kemper Open Golf Tournament, and as a result he was the honored guest at a large banquet of golf enthusiasts at the Waldorf Astoria Hotel in New York. He asked me to be a speaker on the program. The master of ceremonies was Howard Cosell, the famous sports announcer, who didn't know me from Adam. He misread his notes when introducing me and announced that the next speaker had been attorney general under President Nixon. It so happened that *that* attorney general was in federal prison at the time because of a Watergate conviction. The audience caught the mistake immediately and gave me an unusually warm, not to say hilarious, reception. I'm not sure Cosell ever did know that he had slipped.

Back to the story of the 1944 campaign, FDR was nominated for an unprecedented fourth term by the Democrats (having the foresight to dump Henry Wallace and substitute Harry Truman), and the nation was poised for a wartime election campaign with its eyes and its interest fixed primarily on the battlefields of Europe. As it turned out, the contest was closer than predicted.

On the domestic front, the plight of farmers was a major issue. Dewey, as governor, had turned to Prof. Ed Babcock of Cornell University for important advice on agricultural matters. This aroused suspicions among midwestern farmers that Dewey's farm policies were tilted toward the interests of consumers and neglected producers. To counteract this impression I opened up a separate national headquarters in Chicago and persuaded former governor Samuel R. McKelvie of Nebraska to head it (I had delivered papers to his house in my youth). He did so with great competence, having dealt in depth with farm problems as governor and as publisher of the magazine *Nebraska Farmer*, which had a wide circulation in the farm belt.

To promote the candidate among doubting Republican leaders there, McKelvie staged a rodeo on his ranch in the Nebraska Sandhills with Governor Dewey as guest of honor. The Dewey party arrived by special train and disaster struck: The candidate stepped off the train wearing a black homburg hat—no sombrero or ten-galloner for him. He announced that instead of going directly to the grandstand for opening ceremonies, he had to go to the hotel to put the finishing touches on his speech. Eventually he arrived at the rodeo (still with Homburg) while it was in full swing, earning a big boo rather than the acclaim we had hoped for. Back at New York headquarters I received the news with dismay. And a splendid speech on farm policy hardly got off the ground.

Dewey at this point in his career had not developed the geniality in public appearances that characterized his later years. His physical appearance was also a little off-putting. Dewey wore a mustache, which gave him a rather distinguished appearance close-at-hand; moreover, his wife liked it and didn't want it altered or shaved off just to please the politicians. Still, in those pretelevision years the usual way for a candidate to be seen by the voters was on newsreels in the movie houses, and that meant the cameras showed an intermediate-length exposure rather than close-up shots. In these shots, the black mustache loomed out of proportion and made Dewey look like a villain, and many people formed their opinion of the candidate from those newsreels. Our political opponents even circulated Alice Roosevelt Longworth's wisecrack that Dewey looked like "the groom on the wedding cake"—mostly mustache. But the advice of the politicians and PR experts was disregarded, and the mustache survived.

Dewey was also frequently distracted from more important campaign problems because he had not learned to avoid or disregard well-meant advice from personal friends, especially in the Pawling community where he resided, who reflected their rank amateurism in politics. Dewey's friends in Pawling would have Saturday-night get-togethers in the community, freely offering their advice to the candidate. They had sure-fire solutions for Dewey, such as "avoid politicians," "ignore your opponent," and "act statesmanlike." Many of them wanted active roles in the campaign. It bothered Dewey a bit since he hated to face those Saturday-night parties when he was contemplating a political move, and it was harder for me as campaign manager because he would often tell them to see me with their ideas. I would have to interview and placate them, often a time-consuming task in a busy campaign.

Campaigns in those days involved the "retail politics" of extensive trips by train, stopping at cities and small towns along the route to deliver speeches before whatever crowds might assemble. Since there was no television, paid commercial advertising was not as important as it is today. One could not package a candidate in slick thirty- or sixty-second advertisements and thus peddle him wholesale.

One of Dewey's problems in the 1944 campaign, which would recur in 1948, was the counsel he received, oftentimes ill-advised, on how to conduct himself in such a campaign. His Pawling friends, his chief speech writer Elliot Bell, and Mrs. Dewey were of the view that Dewey should always present himself as "presidential." More politically minded advisers, such as myself at national headquarters, wanted more rousing rhetoric. With communications more difficult then, those people around Dewey such as Bell were often able to have direct influence on the candidate that we at headquarters were unable to counter. Bell, for example, was the last person to see Dewey's speeches before they were delivered and would often edit out segments that gave them their real crowd-pleasing punch.

The problem was compounded by the way the success of a campaign was measured in those days. The printed press played a critical role; there were no television news broadcasts, no television anchors, and no covey of television reporters, video cameras in hand, who followed the candidate around. The media's reporting of campaigns was thus different from today. The reporters would usually gauge the success of the candidates' campaigns by the kind of response a crowd would give to a speech, not the substance of the speech or the issues the candidates would try to raise. Dewey's speeches were sometimes like lectures in political science and economics, with the unsurprising result that they occasionally fell flat in front of large audiences. Dewey's positions on the issues needed to be discussed in the campaign, but some of those speeches were more suitable for smaller, select groups such as the Commonwealth Club of San Francisco, not for large outdoor rallies. The more his friends encouraged him to become "more presidential," the more Dewey's public appeal as a candidate suffered. (Truman, of course, benefited from this greatly four years later: his "Give 'em hell, Harry!" style was perfectly suited to what audiences wanted and to what the media would favorably report.)

In the 1944 campaign the problem of Dewey's "statesmanlike" style came to a head in a speech he delivered at the Los Angeles Coliseum before a packed crowd of over 90,000 people, one of the largest campaign rallies in history. If ever there was an occasion where Dewey needed to deliver a rousing, crowd-pleasing speech, this was it. Instead, he and his advisers traveling with him crafted an important but rather boring speech on social security. The speech fell flat. Not only was the crowd unenthusiastic, but Republican contributors were alarmed over Dewey's deliberate embrace of a program that was anathema to them. Dewey was of course right in his stance on social security; he needed to allay fears that a Republican president would abolish this popular New Deal program, but this was neither the time nor the place nor the means—a whole speech—to do it.

Campaign contributions began to dry up, and by the time Dewey reached Oklahoma, on the next leg of his journey, we were almost out of money. I telephoned the candidate and in no uncertain terms told him of our plight and the need to shake up his speech making. Dewey responded immediately and delivered an address in Oklahoma City that stirred the crowd. He attacked Roosevelt for failing to prepare the military for the war: The U.S. was equipped with "plans but not planes." He criticized Roosevelt for failing to prepare the country for peacetime recovery, a problem that FDR "laughed off." He castigated Gen. Lewis Hershey's comment that "we can keep people in the Army about as cheaply as we could create an agency for them when they are out." As to the view that Roosevelt was "indispensable," Dewey retorted that he was indeed indispensable: "He is indispensable to Harry Hopkins, to Madame Perkins, to Harold Ickes. . . . He's indispensable to those infamous machines in Chicago, in the Bronx, and all the others. . . . He's indispensable to Sidney Hillman. . . . He's indispensable to Earl Browder, the ex-convict and pardoned Communist leader."

The media reported the change in Dewey's style: It did wonders for the morale of Republican party activists, and money began to pour in at national headquarters. Yet many of Dewey's nonpolitical associates—even in the 1948 race—would advise him not to make an "Oklahoma speech." Because of his first experience in running for governor in 1938, Dewey was gun-shy about appearing too much the "prosecutor" and so was inclined to heed such advice.

Dewey was also handicapped by President Roosevelt's initial decision not to wage an active campaign. This essentially made him a candidate without an opponent to attack, like a hunter stalking the countryside but without any prey. Roosevelt followed what has come to be termed a "Rose Garden" strategy, by which sitting presidents run for reelection by attending to their duties in the White House. In Roosevelt's case, such a strategy was doubly effective because he was commander-in-chief in wartime conditions, and the war was coming to a successful conclusion.

Roosevelt was not inactive politically by any means, however. In the middle of the campaign, he made a wartime trip to the Pacific—conveniently billed as a nonpolitical trip in the friendly press. It was a clever ploy to enhance his reelection prospects.[3] Returning to the West Coast, he reported to the American people on the progress of the war, by free radio from a military base in Bremerton, Washington. We demanded free "equal time" from the networks for a radio address by Governor Dewey; after an acrimonious discussion, they turned us down. But I think I am right in believing that those discussions dramatized the issue sufficiently so that by the next presidential campaign the doctrine of "equal time" for candidates had been accepted. In retrospect it is interesting to note that while speaking at Bremerton FDR suffered an attack that was later diagnosed as a heart problem, unbeknownst to us or the public until years later.

Another managerial chore was to try to bring Wendell Willkie, the pre-

vious Republican presidential candidate, in line to endorse Dewey publicly. I had not participated in the 1940 presidential campaign so I did not
know Willkie personally. But I was aware that the personal relationship
between Dewey and Willkie was not good, in part stemming from their rivalry for the 1940 Republican nomination and in part from Willkie's efforts
in 1942 to secure his own selection as the Republican candidate for governor of New York.

I described my problem to Harry Luce, founder and publisher of *Time*
magazine and a person for whom I had great admiration. He was a powerhouse in influencing American public opinion in those days when the
weekly news magazines held sway. Luce was not only articulate but possessed an original mind and had gathered an extraordinary group of political analysts on the staff of *Time*. In later years we became personal
friends. He introduced me to Winston Churchill, and at various times he
and his wife Clare Boothe Luce engaged me in the stimulating political di-
alogues for which their dinner table was famous. Luce now arranged a
dinner in a suite at the Waldorf Astoria Hotel for Willkie, himself, and me.
Over cocktails and at dinner Willkie criticized Dewey and his policies; the
attack was vehement. Suddenly he said, "And I want you to know,
Brownell, that your man is going to be defeated and I am going to run for
president in 1948 and will be elected." After a pause he added, "But I like
you, Brownell, and want you to be my campaign manager in '48."

This gave me my opening. After saying I couldn't very well be in two rival camps at the same time, I added, "One thing is clear and will be clear
to you when I state it; you can't expect to get the Republican nomination
in '48 if you don't endorse the Republican nominee in '44." This sank in,
and as I later learned, he soon telephoned Eugene Pulliam, an influential
newspaper publisher in his home state of Indiana (and Vice-president
Dan Quayle's grandfather), asking Pulliam to set up time on a leading radio network as Willkie was going to announce his support for Dewey. Unfortunately, a few days later, instead of listening to the planned speech, I
was attending Willkie's funeral services.[4]

The other difficult character I had to deal with was Col. Robert McCormick, the vehemently isolationist publisher of the *Chicago Tribune*. After
the nomination, I went to him on a peace-seeking mission (an apt
phrase). He had an office on the top floor of the Tribune building, and he
met me accompanied by a dog that was almost as big as he was. I didn't
know if I was going to be torn to pieces or not; the dog stayed at his side

throughout our conference. As much as he disliked Dewey and what he stood for, McCormick agreed to support him throughout the campaign, which he did in part by running a series of unflattering pictures of an ailing Franklin Roosevelt on the front page of his newspaper.

With Helen Reid, the publisher of the *New York Herald Tribune*, and her husband Ogden, I had the opposite task from the one I had faced with McCormick, namely convincing the Reids that Dewey was indeed an internationalist. The Reids had supported Willkie in 1940 and were an influential voice of the Republican "Eastern Establishment." I also tried to cultivate the Cowles brothers, the publishers of *Look* magazine. They had been strong Willkie and then Stassen supporters, and I at least persuaded them not to be anti-Dewey. We also attempted to cultivate columnists such as Westbrook Pegler, George Sokolsky, Walter Winchell, and, with little success, Walter Lippmann. Lippmann accepted Dewey as an internationalist, but the two never struck it off. Both men had strong personalities and held firm opinions; even when they agreed with each other, as in foreign policy, they would often argue over details and come away angry at each other.

We enjoyed good relations with other members of the media. Bert Andrews, one of the chief political correspondents on the *Herald Tribune*, generally gave us favorable coverage, and he became a personal friend. Although the *New York Times* endorsed Roosevelt, James Hagerty, Sr., a top *Times* reporter and the father of Dewey's and later Eisenhower's press secretary, was not only a friend, dating from my years in Albany when Hagerty covered the legislature, but someone I could turn to for advice and who would never break my trust. Dewey's bona fides as an internationalist were strengthened when he publicly refused to endorse the reelection bid of Congressman Hamilton Fish of Dutchess County, one of the strongest isolationists then on the political scene.

The outstanding campaign crisis, from my point of view, occurred over whether we should make an issue of the failing health of President Roosevelt. Although we did not fully know about the president's condition at the time—he had hypertensive heart disease, hardening of the arteries, acute bronchitis, and had even suffered a heart seizure after his Bremerton speech—we did know that the pictures of the president portrayed an ill and tired man. FDR had even secretly gone to Bethesda Naval Hospital under a false name for medical treatment twenty-nine times. Questions appeared in the press about the state of his health to the point that his physician, Vice-admiral Ross T. McIntire, stated publicly that "there is nothing organically wrong with the President at all. He is perfectly OK. The stories that he is in bad health are not true."

My publicity director was Steve Hanigan, the well-known public-relations expert, and he smelled a rat. In light of the president's physical condition and the rampant rumors about his health, Hanigan prepared an elaborate document for Governor Dewey's consideration, which made the president's failing health a major campaign issue and demanded full disclosure. Dewey took it under advisement, but his advisers were split down the middle. Congress was heavily Democratic so we knew there would be no congressional inquiry into the state of the president's health, nor did the press do any investigative reporting on the subject. The governor decided not to use the health issue, which at that time was based on rumor only, fearing a backlash in the wartime atmosphere. Steve Hanigan resigned.

Of course, the end of the story is known. Roosevelt was reelected in November. At the inauguration he suffered severe chest pains, unknown to the public and to his physicians. On April 12 he died, and Harry Truman became president.

During the campaign's later stages, a new phenomenon appeared in American politics, the political action committee (PAC). Sidney Hillman, leader of the Amalgamated Clothing Workers Union (ACWU), contributed large sums of union funds to a fund for the reelection of Roosevelt. Campaign contributions by corporations were then expressly prohibited by law. We thought it was similarly illegal under existing law for labor unions to make such contributions; but our attacks were disregarded, and the Democratic party received great help from this source.

Hillman individually played a large role in the Democratic campaign. Arthur Krock of the *New York Times* published an account of a meeting at the Democratic convention when Roosevelt told the party leaders to "clear it with Sidney" when they sought FDR's direction on an important matter. We sought to dramatize the influence of Hillman's left-wing following among the New Dealers and ran many ads on the "clear it with Sidney" theme.

Toward the end of the campaign, it came to our attention that many states had antiquated voting laws that severely restricted the ability of U.S. troops overseas from voting in the presidential election. Georgia officials for example refused to send ballots to them at the front. We advocated a federal statute allowing the troops to vote, but Congress passed only an inadequate substitute. We were also unsuccessful in obtaining permission for Dewey to make radio broadcasts to American forces stationed overseas.

A proposal that Dewey visit the battlefields of Europe during the campaign was made by Ed Jaeckle. This plan created divisions among the campaign advisers and was rejected by Dewey; he and some of his advisers feared that his lack of a war record might lead him to be criticized by soldiers on the front. Jaeckle believed his appearance at the front would favorably impress the soldiers' families. Dewey's rejection of the proposal was one of the factors that contributed to Jaeckle's later resignation as state party chairman as soon as the election was over. The Dewey camp lost a strong and honorable leader.

The second big cover-up of the Democratic campaign, in addition to FDR's health, involved Pearl Harbor. We had to face a decision about whether to charge the administration with negligence because of its failure to avert the disaster of December 7, 1941, after high officials had been warned that Japanese attacks on U.S. installations in the Pacific were about to occur. A speech was in preparation on this subject, which pieced together the rumors and the known but scanty evidence indicating negligence and demanded disclosure of the facts.

Just at this time, Gen. George C. Marshall, army chief of staff in Washington, secretly sent a messenger to candidate Dewey, who was then campaigning in Oklahoma. The emissary delivered a letter about Pearl Harbor from Marshall that in its first paragraphs sought to pledge Dewey not to reveal the remainder of its contents. Dewey refused to read the remainder of the letter and sent it back to Marshall.[5]

When Dewey arrived back in Albany, Marshall sent a revised letter by special courier. Dewey read this one. In essence, the message stated that if the story of Pearl Harbor was made a campaign issue, the Japanese would realize we had broken their wartime code, MAGIC.[6] This code was still in use by the Japanese, Marshall said, and he added that the United States was daily receiving valuable information from the secretly broken code. We did not know whether Roosevelt had asked Marshall to act for political reasons or whether Marshall had reasons of his own not to want the Pearl Harbor debacle debated at this time. Dewey discussed the letter with Elliott Bell. Because we were still at war, they decided to take Marshall's word at face value and not to deliver a speech charging the administration with negligence. Dewey then asked me to come to Albany, where he told me about the letter and his reluctant decision, which meant a change in our campaign strategy.

Now, of course, fifty years later, we know that an official army-navy secret investigation was conducted during the presidential campaign, but its results were not disclosed to the public. Four days after the election, the report was handed to Roosevelt. It criticized three high officers, one of whom was Marshall himself. It concluded that Marshall failed to keep his deputies fully informed of the break-off of diplomatic discussions with the Japanese government, especially neglecting to keep General Short in Hawaii abreast of the possible outbreak of war at any time. Roosevelt decided on November 21, 1944, to seal the report until the end of the war.[7]

The historical reconstruction of the relationship of FDR and Marshall to the warning messages that preceded Pearl Harbor is continuing, and I doubt that the last chapter about this dramatic story has been told. When British Intelligence Service and Pentagon and White House papers of that period are fully opened to public scrutiny, I feel sure some surprises are in store. If the MAGIC code broken by our intelligence services gave U.S. authorities in Washington detailed information about Japanese plans to attack Southeast Asia (as is today an acknowledged fact), why didn't the coded messages reveal plans to attack Pearl Harbor?[8] And what had British Intelligence told our government from their sources?

Dewey tried faithfully to maintain a bipartisan foreign policy during the war period. He commissioned John Foster Dulles (who would undoubtedly have been secretary of state if Dewey had been elected) to keep in touch with Secretary of State Cordell Hull to further this goal. Dulles was stricken with an attack of gout, however, which limited his activities.

Dewey did step up the pace of the campaign, making several fighting speeches that aroused the crowds. He analyzed the failure of the New Deal to develop a plan to combat prospective postwar unemployment problems. The speeches raised Roosevelt's ire, and he started fighting back, in his brilliant political style, even though he had earlier avowed he would not have to campaign to be able to defeat Dewey. He gave a rousing speech to the Teamsters Union, teasing the Republicans for attacking his dog Fala. Fala had been left behind in Alaska in the confusion of departure, and a navy destroyer had reputedly been sent back to pick up the dog. Some Republican members of Congress, in speeches on the floor of the House, chided Roosevelt for such an extravagance in wartime. The president, however, turned the attack on his little Scottie to his benefit (a gimmick that Richard Nixon used effectively in his 1952 Checkers speech).

The popular vote was surprisingly close for a wartime election against the commander-in-chief: Roosevelt, 25,602,646; Dewey, 22,017,592. Dewey had done the best among all of Roosevelt's previous opponents, lowering FDR's popular vote to 53.4 percent (it had been 54.7 percent against Willkie in 1940, 60.2 percent against Landon in 1936, and 57.3 percent against Hoover in 1932) and gaining the most electoral votes, ninety-nine (compared to Willkie's eighty-two, Landon's eight, and Hoover's fifty-nine). Interestingly, in the British election a few months later the voters defeated their wartime leader, Winston Churchill. In the United States, the political tide was beginning to turn against FDR and the Democratic party.

I stayed on as Republican national chairman after the 1944 election until 1946 at the request of Governor Dewey. As national chairman I was called upon to speak in all sections of the country to arouse enthusiasm (and to raise money) for the Republican party. The party, however, remained badly divided. In each state I usually encountered two factions in the Republican organization. Their local feuds were sometimes temporarily subordinated on the occasion of a visit by the national chairman. But I remember one occasion, after flying through a snowstorm to reach Fargo, North Dakota, I found the two factions having separate dinners at the hotel where I was to speak. I addressed the one faction and was then escorted to the lobby where I was met by a delegation from the other faction, who conducted me to their dinner; there I delivered the same speech all over again.

The Democratic party had been in power nationally for so long that many commentators predicted that the demise of the Republican party was imminent—that it would never regain the White House. My speeches didn't change that prediction! I appealed to my friend Bert Andrews, the White House correspondent for the Republican-minded *New York Herald Tribune* for speech-writing assistance. He told me that professionally he could not write my next speech but would furnish a rousing peroration to stir audience reaction—and, hopefully, headlines.

Armed with his contribution I tried it out on a group of highly partisan Republicans in New Hampshire. Raising my voice to oratorical heights in an attack on the policies of the new Democratic president, Harry S. Truman, I delivered the conclusion: "And Harry Truman is the worst president since Franklin Pierce." I waited for thunderous applause. I was instead met with silence. I had forgotten that Franklin Pierce was the only New Hampshireman to be president of the United States, and all the natives of the state were very proud of him. I escaped with my life but made no new converts to the Republican cause. Later, my assistant, Thomas E. Stephens, organized a club called the Friendly Sons of Franklin Pierce to commemorate my New Hampshire debacle. The bylaws provided that I was to be honorary president but barred me from making a speech at the club's annual meeting.

NOTES

1. I was ably assisted in the campaign by Adrian Van Sinderen, our finance chairman. Our resulting friendship was a generous dividend from the campaign. He and his lovely wife represented distinguished old-line Brooklyn families. Their home was an elegant example of residences of the period in New York City history that my mother used to describe to me when talking about the year she had spent in the city as a schoolgirl. Van Sinderen introduced me to the Brooklyn Club, to the Gage and Tollner restaurant with its gas lamps, to the Brooklyn Museum, and to the spectacular views of Manhattan as seen from Brooklyn Heights. He was a horseman and a world traveler, and these recreations were reflected in his privately printed, illustrated books of his travels and his philosophical reflections, which he distributed to friends at Christmastime.

2. Roorback was the supposed author of a book published late in the 1844 presidential campaign. It contained libelous allegations against the Democratic candidate, James K. Polk.

3. According to one source, "Roosevelt's trip to Hawaii was as covertly political as it was overtly military. By casting himself in this military role as Commander-in-Chief, the president enhanced his re-elections chances." See Ed Cray, *General of the Army, George C. Marshall* (New York: W. W. Norton, 1990), pp. 469–70.

4. See Robert T. Elson, *The World of Time Inc.* (New York: Atheneum, 1973), 2:88, in which Luce describes the dinner:

It was a painful hour. Willkie behaved atrociously—grumbling, growling and saying everything he could think of against Dewey. Dinner was taken away. Whiskey came. The animal force of Willkie mounted as he lashed out in all directions. Finally, around midnight, Willkie got up and lumbered off. Brownell went over to the couch and flopped. I sank into my chair. . . . Neither of us said a word for minutes and minutes. When we finally aroused ourselves, we agreed that maybe the important job had been done.

5. Dewey told Col. Carter Clarke, Marshall's emissary at the Oklahoma meeting, "I am confident that Franklin Roosevelt is behind this whole thing" (Cray, *General of the Army*, p. 480). Just what FDR knew about the matter remains unclear. According to Robert Sherwood, "During the latter part of October of 1944, Hopkins heard from General Marshall the amazing story of how someone, apparently in the armed services, had imparted to Dewey the fact that the U.S. had broken the Japanese codes before Pearl Harbor." Later Hopkins told Roosevelt about the action that General Marshall had taken in persuading Mr. Dewey not to make this fact public. The president was surprised at Marshall's action but expressed no criticism of it. Hopkins said that the White House never discovered who gave Dewey this military information. See Robert Sherwood, *Roosevelt and Hopkins* (New York: Harper, 1948) p. 827.

6. The Marshall letter to Dewey stated: "We possessed a wealth of information regarding their moves in the Pacific . . . but which unfortunately made no reference whatever to intentions toward Hawaii until the last message before December 7th, which did not reach our hands until the following day, December 8th." This document was generously provided to me by Ed Cray, who obtained it following a Freedom of Information Act appeal. The original document can be found in Box POS-64/2, George Marshall Papers, Washington and Lee University. There was hardly a full disclosure, as later investigations revealed.

7. Cray, *General of the Army*, pp. 480–81.

8. Cray, *General of the Army*, reveals that Marshall acknowledged in testimony before a 1944 congressional investigating committee that he did have responsibility for the failure to make certain that the Pearl Harbor army commander was on alert; and he accepted responsibility for his failure on the morning of December 7, 1941, to use the scrambler telephone to warn General Short of the 1:00 P.M. deadline that day. Marshall also acknowledged that the army had failed to appreciate the importance of the series of MAGIC intercepts that might have tipped them off that Pearl Harbor was the target of Japanese attack (pp. 556–57; 559).

The New York Public Library *Book of Answers* (New York: New York Public Library, 1990), p. 13, offers one account:

> Did the United States have warning of the attack on Pearl Harbor? Answer: Ten hours before the surprise attack on December 7, 1941, Americans interpreted a 14-part Japanese message. They deciphered it at 4:37 A.M. Washington time, just hours before the attack, but the message remained in the code room; not until three hours later was it delivered to President Roosevelt. By 11:00 A.M. the U.S. Chief of Naval Operations and the Army Chief of Staff received the deciphered message, which was then transmitted to all areas of the Pacific except Hawaii, where the

receiver was not working. The message did not reach Pearl Harbor until nearly three hours after the attack, which took 3,000 lives.

In its story on the fiftieth anniversary of Pearl Harbor, *Time* magazine (December 2, 1991; pp. 32–45,) reveals that the White House also had other information that might have led to more vigilance against a possible Japanese attack. For example, MAGIC had revealed to U.S. authorities before the Pearl Harbor attack that Tokyo had requested from its consulate in Honolulu information as to the exact location of all U.S. ships in Pearl Harbor. Washington also had information that on December 2, 1941, the Japanese aircraft carriers had disappeared. On the evening of December 6, 1941, President Roosevelt was handed an intercept that the Japanese had rejected the U.S. diplomatic ultimatum. FDR called for Admiral Stark, but when he found that the admiral was at the theater watching a presentation of *The Student Prince*, he decided not to bother him.

In his recent memoirs, James Reston (*Deadline* [New York: Random House, 1991], p. 105) provides some additional information:

In January of 1941, Joseph Grew, the U.S. ambassador in Tokyo, had alerted Secretary [of State] Hull to the possibility of a sneak attack on Pearl Harbor, but added reassuringly, though inaccurately to his diary, "I guess the boys in Hawaii are not precisely asleep." More important, weeks before the attack, Secretary of the Navy Frank Knox predicted in writing to Secretary of War Henry Stimson that "hostilities would be initiated by a surprise attack on Pearl Harbor."

An interesting speculation: Would the outcome of the FDR–Dewey race have been different if the two big cover-ups (the president's health and the Pearl Harbor affair) had been exposed during the campaign?

4

The Election of 1948

❖ ❖ ❖ ❖ ❖ ❖ ❖ ❖ ❖ ❖ ❖ ❖ ❖ ❖ ❖

Mention the 1948 presidential campaign between Truman and Dewey to people old enough to remember it, and they have but one recollection—a cocky, elated Truman holding up the early edition of the *Chicago Tribune* on the morning after election day with the headline "Dewey Elected" and imitating the commentator Hans Kaltenborn in his deep, guttural voice announcing Dewey's election. Truman was entitled to celebrate. He had confounded the pundits. His "Give 'em hell" populist speeches had appealed to the voters. He had won.

No reasonable person, save perhaps for the ever-confident Truman, would have predicted a Democratic triumph at the outset of the campaign in 1947. The reasons for this almost universal sentiment lay in the condition of the Democratic party after FDR's death in spring 1945. The party machinery was rusty because FDR had imposed his personal governance over it after his falling out with the party chairman, James J. Farley. Nor had Truman yet established himself as party leader.

The Republican party, too, was weak at the time of FDR's death in 1945. The GOP had lost the White House in four successive presidential elections, and not surprisingly, morale was at a low ebb. When I became GOP chairman I found the party's national organization in a shambles and set about reorganizing it. The previous chairman, Harrison Spangler of Iowa, was a man in his seventies; he and most of the party professionals were conservative and isolationist, many dating from the Coolidge and Hoover years. It was thus necessary to shake up the personnel of the national organization. As a courtesy, I gave Spangler an office next to mine, although I think he felt that I didn't consult with him as much as he would have liked. But he did deal sympathetically with the old-timers who would drop by with advice. He was a gentleman from the old school, courteous and civil, and I liked him. Although that old group was cordial to me, they felt that the party had made a mistake in nominating Dewey. Because I represented Dewey and his philosophy of a moderate and progressive Republicanism, it was difficult for us to find common political ground.

Similar problems existed in many state party organizations, especially in the South, where some leaders went back even further than Coolidge to the era of Presidents William Howard Taft and Teddy Roosevelt. Their chief concerns were patronage: gaining Republican control of the White House so that they could appoint postmasters, customs officials, and U.S. marshals and recommend appointments for federal judgeships, even though they never succeeded in carrying their states for the national ticket in electing Republican governors. I had to develop, promote, and encourage the factions in state parties that were sympathetic to the Dewey philosophy: leaders who were internationalist, progressive, and pro–civil rights.

Even members of the national committee tended to be parochial because they were selected by the local Republican state organizations. Dealing with the members of the national committee took a great deal of socializing and of getting acquainted personally so that they would cooperate with me in building a new party structure, which I generally was successful in doing.

Reorganization of the national party machinery was long overdue. Mrs. Ogden Reid (Helen), publisher of the *New York Herald Tribune*, had recommended that our party, which had been out of power nationally for such a long period, follow the rebuilding program the British Conservatives had used when they were out of power for many years. Building on her suggestion, I set about developing a reorganization plan that centralized more control of the issues in the national party, with less influence for local party officials. In this way we would be able to present a nationwide alternative to the New Deal that the voters could recognize.

But the change was not without a fight. Soon after Dewey's defeat, the pro-Taft forces sought to remove me as national chairman. In a late December meeting with Dewey in New York, Senators Taft, Vandenberg, Wallace White of Maine, and Kenneth Wherry of Nebraska, accompanied by four GOP House leaders, discussed the issue of my continuing as party chairman. I assured them that I would not be "Dewey's man" and that I would put forward my best effort in leading the party. Taft, Vandenberg, and White seemed satisfied, although Wherry was not. He was probably upset with me for my efforts on behalf of Governor Griswold, a moderate force within the Nebraska GOP and a rival to Wherry for control of the state party organization.[1]

The matter came to a head in January 1945 at a meeting of the national committee in Indianapolis, where I presented my reorganization plan. I stayed at the home of Eugene Pulliam, a prominent newspaper publisher. The spokesman for my opponents was the national committeeman from Arizona, Bud Kelland, a famous and colorful *Saturday Evening Post* writer, who questioned my credentials to continue as party chairman because, as a lawyer, I had "Wall Street clients." One of my supporters replied that only Charlie McCarthy's dummy, Mortimer Snerd, would be qualified under the Kelland formula.

I had worked hard at maintaining a majority of supporters among the national committee, my base on party issues, and in a close vote I prevailed. Governor Warren of California was instrumental in supporting me as party chairman, as were Senator White of Maine and Republican House leader Joe Martin of Massachusetts, who rebuffed Taft's entreaties to have me removed.

My reorganization plan in hand and my position at least temporarily secure, I set about my work. I enlarged the research staff at national party headquarters. I established a foreign-relations section, headed by former Ambassador Hugh Wilson, an expert on Japan, who worked with the Republicans in Congress on coordinating foreign-policy positions. And I strengthened the domestic-policy section, appointing former Sen. John Danaher of Connecticut as my liaison to Congress on domestic policy; Danaher was a conservative who got along well with Taft and House leader Martin.

I also created a new direct-mail fund-raising arm for the national party. This enabled us to start the practice of helping to finance the local congressional candidates from our national headquarters. The direct-mail campaign for small contributions was devised by Albert Cole of the *Reader's Digest* and has become a smashing success over the years. Our ability to raise funds directly also supported the programs of the national party organization and gave a lot more independence to the national chairman. I attempted to establish closer links between the party's financing efforts and those of the Senate and House campaign committees; but congressional leaders balked at this part of my plan, and fund-raising and disbursing efforts remained separate, as they are to this day.

A new section on nationalities was created in order to try to broaden the appeal of the party to various ethnic groups. I appointed Val Washington, a prominent black leader in Chicago, to head it. He remained active in the Dewey and Eisenhower campaigns, effectively organizing black voters in a number of cities in the East and Middle West. Dewey's success in attracting the support of black and ethnic voters was one of our sources of inspiration for this effort. We recognized that if the Republican party was to achieve majority status it would have to appeal to a wider constituency than the middle-class white voters it had relied upon in the past.

I also established a section under Tom Stephens's direction that would encourage development of a better stable of Republican candidates for Congress. Stephens and his staff, working with local Republicans, would identify likely candidates, and using their own considerable expertise, provide them with advice on how to run a successful campaign, another function that has become an important role for the national party in the years since.

By spring 1946 my reorganization of the national party was well established, and it was time for me to return full-time to my private law practice. I also felt that Dewey would run again in 1948 and that I could not assist him properly if I remained at the helm of the national party. I like to think that my efforts as chairman of the party contributed to the Republican sweep of the 1946 congressional elections (Joe Martin, at least, told me he thought it was a major factor), especially by recruiting new Republican candidates for the House of Representatives. Congress passed to Republican control, and for the first time in many years more voters cast Republican than Democratic ballots in the races for the House of Representatives.

But the Republican success in 1946 sowed the seeds—belatedly discovered—for the outcome in 1948. This knowledge is crucial to an understanding of the 1948 campaign. In the first place it released Truman from appearing as an accident in the White House. Many New Deal senators from the FDR years were defeated in 1946, which enabled Truman to lead his party in his own right, thereby raising his stature. On the Republican side, Senator Taft became the outstanding congressional leader of his party; he was known as "Mr. Republican." He fought Truman at every turn—in foreign affairs as well as domestically. He espoused the Taft-

Hartley Act, which was anathema to the labor unions. He was basically an isolationist in foreign affairs. For many voters, especially independents, "Republican" and "Taft" were synonymous.

During the period I served as chairman of the Republican party I had occasion to work with Senator Taft and got to know him rather well. I helped him draft his proposal for federal aid for the construction of hundreds of thousands of housing units, then desperately needed in the postwar period. I enjoyed working with Taft, despite our political differences. He had a fine mind, and as long as we saw eye-to-eye on an issue, our relationship was productive. We both agreed, for example, that the party should favor a policy that would enable the Japanese to keep Emperor Hirohito as the symbol of the state; we thought this would end the war faster and in the postwar era make it easier to work with the Japanese people than if he were tried as a war criminal.

One of my great disappointments was a lack of success in finding more common ground between the Taft and Dewey camps. To a great extent this reflected the mutual dislike that existed between the two principals; their personal ambitions would clash at every Republican convention from 1940 through 1952. Intellectually I think they could have agreed on some common initiatives in domestic policy. The division in their views on foreign affairs, however, was deep, and the tension between Taft's isolationism and Dewey's internationalism not only prevented the party from moving in one direction on foreign policy in the 1940s but forestalled the development of a coherent and widely accepted Republican alternative to the New Deal and the Fair Deal in domestic affairs. It would take the force of Eisenhower's personality, and the death of Taft in 1953, for the Republicans to achieve the kind of political unity that was needed to make them a viable alternative to the Democrats.

It is interesting to note that, forty years later, the tension between the internationalist and the conservative, isolationist wings of the party once again resurfaced in Patrick Buchanan's "America first" challenge to George Bush's reelection bid. One hopes that the divisiveness over foreign policy will be short-lived and that the party will not be haunted again by its experiences of the past.

As the 1948 Republican convention neared, the moderate wing of the Republican party became convinced that Taft's positions, his housing program notwithstanding, were too conservative to appeal to the electorate, that he did not have a commanding political presence that could appeal much beyond the Republican party faithful, and that, in short, "Mr. Republican" could not be elected "Mr. President." This was the setting for the Republican-nomination battle at Philadelphia.

Moderate Republicans had several candidates for the nomination. Sen. Arthur Vandenberg of Michigan had converted from being an isolationist to an internationalist and played a significant role in developing a truly bipartisan foreign policy. He paid the political price, however, of antagonizing those Republicans who were bitter-end isolationists. Harold Stassen was a strong candidate, holding the loyalty of many younger Republicans who admired his earlier role as the "boy-wonder" governor of Minnesota who had forged a coalition that defeated the New Deal in his state and espoused a middle-of-the-road alternative. Gov. Earl Warren, who led the moderate wing of his party to victory in California, had many adherents among the rank and file but never obtained support of prominent party leaders outside his state. Gen. Douglas MacArthur, still serving as military governor of Japan, threw his hat in the ring, but his campaign ended after his defeat in the Wisconsin primary. And, finally, Governor Dewey of New York was a speculative favorite because of the good showing he had made against FDR in 1944 and because of his success in Albany on the state level.

The battle for the Republican nomination was in earnest because the national polls of public opinion showed Truman a sure loser. For example, one poll in January 1948 showed Dewey 50 percent, Truman 28 percent. It was even known through the grapevine that at least two members of the Truman cabinet were ready to vote the Republican ticket.

At the urging of Republican leaders with whom I had worked in the past, I set up a New York office along with my longtime associate Thomas E. Stephens and Congressman William Pheiffer of New York to organize for Dewey's nomination. Dewey announced that he "wouldn't lift a finger" to obtain the nomination. Stephens remarked, after a customary twelve-hour day's work, that even if Dewey didn't know it, a lot of fingers other than Dewey's were being lifted on his behalf.

This may be the appropriate place to tell more about Stephens, my close political and personal friend over the years, who was a major factor in the ensuing Dewey campaign. As my campaign manager when I successfully ran for the state assembly, he developed an uncanny knack for managing campaigns in the rough and tumble of New York politics. His Irish wit made many friends—I never heard that he had an enemy. His first ingenious campaign plan was to rouse support for my candidacy from prospective voters in the Broadway theater district. Many of them had never before voted, and those who had were New Dealers. Stephens recruited the man who played Santa Claus at Christmastime for Macy's department store and a number of talented actors and actresses, who were unemployed at the time, to lead my cause. They arranged a series of beer parties in the Times Square area, starting at midnight when theater employees were returning home from work. As a result many new voters registered and old Democratic voters cast their first Republican ballot.

Stephens used to give an annual birthday party—at breakfast time—for Republican leaders from all around the country and for his friends to attend on their way to work. He hit the jackpot of hospitality one year when he arranged to have his guests greeted at the door, not by the host but by an appropriately dressed, and most friendly, chimpanzee.

His most famous prank, however, occurred while he was in the White House as appointments secretary to President Eisenhower. Previously he had been the campaign manager for John Foster Dulles for United States senator and was well acquainted with Dulles's somewhat somber approach to life. He decided on a practical joke and wrote Dulles on White House stationery (unbeknownst to Ike) that he thought the president would appreciate an original oil painting by Dulles. Dulles fell for the deception and in due course delivered his painfully executed painting to the White House. Stephens was so delighted with his success that he wrote a similar invitation to the other cabinet members and to U.S. ambassadors. Most of them were likewise taken in, and soon a large assemblage was on display outside the Cabinet Room. Clare Boothe Luce's contribution was, as I remember it, the only one with any artistic merit. Mine was strictly from a Woolworth's painting kit—paint green area marked no.1, red in area no.2, and so on. Today, the "Stephens Collection" is owned by the Eisenhower Museum in Abilene, Kansas. On the serious side, Stephens was an able citizen, a warm person, and a capable assistant to Ike.

To return to our account of my participation in the 1948 Dewey campaign, I was soon engulfed in traveling throughout the country to renew my political alliances from the 1944 campaign and to size up the problems and issues for 1948. I got acquainted with prospective delegates to the Republican convention and their families in their own homes.

The contacts I made between 1944 and 1948, especially during my two years as party chairman, were critical to my ability to get Republican support for Dewey once the 1948 nomination race was under way. I knew many of the delegates personally and thus understood on what terms I might make a pitch to them in favor of Dewey. These personal relationships also enabled me to build an intelligence network even among individuals who were not pro-Dewey. I well knew from experience in 1944 that all the campaigning and careful preparation done the year before is compressed into three or four days at the convention. If you have to deal with strangers in garnering support for your candidate, you not only have no rapport with them, you don't know what's going on. And if you don't know what's going on in a particular delegation you can lose support or fail to pick up the support you need. When I was party chairman, for example, one of the vice-chairmen came from Idaho. I went to visit him, and we took a trip up into Glacier National Park, doing a little hunting and fishing along the way. In critical times he would vote with me on the national committee, even though he was a real conservative, a right-winger. He liked me and I liked him, and he would do me a personal favor when he could. When we got to a convention, he would tell me exactly what was going on in the Idaho delegation even though he always backed other candidates, and I could pick off a vote here or there.

I especially had an advantage in coming from the Middle West, where the strength of the Republican party lay, at least in those years. I could understand the delegates' suspicions about Wall Street, New York, and the "Eastern Establishment," a label which our opponents repeatedly stuck on us. Delegates from the Middle West were often relieved that I came from the same area of the country and could talk about agricultural prices or the need for good roads; as a result, they would be more willing to hear what I had to say on behalf of Dewey than might otherwise have been the case. I also seriously supported women in Republican party politics. I had been to a coeducational college, so I was more inclined to treat the women delegates as equals, which a lot of the representatives of other candidates failed to do. I was relatively young compared to the individuals I was dealing with, but this was an advantage. I realized that the older, more conservative delegates might accept a good progressive thought now and then, especially from a "youngster." My legislative experience led me to deal with individuals openly and kept me from getting angry at them if they had a different view. I had been accustomed to working with conservative, upstate Republicans (and with Democrats), so I could apply these skills in working with the kinds of Republicans on the national scene who might otherwise be inclined to support Taft.

The first major problem arose, however, not in getting delegates but in keeping Dewey's name alive as a viable candidate. Dewey had declared that he was not a candidate for president in 1948, and he remained in Albany, busy with his state legislative program. In 1946 he was reelected as governor, with a plurality of almost 700,000 votes and the largest percentage ever recorded for a candidate for governor. Dewey continued to pursue an ambitious legislative agenda, including landmark antidiscrimination laws in employment, a rent-control bill, plans for the creation of a throughway system that would link New York State, north and south, east and west, and plans for the establishment of a state university system, all this with a half-billion-dollar and growing surplus fund. Dewey also began to venture out more in national affairs, giving thoughtful speeches on foreign issues, generally in support of a bipartisan foreign policy. This led to a cry from the Taft camp that Dewey was merely a "me-too" Republican and did not represent a viable alternative to Truman.

Dewey was a shrewd analyst of the current political scene; he did not underestimate Truman's strength. Truman had drawn even in some of the polls by April 1948, and Dewey wrote to his friend Ben Duffy who was helping him in public relations, "I have no doubt that Harry Truman will be a formidable candidate." Dewey noted a poll showing that only 22 percent of the voters rated the performance of the Republican Congress as good or better. He also weighed the chance that Dwight D. Eisenhower might enter the political lists, and he dined with Ike to make his own assessment. No wonder he hesitated.

With this uncertain state of affairs, I joined with New York Republican leaders in deciding to make an all-out drive for Dewey's nomination. Since he held back from declaring his candidacy, we persuaded him to make "nonpolitical" trips around the country. One was to New Hampshire, where he visited the graves of some ancestors. New Hampshire also happened to be the site of the first presidential primary. Another journey was to the Far West, to combine a trip to the annual conference of state governors at Salt Lake City with a vacation trip with his family to Yellowstone Park. Many Republican leaders in the West arranged to meet him.

Although he had still not declared as a candidate, Dewey's popularity in the polls continued to rise. He met with foreign leaders such as Churchill and Italy's De Gasperi. He did not object to our efforts to arrange campaign organizations in the early primary states of New Hampshire, Nebraska, and Wisconsin, and he consented to make brief forays to Wisconsin and Nebraska. But the early primaries showed mixed results. In the New Hampshire race, Dewey captured six of the state's eight delegates; in Wisconsin, he came in third to Stassen and MacArthur. Dewey did a bit better in Nebraska the next week, far ahead of Taft, who had waged a strong campaign, but again behind Stassen.

Not until the Oregon primary date approached in May (with his New York legislature now adjourned for the year) was Dewey finally convinced he should declare his candidacy. With Stassen now the seeming front-runner, Dewey needed to demonstrate that he could still command strong support and that he was the leader of the internationalist and progressive wing of the party. Despite a severe bursitis attack, which made his wife reluctant to have him travel, he went to Oregon and vigorously campaigned. We pulled out all the stops, mobilizing groups in New York such as bankers, dentists, labor, and ethnic groups to contact their counterparts in Oregon and plead Dewey's case; it was the kind of retail politics at which the well-organized Dewey campaign team excelled and that the Stassen campaign was ill-prepared to counter.

Dewey's break came when he debated Stassen on a nationwide radio hookup on the question of whether the Communist party should be outlawed, with Stassen for outlawing and Dewey, taking a civil-libertarian position, against it. Many liberals at that time, Republican and Democrat, favored making membership in the Communist party illegal. Few real issues divided Stassen and Dewey ideologically; however, Stassen had been speaking repeatedly in favor of outlawing the party, which provided us an issue that would differentiate the candidates.

In the debate Stassen hardly deviated from his prepared script, while Dewey, at ease and using his consummate skills as courtroom prosecutor, hammered hard at his opponent. Dewey's success was also aided by the terms he had forced on Stassen for the debate: national radio coverage but no live audience, with the last closing statement to be made by Dewey. In his closing comments, Dewey not only labeled Stassen's position un-American but tarred Stassen with the brush of electoral self-interest. "As I have watched the repeated proposals of this easy panacea for getting rid of ideas we do not like by passing a law," Dewey told the radio audience, "I have been increasingly shocked. . . . I will never seek votes that way from free Americans."

I listened to the debate over the radio while I was in Kansas City, Missouri, trying to gather delegates. I knew immediately that Dewey had scored a success. Barak Mattingly, our chief supporter there, called me at my hotel room and confirmed my reaction. Mattingly told me the whole atmosphere had changed; he hadn't had much success with the Missouri delegates, but after the debate he had sensed growing support for Dewey. Dewey was a clear winner in the polls following the debate, and Oregon went for him in the primary by a 10,000-vote margin.

Oregon turned the tide against Stassen and toward a Dewey victory at the national convention in Philadelphia. If the debate had been a draw, we probably still would have won Oregon, but Dewey's performance had revitalized the campaign nationally.

Dewey, Taft, Stassen, and Vandenberg were the leading contenders as the convention opened in Philadelphia in late June. I had meticulously planned our efforts for the convention. My best resource in garnering delegates' votes was an elaborate card system I had created that listed all the information we could possibly gather on individual delegates so that we would be able to make the right kind of pitch and accurately tally our strength, state by state. If we sensed trouble in a particular state, for example, we could flip through the card file and find detailed information on the state's delegates and on whom we might contact to keep wavering supporters on board. Our supporters in Philadelphia such as Walter Annenberg, the publishing magnate, and Martin Clement, the president of the Pennsylvania Railroad, entertained the delegates elaborately. We also rented a huge ballroom in one of the main hotels, and Marge Hogan, who was our women's campaign director, created an attractive headquarters where our campaign workers handed out various Dewey paraphernalia (Dewey shopping bags were an especially big item), held door-prize contests, and kept a supply of food and refreshments flowing. I remember a lot of compliments from delegates—"You're a lot nicer than the Taft people are"—which, while half-joking, were still significant and helped Dewey's image. For my part, I held regular news conferences, often twice a day, during which I strategically announced new support and hints of more to come, thus creating news that I knew would travel through the convention and create somewhat of a bandwagon effect.

Our skills at knowing where support for Dewey might lie and our ability to use that support, once gained, to build momentum for his campaign are best illustrated by our efforts in Pennsylvania. The Pennsylvania Republicans at the time were divided into two factions, a conservative, Old Guard group led by Joseph Grundy, an aging former senator and long-time local party figure, and a moderate group led by James Duff, the state's liberal governor; neither group could abide the other. Duff and his supporters seemed logical sources for Dewey votes; however, Duff hated Dewey, and we knew it. Our strategy was to cultivate Grundy, which we did through Congressman Hugh Scott. The Duff and Grundy forces had agreed to nominate Sen. Edward Martin as a favorite-son candidate. Fortunately, Martin was a close friend and admirer of Dewey. Dewey called Martin to his hotel suite and prevailed upon him to support Dewey's candidacy, offering him the choice plum of placing Dewey's name in nomination. Downstairs, in my headquarters, I hinted to reporters that a big surprise was in the offing, and later that day I was able to announce Martin's support as well as that of the Grundy delegates, a major break for our campaign.

I had worked myself to the bone at the convention, which almost did me in: On the morning before the balloting I experienced a jolting sensation in my back that almost threw me to the floor. I decided that if this was the way I was to go, so be it; what better way for a Republican loyalist than at his party's convention? My good friend Clifford Carver took me to the Union League Club for a welcome rubdown and a rest. I quickly recovered and went back to work.

The nomination came down to a contest between Dewey, Stassen, and Taft, with Vandenberg, Warren, and others waiting in the wings if a dead-lock should develop. I knew the voting would be close, and it was the only convention in which I was active that I could not predict the outcome until the final roll call came; it was that tight. Fortunately, our opponents made mistakes in their strategy. As the convention opened, Senator Vandenberg waffled on whether to put up a floor fight despite the vigorous efforts of a small band of supporters headed by Congresswoman Clare Boothe Luce; I always held my breath when Vandenberg met with reporters at the convention because if he announced he was an active candidate the convention would break wide open. As it was, his caution prevented delegates from announcing their support for him, fearful they would be left high and dry. Stassen overplayed his hand, announcing support in a particular delegation that usually failed to materialize; after a while the news reporters began to sense he had less support than was thought and discounted his public announcements. Taft's managers thought he could rely on the old methods of securing the party's nomination: controlling the southern delegations and attempting to curry favor with the local party bosses. This strategy brought him some support but smacked of the old-time politics of smoke-filled rooms, and it didn't go down well with the media and the more independent-minded delegates that Taft would need to gain a majority.

Our efforts paid off. At the end of the first ballot, Dewey was in the lead with 434 of the necessary 548 votes for nomination; he was followed by Taft with a surprisingly small 224, Stassen at 157, Vandenberg with 62, and Warren, 59. A second ballot followed, and Dewey took a commanding lead of 515 votes, just 33 short of victory, with gains coming from New Jersey, Iowa, and other states whose delegates had promised second-ballot support. The anti-Dewey forces, on a motion by Governor Duff of Pennsylvania (now supporting Taft!), moved to recess the convention. I didn't have time to consult Governor Dewey but made the decision to have our supporters vote for the recess. Dewey was startled, to say the least, when he heard about it. He was upset that I hadn't consulted with him, but I knew Dewey's deliberative style would have required an hour or so of argument back and forth, "courtroom proof" of which delegates and how many we could expect to gain on the next ballot and thorough analysis of Taft's, Vandenberg's, and Stassen's intentions. There just wasn't time for this, so I trusted my own instincts.

It was a tough and risky decision—maybe Vandenberg would enter the race, maybe he and Taft and Stassen would combine. I worried that the rising Dewey tide might turn if we opposed the motion and lost, thus showing we were short of a majority. I had received promises of further support for Dewey and believed my ties of friendship with the delegates who made those promises were strong enough to hold. But before the convention convened again, the opposition to Dewey collapsed; Taft conceded, and Warren freed his delegates to vote for whomever they wished. On the third ballot, a motion was made to make Dewey the unanimous choice. As Tom Dewey entered the convention hall to accept his party's nomination, we exuberantly thought he would be the next president.

Selection of the vice-presidential candidate was an important part of our election strategy in 1948. I had previously favored Gov. Dwight Green of Illinois. He and I had several conferences during the preconvention period, and I was convinced that he personally favored Dewey's stand in foreign affairs and that he also would be able to swing the Illinois delegation to vote for Dewey. Green was scheduled to deliver the keynote address at the convention but made the mistake of submitting his speech draft to Col. Robert R. McCormick, publisher of the *Chicago Tribune,* for approval; the colonel turned it into an isolationist document. Green's chances for the nomination vanished quickly. Had Green given his original speech, he might have won a place on the ticket. Furthermore, as governor of a large midwestern state, he might have provided better balance for the ticket. Green had greater appeal to the farm belt than Warren had, and Dewey's loss in that region was a major factor in his defeat. At the very least, Green's presence on the ticket would undoubtedly have carried Illinois for Dewey, which he narrowly lost by only 30,000 votes out of almost 4 million cast. If it had not been for that speech, perhaps a Dewey-Green Republican team might have won the election.

With Green out of the picture, Dewey assembled a group of party leaders to advise him on who would make a good vice-presidential candidate. Congressman Charles Halleck of Indiana, the House majority leader, thought that he had been promised the spot. Halleck was a conservative from the Taft wing of the party, but he had brought the Indiana delegation in line for Dewey, apparently thinking he would get the vice-presidential nomination as a result. (It was not the first time Halleck had put politics above principle: In 1940 he had backed Willkie.) Russel Sprague, in charge of rounding up votes in the Indiana delegation, might have discussed the possibility with Halleck of being a vice-presidential contender, but he was not in the position to offer him the explicit promise to be the vice-presidential nominee, as Halleck later claimed. Halleck's name came up in our discussion but generated little support. Other possibilities were entertained, but no consensus emerged. Finally, Warren's name was put forward, and Dewey selected him as his running mate. This time Warren was agreeable to running with Dewey, unlike in 1944. It seemed at the time an ideal ticket: two progressive governors, with impressive records and strong voter appeal, and from two states, New York and California, with large blocks of electoral votes (72 of the 266 electoral votes needed to win). As it turned out, Warren's presence on the ticket did not carry California.

Dewey again selected me to manage his campaign, which I agreed to do, but I did not want to return as chairman of the national party. I wanted to be in a position to go back to private law practice immediately after election day, without feeling obligated to continue as a party official, as had occurred after the 1944 campaign. Dewey selected Congressman Hugh

Scott, a moderate from Pennsylvania, as the new national chairman. Scott had been our contact in the Duff-Grundy fight over the Pennsylvania delegation, and his appointment returned control of the national party once again to the pro-Dewey forces (my successor as national chairman had been Congressman B. Carroll Reece of Tennessee, who was from the Taft wing of the party). Scott later became a United States senator and Republican leader of the Senate.

So much for the background of the Dewey-Truman election campaign. Our optimism for a Republican victory in November was based in large part on Truman's political woes. On the Left of the Democratic party, he was deserted by Vice-president Henry Wallace, who ran for president himself as a Progressive. On the Right he was assailed by southern delegates because of his pro–civil rights stand. They walked out of the Democratic convention and formed the Dixiecrat party under the leadership of Strom Thurmond, then a Democrat. Thus a four-party race was in prospect—really a Republican against a splintered Democratic party.

The strategy of the Truman forces in response to this unpromising outlook was at the time said to have been devised by Clark Clifford, a Truman political adviser and later secretary of defense under President Lyndon B. Johnson during the Vietnam War. It now appears that the Clifford memo was a mild revision of a memorandum written by another White House aide, James Rowe. The report capitalized on Republican weakness—the split between the views of the congressional Republican leaders and of Dewey, the presidential candidate. The Republican national platform had been formulated by Dewey and the moderate wing of the party and was much more progressive than the views of conservative Republican leaders in Congress. Truman shrewdly opened his campaign by challenging the Republicans in Congress to enact that platform into law when he called a special session of the Eightieth Congress. He sought to turn the campaign into a Truman-versus-Republican-Congress contest rather than a Truman-Dewey race. Would Dewey be able to dominate over Taft?

Dewey immediately recognized the implications of Truman's move and dispatched me to Washington to have an off-the-record meeting with Taft at the old Statler Hotel to determine a course of action. I went with olive branch in hand. Taft brought Senator Vandenberg into the meeting. I was hoping they would overlook the bruising convention battle for the Republican nomination. I took the position that the voters, despite Truman's call, would not expect the Congress at a special session in the midst of a presidential campaign to enact legislation to carry out the entire Republican platform. But I proposed that the Republicans in Congress pass a bill revising the restrictive Displaced Persons Act and a bill expanding social security and then adjourn. Those bills would be popular and would foil Truman's strategy. The atmosphere immediately turned icy. Taft made it clear that he would not change his position on any matters where he had been battling Truman. Vandenberg pointed out that the Republican senators were angry at being called back into session in the midst of campaigning at home and regarded Truman's move as so transparently partisan that the voters would not expect any constructive results. The Republican senators, he predicted, would meet and promptly adjourn. Taft finally agreed to consult Sen. Chapman Revercomb of West Virginia, whose committee would consider the displaced persons legislation that I had proposed, but Revercomb promptly rejected the proposal.

I reported the result of the meeting to Dewey, who decided that he would encounter the same results if he intervened personally. If we disclosed the Republican senators' lack of cooperation to the press and the public, we felt that it would reveal a divided Republican party, placing us at a huge disadvantage in the campaign; so we did not tell the story. In retrospect (even at the time I knew it) the failure of the Republican leaders in Congress to accommodate their presidential candidate was damaging. The conservative Republicans in Congress had for too long been accustomed to attacking Roosevelt and his New Deal programs, taking essentially a negative stance. Now with Truman at the helm and the nation yearning for new policies that would move the country forward in peacetime, a more affirmative program by the Republican party was needed. Dewey attempted to develop this approach into a winning strategy but was thwarted by the Republican conservatives on the Hill.

I thought my proposal to have the special session pass the immigration and social security bills a reasonable compromise. Some observers attributed the reluctance of Taft and the other Republicans in Congress to act even on these suggestions to their willingness to write Dewey off as a candidate. Dewey was not the kind of Republican they wanted to have at the head of the party when it regained the White House. If Dewey became president and ran for a second term, it would not be until 1956—and too late—that Taft and Vandenberg, who continued to harbor presidential ambitions, could run again.

This might have been an element, but I would not ascribe to a man like

Taft such a self-serving motive. More plausible is the reason they gave me at the time: They had opposed Truman and his Fair Deal program openly and could not politically and in good conscience turn around and take the other point of view. But I was astounded at their response to the limited proposal I had offered. It still doesn't sound reasonable as I think about it today; they were operating as senators, with limited vision, not as national political leaders who could grasp the strategy that was needed to win the election and move the Republican party forward.

The rift in the Republican ranks enabled Truman to depict the party in a negative light, resuscitating public suspicions of the Republicans as the party of Herbert Hoover and political reaction. Thus, the failures of the Republican-controlled Eightieth Congress—rather than Truman's own record—became the focus of the rest of the campaign, enabling Truman to take the offensive.

The public aspects of the 1948 campaign, and the oratory, have been chronicled elsewhere. Basically Truman turned populist in his appeals, pitting the poor against the rich, the farmers against Wall Street. His rhetoric became harsh. Lessons he had learned earlier in his life as a member of the Pendergast machine in Kansas City surfaced when he accused Dewey of being a front man for the same cliques that had backed Hitler, Mussolini, and Tojo.

Dewey, in contrast, gave a series of high-minded and constructive speeches—just as he had done four years before—rather than indulging in campaign oratory. He presented the policies, foreign and domestic, that he would follow as president. He rejected the advice of those supporters who wanted him to reply in kind to Truman's assaults. It should be remembered that 1948 was the last campaign dominated by radio—no TV. Hence colorful not to say reckless oratory had a big advantage.

My primary job in the fall campaign was to advise as to political developments. Ominously, the Henry Wallace campaign fell apart. He was wildly left wing and embraced Communist party support, losing his following. He was thrown off the ballot by the local courts in Illinois, where he had been expected to be the balance of power as a third-party candidate. The Dixiecrat movement failed to gather momentum outside the South because it appeared as racist. These were negative developments for us but beyond our control.

Then Truman scored a major political point by hastily recognizing the new state of Israel even before that country had completed its formation as a separate, organized nation. His political strategist, Clark Clifford, led an intraparty fight among Democrats to ensure announcement of the recognition during the presidential campaign. This move was bitterly opposed—it now appears—by Truman's chief foreign-policy advisers, Secretary of State George C. Marshall and his deputy, Robert Lovett. Both expressed their reservations privately to Truman; their opposition to the move was not public at the time and has only come to light recently with the publication of the State Department's classified documents on Truman's actions.[2] The move to recognize Israel firmed up Truman's support among liberal voters—some of whom had been leaning toward Wallace—in the industrial states of the North and in California, which Dewey would have to carry.

It is interesting to note in retrospect that both Dewey and Truman had these secret revolts within their respective parties early in the campaign. Dewey could not overcome the concealed congressional Republican opposition. But Truman, exercising the power of the presidency, covertly overrode his cabinet dissenters and outwitted Secretary of State Marshall.

The big blow to the still bright Republican chances was the gradual slippage of the farm vote. Early in the campaign I had again urged more prominence for midwestern agricultural leaders in the Republican campaign, just as I had endeavored to do in 1944. Farmers were suspicious that Dewey was overly influenced by easterners, such as the agricultural economists at Cornell University who advised him on farm issues. I became so frustrated at one point that I fired off my resignation to Dewey. But the wire never reached him, due to the cool-headed action of my assistant, Tom Stephens, who intercepted the telegram and tore it up. My disagreements with Dewey over agricultural policy and the campaign strategies needed to appeal to the farm vote—which I recognized was crucial to a Republican victory—were a source of contention between us in both 1944 and 1948.

Our confidential polls and the midsummer public polls showed Truman cutting down the big deficit he had started out with. The media were still predicting a Dewey landslide, however, and this gave our workers a sense of overconfidence; we still thought we would win by a close margin. I polled the members of the national committee and the state party chairmen, in a recorded multiparty telephone call, to ask them whether Dewey should change his tactics. They responded 90-1 that no change was needed to win, with the dissent coming from Sen. Harry Darby of Kansas. I reported the results to the candidate. Dewey, however, was not over-confident, as is common lore. At about this time he was completing a campaign swing through New York State and west to Ohio; as his train left Buffalo, Dewey rather plaintively remarked to one of his campaign aides, John Burton, "We're in trouble, aren't we John?"

Near the end of the campaign, agricultural prices fell nearly 50 percent, and farmers had to sell their grain at depressed prices. Truman capitalized on this development by showing that the Republican-dominated Eighti-eth Congress had refused to appropriate governmental funds for the con-struction of grain-storage facilities. Dewey had no adequate answer be-cause the charge was true. The Dewey campaign was again stymied by the shortsighted actions of the Republicans in Congress, and again we could not criticize their actions publicly without reopening the Taft-Dewey split in the party. Our problem in this instance was another result of our earlier decision not to break with the conservative Taft Republicans on the Hill.

Vice-president Alben Barkley, the popular "Veep" and an orator of great repute from Kentucky, then went on the hustings to dramatize the issue. Secretary of Agriculture Charles Brannan joined in the fray. The media did not get the significance of the drop in farm prices, but the October crowds in the farm states surely did. I have always credited Barkley with putting the Truman ticket over the top in the last days of the campaign.

Dewey's party loyalty in this instance proved costly. A mere handful of votes in three big agricultural states—Ohio, Illinois, and California—would have swung those states to Dewey and given him enough electoral votes to ensure victory.[3] "You can analyze figures from now to kingdom come," Dewey said after the votes were in, "and all they will show is that we lost the farm vote which we had in 1944 and that lost the election."

There were demands in the press for a recount. Allegations of wide-spread fraudulent voting in Chicago and Texas were circulated. But Dewey rejected these calls summarily because he realized he did not have a majority of the popular vote and that the country would be divided dur-ing a protracted recount period.

The scene at Dewey headquarters as the returns came in has been re-counted in political lore many times over the years. Many Republicans who came to celebrate hadn't even bothered to vote because they had fol-lowed the pundits and were sure of the outcome. Hours before the tide turned to Truman, Dewey's statisticians had analyzed the early returns from key districts throughout the country and told us confidentially that the outcome would be decided by a hair's breadth. Dewey himself was alerted. I was optimistic and asked the crowd, waiting to celebrate, to expect a Dewey victory in the decisive farm states. New York State, with a large farm vote upstate, had gone for Dewey, and that seemed to indicate that the farm vote in other states would go Republican. I stayed with the statisticians all night and did not see the faces of Dewey, his wife and sons, his mother, and close friends from Pawling in Dewey's suite as the returns went sour.

None of us retired. We finally gathered in Dewey's suite and knew by breakfast time that we had lost—Kaltenborn and the *Chicago Tribune* notwithstanding. Dewey himself never lost his composure and methodically drafted his congratulatory message to Truman and prepared for a morning press conference. There were no contributors in line (as I am sure were present at the Truman headquarters) bringing in checks and explaining that they had meant to give them earlier.

After the election upset, the Deweys and the Brownells went to Arizona for a restful vacation on neighboring ranches and got together for a post mortem. When I returned to my law office, the senior partner said, "I'm so sorry about you and Dewey." I asked him what he meant, and he told me that Cholly Knickerbocker, a Hearst columnist, had printed a story that on election night Dewey was so angry at me that he picked up a chair and broke it over my head. Bad news travels fast, and I found that many of my friends believed the column. Fortunately for me, Richard Berlin, head of the Hearst papers, had been in the room with me all through election night and knew the facts of our vigil. He got Knickerbocker to print a retraction.

Some weeks later Dewey spoke off-the-record at the Gridiron Dinner in Washington and recounted a story to describe how he felt on the morning after his loss. An Irishman passed away, he said. At the wake, his good friend Pat was overcome with grief to a point where he drank to excess and passed out. Pat's friends decided to play a trick on him. They irreverently took the corpse out of the casket and put the unconscious Pat in it, placed a lily in his hand, and departed. When Pat awoke the morning after, he looked around, felt the silk lining of the coffin, and smelled the lily. "If I'm alive, what am I doing in these surroundings?" he murmured to himself, "and if I'm dead, why do I have to go to the bathroom?" As on many other occasions, Dewey distinguished himself as a good sport.

Following the 1948 defeat, Dewey continued to serve New York State as an able and energetic chief executive. His plans for a state university system came to fruition as did construction of the massive throughway project (later named the Governor Thomas E. Dewey Thruway in his honor), for which ground was broken well before Eisenhower's interstate-highway system was even proposed. His concern for civil rights led him to complement his employment antidiscrimination bill with laws to eliminate discrimination in housing, public accommodations, and education, each one years before similar efforts on the federal level were to achieve passage. His efforts to develop the Niagara power project provided the cornerstone of a hydroelectric grid that would eventually supply power to most of the Northeast.

Dewey also retained an interest in national politics and was a strong supporter of Eisenhower in 1952. Many of the individuals associated with Dewey became members of Eisenhower's team, including not only myself and John Foster Dulles in the cabinet, but Allen Dulles at the CIA, James Hagerty, who would serve as Eisenhower's press secretary, Tom Stephens, who was appointments secretary, Gabriel Hauge, an economics adviser, and William Rogers, my assistant and later successor as attorney general.

Perhaps Dewey's greatest achievement, even in defeat, was to pave the way for the kind of moderate Republican philosophy that Eisenhower was to follow. Dewey's efforts in the 1940s were instrumental in turning the Republican party from the essentially isolationist views of Taft and the Old Guard toward internationalism, which it has since represented even more strongly than has the Democratic party. Dewey also encouraged acceptance of most parts of the New Deal among most Republicans; the Republican party retained its concern for fiscal responsibility during the Eisenhower years, but there were no serious efforts to dismantle Roosevelt's popular domestic programs.

In some areas, Dewey's domestic programs and ideas were even more creative than were Eisenhower's, but the general thrust of maintaining much of the New Deal—with some fiscal fine-tuning—was carried over to the Eisenhower administration. And in areas such as civil rights and aid to education, the individuals associated with Dewey who joined the Eisenhower team were able to encourage Eisenhower—whose views on domestic politics were somewhat undefined at the start of his presidency—to support progressive legislation. Had Taft lived past 1953, it is quite likely that the Eisenhower years might have taken a different course,

Mr. Brownell's parents, Herbert Brownell and May Miller Brownell.

Mr. Brownell's great-uncle, William H. H. Miller, United States Attorney General under President Benjamin Harrison.

Herbert Brownell with his brothers, sisters, and mother. Front row (left to right): Mary Helm, Gertrude Randol, Ruth Bullock, and Mrs. May Miller Brownell; back row (left to right): Philip C. Brownell, Louise Trow, Herbert Brownell, and Samuel Miller Brownell.

The Brownells with their children, 1960. Front row (left to right): James Barker Brownell, Doris and Herbert Brownell; back row (left to right): Joan Brownell, Thomas McCarter Brownell, and Ann Sloane.

Doris McCarter Brownell, wife of
Herbert Brownell.

Mrs. Brownell's parents, Thomas McCarter and Jessie Pender McCarter,
who moved from Glasgow, Scotland, to Texas where Mr. McCarter was the
chief engineer of the MacFadden Compress Company.

The Record of Assemblyman

TRAINING AND EXPERIENCE

Mr. Brownell was graduated from Yale Law School with high honors in 1927, admitted to the New York Bar and entered the office of Root, Clark, Buckner & Ballantine. He is now a member of the firm of Lord, Day & Lord.

As a member of the Assembly, he was chairman of the Social Welfare Committee during his second term as well as a member of the Judiciary Committee. In 1935 he served as one of the four minority members of the powerful Rules Committee.

PUBLIC ENEMY LAW

Sponsoring New York's widely-heralded Public Enemy Law, Mr. Brownell successfully provided a powerful weapon to help rid the community of gangsters and racketeers who show their fear of the new law by the bitter fight they are making against it in the courts.

CHILD LABOR LAW

Battling for three years, Mr. Brownell finally succeeded in 1935 in passing his bill to strengthen New York's laws against Child Labor by providing that any employer who hires a child in a dangerous occupation in violation to the Rules of the Industrial Board shall pay double workmen's compensation benefits if the child is injured in the course of his employment.

PARKS, PARKWAYS AND PLAYGROUNDS

Mr. Brownell, believing in more parks and playgrounds, sponsored a law creating the new consolidated City Park Department which has improved and made more beautiful Bryant Park, Jackson Square Park and Washington Square Park, all in the 10th Assembly District. The Department also will open two new playgrounds for children in the 10th District this fall.

Unsightly advertising billboards on state parkways in New York City will no longer deface the countryside under another bill which Mr. Brownell sponsored and had passed at the 1935 session.

(*Above and opposite*) Brochure for the 1936 campaign for reelection to the New York State Assembly.

HERBERT BROWNELL, Jr.

ECONOMY

Mr. Brownell successfully sponsored the first law in the history of New York City's pension systems to reduce the cost to taxpayers. The law cuts $150,000 annually off the city budget by providing that out-of-state persons teaching in New York City shall not be entitled to pensions based on prior service unless they pay their share into the reserve fund, as is required of resident teachers.

SIDEWALK CAFES

The modern sidewalk cafes were saved by Mr. Brownell. As chairman of a citizens' committee, he sponsored new legislation which allowed them to continue to operate after having been declared illegal under a former city administration.

PUBLIC SCHOOL No. 41

As a result of Mr. Brownell's continued effort with public authorities, unsanitary conditions at the local public school were eliminated and school rooms were completely repainted this summer.

CHARTER REVISION

A commission now engaged in revising New York City's outworn and cumbersome charter for submission to popular vote, was created pursuant to another of Mr. Brownell's acts.

SOCIAL WELFARE

Assemblyman Brownell introduced and obtained the passage of a bill establishing state supervision of Maternity homes. He also successfully sponsored a bill liberalizing the state's old age pension law.

ALIMONY

A strong believer in preserving civil liberties, Mr. Brownell during the 1935 session added two laws to his series of bills to stop the infamous "alimony racket" under which men who were financially unable to pay alimony could be imprisoned for their debts.

Lord, Day & Lord office party about the time the author was made a partner. The senior partners shown at the head table are Lucius Beers, Henry deForest Baldwin, and Franklin B. Lord. Herbert Brownell is second from the front on the right.

The 1948 presidential Republican ticket—Governor Thomas E. Dewey of New York and Governor Earl Warren of California—with their respective campaign managers, Herbert Brownell and Senator William Knowland.

New York World's Fair of 1939–1940—a day at Yankee Stadium with President of the Fair, Grover A. Whalen (with mustache), and his guests, including Babe Ruth (center) and Herbert Brownell (directly behind Whalen and Ruth).

CAN NATIONAL CONVENTION

(*Above*) Dwight D. Eisenhower accepting the presidential nomination at the tumultuous Republican National Convention, 1952, after winning the crucial preliminary fight for the Fair Play amendment to convention rules. (Photo courtesy of Republican National Committee)

(*Opposite*) The Attorney General–designate with President-elect Eisenhower and an unidentified soldier at Iwo Jima on the 1952 postelection "I shall go to Korea" trip.

(*Above*) The Eisenhower cabinet, prior to the inauguration, at the former Commodore Hotel, New York City. Front row (left to right): Herbert Brownell, George Humphrey, Richard Nixon, the President-elect, John Foster Dulles, Charles Wilson; back row (left to right): Joseph Dodge, Oveta Culp Hobby, Sherman Adams, Sinclair Weeks, Douglas McKay, Arthur Summerfield, Ezra Taft Benson, Martin Durkin, Henry Cabot Lodge, Harold Stassen.

(Above) Swearing in the sixty-first Attorney General of the United States at the White House, by Chief Justice of the United States Fred Vinson with President Eisenhower as witness.

(Opposite) Deputy Attorney General William P. Rogers—himself later Attorney General and still later Secretary of State—greeting Brownell at his induction as Attorney General.

The principal author of the Twenty-fifth Amendment to the U.S. Constitution relating to presidential disability, the Attorney General (second from the right), with the amendment's congressional sponsors, Senator Birch Bayh of Indiana (third from right) and Congressman Emanuel Cellar (far right), and the supporting American Bar Association Committee (from left): Edward Wright, Walter Craig, and Governor Leroy Collins of Florida.

The Attorney General's "cabinet" at the Department of Justice, 1953. Front row (left to right): Charles Metzner, J. Edgar Hoover, William P. Rogers, the Attorney General, Simon Sobeloff, Warren E. Burger, J. Lee Rankin; back row (left to right): Frederick Mullen, Brian Holland, Perry Morton, Dallas Townsend, Warren Olney, Stanley Barnes, James Bennett, Joseph Swing, William Tompkins, Sal Andretta.

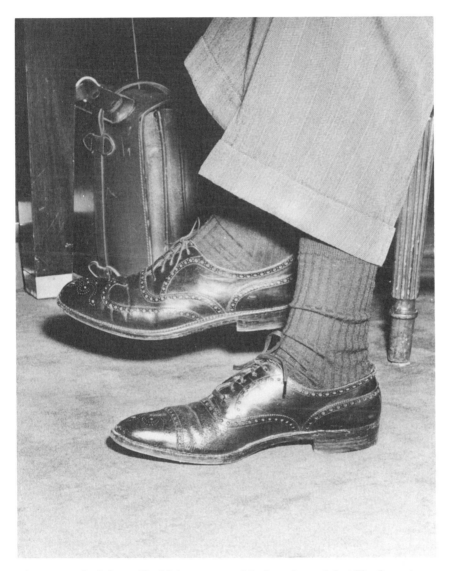

The mismatched shoes: "I told the reporters I had another pair just like these at home" (see pages 227–28).

President Eisenhower and the Attorney General greeting Chief Justice–designate Earl Warren on his arrival at Washington National Airport.

As Special Ambassador to Mexico for solution of the international dispute involving waters of the Colorado River, the Attorney General is shown at a meeting with desalinization experts to consider construction of the world's largest desalting plant (now nearing completion) at Yuma, Arizona.

Former antagonists of the 1957 Little Rock school desegregation constitutional crisis—Governor Orville Faubus of Arkansas and Ernest Green, one of the black high school students barred entry to the high school by the governor—speaking at a commemorative convocation at the Eisenhower Presidential Library, Abilene, Kansas, June 1990. (Photograph by Robert Paull, reproduced courtesy of the Dwight D. Eisenhower Library)

Chief Justice of the United States, retired, Warren E. Burger, Chairman of the Bicentennial Commission on the United States Constitution, and Herbert Brownell, the Vice-Chairman, at a commission hearing.

with Taft supporting Eisenhower's foreign policy but exerting a conservative influence on the domestic front. As it was, Eisenhower was able to develop a moderate Republican program in both domestic and foreign policy.

As Dewey's third term came to an end in 1954, I went to Eisenhower and suggested that he ask Dewey to run for another term. I thought that Dewey would not run again but that the gesture would be good for Ike's relationship with him and good for the party. Eisenhower agreed, and I was authorized to tell Dewey. I caught Dewey at his son's graduation from Princeton and delivered the message. Dewey still wanted to return to private life, but he appreciated the gesture, and his relationship with Eisenhower was indeed better after that.

Dewey changed after his defeat in 1948. He was no longer gung ho to be president; he mellowed and was more relaxed. Socially he was more at ease. He would volunteer advice to others in politics selflessly. He took up golf and was an excellent companion.

For years he and I lunched together at the old Recess Club in downtown New York; in summer season we reverted to our midwestern upbringing and ordered a large slice of watermelon. I always profited by his observations on the current political scene, in which he kept an active and well-informed interest. Especially in the field of foreign affairs, where he had tried to lead his party to an internationalist position and to a bipartisan foreign policy, did he act in the capacity of a private citizen to advance this point of view. He was called upon for advice from time to time by Secretary of State Dean Acheson and by his friends John J. McCloy and Robert Lovett, who had been wartime War Department officials and who continued to advise President Truman. Without a doubt, Tom Dewey would have made a first-rate president of the United States.

NOTES

1. Senator Vandenberg recounts the meeting in his published diaries; see Arthur H. Vandenberg, Jr., ed., *The Private Papers of Senator Vandenberg* (Boston: Houghton Mifflin, 1952), pp. 126–27. Senator Wherry's account of the meeting, which is more negative, can be found in the journals kept by Allen Drury, who was covering the Senate for the UPI wire service; see Allen Drury, *A Senate Journal, 1943–1945* (New York: McGraw-Hill, 1963), p. 319.

2. Truman's secretary of state, George C. Marshall, wrote into the records

of the State Department, declassified about thirty years later, the following comments:

> I remarked to the President [Truman] that, speaking objectively, I could not help but think that suggestions made by Mr. Clifford were wrong. I thought that to adopt these suggestions would have precisely the opposite effect from that intended by Mr. Clifford. The transparent dodge to win a few votes would not in fact achieve this purpose. The great dignity of the office of the President would be seriously diminished. The counsel offered by Mr. Clifford was based on domestic political considerations, while the problem which confronted us was international. I said bluntly that if the President were to follow Mr. Clifford's advice and if in the elections I were to vote, I would vote against the President. (*Foreign Relations of the United States, 1948* [Washington, D.C.: GPO, 1976], 5: p. 975).

It would be fascinating to know whether General Marshall actually did vote for Dewey.

3. The results in the three states were:

	Dewey	*Truman*	*Percentage*	
California	1,895,269	1,913,134	Dewey	47.1
			Truman	47.6
Illinois	1,961,103	1,994,714	Dewey	49.2
			Truman	50.1
Ohio	1,445,684	1,452,791	Dewey	49.2
			Truman	49.5

Neither Truman nor Dewey won 50 percent of the total popular vote cast nationwide.

5

Enlisting Eisenhower

❖   ❖   ❖   ❖   ❖   ❖   ❖   ❖   ❖   ❖   ❖   ❖   ❖   ❖   ❖

In the spring of 1952 I received a confidential letter from General Eisenhower encouraging me to visit him at NATO headquarters near Paris.[1] As it turned out, this invitation led to a lifelong association and friendship with him, and it changed my career.

At this point in my life I was forty-eight years old, happily married with four young children and practicing corporation law. Our family lived in Manhattan in a four-story house designed by an Italian architect, Candella, in a tree-shaded street, known locally as "Block Beautiful,"—Nineteenth Street between Irving Place and Third Avenue, just off Gramercy Park. My wife Doris and I were enjoying a wide circle of friends from all parts of the United States, friendships that had developed from my twenty-five years of legal practice and our active participation in Republican politics at the local, state, and national levels. We were active in community affairs. Doris helped organize the annual Gramercy Park flower show, which still flourishes, and as president of the Gramercy Park Association, I organized the annual Christmas-carol sing in the park.

Our children attended Friends Seminary, a nearby Quaker school, and had a key to fenced-in Gramercy Park, where they could play after school under the benign supervision of the gardener, "Teck" Hannan. Our neighbors and friends included some well-known New Yorkers: Adolf A. Berle—one of Franklin Roosevelt's "Brains Trusters" in the early New Deal days and at this time a Columbia Law School professor—and his wife, a noted public-health physician; Ted Husing, a nationally known radio sports announcer, and his wife, Iris; Ben Sonnenberg, the so-called dean of public-relations advisers; and the widow of George Bellows, the famous American painter of sports scenes.

Many of the houses on our block were converted carriage houses of the worthies who had populated Gramercy Park in Civil War days—Edwin Booth, actor; Cyrus Field, inventor, and his brother David Dudley Field, jurist; and Peter Cooper, philanthropist. We often ate out at the National Arts Club or at Pete's Tavern, which had been a favorite restaurant of O. Henry's. Our street was quiet except for the occasional rumbling of the Third Avenue elevated railroad and, on Saturday nights, the sounds of laughter from The Barrel—a Third Avenue Irish pub. All in all, it was not the typical hustle-bustle of Manhattan's hectic life but a quiet family life, which we thought would continue until the children went away to college. The family did not have a weekend retreat or a summer place out of the city, but we traveled extensively in the Southwest and to upstate New York resorts such as Saratoga and Lake Placid, and, closer to home, to Yankee stadium. Such was our life-style when the Eisenhower letter arrived.

The letter did not come out of the blue. For several months before it came I had been a member of a group dedicated to persuading Ike to run for president of the United States on the Republican ticket. The other organizers of the group were Gov. Thomas E. Dewey of New York, Gen. Lucius D. Clay, who had by then retired from the army,[2] and Sen. Henry Cabot Lodge of Massachusetts.[3] The group met on an irregular basis in the old Commodore Hotel in New York City. It was started and carried forward without any authorization from General Eisenhower. Both Clay and Dewey were instrumental in organizing the Eisenhower forces in these early stages, bringing together a number of political leaders from across the country who had been working independently to draft Eisenhower. Dewey and Clay both knew that although Eisenhower was extremely popular, winning the Republican nomination would require hard work.

Separate from the campaign to obtain for Ike the support of a majority of delegates to the upcoming Republican National Convention in Chicago, a fund-raising effort was needed. The original Eisenhower finance group was composed of a small number of Ike's personal friends who had come to admire him because of his successful military career culminating as commanding general of the Allied forces against Hitler. They played golf and bridge with him, attended his cook-outs and skeet-shooting matches, and talked politics with him. The gregarious leader of the group was Bill Robinson, business manager of the *New York Herald Tribune*. Robinson served as Eisenhower's liaison to his publishers when the general was writing *Crusade in Europe*, his memoirs of the war years, and thus was in frequent contact with him.

The group held an annual Christmas party, hosted by Alton (Pete) Jones, the head of the Cities Service Oil Company, and in 1951 Robinson invited me to attend the affair. All or almost all of the finance group were there—"Slats" Slater of Frankfort Distillers, Bob Woodruff, the head of Coca-Cola, Clif Roberts, a stockbroker in New York, Sid Richardson, a Texas oilman, and George Allen, a businessman who was a close friend of President Truman as well as of Ike.

The Christmas get-together served as a sort of rush party for me, as the group had evidently decided to urge me to take a full-time active role in the campaign to garner delegates to nominate Ike. Bill Robinson, their spokesman, told me the group would undertake to raise the funds necessary for the preconvention campaign, along with the existing fund-raising efforts of Harold E. Talbott, a New York businessman. I told him that if I took a leading part in the campaign it would be as an unpaid volunteer, just as my previous participation in Governor Dewey's campaigns had been.

I was eager to join the effort to gain the presidency for Eisenhower. With Dewey out of contention in 1952, there were few Republicans who were both representatives of the moderate wing of the party and who could wage a winning battle for the nomination and the general election. Governor Stassen was again a candidate, but he had antagonized Dewey because of his political maneuverings in his previous quests for the presidency. Governor Warren was a possibility, and I agreed with his general philosophy of government. But my experience with him as Dewey's running mate in 1948 had led me to question his ability to wage an active and successful campaign; Warren always did well in California where the voters knew him, but he had difficulty in translating his political appeal to party leaders and the voting public outside his home state.

Eisenhower, I knew, not only had such appeal but it was manifest in all regions of the country and it cut across party lines. Here was a candidate who could attract independents and Democrats in ways even a moderate like Tom Dewey was unable to do. Eisenhower's position on foreign policy was an especially important factor in my commitment. Willkie, then Dewey, had battled the strong isolationist sentiment in the party, but only

Eisenhower had the skill and expertise to seal once and for all the Republican party's commitment to internationalism. The long-standing division within the Republican party between isolationism and internationalism had resurfaced after the war, and Taft's candidacy threatened to set the party and the country, if he were to win the presidency, on a foreign-policy course I thought dangerous.

Thus, I was naturally drawn to Eisenhower: He filled the bill perfectly, both in terms of his policy views and his assets as a popular national hero. The only negative I could see was his military background and our American tradition of keeping the military out of politics and civilian affairs. I later found out in conversations with Eisenhower that he had some of the same concerns. Yet I also knew that the country had turned to figures with strong military records at particular points in its history—Washington, Jackson, Taylor, and Grant, even Teddy Roosevelt had a tinge of it—so it was not unprecedented by any means.

I hoped that I could make an especially useful contribution to the effort on Eisenhower's behalf. Because I had managed Dewey's two presidential campaigns of 1944 and 1948 and had been chairman of the Republican National Committee, I knew more Republican leaders and prospective convention delegates personally throughout the country than anybody else in the Dewey-Clay-Lodge group. I had a background knowledge of the factions and rivalries within the Republican party in every state of the Union.

A public-relations problem existed, however, if I was to manage the campaign: The effort to nominate Eisenhower could not be openly linked at the outset with the unsuccessful Dewey campaign of 1948. Many Democrats and independents who had voted the Democratic ticket in 1948 were expected to be drawn to an Eisenhower candidacy in 1952, and a strong connection to Dewey might thwart that appeal. There was an additional consideration that whoever was to manage the Eisenhower campaign needed to know more about Eisenhower's intentions and his views on domestic political issues than he had publicly stated. The group had clearly reached a point where a definite consultation with Ike and an answer from him were necessary.

General Clay was the key to our efforts at this point. In our group he had the closest ties with General Eisenhower, growing out of their association in World War II, and he had access to the general on a confidential basis. As early as January 1952 Ike had written to Clay putting the management of his "political affairs" in Clay's hands. Clay told him of the activities of our group but had received no promises from him.

From January through March, Clay skillfully used his personal association with the general to persuade a reluctant Eisenhower to wage an active campaign for the nomination. We were fairly certain that Eisenhower would accept a draft for the Republican nomination, but we also knew that in the absence of an active Eisenhower candidacy before the convention Taft would probably become the nominee. Clay walked a fine line between pushing the campaign to nominate Eisenhower forward and protecting Eisenhower's personal interests and his reluctance, as a member of the military on active duty, from becoming embroiled in partisan politics in an unseemly way. Eisenhower's decision to run came later, but Clay's efforts were clearly the most important in paving the way.

Henry Cabot Lodge was another central figure in these early efforts to enlist Eisenhower. He was essentially acting as the manager of the campaign and would in fact hold that title officially throughout the 1952 campaign. Eisenhower had a good relationship with Lodge and had dealt with him personally, but as time went on it became apparent to Clay and the others that Lodge needed help, especially in mounting the kind of preconvention effort in getting the delegates needed to win the nomination. Lodge was engaged in his own battle for reelection to the Senate that year, and he also lacked some of the managerial experience and skills I had developed from my prior campaigns with Dewey.

On January 14, 1952, Bill Robinson had written Eisenhower that Lodge needed "organizational help." In this uncertain situation Clay saw an opportunity not only to bring me on board but also to bring more political pressure on the general, and he undoubtedly encouraged Eisenhower to write to me. When the letter arrived, the group urged me to accept. General Clay arranged for me to fly to Paris under an assumed name (since forgotten). The anonymity was deemed necessary to shield General Eisenhower from media speculation about his political plans since he had announced several times that he was not a candidate.

I was met at the George V Hotel in Paris early in the morning, March 24, 1952, and driven to NATO headquarters. I was still traveling under an assumed name, and the meeting was not on the published list of Eisenhower's appointments for the day. I met the general that morning and spent the entire day with him alone, discussing the political situation at home and his future plans.

I had met Eisenhower briefly twice before. Our first meeting occurred in 1948 when he was president of Columbia University; he had spoken on a nonpolitical topic at the Century Association in New York City. I was then managing Governor Dewey's campaign for the presidency and had a brief conversation with him before the speech. I was surprised to learn that he had been following Dewey's campaign in some detail. The second meeting was just before Eisenhower left New York to become the first head of NATO at the request of President Truman. He had taken a leave as president of Columbia, but we met at the faculty dining room there; also present were Dewey, Clay, and Russel Sprague, the Republican national committeeman from New York. The purpose, Governor Dewey explained as we began our discussion, was to inform Ike that we strongly favored his running for the Republican nomination for president in 1952. Dewey told Eisenhower that under no circumstances would he himself run for the presidency again; he had lost twice and had no intention of becoming a latter-day William Jennings Bryan and losing three times. The commitment of the Dewey forces to an Eisenhower candidacy was settled, not only in our minds but also in Eisenhower's.

We received absolutely no encouragement from the general; indeed, when Dewey had set up the meeting with him we had been told that he was not going to make any comment on whether he would become a candidate. But we did have an opportunity to exchange views on political issues and to become somewhat acquainted. During the meal, Ike asked numerous questions about current political issues, especially about the differences between the Dewey wing of the party and the more conservative views of the Republican leaders in Congress. His chief interest at that time of course was to sound out what effect such attitudes might have on congressional support for his forthcoming duties at NATO.

I was encouraged by the meeting. Once again Ike had not positively ruled out a run for the presidency, and our discussion reinforced my impression that he had a good grasp of politics and was certainly not the political neophyte that some people had assumed him to be. As I look back on it, Eisenhower was quite shrewd on the question of whether he would run. Beginning in 1948, when Truman had first broached the issue of the presidency, through the early months of 1952, Ike never put himself in the position of saying he would not run. He never said no absolutely and never took the Sherman-like stance of completely ruling out the question.

My visit with Eisenhower in Paris renewed our initial acquaintance and reopened our discussion of his political plans. It proved to be an important occasion for a confidential and extremely candid exchange of views. He knew and I knew that any leak of information about the meeting would give the false impression that he had made up his mind to run for the presidency.

After a most cordial welcome at NATO, General Eisenhower said he wanted to discuss with me the pressures that were upon him to decide whether he would leave military life and enter politics for the first time. He summarized by saying that many personal friends in the military and in civilian life, Republicans and Democrats alike, had advised him that he had a duty to announce that he would accept the Republican nomination so that as president he could carry out the foreign policies he deemed essential to a strong nation. Most of these advisers told him that his stature in the country was so high that he did not need to fight for the nomination but could merely wait for a sure draft at the Republican convention.

On the personal side, he remarked that he had no aspiration to enter politics. A number of his military friends thought that it would be a mistake for a military man of his prominence to enter the political arena. The long-standing tradition, and the constitutional requirement, that the military be subject to civilian control might be questioned, they believed, if a high-ranking officer ran for president. Eisenhower also made it clear that he had not completed his duties at NATO and that if he decided to resign he would in any event want to make a tour of all the NATO countries to assure them that his leaving would not reflect any change of United States policy toward NATO. This in itself might make it impossible to return to the United States to campaign for the nomination. And he mentioned that military regulations forbade him, as a military officer, from active participation in politics. He was also concerned that the NATO alliance might be compromised if he engaged in partisan debate while heading NATO.

Before settling into a review of the issues and personalities involved in his decision, General Eisenhower told me two facts that were not generally known at the time. One was that he had met secretly with Sen. Robert A. Taft of Ohio, then the leading Republican candidate for president, before coming to NATO. He had told Taft that, despite the pressures on him both in 1948 and currently to run for president, he would announce that he would decline to run if Taft would agree to support the views of the internationalist wing of the Republican party toward NATO and the involvement of the United States in protecting Western Europe against

Communist aggression. He said that Senator Taft replied that he could not in good conscience agree to adopt such views as they were counter to his beliefs and his public record. The meeting between Eisenhower and Taft ended in disagreement.

President Truman was involved in the other incident. Eisenhower said that Truman had offered him his support for the Democratic nomination for president in 1948. Eisenhower had told Truman that he had no intention of entering political life and that he had not even declared himself as a Republican or a Democrat because of the nonpartisan nature of his life-long military career.

The Eisenhower-Truman relationship was a friendly one at this time. Truman had penned a handwritten note to "Dear Ike" on December 18, 1951: "The columnists, the slick magazines and all the political people, who like to speculate are saying many things about what is to happen in 1952. As I told you in 1948 . . . do what you think best for the country." On January 31, 1952, he had written: "You can rest assured that no matter what the professional liars and the pathological columnists may have to say, you and I understand each other." But the warm relations between them were not to last. On April 6, after Eisenhower notified Truman of his decision to run, Truman had answered, rather abruptly, in another handwritten note: "I hope you will be happy in your new role."

During our meeting General Eisenhower stated that he was generally in accord with the domestic principles of the Republican party as he understood them. In the field of foreign relations he thought that the party had become too isolationist in spite of the efforts of a few individuals such as Sen. Arthur Vandenberg and Governor Dewey. He believed the Republicans were going to recapture the presidency in 1952 and that it would be a tragedy for the country if the party pursued isolationist policies from the White House. If he decided to run, his chief motive, he indicated, would be to obtain bipartisan acceptance of a strong internationalist policy. This would preserve and promote the goals that he had sought to achieve as commander of the Allied forces in World War II and as the first leader of NATO.

Then he commented that he would not sacrifice or compromise any of his views as a price for running. This gave me the opening to say that if he would outline his political beliefs to me I would then give him my opinion as to whether he could be elected. I told him I believed his internationalist views, which were well known, would be endorsed by a majority of

Americans, but I confessed to him that I was not fully familiar with his views on domestic policies.

As an opener, he outlined the content of two speeches that he had made, the Guildhall speech in London at the end of World War II and a speech before the American Bar Association in St. Louis, Missouri, on Labor Day 1949, favoring a middle-of-the-road policy in public affairs.[4] It became quite clear to me that as a general proposition he fully supported a system of free enterprise that did not involve the federal government when state governments could operate more effectively and, further, that did not involve the state and federal governments in areas where the private sector could do a better job. He also stated his belief in a balanced budget on the grounds that the United States could not be strong on the world scene unless it was solvent and maintained a strong economy at home. He especially expressed his shock at the recently announced Truman budget, which envisioned a $14-billion deficit, a startling sum at the time.

I learned for the first time the extent of his experience in the Pentagon representing the armed forces in the presentation of the annual military budget to Congress. He understood the essence of budget making and the system of compromises entailed in dealing with Congress in formulating the nation's fiscal policies. His military career, not only as supreme commander of the Allied forces but earlier as an aide to Gen. Douglas MacArthur, then Army chief of staff, and later as aide to Gen. George C. Marshall, had given him an overall view of the nation's needs for a strong national defense.

As Eisenhower propounded his views, I fully realized the truth of the statement by the journalist and author Theodore White, who had interviewed Eisenhower in Paris during this same week and had told me that Eisenhower had more candidate skill than any amateur on the first run that he had ever known. Not only was Eisenhower politically astute in his views, but he was strategic in his political moves: Throughout the turmoil of political pressures on him from 1950 to 1952, I had observed that Ike had never definitively closed the door on accepting a Republican nomination and at the same time had preserved his image as a noncandidate.

Eisenhower volunteered that he had recently taken a position on the politically explosive Texas tidelands controversy. He had read the agreement on the ownership of the offshore tidelands (so rich in oil), reached when Texas was admitted to the Union. He sided with Texas and opposed

President Truman, who vigorously proclaimed that the federal government—not the state of Texas—owned the tidelands off the Texas coast. Eisenhower's position, taken at a time when he was not in politics, later proved a political asset to him in garnering support in Texas.

I asked about his position on civil rights, and he described his actions during the war in breaking down racial barriers in the army. He stated flatly that if elected, as a first order of business he would seek to eliminate discrimination against black citizens in every area under the jurisdiction of the federal government. Although his views did not encompass the full reach that civil rights would achieve in the 1960s or even reveal the extent to which Eisenhower's own beliefs were to evolve during his presidency—the qualifier *federal* jurisdiction was quite limiting in his 1952 position—he clearly stood on what was then the progressive side of the issue.

It must be remembered that *Brown v. Board of Education* (relating to discrimination against black children in the public schools) had not yet been decided by the Supreme Court. The infamous 1896 ruling by the Supreme Court in *Plessy v. Ferguson* was still the law of the land: It had allowed such segregation and had stood as an authoritative interpretation of the Constitution by the Supreme Court for several generations. Under the *Plessy* doctrine, segregation in the primary and secondary schools, as well as other practices of segregation, was not a matter under federal jurisdiction (and also was in accord with the Constitution).

Nor in national politics was there any widespread recognition that discrimination on the basis of color could not be realistically eliminated from our society unless public schools were desegregated. *Brown v. Board of Education* was to be the turning point. But at the time of my meeting with Eisenhower, the nation had not faced that question—neither had Dwight Eisenhower. Although I did not ask him about his opinion on desegregation of schools, a politically charged issue that would soon erupt once he became president, I was relieved that his views were generally in accord with the pro–civil rights stance of the moderate wing of the Republican party and would not cause difficulty to himself or to the party.

Our discussion of civil rights led to a discussion of the prevailing conservative-moderate split in the Republican party. The conservative Taft wing acquiesced tacitly in the so-called "southern strategy" of the prevailing Democratic congressional majority. This strategy allowed civil rights legislation to be buried by filibuster in the Senate year after year and in return fostered some Democratic support for Republican proposals in other

areas of legislation. I noted that the core of Eisenhower's Republican supporters were in the moderate wing of the Republican party and were civil
rights advocates. For example, Dewey had led the fight for a compulsory
Fair Employment Practices Act in New York. Other leaders of the Republican moderate wing, Gov. Earl Warren of California and Gov. Harold Stassen of Minnesota, had acted correspondingly in their respective states.

Eisenhower commented that he had been urged to run for president by
a number of southern Democratic leaders who opposed civil rights legislation. I felt that Eisenhower's heart was in the right place on civil rights,
but his statement signaled to me that he would not lead the charge to
change race relations fundamentally in the United States. It also implicitly
cautioned that he was not going to be the creature of the Dewey wing of
the party and that he had broader support both within the party and the
nation as a whole. The way he handled the issue with me was quite interesting. He did not pursue the matter in detail, drawing out our respective
positions, analyzing their strengths and weaknesses, and perhaps ending
in disagreement, as had been my experience with Tom Dewey in discussing subjects of political controversy. Rather, Eisenhower broadly hinted
at his position, and I was supposed to be smart enought to recognize
where he stood.

Little did I realize that within a year I would be attorney general and
charged with the responsibility of developing a civil rights program for
Eisenhower on a national level. The insight I gained at our Paris meeting
about Ike's approach to civil rights and to the federal government's role
was invaluable. From a historical standpoint, the fact that he knew about
Earl Warren's general position on civil rights as early as this meeting was
significant.

By this time I had a good enough grasp of the general's philosophy of
government and his stand on issues to advise him that it was my judgment that he could win the presidency without compromising his firmly
held views. I told him as forcefully as I could, however, that it was entirely
unrealistic to expect a draft. He would have to fight for the nomination.
This appeared to surprise him, and I believe it was an important turning
point in his thinking about running.

He had known about and expressed his appreciation to various friends
and volunteer groups advocating his nomination and done nothing to
stop them. Indeed, when his name was entered in the Republican primary in New Hampshire he stated that he had voted as a Republican in

the past, and if offered the Republican nomination he would accept, but he would not seek the nomination. Although he was ready to come home before the convention, he seemed not to realize that he himself would have to act affirmatively and conduct a preconvention campaign.

This was an especially difficult point in my conversation with him. Those advisers and friends around him and those who had discussed the matter with him in the past had emphasized, in urging him to run, that he had strong popular support and that he should not turn the nomination down when the opportunity came. Such was the tenor of the advice he had received up to that point; the nomination was essentially his for the taking. Yet these same people had failed to impress upon him the political work that needed to be done to secure his nomination. This was one of the chief reasons, I believe, that Clay had sent me to Paris: It was my task not only to get him to run but to disabuse him of any ideas he might have about the easy prospect of his nomination.

I felt that the role I now had to take was a bit brash. I had no military connection to him, nor was I a friend or confidante. And I knew that Eisenhower was a bit suspicious of those individuals with long-standing involvement in party affairs who might be using him simply to regain Republican control of the White House. But I knew that I had to say what no one else was willing to tell him.

I had decided beforehand that the best way to broach the issue was to hit him straightforwardly with the political facts as I knew them. I thus explained that Taft already had 40 percent plus of the delegate votes sewed up. The remaining 60 percent were available for moderate Republican candidates, including himself, if he ran, and for three favorite-son candidates—Gov. Earl Warren of California, Gov. Theodore R. McKeldin of Maryland, and former Gov. Harold Stassen of Minnesota, all of whom were already campaigning for the nomination. A small group was not committed to any faction. If Eisenhower did not soon declare publicly that he was a candidate, Taft would be the nominee. I thought that Eisenhower, to be successful, would have to return to the United States at least a month before the convention, declare himself a candidate, speak in various parts of the country on the issues, and above all meet personally with as many delegates as possible before and at the convention. I predicted that Taft would be defeated if this program were followed.

Thus our ten-hour private talk ended. For me it was an experience of a lifetime. Eisenhower, already a legendary world figure, struck me as a plainspoken, warm individual, ready to approach the nation's problems and apply his considerable experience to resolving them. He was dressed in military uniform, surrounded by flags and other symbols of his high rank, but otherwise his office appeared almost spartan. As I sat beside his desk, I felt at ease throughout the long conversation. Apparently he had neither notes nor agenda. Except for a lunch brought in on a tray by a uniformed aide, we had no interruptions by telephone or visitors. His eagerness for information about political personalities and current political issues and developments was insatiable. Despite his friendliness at every turn, there was an absence of small talk. For example, I told him I had attended the Folies Bergère the night before—that fell like a lead balloon. Indeed, throughout the years, I never sensed any interest on his part in mixing official business with repartee or in swapping stories with me, largely because I am not a golfer or a bridge player or an outdoor sportsman. With friends who possessed these companionable skills, Ike was an entirely relaxed, first-name-basis, popular companion. But I liked my role and never lost the admiration I had gained at that first meeting for his leadership qualities, his innate political skills, and his comprehension of America's role as a superpower. I came away with a thorough knowledge of Eisenhower's private views on the issues and personalities of the day. But I did not have the answer to the sixty-four-dollar question: Would he fight for the nomination?

I knew from his comments he had been pleased by the returns from the New Hampshire primary, where he had beaten Taft decisively,[5] and by the outpouring of independent support shown by the write-in campaign for him in Minnesota, where he had gained more than 100,000 votes. He was also pleased with events such as the mammoth Eisenhower-for-President rally held in Madison Square Garden on February 8 and with the popular response to the "I Like Ike" song by Irving Berlin (which later became the campaign slogan).[6] These events showed strong popular support even in the absence of Ike's participation in party politics over the years—normally regarded as a sine qua non for a presidential candidacy.

But I concluded he was genuinely undecided about waging what was sure to be an acrimonious intraparty fight against Senator Taft. I remembered that Gen. John J. Pershing, the victorious American commander in World War I, had been willing to accept a draft at the Republican convention in 1920 but did not wage a campaign for the nomination, which went to Warren G. Harding. Whether Ike remembered that, I didn't know. It would be futile, I was convinced, to urge him to run to satisfy personal ambition or desire for power. His distinguished place in history was already secured. He had devoted his life to service to his country; he was a national hero. The Western world looked to him for leadership in his role at NATO to protect freedom and democracy in peace as he had in war. And he was enjoying the independence of private life with a host of admiring friends here and abroad. From his words and his training, I deduced that he would have to be convinced on the basis of "duty to country" (as he had been trained at West Point and throughout his military career).

General Clay deserves the lion's share of the credit for persuading Ike to make the ultimate decision to run. Clay's father had been a Democratic U.S. senator, and he himself had voted for Truman in 1948. But in 1952 he was enthusiastically for Ike for president. Eisenhower had complete confidence in Clay's judgment and in his integrity and personal loyalty. For our part, we relied on Clay to inform us about Eisenhower's inner thoughts, and more important, to force Eisenhower to make a decision. Clay had thought at several stages (especially at a meeting with Ike in London on the occasion in mid-February of the funeral of King George VI) that Eisenhower had made the decision to run, but no public declaration followed. On this occasion Clay flew to London to meet Ike for what he considered a showdown. But arriving at Eisenhower's suite, he found Ike having dinner and a game of bridge with friends from Texas; the friends stayed on and on. Finally, Clay told me he lost his temper and insisted on a private talk and broke up the game. Ike came the closest he had ever come to saying he would run, but again, no action. Ike was exhibiting a tactical skill that featured in his presidency later on—he kept all his options open, confounding the news media, his political adversaries, and even his friends and political confidantes—until he was ready to act decisively.

Eisenhower's intentions notwithstanding, when I met with the group at the Commodore Hotel on my return from Paris it was our unanimous opinion that a public declaration of candidacy by Ike and an affirmative, personal preconvention campaign were needed—further delay would be fatal. The Taft bandwagon was on the verge of success.

Clay relayed this opinion to Ike and succeeded in getting a flat oral commitment from him to run, to battle Taft, and to follow the time schedule we thought necessary. When the moment for a decision finally arrived, only Clay had the ability to tell Eisenhower, "Goddamn it, Ike, it's time to do this. All the politicians say it's time to decide or it will be too late." Only Clay could deal with Eisenhower so directly; whether in a shouting match or a reasoned conversation, he was the individual who could be completely candid with Eisenhower about his political situation and force him to make up his mind. His efforts were especially crucial, not just in getting Eisenhower to announce his candidacy but in impressing upon him the need to leave his NATO command and resign from the army—no small matters to Eisenhower—in time to be able to wage an active campaign before Taft had all the delegates locked up. Eisenhower's public statement announcing his plans followed shortly. He resigned from his NATO post and from the army as of April 11; then he returned home to start his political career.

NOTES

1. The letter is reproduced as appendix A.

2. General Clay, after a distinguished record in World War II, had ably served as military governor of occupied Germany and had orchestrated the Berlin air lift. During this period, he was president of the Continental Can Company and Dewey's director of civil defense. In the Eisenhower administration he directed the building of the national interstate-highway system.

3. Others who were active in the Commodore group included Senators Harry Darby and Frank Carlson from Eisenhower's home state of Kansas, Sen. James Duff of Pennsylvania, Russel Sprague, Republican national committeeman from New York, and Thomas E. Stephens, who would later serve as appointments secretary to President Eisenhower.

4. The Guildhall speech was delivered on June 12, 1945; the American Bar Association speech was delivered on September 5, 1949.

5. The vote was Eisenhower, 46,661; Taft, 35,838. Our Commodore group had helped organize the New Hampshire campaign, and one of our members, my associate Tom Stephens, played a leading role. Stephens had helped me in that state in the Dewey campaigns of 1944 and 1948.

6. The text of the song was:

> I like Ike,
> I'll shout it over the mike
> Or on a phone, or from the highest steeple;
> I like Ike, and Ike is easy to like,
> Stands alone, the choice of We the People;

Chapter Five

A leader we can call, without political noise,
He can lead us all, as he led the boys;
Let's take Ike, a man all of us like,
Tried and true, courageous, strong, and human,
Why even Harry Truman says, "I like Ike!"

6

The Battle for the Nomination, 1952

❖ ❖ ❖ ❖ ❖ ❖ ❖ ❖ ❖ ❖ ❖ ❖ ❖ ❖ ❖

The Republican National Convention of 1952 opened in Chicago only a few short weeks after Eisenhower's declaration of candidacy, and it proved to be the most exciting since the Republican nomination battle in 1912 between the forces of the conservative candidate, President William Howard Taft, and his Progressive Bull Moose challenger, former President Theodore Roosevelt. In fact, the repercussions of 1912 figured significantly in the 1952 convention outcome: A similar split within party ranks complicated our effort to nominate Eisenhower, and disputes over which delegates would be seated determined the outcome.

At the outset, the broad outline of our campaign strategy was clear. The nomination campaign, it should be remembered, seeks to obtain approval of a majority of one's party. The November election campaign seeks to obtain approval of a majority of all the voters of all parties. A Republican candidate for nomination thus faces a more conservative audience at the convention than during the fall election campaign. Our task was to gain the support of enough delegates without forcing Eisenhower to appear to be too conservative, thus compromising his appeal to voters at the general election in November.

At the start in 1952 Taft was the ideological favorite of a majority of the convention delegates. His status as the leading candidate was accentuated by the party rules governing the convention. Some delegates were allocated to every state, even though that state had never voted Republican in any previous election. In other words, the then-Democratic "solid South" sent many delegates entitled to vote for the Republican presidential nominee. These delegates represented almost no one at home because the Republican vote in those states had been so small in November elections in the past, but they constituted a sizable bloc in the 1952 convention's balloting, and by and large they were Old Guard conservatives strongly in favor of Taft.

We were convinced—and thus argued—that Taft was so conservative he could not win in November. We used Eisenhower's strength shown in early primaries in New Hampshire and Minnesota as proof. In New Hampshire, despite a concerted effort by Taft, Eisenhower had won all fourteen of the delegates at stake, racking up over 46,000 votes to Taft's 35,838; Stassen trailed with 6,574, and MacArthur received 3,227. Eisenhower ended up with more votes than all his opponents combined. In Minnesota, Stassen's home territory, Stassen won with 129,000 votes, but Eisenhower garnered an amazing 108,000 write-in votes; Taft captured only 24,000 votes.[1]

The overwhelming win in New Hampshire and the impressive showing in Minnesota, both by an undeclared candidate, demonstrated Eisenhower's wide voter appeal. The battle was drawn on this line. Taft's appeal, in particular, was limited to the conservative segment of the Republican party and was unable to attract the large numbers of independent and Democratic voters necessary to win in November. We believed that the favorite-son candidates—Warren, Stassen, and McKeldin—agreed with us on this point and were closer to us in policy positions, so if and when their candidacies faded, they would favor Eisenhower over Taft.

An Eisenhower convention victory was far from assured, however, when the general resigned his NATO post and left the army to run for the Republican nomination. In the preconvention fight, the Eisenhower forces consisted basically of two groups. The Commodore Hotel group had chosen Sen. Henry Cabot Lodge of Massachusetts as our chairman; he would handle public relations. He could work only part-time on our campaign, however, because he was at the same time running for reelection to the U.S. Senate against John F. Kennedy. I was chosen to head an autonomous effort to obtain Eisenhower delegates although no public announcement of this choice was made: My close association with the 1948 Dewey campaign was deemed a political liability. Dewey and Clay continued their general advisory role, and together we recommended the staff members who were to handle press relations, speech writing, and the scheduling of Ike's campaign appearances. Of this group, the best known was Jim Hagerty, who later became White House press secretary and played an important role in the success of Eisenhower's presidency.

The other political force that was an important part of the effort to capture the nomination was the "Citizens for Eisenhower" group. It was put together in February 1952 and headed by Paul Hoffman, a close personal friend of Eisenhower and a well-known businessman with an internationalist point of view. Arthur Vandenberg, Jr. (son of the Michigan senator), Mary Lord, Sigmund Larmon, and Jackie Cochran, the aviatrix, were other prominent members. The Citizens group was made up mostly of volunteers who had had no experience in organized politics. They believed that volunteers, by expressing their opinions openly, could force the national convention to act, citing the Willkie nomination in 1940 as an example. Unfortunately, their sense of the situation had little relation to current political realities; in 1940 no one had anywhere near a majority of the delegates before the convention, as Taft had in 1952, so it had been possible in 1940 to organize around a dark-horse candidate. Nevertheless, the Citizens for Eisenhower played a significant role in mobilizing support from Democrats and Independents.

Included in the Citizens group, it should be noted, were many influential individuals who had met and worked with Eisenhower when he was president of Columbia University and was promoting the organization and financing of the nonpartisan American Assembly. The assembly's goals were basically to study the values of our democratic society, as opposed to Communism, and to further study the value of and necessity for international cooperation to achieve our national goals. Eisenhower envisioned that the assembly would be a great cultural center—as indeed it has become—"where business, professional and governmental leaders could meet from time to time to discuss and reach conclusions concerning problems of a social and political nature." After Averell Harriman donated his family estate, Arden House, to launch the assembly, Ike spoke throughout the country to raise its endowment funds. Among the influential citizens who helped and later took an active role in the Eisenhower campaign for the Republican nomination were Jack Porter, Lloyd McCollum, and Oveta Culp Hobby of Texas, Harry Bullis of Minnesota, and Ed Birmingham of Alabama—but there were many more.

The nomination fight required know-how about the mechanics of selecting delegates in each of the states as well as mastery of the rules governing the national party convention. In 1952 a presidential campaign was essentially a collection of forty-eight state campaigns centered around state party organizations. Since there were few primaries, the chief means of getting delegate votes was to try to win support in the individual state party organizations because they played a major role in determining who would be selected as delegates. Personal acquaintanceships with the dominant faction in every state Republican organization, of the sort I had developed in my previous effort on behalf of Tom Dewey and as chairman of the party, were thus invaluable.

We were off to a very late start. For example, no arrangements had been previously made for space for the Eisenhower forces at the upcoming convention in Chicago; until Eisenhower became a declared candidate, his supporters had no standing to ask for accommodations to be allotted. Hotel space had been reserved for the headquarters of the other candidates, and no prime locations remained. Fortunately, I had excellent contacts in the hotel industry because I was general counsel to the American Hotel Association. I obtained the grand ballroom in the old Stevens Hotel with the immense help of Vernon Herndon and Robert Quain of the Hilton hotel chain. How they accomplished this feat at that late date is still unknown to me, but we now had the most central and advantageous place to meet and entertain the delegates.

The upcoming arrangements for the national convention were firmly in the hands of the Taft forces through their control of the Republican National Committee, which was the governing board of the party between presidential elections. They chose the convention speakers, featuring former President Herbert Hoover and Gen. Douglas MacArthur, both of whom supported Senator Taft's candidacy. They appointed the Rules Committee, which governed convention procedure, and the Credentials Committee, which made preliminary decisions about who should be seated as delegates in those states where two opposing slates were vying for the right to be seated. The Taft forces controlled many state party organizations as well and thus delegations at the convention, especially in the South.

This control of the party apparatus—both national and state organizations—somehow had to be overcome. My task was to get friendly delegates selected in each state, form a coalition of those delegates opposed to the Taft nomination but initially favoring the favorite-son candidacies of Warren, Stassen, and McKeldin, and last but not least, break Taft's control of the convention machinery.

The bright spot in our preconvention campaign was Eisenhower himself. In civilian dress for the first time, he captivated audiences across the country much as he had done on his victorious homecoming at the end of World War II in his five-star military uniform. The media increasingly predicted that he could beat Taft—the frontrunner and still "Mr. Republican"—and that lent an air of impending success.

We brought many delegates to New York City to meet personally with Eisenhower. He won them to his cause by his friendly manner, candor, and obvious sincerity. In addition, with the help of Winthrop W. Aldrich (who later became ambassador to the Court of St. James's in London), I went to Harrisburg to court Gov. John Fine and his uncommitted Pennsylvania delegation. In Pennsylvania, as in so many cases, personal friendships between the leaders of the state delegation and the presidential candidate's manager (friendship that could result in gaining the ear of the successful candidate) overrode ideology. For example, in 1948 I had won over to my candidate the conservative faction in the state; now I won over the moderate faction controlled by Governor Fine. In both instances, personal ties acquired in the preconvention maneuvering were invaluable.

I also went to Detroit to seek friendly delegates from the uncommitted Michigan delegation headed by Arthur Summerfield (he became Republican national chairman after the convention and later served in the cabinet as postmaster general). I knew Summerfield personally from past campaigns; indeed I knew delegates from every state from past campaigns. In 1944, 1946, and 1948 I had visited in their homes, met their children, helped dry the dishes in their kitchens, and learned their local political problems.

But still we didn't have a majority committed to Ike. It became apparent to me that control of the convention would be determined by the decision as to which slate of delegates would be seated from among the contesting delegations from Texas, Louisiana, and Georgia. We needed a large bloc of votes from those three states; unless our slate from those states was seated, we would quite likely lose. In any situation where two opposing slates of delegates from a state claimed the right to represent the state, the Taft-controlled National Committee and then the Taft-controlled Credentials Committee made the preliminary decision. These committees would undoubtedly place the Taft slates from those states on the temporary roll of convention delegates. It was too late to remedy that. Could that preliminary decision be overturned by the convention before the balloting for president took place?

My experiences in party politics in four previous national conventions and as party chairman truly counted here. I knew that at the Republican convention of 1912 the outcome of the contest between William Howard Taft (Scn. Robert A. Taft's father) and Teddy Roosevelt had been decided by a ruling from the chairman of the convention on which slate of delegates temporarily seated from contested states should be seated permanently. Similar parliamentary maneuvers would decide the 1952 race.

Quietly, I disappeared from the headquarters of the Eisenhower forces in New York for a week. This I could do without media attention since my role in the preconvention campaign had never been made public. I settled in at the New York Public Library on Forty-second Street to read the entire minutes of the 1912 convention as well as contemporary accounts of maneuvering between the opposing conservative and moderate forces.

At the 1912 convention a resolution was first adopted setting forth the rules that would govern the convention. These rules provided that the Republican National Committee and the convention's Credentials Committee would select the delegations to be seated temporarily. Only the convention delegates themselves could overturn the decision. But in cases where there were two groups contesting the right to represent their state, it was not clear who could vote on the motion to overturn the action of the National Committee and the Credentials Committee. Could the delegates temporarily seated vote on the question of whether they themselves should be permanently seated?

Governor Hadley of Missouri, representing the Roosevelt forces, presented a motion that the temporary roll of delegates as prepared by the National Committee controlled by William Howard Taft be replaced by a roll he presented, which contained the names of about ninety delegates who favored Teddy Roosevelt. The presiding officer, National Committee Chairman Victor Rosewater of Nebraska, declined to entertain the motion. He pointed out that the rules governing procedure at the convention had already been adopted. The rules, in his view, provided that once a delegate had been placed on the temporary roll of delegates he was entitled to vote on all matters, thus giving the contested delegates the right to vote on contested delegations, even their own. Rosewater then proceeded to the next matter of business, the election of a temporary chairman. The highly respected Elihu Root, former secretary of state, won the position over the opposition of the Roosevelt forces and immediately supported Rosewater's initial ruling as complying with the adopted rules of the convention.

The 1912 lessons for us were clear. First, we had to amend the convention rules so that they could not be used, as in 1912, to prevent even the consideration of changes in the temporary-delegate roll and discussion of whether contested delegates could vote on contested delegations. Second, we had to present our arguments in carefully prepared briefs. In 1912 the successful Taft forces had presented their arguments in a clear, lawyerlike manner, but the Roosevelt force's arguments were mere generalities in which the words "fraud," "thievery," and "robbery" predominated. We would not repeat Roosevelt's mistakes.

I then went to work with a Boston lawyer, Ralph Boyd, to prepare what later became known as the fair-play amendment to the rules of the convention. It provided that persons who were temporarily placed on the convention rolls by the Credentials Committee from states where the delegation was contested by more than one-third of the National Committee could not vote on the question of whether contested delegates should be seated permanently. Only the uncontested delegations could vote on that question.

If we won such a rule change, we had to prepare our battle to convince the uncontested delegates to seat our delegates from Georgia, Louisiana, and Texas instead of the Taft delegations from those three states. In Georgia our forces challenging the Taft-controlled state organization were ably led by Elbert Tuttle, a lawyer with previous political experience. He knew the importance of careful legal planning for every procedural step. In Louisiana, John Minor Wisdom, also an attorney, led the fight. He had an uphill battle in every precinct of the state and likewise did a superb job. I could count on these two state leaders to present first-rate briefs to the convention.

Texas then loomed as the key contested state. Stories of a giant "Texas steal" of delegates by the Taft forces were building in the national press, based on the Taft forces' position that only those voters who were registered as Republicans in the previous presidential election (1948 in this case) could vote in the precinct caucuses. Of course, if that position prevailed, the Republican party in the state would never increase in strength because large numbers of potential new Republicans would be excluded from participation in party affairs, hardly an incentive to join the party. The Eisenhower forces said that any voter who declared his intention to vote for a Republican for president in the coming election was eligible to vote at the Republican precinct caucuses. If our forces were excluded from the regular organization precinct caucuses, as they often were, they held their own precinct caucuses and elected their competing slate of delegates. When our forces were able to prevail at a local precinct caucus, the Taft forces often walked out and held their own closed caucuses. These tactics were repeated at district and state conventions in Texas and elsewhere, producing two competing slates of delegates to the national convention.

Jack Porter was the Republican state chairman and the Eisenhower leader in Texas. He had been one of the first persons to urge Ike to run. He realized that the existing statutes of Texas governing selection of delegates of the Republican party to its national convention ensured that the local bosses—who supported Taft—could select the delegates. He had the great foresight to obtain a 1951 amendment to the Texas Civil Statutes authorizing open caucuses in the Republican party.[2] This legislation also prevented local party officials from secretly changing the place, date, and hour of the caucuses as they had done in the past to preserve their control.

My collaboration with Porter in his effort in 1951 and our resulting friendship made it easy for the two of us to be well prepared for the state Republican convention at Mineral Wells, Texas, where the makeup of the Texas delegation to the national convention was to be decided from the rival slates chosen at the Taft and Eisenhower precinct and county caucuses.

I took the train to Mineral Wells. On the same train was Oveta Culp Hobby, who had been head of the Women's Auxiliary Corps, providing invaluable service to U.S. troops in World War II; she had worked with General Eisenhower in that capacity. She and her husband, former Texas Governor Will Hobby, were publishers of the *Houston Post*. She was a powerhouse for gathering Eisenhower support in her state.

This was not my first experience with Texas Republican politics. In 1944 when Dewey faced Taft for the Republican nomination and I was a neophyte in the art of getting delegates, I went to the Texas state Republican convention where the delegates to the national convention were to be chosen. The political czar there at the time was "Colonel" R. B. Creager, locally called "the Red Rooster of the Rio Grande" (his unwritten biography would have included an incident in which he jumped from a second-story window when surprised by the angry husband of the woman he was "visiting"). I couldn't make inroads on his tight control of the state convention, but he invited me to have breakfast with him in a room just off the convention floor. I told him of my plight and how crestfallen I was to have to go back to New York to tell Governor Dewey that my first venture into the "solid South" was a flop. At that he called in one of his henchmen and instructed him: "This young man is just starting in politics. I think we ought to give him a break. Tell the chairman of the convention to change that roster of delegates I sent out to him and give Dewey one delegate." That lone Texas delegate for Dewey attended three later Republican National Conventions and always voted for the candidate I favored. Thus I soon learned that camaraderie and friendship sometimes overrode ideology in the voting procedures followed in those days. Thereafter I tried to cultivate at least one personal friend in every state delegation to be my contact and to let me know what was going on.

In Mineral Wells this time, without publicity, I carefully guided the Eisenhower forces to take all legal steps required by the rules of the Republican National Convention to enable us to present an airtight case for seating the Eisenhower delegates once we got to Chicago.

The scene at Mineral Wells resembled a full-fledged party convention. Several thousand Republicans arrived in the small, overcrowded resort town, the campaign managers for Taft and Eisenhower were there in force, and the media turned out in large numbers to observe this crucial test of wills between the rival camps.

The situation we encountered there foreshadowed the problem we were to face at the national convention in Chicago. The Taft forces controlled the proceedings and systematically ran rough-shod over the Eisenhower delegates. Six hundred delegate seats were in dispute between the Eisenhower and Taft camps. In a heated marathon session lasting twenty-four hours, we carefully documented our case that the Eisenhower delegates should be seated, but the convention leaders would not budge and ruled in favor of all but ten of the Taft delegates. These Taft delegates, in turn, took their seats and were able to vote on the challenge we raised to their credentials on the floor of the state convention: Not surprisingly, we lost 762 to 222. With the Taft delegates seated, the convention selected a delegation to the national convention that heavily favored Taft. The Eisenhower delegates walked out of the convention at this point and held their own meeting, choosing a slate with thirty-three Eisenhower delegates and five for Taft. The action now moved on to Chicago.

Although the battle at Mineral Wells was a technical victory for Taft, it would help us win the bigger war at the national convention. We were able to occupy the moral high ground by showing to the party and the nation the tactics that had been used by the Taft camp in getting their delegates selected. The tide of public sentiment in Texas in favor of Eisenhower had been ignored by the Old Guard politicians who controlled the state party, and Taft's "Texas steal" further strengthened our point that Taft lacked popular appeal and could only win the nomination by the wheeling and dealing of backroom politicians. As I told the media when I was leaving Mineral Wells, "the Taft forces are now convinced he cannot win the nomination fair and square, so they are out to steal it."

Mineral Wells also provided another useful lesson about the attention we would have to pay to the party's rules and procedures. With Eisenhower behind in the delegate count, we would have to be astute in making sure that the rules did not permit Taft's contested delegates to vote on their own credentials as they had done in Mineral Wells and as Taft's father's delegates had done forty years earlier against Teddy Roosevelt. My estimates showed that the fight between Eisenhower and Taft might come down to sixty or seventy votes, just about the number of contested Texas, Georgia, and Louisiana delegates. The fair-play amendment had to pass. If we lost on the seating fight, Taft, not Eisenhower, would probably become the party's nominee.

We were now playing for some very high stakes, and Governor Dewey performed an important role at this juncture. At the conference of the Republican governors just prior to the national convention, he obtained a nearly unanimous vote favoring the adoption of our proposed fair-play amendment even though some of the governors personally preferred Taft as the nominee.[3] This action led to strong media coverage of our drive to adopt our rules amendment.

Then came the convention in Chicago. Eisenhower at first resisted the idea of personally attending. Senator Lodge and I flew to Denver to convince him that his presence was essential and would be helpful in winning over delegates to his candidacy. Also, since the convention's proceedings were to be carried live over television—unlike in 1948, television was now common in many American homes—Eisenhower's presence would help increase national support for him in his efforts to win in November.

Television coverage was also an asset in our efforts to seat our contested delegates. For the first time in the history of Republican conventions, at least that I can recall, the Credentials Committee, dominated by the Taft forces, met behind closed doors in making its decision to place Taft delegates on the temporary roll of the convention; they did this entirely on their own. We recognized, however, that this could be turned to our benefit since it violated the public's and the media's sense of a "right to know" and smacked of party bosses making decisions in smoke-filled rooms. Television coverage of our attempt to make the Credentials Committee's decisions open to public view would build public support for our cause and perhaps even gain sympathetic treatment by the media. Therefore, one of our first steps in the fight over contested delegates was to alert the media that we were going to demonstrate in front of the closed doors of the room where the committee was holding its meetings, and we did. A group of our delegates marched around outside the room with placards demanding "fair play" and "open deliberations" and other signs proclaiming "Rob with Bob" and "Taft steals votes." And at the right moments, with television cameras rolling, our delegates made speeches, with appropriate rhetorical outrage at this violation of basic democratic process. The geography of the setting tempted members of the media to become involved. I still recall John Chancellor, then a young reporter covering the convention for one of the television networks, knocking on the door of the room and asking to be let in, only to be refused.

Our strategy worked. Finally, after convention officials had received a flood of telegrams from the public supporting our cause, we were allowed in behind the closed doors. William P. Rogers, who later became my deputy attorney general, supervised our legal arguments and our expertly documented briefs. The public, eager to see its first nationally televised political convention, had followed the controversy and responded favorably to Ike's side.

Taft prevailed in the Credentials Committee, winning fifty of the sixty-eight contested seats in the three key states. Yet we were able to make some inroads. Taft was awarded all of Georgia, but we were given sixteen of the thirty-eight Texas seats and two in Louisiana. I realized, however, that those numbers would still leave us short; we needed to press on with the fight.

A last-minute compromise proposal to split the votes from Georgia, Louisiana, and Texas—fifty-fifty—was received from the Taft camp and created a crisis because some of our group favored accepting the compromise. But I knew we needed most of those votes and rejected Taft's overtures.

We invited delegates whom we thought were favorable to the fair-play amendment to a strategy meeting on the night before the vote on it. I presided and predicted the outcome of the vote on the amendment (and missed by only two or three votes). Doubtful delegates swung our way. The favorite-son delegations agreed to vote with us. That was crucial, but we had anticipated their reasoning that if the amendment lost, Taft would be nominated. If it carried there could be a deadlock, and their favorite son might have a chance; their hopes would indeed prove crucial in the intricate parliamentary maneuvering that would soon preoccupy the convention.

The next day, the convention considered the amendment; it was a divisive moment in Republican party history. Taft's managers had not done their homework as well as we had. When Gov. Arthur Langlie of Washington stood up to present the fair-play amendment to the convention's rules, Taft's floor leaders made a crucial mistake by offering an amendment to the fair-play amendment that would have excluded some of the Louisiana delegates. Taft's manager, Clarence Brown, argued that eight or so of the Louisiana delegates should be seated because Louisiana party officials had followed the technicalities of the party's rules. The scene in the convention hall was utter pandemonium; the aisles were filled with people, and speeches could hardly be heard over the noise of the emotion-charged delegates. Finally, a vote on Brown's amendment-to-the-amendment was taken, and it was resoundingly defeated, 658 to 548.

The vote was revealing. Because it came before the fair-play amendment, Taft's contested delegates were able to vote on the motion. But even with these 50 or so votes, Taft was well short of the 604 votes needed to nominate. The vote also exposed Taft's weakness with respect to the favorite-son and uncommitted delegations: States such as Michigan, California, Minnesota, and Pennsylvania voted overwhelmingly against the Taft position, signaling little Taft support in these states. The fair-play amendment then came up for a vote. Delegates again loudly booed or cheered, depending on whether they supported Eisenhower or Taft; even a few fistfights erupted on the floor. But the amendment passed overwhelmingly.

The procedural issues settled, the drama moved on to the question of whether the Eisenhower or Taft contested delegations in Georgia, Texas, and Louisiana should be seated; the vote would now be determined only by those delegates from the remaining states in which no seating contest existed. The test vote came over the motion to seat our delegates from Georgia. This point in the convention's proceedings was the memorable occasion when Sen. Everett Dirksen of Illinois, the spokesman for the Taft forces, pointed his finger down at Dewey sitting below him in the New York delegation, chastising: "We followed you before and you took us down the road to defeat. Don't do this to us." Dewey remained calm if not impassive during this personal attack.

For our part, we took the high road when our turn came to speak. We gave recognition to the Young Republicans, who were enthusiastic for Ike, by selecting the telegenic young attorney general of Washington State, Don Eastvold, to make the main speech explaining the fair-play amendment on the convention floor. Our carefully prepared briefs and arguments were convincing, and we won the roll call on Georgia 607 to 531. After that, Taft capitulated. Taft's managers agreed to seat our Louisiana delegation as a "good will gesture," and, at 1:30 in the morning, the convention voted to seat our Texas delegation.

It had been a disastrous day for Taft. Even with his contested delegates voting on the initial Brown amendment, Taft was fifty votes short of victory; that, coupled with the subsequent loss of the fifty or so contested seats, dropped his total to one hundred short of the votes needed to nominate. His string of losses on the roll calls over the Brown and fair-play amendments, then on the contested delegations, again branded him a loser.

The momentum had shifted toward Eisenhower. The votes revealed that he was within striking range of the nomination. The favorite-son and uncommitted delegates still held the balance of power, but a deal between Taft and one of the larger delegations would not be enough to give Taft the nomination. It was Eisenhower, now, who was the clear front-runner and probable victor.

In the midst of receiving delegations in his hotel suite, Eisenhower was seized with severe cramps and an almost unbearable pain. We made makeshift arrangements to provide substitutes to receive the arriving delegates and hoped for the best for the suffering candidate. In the light of subsequent history this must have been an attack of ileitis, such as he had later on in his presidency. Fortunately by the following day, the pain subsided and the general resumed his heavy load of campaigning, with his famous grin belying his discomfort.

The other crisis involved the vote of the New York State delegation. Taft announced he had split the delegation and taken it away from Dewey's control. If true, that would have ensured Taft's nomination. But Dewey prevailed and cast a practically unanimous New York vote for Ike.

One incident that is alleged to have occurred at the convention deserves historical clarification. I learned some years later that Judge Elbert Tuttle, in the oral history of his life, recalled a conversation with Warren E. Burger after Burger had become chief justice of the United States. In this conversation Burger was supposed to have said that at the 1952 convention he had met with Governor Warren to offer him a Supreme Court position (obviously if Eisenhower was elected) if Warren would deliver the votes of the California delegation to Eisenhower. I was sure that this recollection by Tuttle was faulty because Burger was a leading supporter of Gov. Harold Stassen and had no part in the Eisenhower campaign during the convention. No one could have imagined he could speak for Eisenhower. I contacted Chief Justice Burger who wrote Judge Tuttle that such a meeting never occurred—that Burger was representing Governor Stassen at the convention and did not know Ike and hardly was acquainted with the Eisenhower convention leaders. I mention this incident out of fairness both to Eisenhower and Warren, so that the true story will be known if the Tuttle oral history receives public attention.

The ensuing balloting for president was, of course, the high point of the convention for the press and the public. But for the Eisenhower managers, the result was almost a certainty. The carefully prepared floor team knew every move they had to make. It included Senator Lodge, Governors Dewey, Sherman Adams, Alfred Driscoll, John Lodge, and Arthur Langlie and a team of aides in each state delegation. I stayed throughout the balloting with General Eisenhower, his wife, his brother Milton, and my immediate aide Thomas E. Stephens in the Eisenhower suite at the Blackstone Hotel, but I was in communication with our managers on the floor of the convention where the balloting was taking place.

At the end of the first ballot, taken under the eye of the permanent chairman of the convention, Congressman Joseph W. Martin of Massachusetts—experienced and impartial—we were a few votes short of the required majority but well ahead of Senator Taft. Eisenhower stood at 595 (9 short of the number needed to nominate), Taft had 500, Warren 81, Stassen 20, and MacArthur 10.

General Eisenhower was watching the balloting on television and seemed shocked by the close vote. I explained that we had received commitments for second-ballot votes from enough delegates who had not voted with us on the first ballot to decidedly push us over the top. Among these commitments were additional votes from Pennsylvania—enough to ensure Ike's nomination. But before the results of the first ballot were announced, Governor Stassen made a second ballot unnecessary by switching the votes of the entire Minnesota delegation to Eisenhower. Unknown to Stassen, we had received commitments from several Minnesota delegates to vote for Ike on the second ballot even if Stassen remained in the race. The second favorite son, Governor McKeldin, had earlier switched to Eisenhower when I arranged for him to deliver the speech placing Eisenhower's name in nomination. The third favorite son, Governor Warren, refused to switch the vote of the California delegation.[4] We had a majority, however, and Ike was the nominee.

For many years I was puzzled as to why Governor Warren refused to switch the votes of the California delegation to Eisenhower once the general had gone over the top. A recent biography of Richard Nixon by Roger Morris offers one plausible explanation.[5] According to Morris, Sen. William Knowland, Warren's campaign manager, had been called upon by a group of Taft supporters headed by Senator Dirksen, who promised to swing Taft's votes to Warren if Taft and Eisenhower deadlocked. If this had happened, Warren would have been nominated. The motivation for Dirksen's action, according to this recent account, was the bitterness of the Taft delegates against Governor Dewey, their nemesis. I cannot vouch for the accuracy of this story, but if it is true, it would account for Warren's believing to the end that if he did nothing to ensure Ike's nomination, he himself would be the nominee.

I should note, however, that this is only one interpretation of Warren's motivation. In a recent conversation, Warren Burger offered me another one. According to Burger, Warren's character, especially his sense of personal probity, was such that he felt that if he did anything to favor Eisenhower he would later be accused—if he took a job in the Eisenhower administration—of making a political deal.

As it turned out, Warren's California votes were not needed to push Eisenhower over the top. I turned to shake hands with the general, who admitted he was mystified by the maneuvers of convention politics. He immediately prepared to walk across the street to shake hands with Senator Taft. En route, he was swamped by a wildly cheering crowd of admirers so that he could barely reach Taft's suite. This was the beginning of a four-month election campaign against the Democratic nominee Gov. Adlai E. Stevenson of Illinois—one in which similar wildly cheering crowds followed Eisenhower's every appearance.

I had dinner alone with Eisenhower that night and explained the procedure for nominating a vice-president. He expressed surprise that for all practical purposes he could select his running mate by letting the delegates know his personal choice. He decided that he wanted the advice of Eisenhower leaders among the delegates. He wrote out a list of six or seven names, without any prompting from me, who would be acceptable to him and handed it to me. It included Sen. Richard M. Nixon of California. He had met Nixon at least twice previously—once in 1949 at the time of the Hiss-Chambers confrontation and once in 1951 in Europe. I did not show the list to others as the occasion never arose to make it necessary. The nominee then authorized me to call a meeting of the Eisenhower convention leaders for the next morning to recommend a vice-presidential candidate.[6]

I initially chaired the meeting, which met in my outer office, and told the assembled leaders of Eisenhower's charge to them to provide advice about a vice-presidential candidate. I then said that anyone who wished to be considered as a candidate should leave the room; no one moved. I went to my own office next door in order to be in touch on the phone with Eisenhower, although I was in and out of the meeting as it progressed. Taft's name was proposed by Sen. H. Alexander Smith of New Jersey, and Sen. William Knowland's of California was brought up by Arthur Summerfield; the names of one or two others were also discussed. But Governor Dewey carried the day when he presented Nixon's name.

Again Dewey had played an important behind-the-scenes role in the 1952 campaign. After a speech by Nixon at a dinner of the Republican State Committee of New York in spring 1952 Dewey had decided that the young senator from California would make an ideal running mate for Eisenhower. At the Gridiron Dinner in May, Dewey had told Nixon that he was Dewey's candidate for the position. I had met Nixon on these occasions, and Dewey had told me of his decision to secure a place for Nixon on the ticket and for several months pledged me to keep it a secret, which

I had done. Thus, before the meeting was ever convened, I knew that Nixon was the candidate of the Dewey forces in the party. I had even told Eisenhower beforehand what the outcome would be unless he personally offered another choice. Eisenhower quickly approved the recommendation of the leaders, and Nixon was nominated.

At the dinner with Eisenhower the preceding evening, I had told him that I must return at the close of the convention to private law practice for personal financial reasons. I added that I felt comfortable in doing so because I thought he would have a landslide victory over Governor Stevenson in November.

I flew back to New York with Senator Lodge, my wife, and our daughter Joan. When I learned that the vice-presidential candidate was coming to New York City, I entertained him at a Yankee baseball game, where the crowd obviously enjoyed his enthusiasm. Thereafter I had nothing to do with the management of the postconvention campaign. I thought my active participation in the 1952 election had come to a happy close. Events soon arose that dictated otherwise.

NOTES

1. The remaining primaries were largely inconclusive. Unlike today, the candidates did not always face each other in a head-on race. In Nebraska, Taft beat Ike 79,000 to 66,000, but in Illinois, Eisenhower was not on the ballot, and Taft took the state. Eisenhower scored impressive victories in New Jersey, Pennsylvania, and, as a write-in candidate, in Massachusetts. Taft bested Stassen in Ohio and in state conventions in West Virginia, North Dakota, and Wyoming. Eisenhower won Oregon, Rhode Island, and Vermont. Dewey led a largely pro-Eisenhower slate to victory in New York. Warren led a favorite-son slate to victory in California.

2. Texas Civil Statutes, Art. 3158(a); Acts of 1951, chap. 44.

3. Twenty-three of the twenty-five Republican governors signed a manifesto supporting the fair-play amendment at their June convention in Houston.

4. In the actual convention proceedings, a motion was made to make the nomination unanimous, which then carried.

5. Roger Morris, *Nixon* (New York: Henry Holt, 1990), p. 925.

6. In attendance at the meeting, as best as I can now recall, were Dewey and Sprague of New York, Lodge and Congressman Christian Herter of Massachusetts, Gov. John Davis Lodge of Connecticut, Gov. Sherman Adams of New Hampshire, Gov. Alfred Driscoll and Sen. H. Alexander Smith from

New Jersey, Gov. John Fine and Sen. James Duff from Pennsylvania, Gov. William Beardsley of Iowa, Gov. Theodore McKeldin of Maryland, Gov. Dan Thornton of Colorado, Gen. Lucius Clay, John Minor Wisdom of Louisiana, Elbert Tuttle of Georgia, Jack Porter of Texas, Barak Mattingly and Roy Roberts from Missouri, Arthur Summerfield of Michigan, Senators Harry Darby and Frank Carlson of Kansas, and Gov. Arthur Langlie of Washington. Several other party leaders were invited but were unable to attend as they had already left Chicago.

7

Election and Transition to

the Presidency

❖　❖　❖　❖　❖　❖　❖　❖　❖　❖　❖　❖　❖　❖　❖

In September, with the fall campaign just getting into full swing, I received a call at my law office from the Eisenhower campaign train then rolling through the Middle West. Eisenhower had just spoken with General Clay, who had advised him to discuss with me a serious problem concerning the vice-presidential candidate, Richard M. Nixon, before Eisenhower reached any conclusions. Eisenhower requested that I visit him after midnight the following day when his train would be in the railyards in Cincinnati. The subject was to be the Nixon "secret fund."

The supposed scandal surrounding Nixon first broke into print in the *New York Post* and was immediately picked up by the national media. The *Post* reported that Nixon had maintained a slush fund raised by his California supporters. The fund—some $18,000—had been established without publicity and apart from his published campaign contributions; its ostensible purpose was to pay his incidental expenses as a member of Congress that were not covered by governmental reimbursement. The secret fund created a national stir. Today we are accustomed to reading about honoraria available for personal use of members of Congress many times the amount of the Nixon fund, even with inflation factored in. But the Nixon fund had been kept secret, and in the midst of a hot presidential race, demands were made by Democrats and a few Republicans that Nixon resign his candidacy. The charges, if proved, would weaken the credibility of our campaign theme of attacking the corruption in the Truman administration.

By the time I arrived on the campaign train in Cincinnati, it had been disclosed that the Democratic presidential candidate, Adlai Stevenson, while governor of Illinois, had kept a similar fund. In Stevenson's case, funds had been directly given to members of his staff as a supplement for their salaries. Stevenson's fund seemed more ethically and politically questionable since money went straight into individuals' pockets. But it was Nixon's fund that caught the media's and the public's attention, and the furor continued unabated. In the Republican camp, the alarm spread. Most of the people around Eisenhower who were the amateur enthusiasts felt that anybody who interfered with Eisenhower's plans should be dismissed immediately. Helen Reid of the *Herald Tribune* and Bill Robinson of our campaign finance committee believed that Nixon had to go. I also spoke with both Tom Dewey and Lucius Clay about the problem. Dewey, who had been a strong supporter of Nixon, told me that he had advised Nixon to tell the facts, justify his actions, and then resign from the ticket. Clay was livid and thought Eisenhower should remove him from the ticket as soon as possible.

Eisenhower was exasperated if not shocked over the revelations, and my impression was that he was close to throwing Nixon off the ticket, especially given Clay's angry reaction to the situation. I don't think Eisenhower was morally outraged, but he saw it as a political problem that had to be solved, and he didn't have enough background in politics or experience in campaigning to feel sure of himself. He was not sympathetic to Nixon's predicament and felt that it was up to Nixon to justify his actions and that if he could not do so convincingly he had to leave the ticket. Eisenhower certainly wasn't going to take Nixon's word for it.

I suspect if I had told him to get rid of Nixon he would have done it without any question. Up to this point, however, I had not taken sides in the arguments as to whether Nixon should be asked to resign. When Eisenhower asked my political opinion, I answered that if it turned out upon audit that Nixon had used any of the fund for personal expenses or had granted political favors in exchange for contributions, he should resign. Assuming these possibilities did not eventuate (and they did not), if Nixon was forced off the ticket, a special Republican National Convention would undoubtedly be demanded by many unfriendly persons to nominate another vice-presidential candidate, or the decision might be turned over to the Taft-dominated Republican National Committee. In either case, I envisioned a resumption of the Taft-Eisenhower fight and that the Republican campaign would be left in disarray—probably fatal disarray. I was reminded of that advice when in 1972 the Democratic vice-presidential candidate, Sen. Thomas Eagleton, was forced off the ticket in the midst of a presidential campaign. The result was disastrous for the Democrats.

For several days Nixon would defy Eisenhower's request that he meet with him and disprove the charges. As I learned from Bill Rogers, who was managing the vice-presidential campaign, Nixon knew that Eisenhower had the power to dismiss him from the ticket, but he felt that they had become partners by that time and that Ike should accept Nixon's word and otherwise back him up. Eisenhower saw the situation very differently; he wasn't close to Nixon at that time, and he made it very clear that Nixon was on trial so to speak and that he had to prove that he had not done anything wrong.

Cooler heads finally prevailed, and Nixon decided to deliver a forceful and passionate defense of his actions before a nationwide television audience. He carefully explained the nature and operations of the fund and, unprecedented in American politics, revealed intimate details of his personal finances. He shrewdly pointed out that his wife Pat, who sat near him on the set, owned only a "good Republican cloth coat," a thinly veiled reference to the mink coats some of the wives of members of the Truman administration had received in exchange for political favors. The most memorable line from the address came when Nixon dramatically announced he had accepted a gift—a cocker spaniel puppy named Checkers—but no matter what his critics might say he would not return it since his daughters had come to love it so much. Few dry eyes were left after Nixon finished.

Nixon was particularly shrewd at the end of his speech when he told the audience to write or wire the Republican National Committee (and, by implication, not Eisenhower) about whether he should remain on the ticket. The national party organization was quite supportive of Nixon during this period and was angry at Eisenhower for "temporizing," believing that Eisenhower should have backed up his running mate completely without waiting for an investigation. Nixon's gambit took the control over measuring public reaction to the speech away from the Eisenhower campaign and gave it to the party organization, control that might have become crucial if the response had been more mixed. Fortunately for Nixon the public outpouring of support was overwhelming, and Eisenhower kept him on the ticket.

I thought Nixon's speech was good and quite effective politically, although Dewey and others in the New York group remained unconvinced. I was especially influenced by the auditors' report on the fund. I had a law-school classmate, Herbert Sturdy, in the Los Angeles law firm that commissioned the report, and independently I kept in touch with them on the auditors' findings. I had complete confidence in him, and he assured me that the audit had indicated no wrongdoing, which removed any worry on my part.

In any event, the Nixon secret-fund story and the Checkers speech are history. Personally, the chief result of my midnight visit with Eisenhower was unanticipated. Eisenhower told me he was dissatisfied with the way the campaign was progressing. He complained that Arthur Summerfield, his campaign manager and the new chairman of the Republican party, and other representatives of the Republican National Committee had presented him with a "take-it-or-leave-it" plan for the campaign without consulting with him; they had just handed the plan to Eisenhower. He said that he was not used to dealing with matters that way and was not happy with the system. "I don't like what they are doing," he continued. "They are working me to death without regard to my physical stamina. I want you, Brownell, back at national headquarters to represent me."

I knew beforehand that problems were brewing with the campaign. A friend of mine, Jock Lawrence, who had been with Eisenhower during the war and had held responsibilities in the area of public relations, came back from Denver after visiting with Eisenhower and told me a story that illustrated Eisenhower's dissatisfaction. He had asked Eisenhower how he was getting along, and he had replied, "I don't like this business; these politicians are terrible." Eisenhower then had gone over to a corner of the carpet on which he had been standing, lifted it up, and said to Lawrence, "You see them crawling out from under there."

Summerfield and the other national committee leaders were orthodox party officials in their method of running the campaign. They thought it was as important to elect senators, members of Congress, and governors as it was to elect a president. Thus they wanted the popular Eisenhower to travel around and help out congressional and state campaigns across the country. They used the candidate, just as any political organization does, as an asset, without regard to his health, his wife, or the ideology of those candidates on whose behalf they had expected Eisenhower to campaign. Eisenhower was especially irritated that he had been booked to speak in Wisconsin—the home state of Sen. Joe McCarthy—in opposition to his expressed wishes. Eisenhower detested McCarthy's political tactics, especially his accusations against Gen. George Marshall, Eisenhower's revered friend and mentor.

I was sympathetic to Eisenhower's problem and was quite aware, because of my experience in past presidential campaigns, that the candidate for president needs a representative or a buffer between himself and the national party organization to guard against demands that are personally unpalatable to the candidate or that overtax his physical stamina. He asked me to spend the balance of the campaign as his full-time personal representative in his national campaign headquarters in New York City. I consulted my law partners, who generously agreed to my accepting the request. Early in October I was back in the fray.

One of my chief goals was to lighten up Ike's campaign schedule. I spoke with Mrs. Eisenhower and with his brother, Milton, to get their assessment of the situation. I looked over his speeches with C. D. Jackson, and I worked with the Citizens for Eisenhower group who at that point felt that they had been left out of the campaign. When Eisenhower would return to Morningside Heights from a campaign swing I would often meet with him late in the evening to discuss the campaign's progress and what lay ahead. I took on a kind of counselor role as someone he could talk to who could advise him on whether he was being effective. Sometimes I was critical in my advice, but he took it in stride.

On the campaign trail, Eisenhower especially disliked having to extol the virtues of local candidates because he did not know them and felt that it sounded false, but he also felt he was shirking his responsibilities if he didn't do it. I would reassure him that it was not his duty to worry about the political fortunes of the other Republican candidates. Although I knew that he could be of great help to them, I also knew that it was more important that he be at ease in his public appearances, and I tried to eliminate the nonpresidential aspects of these appearances as much as possible. Such efforts, of course, did not endear me to the party organization, and I would get calls from Summerfield and others at the national committee taking me to task for not having Ike mention Congressman Smith or Jones in his latest speech. But I recognized that Eisenhower was not a typical professional politician and that we had to let Eisenhower be Eisenhower if we wanted to win the election.

At headquarters I learned that increasing sentiment was spreading among newspaper people that Ike's campaign had stalled. Stevenson's literate and entertaining speeches were prominently featured in the media, and Eisenhower appeared to be on the defensive. Shades of the 1948 Dewey-Truman campaign were on my mind; we needed something daring to electrify the campaign.

Emmett Hughes, a campaign speech writer on Eisenhower's staff under the direction of C. D. Jackson, formerly of *Life* magazine, had invited me to dinner at his Greenwich Village apartment. He was alert to the problem in Eisenhower's campaign. Over dinner, we debated at length various subjects for forthcoming speeches by the candidate to counteract the crisis. We agreed on the need to attack, not to defend against attacks. I said I sensed a growing restlessness in the electorate over the seemingly futile nature of the Korean War and the continuing heavy loss of life and casualties in our armed forces. We finally agreed that settlement of the Korean conflict was the unspoken number-one issue. Hughes put still another sheet in his typewriter and before long he had finished a draft of a speech. One short phrase would prove memorable: Eisenhower's pledge, "I shall go to Korea."

It was a brilliant stroke. When the speech was complete, I took on the assignment of selling it to the candidate. He had some changes to make in the text but not in the vital pledge. When Eisenhower delivered the speech to a nationwide television audience, it marked the beginning of an era in which television dominated presidential campaigns. This development was accompanied by the first extensive use of television ads in a presidential campaign in a series called "Eisenhower Answers America."

Truman cried "Politics," and as was his custom engaged in a personal attack—this time on Eisenhower. Stevenson answered, saying in effect, "I was thinking of going there myself." The public, however, eagerly accepted the pledge of Eisenhower, the great military leader, and interpreted it as a decision by him, if elected, to bring the bloodshed to a speedy conclusion, which of course is what Eisenhower did as president. No more complaints arose from the media about a dull campaign. And for us, after the speech was delivered the Eisenhower campaign never faltered.

The Korean speech further strained whatever friendly bonds still existed between Truman and Eisenhower. Even after Eisenhower was elected, Truman expressed the view that the pledge to go to Korea was purely political. After the election, Truman offered to put a plane at the president-elect's disposal for the trip, somewhat caustically adding in his telegraphed offer, "if you still desire to go to Korea." The break between the two men had begun in August after Eisenhower had been nominated for president and he had declined an invitation from Truman to sit with him and the Truman cabinet. In response to this unprecedented request, Eisenhower wrote, "In my current position as standard bearer of the Republican party and of other Americans who want to bring about a change in the national government, it is my duty to remain free to analyze the policies and acts of the present Administration whenever it appears to me to be proper and in the country's interests." This declaration was greatly significant to the success of the campaign. Since Eisenhower had not been an enrolled Republican and had served in important capacities in Democratic administrations, many Republicans, especially in the conservative wing of the party, wondered whether Ike would act independently. They were greatly reassured by the letter.

For Truman, who had offered at one point to back Eisenhower for the Democratic nomination in 1948, it was political betrayal. In his handwritten reply to Ike's letter on August 16, Truman told Eisenhower that, "I am extremely sorry that you have allowed a bunch of screwballs to come between us. You have made a bad mistake . . . from a man who has always been your friend and who always wanted to be."

The final break between the two men came late in the campaign when Truman bitterly and personally attacked Eisenhower for the advice he had given Truman at the Potsdam Conference at the end of World War II. Eisenhower thought that Truman was calling him a liar and was quite offended. I am indebted to Bernard Shanley, who served as special counsel to President Eisenhower, for the firsthand account of the events that followed. Shanley and Gabriel Hauge were campaigning through Montana with Ike, and Hauge brought in a teletype of Truman's speech. Ike's outrage exploded: "I'll never ride down Pennsylvania Avenue with him. I'll meet him at the Capitol steps. Just how low can you get!"

Ike, for his part, attacked Truman's record in a speech at Richmond, Virginia, which, as it turned out, broke the "solid South" for all time. After the election, their relationship further deteriorated. During his meeting with Truman in the Oval Office to discuss the formalities of transition, Ike was cold and uncharacteristically taciturn, which Truman later insinuated (mistakenly) was evidence that Ike was stunned on learning some of the complexities of the presidency.

Eisenhower did meet Truman at the White House on inauguration day, as is customary, but during the ride down Pennsylvania Avenue and for the remainder of Eisenhower's presidency, the relationship on Ike's part was strictly formal. Truman's reaction was different. His resentment of Ike's criticism of the Truman administration's pockets of corruption, his policies toward the Korean War, and Communist infiltration into government took a personal turn. Truman's rancor continued, as shown by his slighting comments—even after Eisenhower had left the White House—about Eisenhower's lack of ability as president.[1]

A significant, unpublicized event near the end of the campaign occurred as Eisenhower was traveling by train across New York State. Governor Dewey was with him. Ignoring the tension of the candidate, who was under the pressure of making frequent appearances, the governor persisted on giving Eisenhower advice on ways to improve his speaking, pointing out the flaws he found in Ike's delivery. It was typical of Dewey: He would have considered it his responsibility to see that "his candidate" did a good job. He prided himself on his elocutionary ability, honed during many years of voice study. Dewey's speaking style was, however, completely different from Eisenhower's. (I think Dewey was wrong; although Eisenhower was not a polished speaker, he communicated his ideas simply and effectively and was especially masterful with his smile and gestures in relating to the crowds.)

Eisenhower was exasperated with Dewey and after Ike returned to New York City, he described the episode to me with considerable pique if not some anger. The tension between the two men persisted. During the period leading up to the inauguration he was cool toward Dewey, which later was completely forgotten. But from time to time, Eisenhower's feelings about Dewey would reemerge. During Eisenhower's first year as president, a vacancy developed on the Supreme Court and Eisenhower told me, "I'll never consider Tom Dewey for that job; he has about the least judicial temperament that I have ever known."

From the long-range point of view of American politics, Eisenhower's decision to campaign in the deep South was the forerunner of a basic change in the political complexion of presidential campaigns, especially by the Republican party. It was a personal decision of the candidate against the advice of a number of the professional politicians. The latter

considered campaigning in the southern states to be a waste of time because the region had been the "solid South"—almost always delivering
huge majorities for the Democratic candidate for president—ever since the
Civil War.[2] But Eisenhower, foreshadowing his stance after the election
that the president is head of state and represents all the people, insisted
on campaigning there. He was met by huge crowds and as it turned out
carried four southern states in the general election.[3] The "solid South"
was smashed and has never been solid since that time. Eisenhower's national victory on election day was also impressive: He garnered 55 percent
of the popular vote to Stevenson's 44 percent, and Eisenhower bested his
opponent 442 to 89 in the electoral vote.

I played an active managerial role in the three presidential campaigns
against three Democratic candidates: Franklin D. Roosevelt, Harry S. Truman, and Adlai E. Stevenson. Stevenson was by far, in my opinion, the
most likable and erudite of the three. He was an overwhelming favorite on
college campuses, including Columbia University where Eisenhower had
been president, among faculty and students alike. He was an entertaining, literate, and witty speaker. But as a presidential candidate he fell
short. He talked over the heads of the average audience and seemed to be
lecturing them. He appeared ambivalent. On matters of civil rights and
civil liberties he inveighed against Sen. Joe McCarthy, but he chose a segregationist senator, John Sparkman of Alabama, as his running mate and
when campaigning in Mississippi endorsed the leading segregationist,
Sen. James Eastland, for reelection. He praised Truman but agreed that if
elected president he would "clean up the mess in Washington." And he
did not capitalize, as did Eisenhower, on the opportunities that the new
medium of television offered.

On election day, before the polls closed, Eisenhower telephoned me at
my home and asked me to come to see him. Columbia University had lent
him the use of its President's House for the duration of the campaign. I
found him on the top floor, which he had turned into a studio. In an artist's smock he stood before his easel, brush in hand. He was copying a
landscape scene that he had propped up before him.

He asked me how the vote was going, and I predicted a landslide.
"Well," he said, "then I guess we'd better get busy planning how to run
the White House." Here and throughout the conversation, he would
pause between sentences to add a brush stroke to his painting. He was far

more relaxed on this election day than was I, even though the first returns and the informal exit polls at the voting booths were encouraging.

"I am going to organize the White House in a manner that I have been used to in the military," he said, "with a Chief of Staff at my side." Then came a pause, a sketching in of another branch, and the blockbuster: "And I want you to be Chief of Staff." Ike's decision to have a chief of staff has had immense importance in American political history; all succeeding presidents have followed his lead.[4] It has been called one of the key moments in the development of the modern presidency. The decision was misunderstood at the beginning by some political scientists, who pointed to it as an indication of a "passive presidency." They linked it to Ike's love of playing golf, implying that he was not keeping in touch with the duties of the office. Time has shown, however, the inaccuracy of this early assessment. With the opening of Eisenhower's papers to the public, it is now clear that the reorganization of the White House by the appointment of a chief of staff was a great contribution to the efficient operation of the Oval Office. Eisenhower himself kept the reins of government strictly in his own hands, but he did so through using a chief of staff who coordinated the activities of the executive branch for him yet did not make important policy decisions. The result left Eisenhower free to concentrate on the major issues before the country.

I expressed my gratitude for his confidence. After another pause and another stroke of the brush, I said, "You know I'm a lawyer, and I have a deep interest in the law. I've spent twenty-five years at the bar and want to spend another twenty-five there." "So you want to remain a lawyer," he commented; "well, how about being attorney general?" I really was astounded but thanked him profusely. It was left that I would return later, when the polls closed in New York, to give him an answer and accompany him to his election headquarters.

I called Gen. Lucius Clay and told him about the offer, and good friend that he was, he expressed his pleasure. (I learned years later that Clay was the person who had recommended me for the chief-of-staff position.) I asked him how much it would cost me from savings, over and above the salary of $22,500 per year, to accept the cabinet post. I had saved just about enough, he thought, to last four years. After consulting my wife I returned to Morningside Heights and accepted the post. We drove to election headquarters and joined the celebration as the returns came in. Later, my wife and I celebrated by drinking a toast to my selection as attorney general.

It would be hard to imagine another year such as I had in 1952, working at top speed from morning to night—under pressure constantly—in a confidential relationship with three of the most dynamic, powerful men of our time: Dwight D. Eisenhower, Lucius D. Clay, and Thomas E. Dewey. Each man had experienced triumphs in his own field in spite of great odds against success. Now they united in a single cause—developing a lasting bipartisan coalition to ensure that the United States would lead the Western world to oppose Stalin's aggression and to bring Germany into a united Europe with the United States as a reliable partner. They accomplished this through Eisenhower's election as president to replace the fading New Deal at home. It was a peaceful political revolution such as could occur only in a democracy.

With no let-up in his pace, the president-elect took over an office of the campaign headquarters at the Commodore Hotel to receive visitors and conduct his political affairs. Gov. Sherman Adams of New Hampshire meanwhile had accepted the position of chief of staff and joined us at the Commodore to organize the mass of mail and calls.

Eisenhower appointed a committee of three to advise him on cabinet appointments. The selection committee consisted of General Clay, Thomas Coleman of Wisconsin (who had been one of the top advisers to Senator Taft), and myself. Later Tom Coleman withdrew because he felt that the bulk of our recommendations did not represent the Taft point of view.

Eisenhower generally instructed us not to leave Taft's people out of the cabinet, telling us he wanted all points of view represented, but beyond those general orders Clay and I had a remarkably free hand in the process. On the major appointments we would sometimes have a preliminary talk with Eisenhower to ascertain if there were any particular skills or expertise he wanted to see brought to the position, such as his desire to have a good organizational manager rather than a policymaker as secretary of defense. We would inquire about any preferences he might have for particular candidates for a position, but he usually did not have a list of his own. He listened to our recommendations, and we would usually forward only one name to him for his final approval. The work of cabinet selection coupled with long hours preparing to assume the office of attorney general occupied my time until inauguration day.

Political scientists search rather fruitlessly for the principles governing selection of cabinet members. No textbook that I know of has the answer. The cabinet is an advisory body formed *by* the president, *for* the carrying out of the president's policies, and made up *of* the various support groups that brought about the president's election. Cabinet members are advisers to the president and should be personally compatible with him to achieve the best results (although Abraham Lincoln would have disagreed that compatibility was essential). No two presidential approaches will ever be alike. The core of the cabinet—the secretaries of state, treasury, defense, and the attorney general—have across-the-board policy-making responsibilities; the other members are policymakers and administrators in specialized fields. Cabinet members are dispensable at the will of the president. A host of considerations are involved in producing a group that commands public confidence. In addition to competence and character, a president must have in mind his relations with Congress, his responsibility as head of his political party, geographical distribution, ideological balance, and the desirability of including representatives of minority groups whose interests might otherwise be overlooked. Above all, loyalty to the president and the ability to function as part of a team are required. Many times there are gaps remaining after the cabinet is selected, and the president chooses personal advisers who become more powerful than cabinet members. In 1952, for our part, we faced a particular difficulty in that the Republican party had been out of power for such a long time that there were few if any persons in the party with administrative experience in the federal government.

A quick consultation by the cabinet-selection committee with the president-elect made it clear that John Foster Dulles would be the choice for secretary of state (although the possibility of John McCloy was also discussed). Public announcement of this appointment was promptly made, enabling Dulles to meet with Britain's foreign secretary, Anthony Eden, who was then in New York. It is often thought, mistakenly, that Dulles had free rein in the State Department, but even from the start Eisenhower placed some of his own associates in whom he had great personal trust in key positions in the department. He appointed Walter Bedell Smith, his wartime chief of staff, as undersecretary of state, the number-two position in the department, without consulting Clay or me; I think he even appointed Smith without telling Dulles beforehand.

Eisenhower asked us to consider K. T. Keller of Chrysler as secretary of defense. But General Clay took the lead in persuading Charles Wilson, head of General Motors, to take that position. Clay was also instrumental in the selection of George Humphrey, head of the Hanna Corporation of Ohio, to be secretary of treasury. Wilson and Humphrey were friends with Clay and with each other in the Business Advisory Council, a nation-wide organization of chief executive officers of large corporate enterprises. Each man agreed to accept only if the other did. Since Humphrey came from Ohio and had been a financial supporter of Taft, Clay and I thought his selection would repair our bridges with the Taft wing of the party. We consulted Senator Taft, who testily replied that while Humphrey was a fine businessman, he didn't want Eisenhower to think that he was doing Taft a political favor by selecting Humphrey.

My later association with Humphrey and Wilson was open and friendly, and our families became friends as a result. George Humphrey was more conservative than I, and we disagreed on my civil rights program and the need for budget expenditures for some social programs; but in the main we collaborated on major policy matters. He was forceful and disarming, and he almost single-handedly pushed through the program to create the St. Lawrence Seaway. He was a close companion of the president socially. My wife and I enjoyed the hospitality of the Humphreys in their homes in Ohio and Georgia and in get-togethers at the baseball field and the race track. Charlie Wilson and I thought alike on most issues. He was famous for his impolitic remarks and off-the-cuff public statements, which often got him into political hot water, but he managed defense policies with skill and in close collaboration with a president who was expert in these fields. Wilson's talkativeness irritated Eisenhower at times, but they worked closely on Pentagon policies.

Ezra Taft Benson, as secretary of agriculture, became known as the lone representative of the Taft wing of the party in the new cabinet. Harold Stassen recommended Martin Durkin, a Democrat, as secretary of labor, and he was chosen. There was considerable sentiment for Governor Warren for secretary of interior, but Clay and I discussed it with Warren and found out that he wasn't interested. Governor Langlie of Washington State was asked to take this post but declined as he had just been re-elected for a four-year term. So the post went to Gov. Douglas McKay of Oregon.

Former Sen. Sinclair Weeks of Massachusetts, at commerce, Arthur Summerfield of Michigan for postmaster general, and Oveta Culp Hobby of Texas for secretary of health, education, and welfare completed the list. Three other posts that Eisenhower decided merited cabinet-level status went to Sen. Henry Cabot Lodge (who had just been defeated for reelection to the Senate by John F. Kennedy) as representative to the United Nations; Harold Stassen, who became head of the foreign-aid program; and Joseph Dodge as budget director. Dodge had previously worked with Eisenhower at NATO on European recovery programs and was to play a key role in Eisenhower's remarkably successful attempts (since unrepeated) to balance the national budget.

When the cabinet was completed it was tagged in the press as consisting of eight millionaires and a plumber. I knew I wasn't the plumber (Durkin had been a high official in the plumbers' labor union), and my family certainly knew I wasn't a millionaire. But the press's label stuck for a time until the new cabinet members, most of them still a mystery to the Washington establishment, became known there.

Before any announcement was made of my appointment as attorney general I received a call from Nelson A. Rockefeller. At that time it had been announced that he was going to Washington as deputy secretary of health, education, and welfare. We agreed to meet to celebrate Eisenhower's victory at his sometime office above Radio City Music Hall in Rockefeller Center. I had known him and his wife for a number of years as they had been generous supporters of both Dewey and Eisenhower. Nelson served a glass of Dubonnet and a rather meager lunch, I thought, for a celebration of Eisenhower's election. He soon revealed another purpose for the get-together: to discuss his political future. He said he was aiming his sights to run for president of the United States and asked me to manage his political affairs. He was an optimist by nature and painted a rosy view of his chances. He described various perquisites that could come my way—if I accepted—such as directorships in prestigious corporations. But I disclosed my upcoming appointment as attorney general, which made it impossible for me to pursue political activity.

Rockefeller, as a member of the Eisenhower administration, was especially interested in foreign policy. He, along with Stassen, is credited with originating a number of proposals, such as the open-skies proposal for use in disarmament negotiations with the USSR, an offer to allow mutual aerial inspection of military facilities and thereby protect against surprise attacks. The president adopted the proposal.

At times Rockefeller could be a loose cannon, clashing with Secretary of

State Dulles and Secretary of the Treasury Humphrey when he made public proposals for new initiatives in their fields without prior consultation with them. Each time this happened I thought back to our conversation over lunch and his ambitious plans for his own political future.

When I returned from Washington in 1957, Rockefeller again asked me to lunch, this time at the Downtown Association in the Wall Street area. He said he noticed in the press that there was a movement among some Young Republican groups to draft me as a candidate for governor of New York. I made it clear to him right away that I was not interested. He then asked me to help him to get the nomination, and I did support his candidacy. When he was elected, my wife and I attended the private swearing-in ceremony at the Executive Mansion in Albany on New Year's Eve. Later, when he ran for president in 1964, I supported him in his search for delegates before the nominating convention. But when I warned him that his impending divorce would destroy his chances for the nomination, he did not like the advice, and I dropped out of the active circle of his political advisers. Later, when I was supporting John Lindsay (who had been my executive assistant in the Justice Department) as the Republican candidate for mayor of New York City, and then during his mayoralty, those two men began jockeying for position in the moderate wing of the Republican party. I admired them both but did not become involved in their disputes, which led eventually to Lindsay's defection to the Democratic party. Lindsay's decision was unfortunate for the Republicans since there was no one with leadership qualities and name recognition to lead the GOP in New York after Rockefeller left Albany—a problem from which the state party has yet to recover.

With the selection of the cabinet completed, the president-elect honored his pledge to go to Korea. He wanted to make the trip and return by Christmas. He asked the new secretary of defense-designate and several of the military brass from the Pentagon to accompany him. I was engaged, almost on an hourly basis, with plans for the new administration, but he asked me to join the group also. Strict security, wartime in nature, had to be observed; no one was to know the date of the departure. As a cover, the press room prepared a series of announcements to be issued each day in Eisenhower's name.

On the departure day, November 29, Charlie Wilson and I were picked up by the Secret Service well after midnight from our allotted street corners in New York and rushed to the airport where Eisenhower was waiting. The flight plan included stops at a military base in California and in Hawaii, Midway, and Iwo Jima.

The president-elect asked me shortly after takeoff to join in a bridge game. Knowing his reputation for being disdainful of poor card players, I declined—and thereafter was never asked to join any of the White House bridge games, just as well for our friendship, I thought. I occupied myself in conversation with the other travelers and by watching the gooney birds at the Pacific stops we made.

Upon our hush-hush arrival in Korea, we were fitted with parkas because of the winter weather and flown to the front lines where Eisenhower inspected the troops, who came under shellfire from the North Koreans. No one knew whether this signaled that the North Koreans had been tipped off that the presidential party had arrived. But we ate our K-rations and, Eisenhower's tour of the front complete, flew back to Seoul.[5] We met with President Syngman Rhee and watched the South Korean troops being trained under the direction of Gen. James Van Fleet.

The president-elect also had intensive discussions and participated in inspection tours with Generals Omar Bradley, Mark Clark, and James Van Fleet, as well as with Adm. Arthur Radford and lesser military officers, both American and South Korean. Van Fleet outlined to him a contingency plan from the Pentagon for expanding the war into China.

Many years later, Van Fleet told me the secret of Eisenhower's decision about how to deal with the Korean War, as Ike himself told him. As General Van Fleet and I later compared notes, Eisenhower's visit to the Korean front and his own assessment of the war led him to the conclusion that the public was tiring of the war and probably would not continue to support it (shades of Vietnam). He decided that the South Korean forces were competently trained and could continue to hold South Korea. He determined at all costs to seek an armistice and not to accept the military plan to expand the war or to seek a bloody military victory. I believe the president-elect knew his course of action by the time he returned home, but he did not disclose it then, even to his top advisers.

I have no knowledge of Eisenhower's supposed threat to use atomic weapons in Korea if the North Koreans did not agree to an armistice. But I do know that on a number of occasions he received advice from Adm. Arthur Radford, the chairman of the Joint Chiefs of Staff, and from Dulles on the possible use of atomic weapons; Eisenhower never came close to entertaining the notion. On several occasions I tried to sound him out on his view of Truman's use of the atomic bomb at Hiroshima and Nagasaki. Although he would not answer me directly, I came away with the impression that he felt that it had been a mistake.

On returning home, Eisenhower completed his fact-finding tour with a visit to Gen. Douglas MacArthur. The relationship between these two men has always fascinated me. In the beginning, of course, Eisenhower was an aide, low on the totem pole, to Army Chief of Staff MacArthur. Then Eisenhower's skill caught MacArthur's eye, and Ike became his personal assistant. Eventually, during the war, they held equivalent rank. It was a typical case, so often repeated, in which a strain results between two individuals from the readjustment necessary when an assistant becomes a peer. This strain sometimes showed in both generals and was accentuated by differing personalities—the imperious MacArthur and the open friendliness of Eisenhower.

I suspect that MacArthur's willingness to use force, even the atomic bomb, may have had a kind of reverse impact on Eisenhower, cautioning him against using American troops in foreign combat or dropping the bomb. He never looked to MacArthur for advice. And I think that on those occasions when use of the atomic bomb was discussed, he was helped in his decision not to use it because people like MacArthur were urging him to.

The news of Eisenhower's trip broke only after he had flown out of Korea and reached the naval cruiser *Helena*, under command of Admiral Radford, whom he asked to become chairman of the Joint Chiefs of Staff. There at Wake Island, we were joined by Dulles, Humphrey, and Clay, and sessions were held on board to discuss pending cabinet-level matters.

I was looking forward to seeing Pearl Harbor and Honolulu, but on deck as we were landing Eisenhower handed me a sheaf of papers relating to candidates for appointment for governor of Hawaii and other federal territorial offices, including judicial appointments there. So I spent my time on my first visit to Honolulu in a hotel room, interviewing applicants for presidential appointments.

I did, however, have the experience of a ride with General Bradley in a car behind the president-elect's car in a tumultuous motorcade. Many shouts of "Bradlee-Bradlee" were directed at our car, and I told the general he should run for mayor of Honolulu.

On January 12, 1952, Eisenhower held his first cabinet meeting in the

Commodore Hotel, and read aloud his proposed acceptance speech, and received comments on his draft. The time then arrived for the Brownells to break camp, and I gathered my wife, four children, and baggage for a train trip to Union Station, Washington. Our belongings went by truck, and among the lost items was my Homburg hat. I didn't discover the loss until just an hour before we were scheduled to join the inaugural parade down Pennsylvania Avenue (Homburg hats, instead of silk top hats, had been prescribed by the president-elect for the parade). An assistant obtained an oversized hat in the nick of time.

In Washington, we moved into a home in Wesley Heights near the American University campus. Our neighbors, of course, included many leaders who were in the limelight of official life. Vice-president Nixon, with his lovely family, was among them. Another neighbor was former Attorney General Homer Cummings. We became happily acquainted, too, with Philip Young and his family (he was Ike's civil service commissioner) and with Ambassador Jack Simmons and his wife Caroline. The neighbor who made our arrival memorable was Gen. Bedell Smith, the crusty army officer of World War II fame, who was now undersecretary of state. He maintained a bird sanctuary at his residence across the street. And when we moved in we brought our family cat, who had learned to roam on the every-cat-for-himself streets of New York City. On our first night in our new home, the kitty ventured into the inviting premises of Bedell Smith, only to be met by the general, who was guarding his sanctuary with his military efficiency. He accurately aimed a few shots of his B-B gun, and our kitty came limping home. Later diplomatic relations between the two households were restored by Doris Brownell and Nory Smith—and the good-neighbor policy triumphed for the rest of our stay in Washington.

Before I could be sworn into office by Chief Justice Fred Vinson I had to be confirmed as attorney general by the Senate Judiciary Committee. I was questioned about a number of matters of constitutional law, and the interrogation was then turned over to the colorful Senator Pat McCarran, Democrat from Nevada. "Mr. Brownell," he began, "have you resigned from your law firm?" "Yes, Senator." "Did you take your name out of the lawyer list in the telephone book?" Again the same answer. "So from now on you have no direct or indirect interest in the profits of your old firm?" "That's right, Senator." "Well, Mr. Brownell, what investments do you own?" "Such few as I had, I disposed of before I came to Washington," I replied. He countered: "What did you do with the proceeds?" "I put them into government securities," I noted smugly. He then leaned over to the television camera and said in a loud voice, "Say, Brownell, you're in a hell of a fix if we don't confirm you."

So I had my first lesson in the ways of political Washington—a combination of serious policy discussion, a touch of cynicism, and a large dose of camaraderie. I was unanimously confirmed and served as the sixty-second attorney general from January 1953 to November 1957—longer than anyone else has held that post, except for William Wirt early in the nineteenth century and Homer Cummings during the New Deal years.

NOTES

1. See Margaret Truman, ed., *Where the Buck Stops: The Personal and Private Writings of Harry S. Truman* (New York: Warner Brothers, 1989), pp. 60–73.

2. The major exception was Herbert Hoover in 1928. Hoover, running against the first Catholic nominee of a major party, Gov. Alfred Smith of New York, carried several southern states.

3. Eisenhower carried Virginia, Tennessee, Florida, and Texas; he also carried the border states of Maryland and Missouri.

4. John Kennedy and Lyndon Johnson might be considered exceptions to this pattern since neither had an individual with the formal title or full responsibilities of a chief of staff. Both, however, had chief advisers—Sorensen in Kennedy's case, Bill Moyers and Harry McPherson in the Johnson White House—who were singularly powerful "first among equals" and performed many of the duties associated with the role of chief of staff.

5. In our spare time in Seoul, Charlie Wilson and I shopped for jewelry, and he outbid me for a handsome necklace. Whenever I saw the necklace around Jessie Wilson's neck, I would always kid her that I was its rightful owner. She and I became great friends. Protocol dictated that the attorney general be seated at all State dinners next to the wife of the secretary of defense. Jessie had trouble keeping her stiff linen napkin from slipping onto the floor, and I would have to dive under the table to retrieve it. Finally we devised a remedy. I kept a large pin under the lapel of my white-tie outfit. When we sat down I would hand her the pin, which she would use to fasten the napkin to her dress. At the end of the dinner, I retrieved the pin and returned it to my lapel, where it remained until the next State dinner.

8

At the Helm of Justice

❖ ❖ ❖ ❖ ❖ ❖ ❖ ❖ ❖ ❖ ❖ ❖ ❖ ❖ ❖

A cold meat sandwich and an apple were all I was served at lunch with my predecessor, Attorney General James McGranery, when I first entered the Department of Justice building. His description of the condition of the department in the waning days of the Truman administration was as bleak as the meager fare he offered.

Sadly, the Justice Department was a part of the "mess in Washington" described by Eisenhower in the 1952 campaign. Even Adlai Stevenson had promised in the campaign that he would "clean up the mess in Washington." Scandals abounded. The department had failed to prosecute allegations of corruption against the commissioner of internal revenue and a group of twenty collectors of internal revenue. The head of the Justice Department's own Tax Division, Lamar Caudle, had been accused of playing favorites in the prosecution of cases, and the department's Bureau of Alien Property was under suspicion of improprieties in disposing of property in occupied Germany. President Truman's practice of not publicizing the names of individuals who had been granted presidential pardons also raised concerns, especially following the pardon of George Parr, a Texas political boss who had been under suspicion of stuffing ballot boxes in Lyndon Johnson's 87-vote victory in a Senate race with Gov. Coke Stevenson. Cases dealing with vote fraud in Kansas City also had not been resolved, and Truman—who had the support of the infamous Pendergast machine in Kansas City during his political career—was suspect there as was the former attorney general, Tom Clark.

The news media hammered away at the department, and morale declined as each of these allegations unfolded. Even the Democratic-controlled Congress was fed up with the situation at Justice and appointed a special committee, headed by Congressman Frank L. Chelf of Kentucky, to investigate the department.

Earlier in 1952 President Truman had been forced to appoint a special prosecutor to clean things up and had selected Newbold Morris, a Republican reformer and former officeholder in the LaGuardia administration. Morris, however, encountered resistance in the department to his investigations. The attorney general at the time, J. Howard McGrath, a former Democratic senator from Rhode Island and chairman of the Democratic National Committee, refused to grant Morris full access to the department's files, and Morris quit. Truman replaced McGrath with McGranery, a federal appeals court judge from Philadelphia, in an attempt to stem the congressional and media criticism of the department. But McGranery had a tenure of only a few months before I was chosen to succeed him, and despite his good intentions, he too was stymied in his efforts.

In walking down the corridor to the attorney general's office I was at least pleased to see the portrait of my great uncle, William H. H. Miller who had been attorney general under President Benjamin Harrison; I arranged to have his portrait hung in my inner office during my term. Beside it was a volume of his published opinions as attorney general, which had been given to me by my mother. These reminders of happier times at the Justice Department were no small consolation as I knew I had my work cut out for me.

My first task was to assemble a first-rate team that would ably and professionally assist me in the reform effort I planned to undertake. I chose them for their professional competence, but given the need for cooperation with Congress in securing the legislation needed for reform, I also recognized that they had to be knowledgeable about how our political system works, either from prior governmental experience or from previous political activity or both. As I look back at the achievements of these assistants in later life I realize how fortunate I was to have had the benefit of their counsel and professional skills. I was also fortunate in having the full support of President Eisenhower in my efforts, and he accepted my selections without political interference or consideration, as had often been the practice in the past.

For deputy attorney general, I selected William P. Rogers. Rogers had served as counsel to the Truman Committee during its wartime investigation of fraud in federal contracts, and he had earned the respect and confidence of Senate leaders on both sides of the aisle. These contacts were an invaluable asset for us in the work of the Justice Department. Rogers had also been an assistant prosecutor on Thomas E. Dewey's staff in New York and was highly recommended by the governor for his professional competence, diligence, and loyalty. He ably coordinated the activities of all agencies within the Justice Department. Rogers succeeded me as attorney general and during the Nixon administration served as secretary of state. Still later, back in private law practice, he effectively headed the investigation of the Challenger space-shuttle disaster.

I appointed Warren E. Burger of Minnesota as head of the Civil Division. I had become acquainted with him during the 1952 political campaign—he was backing Harold Stassen for the nomination—and was impressed by his record as a trial lawyer. His later record as chief justice was one of great distinction, and his leadership in improving our judicial system is universally recognized. After his retirement from the bench, he became chairman of the Bicentennial Commission on the U.S. Constitution, and I had the pleasure of working closely with him as vice-chairman.

J. Lee Rankin of Nebraska agreed to become assistant attorney general heading up the Office of Legal Counsel, which has the crucial duty of developing and researching the attorney general's most important written opinions. Many of these opinions are requested directly by the president and call for interpretation of the Constitution. Furthermore, they are binding throughout the federal government unless later overruled by the Supreme Court. Accordingly, the person selected to head the Office of Legal Counsel had to be a first-rate lawyer and one in whom I had the utmost confidence. Lee Rankin and his wife Gertrude had been personal friends since college days, and I had worked closely with him in a number of intricate cases while I was engaged in private practice in New York. He was the only one of the new group selected to run the Justice Department whom I had known and worked with over a long period of time, and I knew I could depend upon him (as I did) to uphold the highest standards of professional conduct in a time of crisis when political pressures crowded in upon us. He later became solicitor general of the United States, corporation counsel of New York City, and chief counsel to the Warren Commission during its investigation of the assassination of President Kennedy.

I selected Simon Sobeloff of Maryland for the important post of solicitor general. Sobeloff had been a prominent civil rights lawyer and later became an outstanding member of the U.S. Court of Appeals for the Fourth Circuit. Warren Olney, who had been a prosecutor on Earl Warren's staff, was chosen to head the Criminal Division and later became director of the Office of the Federal Court System. I appointed Stanley Barnes as head of the Antitrust Division. Barnes had been chief judge of the superior court in Los Angeles, the largest trial court in the country, and later became a federal circuit court judge in California. Brian Holland of Massachusetts, recommended to head the Tax Division by my former tax partner in private practice, had had prior exprience in the federal government. Afterward he continued his distinguished career at the Boston bar. Perry W. Morton, assistant for the Lands Division, was a successful practicing lawyer from Nebraska and later became an executive of a major life insurance company. After we created a new internal Security Division, it was headed by William F. Tompkins of New Jersey, whom I had known as U.S. attorney for New Jersey, and he would later successfully prosecute the Russian spy Rudolf Abel. As chairman of the parole board, we selected Scoville Richardson of St. Louis, who later became the first black judge of the U.S. Customs Court. Assistant attorney general Malcolm Wilkey of Texas, who also arrived later, had served with us as a U.S. attorney and would go on to serve as a judge on the Court of Appeals of the District of Columbia and then as ambassador to Uruguay. Unfortunately, no women lawyers were in the group; today, of course, with women lawyers successfully competing in the law profession in great numbers, it is a different situation.

I was also greatly assisted in my duties as attorney general by three able executive assistants. The first, Charles M. Metzner, became a federal district judge in New York. His successor, John V. Lindsay, served in Congress and then became mayor of New York City. His successor, in turn, was Harold Healy, who became president of the prestigious Unione Internationale des Avocats.

An extra word about John Lindsay is in order. After I left Washington, he successfully ran for Congress and then for mayor of New York. My family and I enthusiastically supported him and admired his record. When Lindsay became mayor he faced a particular problem: many citizens thought that the police department was not organized properly to deal with racial disturbances and that minority citizens were not treated fairly in law enforcement, a problem that still remains with us in many communities across the nation. Both of us favored a plan for the establishment of an independent Police Review Board, with a majority of members from outside the police department, who would review charges of police brutality or other misconduct and make public their findings. Lindsay was prepared to establish such a board and wanted me to be its chairman. He was blocked, however, when a plebiscite was held and the voters of the city rejected the idea. In retrospect, Lindsay has not been given nearly enough public recognition for the effective leadership he displayed as mayor in keeping the City of New York calm during the turbulence of the urban riots in the 1960s.

Lindsay's sense of humor sustained him throughout his public career. He furnished me with one of my favorite political stories illustrating the artificialities that creep into public life at times. When he was mayor, the apocryphal story goes, he became ill and was confined to Gracie Mansion, where he received a telegram from the presiding officer of the City Council: "Council passed resolution today wishing you a speedy recovery and an early return to City Hall. P.S. The vote was 6 to 5."

Several times a week, my assistants and I lunched together. This ensured that each of them had ready, personal access to me, an innovation that fostered a close team relationship among the members of our group. We were often joined by the heads of the four bureaus attached to the Justice Department: J. Edgar Hoover, longtime director of the Federal Bureau of Investigation; Gen. Joseph Swing of the regular army (and a classmate of Eisenhower at West Point), who served as head of the Immigration and Naturalization Service; James V. Bennett, head of the Federal Prison Service, who was retained when we decided to make this position a career post; and Dallas Townsend, who, as director, ably reorganized the Office of Alien Property.

One immediate problem that had to be dealt with swiftly was ridding the department of the political deadwood that had accumulated over the years. Some jobs in the Justice Department had come to be regarded as choice political plums, and these positions were sometimes filled by individuals with little competence and legal expertise. This was not just my assessment as the incoming nominee of a Republican president; it was the view of my predecessor in a Democratic administration. At our lunch, McGranery had handed me a list of about twenty-five lawyers in the department who, he said, were incompetent but had important political sponsors. He had been unable to fire them during his brief incumbency but urged me to get rid of them as soon as possible. I immediately divided up the names and distributed them to my newly selected division heads for investigation.

One repercussion of my attempts to replace these individuals illuminated the ways of Washington politics. In the Civil Division, Assistant Attorney General Warren Burger conducted a thorough investigation and confirmed McGranery's allegations. We then terminated the services of the lawyers pursuant to regulations. Several year later, President Eisenhower, who had worked personally with Burger on important matters involving nationwide labor disputes, appointed him as a judge of the Federal Court of Appeals of the District of Columbia. After his nomination went to the Senate Judiciary Committee for confirmation, weeks went by with no action. Finally we discovered that the discharged employees had held up the hearings on his confirmation by claiming to the committee staff that they had been fired by Burger because they were Catholics. To support the nomination we had to bring in the Roman Catholic bishop of St. Paul, who testified to Burger's unimpeachable record of leadership in his hometown in charitable and interdenominational causes. The nomination was then unanimously confirmed, but the incident revealed how difficult it was for department heads to improve the quality of personnel.

At our lunch McGranery had also described the status of the Chelf subcommittee's investigation of wrongdoing in the department. I learned that I would soon be called upon to appear before that subcommittee to outline my plans for reorganization. First I consulted with Chelf, who had already conducted a number of hearings, and solicited his views about needed reforms. I also worked closely with my new deputy attorney general, William Rogers, who had been following the Chelf subcommittee's deliberations. Reforms were needed in the appointment of U.S. attorneys, who represent the department at the district-court level; improvements were required in the ability of the department to attract first-rate attorneys; the organization of the department needed to be made more efficient; and the scandals that had plagued the department during the Truman administration needed to be resolved.

I soon found out that some of the media eyed me suspiciously because I had played such an active part in political campaigns of the past. Was I going to be a "political" attorney general?

The initial test came with the appointment of U.S. attorneys to represent the department in local districts throughout the nation. Previously they had served on a part-time basis and were allowed to continue to practice privately. This system had led to many conflicts of interest and re-sulted in yet more suspicion that some persons in the Justice Department in the Truman administration were motivated by the pursuit of personal gain. I quickly discovered that these charges of conflict of interest were prominent in the list of complaints in Congress about the Justice Depart-ment. As a result, we moved to require that newly appointed U.S. attor-neys and their assistants serve on a full-time basis and not engage in private law practice. President Eisenhower arranged for commensurate salary raises, and the resulting improvement in morale in the department was noticeable.

We strengthened our hand in appointing qualified U.S. attorneys by es-tablishing an Office of U.S. Attorneys under the supervision of the dep-uty attorney general that would review prospective appointments and otherwise monitor their conduct. We also relied more strongly than in the past on the advice and recommendations of state and local bar associa-tions. Our success at appointing qualified nominees was especially en-hanced by Deputy Attorney General Rogers's knowledge of congressional politics and his adeptness at handling powerful members of Congress without creating antagonism or animosity.

I also sought to reduce the temptation of corrupt practices. In the past the local U.S. attorneys prosecuting cases had the power to grant excuses from prosecution for reasons of health. Defendants would sometimes pro-duce certificates from physicians describing temporary and minor ail-ments that the local U.S. attorney, often for political considerations or for personal gain, would accept. Abuse of these excuses was prevalent partic-ularly in the Tax Division and a source of its problems under our predeces-sors. As a solution we required approval of such excuses by departmental officials in Washington.

The federal prison system was another unit of the Justice Department that I sought to insulate from partisan politics. When I arrived on the scene the director of prisons was James V. Bennett. I was besieged by ap-plicants for his position. I looked into Bennett's record and found that he was a superior and progressive administrator; no uprisings had occurred in prisons under his control (a record he maintained during the five years that I was attorney general). Republican applicants for his post pointed out that his wife was active in liberal Democratic politics. But I believed in the famous dicta enunciated by Fiorello LaGuardia that "there is no Re-publican or Democratic way of fighting fires or cleaning the streets." I could not see that party affiliation should have a part in prison adminis-tration. President Eisenhower accepted my recommendation that the po-sition be made a career post, and Jim Bennett was retained.

Another major problem facing the department was the need to recruit first-rate lawyers. A wide discrepancy existed between the starting salary for lawyers in the department and lawyers starting in private practice. At the time, graduates of the best law schools did not seriously consider coming to the Justice Department. We therefore developed the Attorney General's Honors Program for outstanding third-year law students. Selec-tion of students for the program was made on the basis of scholastic standing, law-review work, legal-aid experience, legal-clinic work, and other extracurricular activities such as moot-court work, student-bar-asso-ciation activities, and the like. Salaries were raised to entice the best appli-cants, and recruitment took place in all law schools. The participating stu-dents agreed to stay with the department at least three years.

I announced the program in a speech at the University of Texas Law School, and the response was gratifying. Years later I participated in a cer-emony at the department commemorating the thirtieth anniversary of the program. I learned that a large number of former honors-program recruits formed a core of the department's present leadership. In addition, two have been elected to Congress—Sen. George J. Mitchell of Maine, the Senate majority leader at the time of this writing, and Congressman John E. Porter of Oregon. Other notables included the late Patricia Harris, sec-retary of health, education, and welfare in the Carter administration, Rob-ert Pitofsky, former dean of Georgetown University Law Center, and Der-rick A. Bell, Jr., former dean of the University of Oregon Law School. Many attorneys who began their careers in the honors program have dis-tinguished themselves in the judiciary, government, private practice, and industry.

I also sought to get the Justice Department's house in order by reorgan-izing internal operations. One major change was to make the deputy at-torney general the number-two man in the department instead of the so-licitor general, as had been the practice in the past. I enlarged the staff at Rogers's disposal as well as his responsibilities. The solicitor general's pri-mary duty has always been to prepare the government's case in litigation that comes before the Supreme Court and to argue the government's posi-tion before the Court. I felt that these were important responsibilities in their own right and that the solicitor general should not be given the added duties of administering on the attorney general's behalf a department that at the time had some 30,000 employees as well as overseeing the four bureaus attached to the department: alien property, immigration and naturalization, the FBI, and the federal prison system. I also thought that the deputy attorney general was better qualified to sit in whenever necessary for the attorney general at cabinet meetings and other occasions that required the attorney general's attendance.

The creation of the post of deputy attorney general as I defined it had other advantages. In the past, some ten individuals (the four bureau chiefs and the heads of each of the divisions within the department) reported directly to the attorney general. In my view this arrangement with its wide span of oversight required from the attorney general was inefficient and cumbersome. Too many individuals reporting directly to the attorney general enabled bureaus and divisions to escape needed supervision and scrutiny, which may have encouraged some of the malfeasance that had occurred in the Tax Division and in the Bureau of Alien Property. By making the deputy attorney general in effect my chief of staff, I also maximized my ability to focus on those areas of judicial policy and the department's operations I believed were most important.

Later in my tenure as attorney general I created two new divisions, one dealing with civil rights and the other with internal security. Civil rights matters had been woefully neglected. Only three lawyers had been budgeted by Congress in a subdivision of the Criminal Division to handle such matters. Before I left the department in 1957, we had succeeded, by obtaining passage of the Civil Rights Act of 1957, in establishing a well-funded Civil Rights Division under the auspices of a newly created Office of Assistant Attorney General.[1]

One further matter had to be attended to before our departmental reorganization plan could be considered complete: following through on the indictments and convictions of corrupt officials in the previous administration. The scandals of the Truman administration centered on illegal activities in the Internal Revenue Service and in the Justice Department's own Tax Division. We took quick action, and the former commissioner of internal revenue and more than twenty collectors of internal revenue were tried, found guilty, and imprisoned. Lamar Caudle, the former head of the Tax Division, and President Truman's appointments secretary, Matthew Connally, were also convicted and sent to jail.

I was now ready to report my efforts to Congressman Chelf's subcommittee. The work we had done in the Justice Department drew praise from the subcommittee in its final report. The cloud that had hung over the department lifted. I took special satisfaction from an article by Dean Erwin N. Griswold of Harvard Law School in *Nation's Business* magazine:

> Attorney General Brownell took charge with a firm and sure hand. This was made plain when he named excellent lawyers as assistant attorneys general and as heads of the various divisions in the department. . . . These men quickly won each other's respect, and demonstrated capacity for teamwork. The atmosphere in the department was cleared up within a few months. The restoration of morale was dramatic. The department began functioning once again like a first-class law office. This was a great contribution to the administration of government.[2]

It was gratifying to be able to make these changes in light of the fears that I would be "too political" as attorney general. Those critics who held this view often neglected to understand my long career as a practicing attorney and active member of the bar.

The scope of jurisdiction of the Department of Justice is breathtaking, and as attorney general I was involved in a number of interesting matters of public policy. One law-enforcement problem facing the attorney general when I assumed that office was the influx of illegal entrants to the United States over the Mexican border, literally hundreds of thousands each year. I arranged to visit the border area personally, with Assistant Attorney General Rankin, to get a firsthand view. At night we watched the "illegals" steal across the river separating the United States from Mexico. We inspected the inadequate reception centers of the understaffed border patrol. We visited local law-enforcement and social-welfare agencies in California to learn of the problems confronting the illegals who, since they were living outside the law, were preyed upon by exploiters.

With the aid of President Eisenhower, I consulted General Swing at the Presidio in San Francisco to get his advice on procedures to combat the illegal flow. This contact was most fortunate as it led to Swing's acceptance of the post of commissioner of the Immigration and Naturalization Service in the department. He developed a brilliant plan, in cooperation with Mexican local officials along the border, to stem the influx. Within a couple of years, he was able to report to Congress that the problem had been brought under control. Later he played an important role in implementing President Eisenhower's humanitarian decision to allow the victims of Stalin's invasion of Hungary to enter the United States as refugees in 1956. My legal opinion opening the way for the president's program described the important role that Hungarian immigrants to the United States have always played in the development of our country.

James Bennett, head of the federal prison system, was another bureau chief who performed admirably. The most important reform I was able to accomplish for Bennett was to obtain appropriations that enabled him to accelerate his program to separate youthful first offenders from hardened criminals in the federal prison system. Bennett took me on tours of a number of federal prisons to demonstrate the problems from overcrowding and idleness—Alcatraz, Leavenworth, and, finally, the women's prison at Alderson, West Virginia. At Alderson I was able to institute a number of reforms, and when I resigned as attorney general, the inmates (including Axis Sally who had been imprisoned for her activities during World War II in broadcasting appeals to our GI's to desert) presented me with the Justice Department's flag, which they had sewn by hand. This memento, along with a badge as an honorary agent of the FBI, I keep in my home as souvenirs of my Justice Department years.

By Eisenhower's direction, I personally supervised the exercise of the president's pardoning power. Truman's policy had been not to publicize the pardons he granted, which led to conflict with the media and widespread suspicion of a cover-up. Eisenhower adopted my recommendation that all pardons should be made available to the press at the time they were granted but that the press should be asked not to publicize the event unless they felt some public reason would be served. In the ordinary case, it was humane not to give publicity to the pardon because the person pardoned could be damaged by it in the home community where he or she was leading a new life. The press always observed this request during my years in office.

The most poignant instance I remember of the use of presidential pardoning power involved the case of a young man who had opposed the draft during the war against Hitler; he had been convicted of draft dodging. After he served his prison sentence, he went to Columbia Law School and achieved a brilliant academic record. But he could not be admitted to the bar because his conviction carried with it the loss of civil rights, including the right to vote and to enter a licensed profession. The young man's professors joined in urging a pardon.

I put the facts of the case to Eisenhower. "How can I pardon this man?" the president demanded. "When I think back to the war days, one of my most distressing morale problems in the midst of the war was dealing with the bitterness of the GI's when they read in the *Stars and Stripes* newspaper about cases of draft evasion on the home front." But after some hesitation he said, "I just can't do it now—bring the case back to me next year." So the next year, in a list of "Christmas pardons," I brought the case to his attention again. "I've thought about it a lot," he said, "and I've decided to grant the pardon to give the young man a second chance."

An important aspect of the responsibilities of an attorney general is the enforcement of the antitrust laws—the statutes designed to prevent conspiracies to fix prices, stop unfair trade practices, restrain corporate mergers, and block industrial monopolies. Although the Justice Department is the chief agency for prosecuting violations of these trade laws, other departments—Commerce, State, Defense, and Agriculture—are vitally interested. Delicate issues of intragovernmental relations, which can often be settled only by the intervention of the president, are involved. Such issues require tact and diplomacy in dealing with fellow cabinet officers.

When I assumed office there was a strong demand from the business community for changes in antitrust enforcement. Since the time of Roosevelt's New Deal, it was claimed, a powerful antibusiness bias had existed in Washington, and antitrust cases had languished in the courts for years, resulting in huge litigation fees. There was great speculation when I was appointed that all this litigation would end, and I was often queried on the matter in my early press conferences. I answered that the whole matter should be reviewed and that the charges of antibusiness bias against the Roosevelt and Truman administrations and their political motivations would be thoroughly investigated. As a consequence, with the president's approval, I created an Attorney General's Commission to study the antitrust laws and their enforcement. Many of its recommendations were adopted by Congress, and our enforcement policies during the ensuing five years were likewise guided by the commission's report.

We had a strong antitrust enforcement program throughout the Eisenhower years, which I think surprised many people in the business community. Initially I had suspected that some of the staff members in the Antitrust Division, many of whom dated from the New Deal, had been politically motivated in their enforcement efforts. These suspicions led me, in fact, to go outside the department to pick Judge Stanley Barnes to head the division. Based on my own analysis of the cases and the on-going work of the commission, however, I became convinced of the merit of the department's efforts.

We also began to enforce provisions of an antimerger act passed by Congress some years earlier. The act had been sponsored by Congressman Emanuel Celler of New York, and he always insisted that in my speeches and public comments I should call it the Celler Act, not the Antimerger Act (I suspect he was as much interested in the title as in the enforcement of the statute). We brought test cases to establish the parameters of the act, covering horizontal mergers, vertical mergers, and conglomerate mergers.

I shall not attempt to describe these enforcement efforts in complex detail as they have been written about from a scholarly standpoint elsewhere.[3] But I was especially appreciative of the efforts of our enforcement chief, Judge Barnes, for his evenhanded administration of these laws. Because proposed litigation under the antitrust laws required the personal signature of the attorney general, I worked closely with Barnes in reviewing the pending cases. Careful review was especially necessary once I discovered that a large stack of cases would suddenly arrive on my desk in June. June was the last month of the federal government's fiscal year then, and lawyers in the division were in the habit of generating large numbers of cases that month to justify their budget for the coming fiscal year. Barnes also served to deflect any partisan criticism when we did not pursue enforcement in a weak case: He had an absolutely impeccable reputation as the chief judge of the largest court system in the country, and he was quite effective in rebutting any challenges to our decisions.

I should note that our enforcement efforts drew the department into litigation against political and personal associates: One of the antimerger cases involved Continental Can, headed by General Clay, and others included General Motors, which Charlie Wilson had just left before becoming defense secretary. One particularly controversial case concerned the activities of American oil companies doing business in the Mideast. I believed the criminal charges in the case should have been dropped, and the department negotiated what I considered a reasonable consent decree in the civil action. Although I thought my actions were fully justified, I feared possible charges of scandal since Eisenhower had had strong support from Texas oil interests in the 1952 election. Fortunately, I came across

a memorandum from President Truman, written just before he left office, in which he recommended just about the same course I had taken.

In my view, it is time for another antitrust study commission to be convened. The Sherman Antitrust Act focused on competition within the United States. Now our most important market areas are worldwide, and competition in industry is international. Our antitrust laws should be updated to reflect these economic changes, especially so that foreign businesses are not unduly advantaged in their competition with American industry.

Conservation of natural resources—which now has its own niche in the legal profession as environmental law—was undergoing a metamorphosis during the Eisenhower years. States' rights were giving way to the assumption by the federal government of preeminence in this field. The particular area where this transition of power was most evident was water rights. Congress had not yet enacted comprehensive federal environmental laws, and the states in the western part of the country still fought for exclusive control of water rights. In the Justice Department we upheld the powers of the federal government, which brought us into direct litigation with the states. Assistant Attorneys General Rankin and Morton bore the brunt of these legal battles.

A particularly vexing issue was the question of who owned the right to exploit the oil deposits under the oceans along the coastal waters of the United States, especially in the Gulf of Mexico. This legal issue was unde cided when I entered the Justice Department. President Truman had claimed these rights belonged to the federal government, but Eisenhower, while still in private life, had sided with the states. The matter was so important at the time that it was one of the issues that had come up in my discussions with Eisenhower in Paris. The issue of offshore oil rights raises intricate legal and constitutional problems. But as attorney general, I thought one way around the problem was to draw an actual line on a map to designate the respective areas of federal and state jurisdiction. Unfortunately, the statute as passed by Congress was expressed in general terms and resulted in complex, extended, and expensive litigation.

My work as attorney general brought me into contact with some of the more interesting figures in American political life, for example, J. Edgar Hoover, who had been director of the FBI since the 1920s. The FBI was both powerful and well respected in law-enforcement circles. Its public exhibit of the artifacts surrounding the capture of famous gangsters and its displays of other fabulous feats in the bureau's history were among the most popular tourist attractions in Washington.

Hoover ruled the FBI with an iron hand. Because of his long tenure, he was widely known throughout the United States, especially among youngsters, as the "number-one G-man." Indeed the favorite story of all attorneys general in those years recounted the incident when Attorney General Francis Biddle, who served under FDR, went to his office on a Saturday morning in wartime. He was stopped by the security guard because he'd forgotten his pass. "But I'm the attorney general," Biddle protested, to no avail. The guard said, "I wouldn't let you in without a pass if you were J. Edgar Hoover himself." Hoover's knowledge of the careers of famous outlaws was phenomenal, and at our staff luncheons he regaled us with those stories. His opinions were strongly held and stated—he either liked or disliked a person with a passion.

The FBI, as a unit within the Justice Department, had exclusive jurisdiction to conduct the investigations of all offenses set forth in federal statutes: crimes such as interstate killings, kidnappings, thefts of property, antitrust violations, and so on. It had vast laboratory facilities to assist state and local law-enforcement officials. Many prosecutors who entered the federal system for the first time had been accustomed to conducting their own investigations preliminary to trial. They often resented the system of relying exclusively on FBI investigators in order to prepare their cases for trial. But over the years the federal system has worked well to keep personal ambition and favoritism in law enforcement at a minimum.

In its investigations of violations of federal statutes, the bureau's record received almost unchallenged public approval during the Eisenhower years. In the separate area of investigating suspected violations of internal-security matters, its activities were always controversial (see chapter 13).

Conflicts of interest, real and imagined, always create personal and public-relations problems for a high public official. I experienced such a situation when Aristotle Onassis, the shipowner, tangled with the Department of Justice. Shortly before I became attorney general, Onassis had been indicted by a federal grand jury for violation of certain shipping laws. It was alleged that he and other shipowners had turned over to foreign control certain ships they had bought from the United States government despite a commitment to keep them under U.S. control because they were important for international transportation of oil in case of national emergency.

Before I went to Washington my law firm had given legal advice to Onassis on shipping matters other than those involved in the indictment. Onassis publicly claimed that the firm had advised him on the transfer of the ships to foreign ownership and that as attorney general I was prosecuting him for doing the very thing that the firm—and by implication that I—had okayed. When Onassis appeared at the department to see Assistant Attorney General Warren Burger, he announced to the news media afterward that he had asked the attorney general, "What's the ransom?" implying that he was dealing with brigands. It made news, as he had hoped. But it did not interfere with a government victory, and Onassis paid a heavy fine in the civil case. We thought the previous administration had not had enough evidence of illegal intent to justify a criminal charge, so we dropped the indictment.

For my part I had to spend many hours preparing for a congressional hearing on the department's handling of the matter. I showed that I had never personally had anything whatsoever to do with advice to Onassis and that the advice given by the firm, as shown by detailed records and bills for services, did not relate to the matter for which he was being prosecuted. The congressional committee did not even bother to issue a report.

A final footnote closed the story as far as I was concerned. Years later, after I was back in private law practice, I received a call from Onassis. At his request I met him for cocktails at his posh New York residence on the East River. He had a battery of assistants present for the meeting. In due course he asked if I would represent him as his attorney in certain pending matters; I inquired as to what those matters might be. Without blinking an eye he said that he would want me to "undo what I had done to him as attorney general." I refused the retainer of course, and that brought the meeting to a quick conclusion.

The attorney general, in his role as the federal government's chief prosecutor and law enforcer, is bound to create antagonisms and lose friends. A distinguished British attorney general, Peter Rawlinson, recently pointed out some of these problems in describing how an attorney general is perceived by others as he goes about his job:

What is certain is that an attorney general . . . has to fulfill a task which, in popular sentiment, must appear remarkably unsympathetic—the figure in the dock (the defendant, oftentimes) becomes the hunted and the prosecutor becomes the hunter—the media do not love him. Historically he is always the villain whom the public and now the media love to hiss. Even among his own colleagues he has to play the restraining role, guarding against the legislative misuse of power, reviewing and sometimes advising against the pet proposals of ministers on the grounds of their dubious legality. . . . So the Attorney General becomes, to friend and foe alike, the bogeyman, a popular target for popular commentators. What is absolutely certain is that an Attorney General who becomes popular will not be doing responsibly that which his office demands.[4]

Rawlinson's observations are on the mark, and his description of the problem matches some of my own experiences in office. To illustrate, one day I received a call from Herman Phleger, legal adviser to Secretary of State John Foster Dulles. I had known him in private law practice when he was a senior partner in a distinguished San Francisco law firm. When my family and I first went to Washington and were living in cramped quarters in a tiny Georgetown house while looking for a larger home, the Phlegers lived across the street. They had invited us to Sunday lunch, and a delicious Chinese meal was cooked and served poolside by their chef. I had commented enthusiastically about how fortunate they were to have such a great chef. Now, over the phone, Phleger asked if I knew what I had done to him. "You remember our chef," he said. "Well, you have just indicted him as a ringleader of a group allegedly smuggling aliens into the U.S. illegally." The chef was tried and convicted. This, I was to learn, was only one of many such incidents demonstrating the truth of the observations of my British counterpart. Fortunately, Mr. Phleger and I remained good friends.

Other cases I pursued proved politically and personally controversial. At one point, the department prosecuted an appeal originating before our time of the wife of a fellow cabinet member in a tax case. At another point it sued, for tax delinquencies, the physician who had delivered the babies in the family of another cabinet member, much to the unhappiness of that member. Under the antitrust laws it sued the company presided over by one of my close friends, General Lucius D. Clay, and it also brought suit against the General Motors Corporation, which had recently been headed by Secretary of Defense Charles Wilson, as previously noted.

The General Motors case had unforeseen personal consequences. When I resigned as attorney general, I was offered the presidency of a large commercial bank. While I was considering the proposal, the chairman of the bank received a call from Albert Bradley, a General Motors executive, to the effect that if I became bank president, General Motors would withdraw its business from the bank because of the antitrust litigation (which he claimed I had "instigated"). My career in banking ended at that point: The General Motors account was the largest in the bank. I should add that I am confident this action was taken by General Motors without the knowledge of Secretary of Defense Wilson.

We prosecuted Republican and Democratic members of Congress, thereby incurring the wrath of many legislators. One of the congressmen, a member of the House Judiciary Committee, which handled the legislative proposals and the oversight of the Justice Department, was prosecuted for failure to pay taxes on sums that he had stashed away in savings banks throughout the country. When he was convicted I was puzzled that the judge sentenced him to a jail term—not for the orthodox sixty days or one year but to an odd number of days previously unknown in such cases. It turned out that this sentence allowed him to emerge from jail just in time to circulate petitions for reelection, and he was triumphantly reelected. Once again appointed to the Judiciary Committee, he voted upon Justice Department matters for the balance of my term.

Entering into the Washington spotlight I had to deal with the problems of press and media relations. I already had cordial associations with many of the journalists in the Washington press corps who had covered the presidential campaigns of 1944, 1948, and 1952. They were now covering the White House primarily, but our pleasant relationships continued throughout my Washington years. The press associations assigned reporters to the Justice Department. I had not known any of these reporters before coming to Washington, but I can attest that they reported our departmental activities fairly and accurately. The television political programs and the national news magazines gave me extensive coverage that was balanced and perceptive. There were some reporters, of course, who were partisan Democrats, and they undoubtedly remembered my own partisan Republican days before I took public office and wrote with that in mind. If left-wing Democrats, they attacked our Communist prosecutions. If right-wing, they attacked our civil rights activities. But generally these accounts were within the boundaries of fair comment. Sometimes, too, such attacks engender replies that give the public information that it has the right to know and thus serve a good purpose. In my experience, the public enjoys reading such attacks but usually discounts them if they are too biased.

During the whole period I had only two unfortunate experiences. One was with Drew Pearson, the columnist. Shortly after I became attorney general he called upon me to say that he had had a confidential relationship with J. Howard McGrath, a Democratic attorney general under Truman, whereby he would receive exclusive tips on criminal investigations being conducted in the Department of Justice. He said that he wanted to establish the same relationship with me. I explained why I could not do this in fairness to the persons being investigated, many of whom could turn out to be innocent. After this conversation, he turned on me, writing over two hundred columns or items in his columns during my years as attorney general in which my name appeared; every one was unfavorable, some snide and some vitriolic. He quite evidently had greatly valued the unfair advantage over his fellow journalists that he had previously enjoyed in his bootleg exclusives.

The other unfortunate press relation was with George Sokolsky, a columnist of conservative stripe. When my appointment as attorney general was announced, he was one of my first callers. He asked me to appoint Roy Cohn as my deputy. Cohn, he said, was a brilliant lawyer and an able prosecutor. I knew Cohn, by reputation only, as an assistant on the staff of Sen. Joe McCarthy, and I thoroughly disapproved of his tactics and ruthlessness. Thus I turned down Sokolsky's request. I always thought that the rough treatment I afterward received in Sokolsky's column reflected his resentment of my refusal to appoint Cohn. With these two exceptions, I admired the way in which the media carried on their all-important role of exercising their First Amendment constitutional rights to freedom of the press and of speech.

On a very personal note, I want to say that throughout my years in Washington my sisters and brothers and my wife Doris and our children never caused the slightest public-relations problems for me. In view of the controversies in many fields in which I was necessarily engaged, I owe them a deep debt of gratitude. When I see the way other public officials have been embarrassed in performing their official duties by the actions of their relatives—often unintentional—I am doubly appreciative.[5]

From time to time suggestions are made that no one should be appointed as attorney general who has been active in politics. I disagree, unless of course the activities in politics have led to some dishonorable act or have demonstrated a flaw in personal character. The Constitution established a political system to operate our democracy, and the attorney general's post is an integral part of that system. As is true in every walk of life, experience counts. Previous political participation gives one a chance to understand people's reactions to the opportunities and pressures generated by the system. It gives one experience in dealing with the frailties of human nature and the temptations and limits of governmental power. It impresses upon one both the need and the opportunities to protect the vulnerable members of society. In the office of attorney general, such knowledge is especially invaluable—almost as important as technical knowledge of the law.

As one result of the Watergate scandals, the Carter administration tried to isolate the office of attorney general from politics. As I have heard firsthand from Attorney General Griffin Bell, all calls from the White House to the Department of Justice (and vice versa) were recorded. All involved personnel were instructed not to deal with political questions, only with legal matters. Legislation was drawn up to place an additional officer on the staff of the Justice Department to deal with political affairs that would otherwise engage the attorney general. No one could be appointed attorney general who had participated in party politics in any significant way. Judicial nominations were to be handled by committees outside the department.

The experiment collapsed despite good intentions. The political system needed legal advice. The lawyers needed to know the political facts on which their opinions were to be based. No practical dividing line existed between the two mythical worlds; one could not operate without the other. In the final analysis, the integrity of the individual officials turned out to be the key ingredient in reaching proper conclusions.

Another well-meant experiment, also growing out of Watergate, is being tried: the appointment of a special prosecutor from outside the Justice Department to handle cases in which the attorney general is called upon to investigate another member of the executive branch. In such cases, there is or may be a public perception that the attorney general would not vigorously investigate and prosecute. This experiment is still being tested, although the special-prosecutor statute is temporary by its terms.

My own reaction is to rely on the watchdog supervision of the attorney general by the president, the Congress, the courts, and the media rather than to set up a statutory observer to do the watching. Any attorneys general who value their reputations will voluntarily separate themselves from situations where a legal conflict of interest exists or where personal or political ties create a public suspicion of favoritism or laxity. Otherwise he or she must be prepared to face the wrath of the president, Congress, or the media and have professional reputations tarnished or destroyed. These are strong sanctions. One other drawback to a special prosecutor statute is the extraordinary media publicity engendered by the mere naming of a special prosecutor. In any event, Congress should not exempt its own members if a new special prosecutor act is to be passed.

NOTES

1. For an impartial account of the day-to-day activities of the Civil Rights Section while it was still a part of the Criminal Division, see John T. Elliff, *The United States Department of Justice and Individual Rights, 1937–1962* (New York: Garland Publishing, 1987).

2. Erwin Griswold, "Good Men . . . Good Lawyers,"*Nation's Business* 42,1 (Jan. 1953): 40.

3. See Theodore P. Kovaleff, *Business and Government during the Eisenhower Administration* (Athens: Ohio University Press, 1980). See also Raymond J. Saulnier, *Constructive Years: The U.S. Economy under Eisenhower* (Lanham, Md.: University Press of America, 1991).

4. Peter Rawlinson, *An Autobiography* (London: Weidenfeld and Nicholson, 1989), pp. 146–47.

5. A final point about aspects of my social life in Washington also deserves mention. Nowhere on the organizational chart of the Department of Justice is there mention of foreign-embassy cocktail parties and receptions. But I soon learned that official business is often discussed on these occasions and that foreign ambassadors will mention matters of concern that are within the attorney general's sphere—foreign antitrust problems, tax-treaty problems, extradition problems, and the like. This method of mixing business and pleasure is a real part of the Washington scene. I always enjoyed these occasions, especially the receptions in the Latin American embassies—they reflected an unexcelled joie de vivre. Perhaps it was because I was adopted by the Peruvian ambassador, Fernando Berkemeyer, and his wife. When he found out that I was born in Peru, Nebraska, he never failed, at the height of his parties, to introduce me as the only native of Peru who was a member of the cabinet of a president of the United States.

9

Appointing a New Chief Justice

❖ ❖ ❖ ❖ ❖ ❖ ❖ ❖ ❖ ❖ ❖ ❖ ❖ ❖ ❖

Nominating an individual to the position of chief justice of the United States Supreme Court is one of the most important exercises of a president's constitutional powers. It is far-reaching in its effects, with its impact often lasting decades after the president himself has departed from office. Over the last forty years only Richard Nixon, Ronald Reagan, and Dwight Eisenhower have had the opportunity to make such an important choice and to see their nominees serve on the highest court of the land.[1]

The relationship between President Eisenhower and his choice for chief justice, Earl Warren, has been the subject of much speculation. I was asked by the president to interview Warren when he was governor of California, preliminary to his possible appointment as chief justice, and as attorney general I was frequently privy to the president's reflections on Warren's service as chief justice; thus, I am in a position to address some of the theories. First I offer an account of my prior experiences with Governor Warren, which may shed some light on the reason I was selected for the delicate task of exploring the possibility of his appointment to the Court. I became acquainted with the governor when I was chairman of the Republican National Committee from 1944 to 1946. He supported my contested reelection as Republican National chairman after the Dewey defeat in 1944, and during the rest of my chairmanship he continued to be of assistance, as I developed a program to help the Republicans in Congress offer an affirmative alternative to the fading New Deal. In a letter to me on October 6, 1945, Warren wrote: "We must have an affirmative program which we offer to the public for the solution of our basic problems. Until this is done it will be difficult to convince a majority of the people of our desire and ability to raise the standards of American living."

When the 1948 presidential campaign started, both Governor Dewey and Governor Warren were candidates for the Republican nomination and I was again Dewey's manager. Dewey won the nomination, and selected Warren as his running mate. As manager of the ensuing presidential campaign, I became well acquainted with Warren and his attractive family. One personal incident in the campaign remains in my memory. Mrs. Brownell and I had arranged to entertain the Warrens following a campaign rally in Baltimore. Party leaders from the area were invited to meet the vice-presidential candidate and his wife. While the reception was in full swing, Mrs. Warren suddenly grew pale and appeared about to collapse. "Is there a cat in the house?" she asked my wife. Sure enough, our family cat was busily fraternizing with the guests. Senator William F. Knowland, Warren's manager, and I finally captured Kitty and locked her in the basement for the duration. It was a favorite story we often laughed about with the Warrens whenever we met socially and at Republican affairs years later.

After Eisenhower was nominated in 1952, Warren directed the California campaign for the Republican ticket and spoke for the ticket in other areas of the country when requested by the national campaign headquarters to do so. The two men had friendly meetings at rallies when Eisenhower spoke on the West Coast. Eisenhower told me he admired the nonpartisan way in which Warren governed the state and Warren's broad public appeal. Eisenhower also appreciated the practical political advice Warren gave him on these occasions. In one instance, the media reported that a group of conservatives in California were planning to enter General MacArthur's name on the ballot as a third-party candidate. Eisenhower was worried that a sizable MacArthur turnout might split the Republican vote and give the state to Stevenson. Warren told Eisenhower it was just a figment of someone's imagination and that MacArthur couldn't get more than a half-dozen votes. As it turned out, Warren's advice was on the mark, and the MacArthur effort never amounted to anything.

After the 1952 election, just as the selection of the new cabinet was being completed, the president-elect walked unannounced into my office in the Commodore Hotel. Eisenhower remarked that even though Warren was not to be in the cabinet, he wanted a continuation of the friendly relationship established during the campaign.[2] Out of the blue, Ike told me that he thought Warren would make a fine Supreme Court justice and added, "Why don't we call him up and tell him?" He picked up the receiver, and I heard his end of the conversation, which concluded with his saying that he planned to offer the "next vacancy" on the Court to Warren. That was in December 1952, after the election and just before Eisenhower left for Korea.

This firsthand account will, I hope, put to rest for all time the rumors that Eisenhower and Warren had made a deal for Warren's appointment to the Court when they were both candidates for the Republican presidential nomination. Eisenhower first considered a Warren nomination to the Court well after the election. The votes of Warren's delegates to the convention certainly did not play any part in Ike's convention victory, as I noted in an earlier chapter.

In spring 1953 during a conversation in the Oval Office, I told the president I was having a difficult time finding the right man for solicitor general to recommend to him. He responded in a day or two. "You remember my telephone call to Governor Warren," he said. "I've been thinking [that] some fresh legal experience for him, if he is to go on the Court, would be a good thing—how about solicitor general?"

It was arranged that I would talk to Warren about the post when he came East on his way to Stockholm and London (Eisenhower had appointed Warren to the U.S. delegation to attend the coronation of Queen Elizabeth). In connection with the appointment, Eisenhower met with Warren and afterward recounted the event in his memoirs. He stated that the meeting gave him an opportunity to talk to Governor Warren "about his political philosophy" and that he found him to be "a man of high ideals and common sense." Eisenhower and I had discussed Warren's political views during our meeting in Paris earlier in the year as part of our exchange over leading figures in the Republican party and likely candidates for the 1952 nomination. I noted that Warren had a solid reputation as an internationalist and as a supporter of the United Nations, and in domestic affairs he was considered a progressive who supported legislation for fair-employment practices for black citizens. He was also in favor of public-health and social-security programs.

When I talked to Warren, he seemed to like the idea of being solicitor general and arranged to send me an answer in coded form. The text of his reply, dated August 3, 1953, and sent from Stockholm, was, "Thanks for message. Stop. Have been refreshed by trip. Stop. Looking forward to my return to work." This represented the method that we had devised to tell the president that he accepted the post of solicitor general. After I advised the president, I cabled back, "We are both gratified to receive your cable."

From London Warren returned directly to California and quietly started to wrap up his official and personal affairs, but there was as yet no public announcement of his appointment. Suddenly, Chief Justice Fred Vinson died. No one had considered whether the "next vacancy on the Court" encompassed a vacancy in the office of chief justice.

The president had asked me to compile the records of four or five persons whom he thought should be seriously considered, including Warren. Chief Justice Arthur Vanderbilt of the New Jersey high court was on the list, but it came to light that he had suffered a heart attack although that was not generally known. Two distinguished federal judges known personally to the president, Orie Phillips and John Parker, were also on the list, but they were advanced in years. In his memoirs, President Eisenhower reports that he offered the chief justiceship to John Foster Dulles, but neither he nor Dulles mentioned it to me.

No sitting member of the Court was seriously considered other than Robert Jackson, whose record I greatly admired.[3] But two factors were weighed that ruled him out. First, Jackson's acceptance, while still remaining on the Court, of the post of prosecutor for the United States at the Nuremburg Trials of Nazi war criminals had aroused considerable senatorial hostility toward him. Second, Jackson's previous advocacy of FDR's Court-packing plan when he had been solicitor general was on the debit side. Jackson's name was dropped from the list of possible appointees; this meant that the nomination would go to someone other than a sitting justice.

The president pondered if Warren would think that Eisenhower would be breaking his word if he took the position that in their earlier telephone conversation he had been considering an associate justiceship and had not envisioned a vacancy in the chief justiceship. That was one reason he asked me to go to California to confer with Warren; the other was to complete our study of his legal career, including his experience as attorney general of California.

By this time I had learned the gist of the president's approach to appointing a new chief justice, and it was somewhat different from his approach to other judicial vacancies. He believed (and I agreed) that previous experience in public affairs and administrative skill and abilities were qualities to be desired in addition to the usual requirements of judicial competence and integrity. He wanted a chief justice who would command instant public confidence—not only for integrity and professional competency but for proven success in public life. We discussed Charles Evans Hughes and William Howard Taft as exemplars. They had been tested in public life as well as in their professional careers before their appointments.

The president emphasized that partisan politics should have no place in the selection of a member of the Supreme Court, and he noted approvingly Governor Warren's reputation for running a nonpartisan administration in California. We also discussed the desirability of having a chief justice with broad administrative skill if not experience because of the increasing involvement of the chief justice, as head of the Judicial Conference of the United States, in matters of judicial organization and administration.

At this point, although the president had not firmly made up his mind on Warren, he instructed me to study the governor's public record. He also asked me to confer personally with Warren about whether he preferred to serve as solicitor general for a time or to plunge immediately into the work of the Court.

I was the sole occupant of the presidential plane on the trip to California. I met Warren by prearrangement at McClellan Air Base near Sacramento. He arrived, with no publicity, fresh from a hunting trip and dressed in his hunting outfit. Our two- or three-hour conference was low key. He familiarized me in detail on his professional career. His political opponents in California had raised controversies over some of his actions as governor and as state attorney general (as recited later at his confirmation hearing), and I wanted to assure myself that these charges had no substance.

Warren made it plain that he regarded the present vacancy as "the next vacancy," although he recognized that the president could fulfill his commitment if he took one of the sitting associate justices as Chief and nominated him, Warren, to the resulting vacancy in an associate justiceship. I am often asked if we discussed *Brown v. Board of Education* or any other case that was pending in the Supreme Court at the time. The answer is no. I believed (and still do) that the president should not exact a pledge on how the prospective justice will vote on any matter likely to come before the Court any more than the Senate should during confirmation hearings.

Otherwise our system of government will lose one of its main pillars—an independent judiciary.

During the course of our conference, Governor Warren volunteered that he had followed the administration's actions with great interest and was in accord with its policies as they had unfolded. He also stated that his previous agreement to serve as solicitor general had already led him to make arrangements to leave the governorship, and thus if appointed to the Court, he was prepared to take his place on the bench at the opening of its fall session.

The conference ended with an exchange of views on the proper relationship between the executive branch (and specifically the attorney general) and the Court on the administration of the federal court system. We agreed that, despite the doctrine of separation of powers, certain areas of cooperation were essential. One example was in the development of programs to expedite judicial procedures and to eliminate backlogs in court calendars; another was in the need to enlarge the membership of the Judicial Conference (an administrative body of the federal court system presided over by the chief justice and composed at the time of senior members of various federal appeals courts) through the addition of younger federal judges.

I reported to the president on my return to Washington, and the following day he chose Warren. I held an off-the-record press conference with a number of individuals I selected from the Washington press corps to brief them on the background of the impending nomination. When Warren later arrived in Washington he was greeted by the president at the airport. In looking back at Warren's selection one may observe, first, that Eisenhower had considerable personal contact with Warren prior to the appointment, and second, that Eisenhower took the initiative in selecting Warren for solicitor general and then as chief justice.

Considerable controversy arose when the Senate Judiciary Committee held hearings on Warren's nomination. The chairman of the committee, Sen. William Langer of North Dakota, was unfriendly and allowed the widest latitude to opponents to express their views. It was rumored that the senator was unhappy because the White House had ignored him on the appointment of several postmasters in North Dakota (the senator denied the rumors).

Other critics joined the attack. A professor of law at the University of Virginia wrote:

Of course I have read the gossip indicating that Governor Warren may be named either to succeed Chief Justice Vinson or to a position on the Ninth Circuit bench. In Heaven's dear name, why? The man has had no judicial experience, and he is not a lawyer in any proper sense of the term. And I cannot believe that the President owes him anything. If that appointment is made, it will almost rank in flagrant inappropriateness with the _____ and _____ designations, which certainly achieved an all-time low.

A nationally prominent California attorney and former president of the American Bar Association who had had political differences with Governor Warren wired:

I call . . . the president's attention to the fact that Warren is not a Republican, he is not a lawyer nor an executive in the sense of the judiciary. Thousands of Americans and thousands of lawyers look to this administration to cease the unconscionable practice of putting politicians on the federal bench.

Senator Langer sent investigators to California to look into anonymous charges against Warren, which were listed as follows:

1. That the nominee was at one time "under the domination and control of a notorious liquor lobbyist" (Arthur Samish).
2. That the nominee has had improper connections with "the czar of illicit enterprise in California."
3. That the nominee as Attorney General and Governor "permitted organized crime to establish national headquarters in California."
4. That the nominee, as Governor, willfully protected corruption in his administration, and visited reprisals upon those who complained of such corruption.
5. That the nominee lacks sufficient judicial experience.
6. That the nominee has a "100 percent perfect record of following the Marxist revolutionary line."
7. That the nominee is "biased for the AFL labor monopoly."
8. That the nominee, when he was State Attorney General, was guilty of nonfeasance in failing and refusing to bring about prosecution in the case of more than 1,000 bookmaking violations concerning which evidence was presented to him.

9. That the nominee, while Governor, "owned and operated" an "escrow racket."

10. That the nominee, while Governor, "knowingly appointed dishonest persons as judges and thereafter elevated them."

As a result of these and similar unsupported allegations, Sen. Olin Johnston of South Carolina demanded an unprecedented full FBI investigation of Governor Warren before the committee voted upon his confirmation as chief justice. Other members of the committee denounced the charges as "tommyrot" and "rubbish."

The affirmative support for Warren's confirmation was impressive. The Standing Committee on the Federal Judiciary of the American Bar Association urged the confirmation and stated that Governor Warren was

> well qualified . . . and should be confirmed. . . . He has been subjected to the most searching and critical examination of the Bar and it is a great pleasure to report that he has presided over the Court with great dignity and distinction which gives assurance that if he is confirmed he will continue to grace the Court after the manner of its great Chief Justices.

The Board of Governors of the State Bar of California wrote that it

> unanimously and without reservation approves the qualifications of Earl Warren as Chief Justice of the United States. The Board of Governors believes that the same opinion is overwhelmingly the opinion of the lawyers of Caliornia.

At this point Eisenhower spoke out: "I think he is one of the finest public servants this country has ever produced." At the Justice Department I held a reception for the chief justice-designate to show our continued support for his confirmation.

Warren took his seat on the high Court with the president making an unusual personal appearance. Normally, Senate confirmation would have come first. My research, however, had shown that the first chief justice, John Jay, similarly had sat before Senate confirmation. Warren's action was criticized by some. The *Harvard Crimson*, for example, carried quotations from five professors of the Harvard Law School objecting to the chief justice sitting before he was confirmed; in one professor's view:

> If Governor Warren takes his seat as chief justice next Monday and then proceeds as a temporary judge to participate in the decision of

cases before his nomination has been confirmed by the Senate, he will in my judgment violate the spirit of the Constitution and possibly also its letter. No doubt the technical question is open to debate. . . . The permanent appointment will be subject to three future contingencies: (1) the decision of the President to forward his nomination to the Senate; (2) the decision of the President not to withdraw the nomination before it has been acted upon; and (3) the decision of the Senate to confirm the nomination. . . . I can not believe that the Constitution contemplates that any Federal judge, let alone the Chief Justice of the United States should hold office, and decide cases, with all these strings tied to him.[4]

I had been advised, however, by Justice Frankfurter, speaking for several members of the Court, that a number of important cases were before the Court at the opening of the October term. Warren's presence during oral arguments before the Court was necessary in order for him to participate in the Court's eventual decisions (rendered later in the term when he would presumably have been confirmed). Warren's vote might be critical. The Justices thus felt that he should sit with the Court at the opening of the fall term even though he remained unconfirmed. Their judgment proved correct; although President Eisenhower forwarded Warren's name to the Senate on October 2, 1953, he was not confirmed until March 1, 1954. Had Warren not sat with the Court, he would have missed over half of its nine-month term (the Court begins its work in October and generally recesses in June), including the reargument, previously ordered by the Vinson Court, in the landmark case of *Brown v. Board of Education*. In light of Warren's crucial role in the *Brown* decision in obtaining the support of a unanimous Court against segregation of public schools, it is not unreasonable to speculate that the decision might have come down differently, perhaps as a divided vote, and that the struggle for civil rights might have taken a different, more divisive course had Warren not taken his seat on the Court in October.

Warren and I enjoyed a good personal relationship: I had him over to dinner on several occasions, and we sometimes went to athletic events together. We discussed current events, items in the newspapers, and other issues of the day. But after he became chief justice, I was reluctant to converse with him about anything that was before the Court. Only once did we discuss a current controversy, and that concerned a matter he raised with me. It involved the power of a federal trial judge to hold a person in contempt of court without a jury trial. This was a matter of some importance then because contempt orders were one of the few weapons at the disposal of the federal courts in their attempts to enforce court-ordered integration. Warren's thought was that a judge should not be able to send someone to jail for more than six months.

Warren also tipped me off the day the *Brown* decision was to be handed down so that I would be in the Supreme Court's chambers on that historic occasion (although he didn't tell me what the Court's ruling would be). He later told me that Hugo Black was furious with him for leaking the information to me.

I am often asked whether I think Warren became more liberal once he joined the Supreme Court. To some extent, many of his rulings could have been anticipated because of his prior experience as a moderate if not a progressive Republican, especially in the area of civil rights. In other areas, I do think Warren became more liberal. This difference represents not so much a change in views but their evolution and development as he was forced to deal with new constitutional issues and problems that he had not encountered before. Although Warren's general judicial philosophy was cast in the right direction and his judicial instincts were good, when he joined the Court he lacked a sophisticated view of constitutional history and jurisprudence and was ripe for being influenced by other members of the Court.

In general, it is my view that much of Warren's increasing liberalism was due to the influence of Hugo Black. Intelligent and articulate, Black held well-defined views on most of the matters that came before the Court, and Warren did not. He learned a lot from Black. If John Marshall Harlan had been on the Court at the time, I suspect Warren's constitutional reasoning might have taken a different course. In fact, Harlan was able to exert some influence on Black in later years.

Felix Frankfurter was another great figure on the Court who potentially could have exerted some influence on Warren; I suspect he tried. But Frankfurter was a bit like Tom Dewey: too dogged and self-assured, if not a bit patronizing, in his dealings with others. This didn't work with Warren. After Warren was on the Supreme Court for about a month, Frankfurter told me, "That was the greatest thing you ever did. He is an excellent Chief Justice." But over the years, Frankfurter became disillusioned with Warren's increasingly liberal leanings. Black was much shrewder in his approach to Warren. He carefully tutored him in his views on the Fourteenth Amendment, for example; I suspect Warren had never even thought about the Fourteenth Amendment when he was involved in the internment of Japanese-Americans in California during World War II.

Whatever one thinks about the wisdom of the Warren Court's rulings, the Court was a definite improvement over what it had been in the Truman years. When I came to Washington in 1953 I thought many of Truman's appointments had been mediocre. Sherman Minton, Harold Burton, and Fred Vinson, for example, were all pals of Truman. And the Court, in my view at least, was very political. Frankfurter and William O. Douglas were active in trying to influence people in the executive branch; Douglas had harbored presidential ambitions, and both men talked freely about cases pending before the Court. The Court's reputation improved once Warren took over as chief justice, and it was further enhanced by the caliber of the appointments Eisenhower was subsequently able to make.

Did Eisenhower in later years say that the Warren appointment was one of the worst political mistakes he had ever made? He certainly never made such a comment publicly, or to me in private. Variations of this story have been published, but nothing in the memoirs of either man bears it out. It is so uncharacteristic of Eisenhower as to make me doubt it.

The only written source for the alleged statement that I have been able to locate is from an oral-history interview given in 1969 by Ralph H. Cake, a former Republican national committeeman from Oregon. Cake was a longtime political enemy of Warren, and when Warren was about to be nominated for chief justice, Cake called on Eisenhower personally to oppose the nomination. Furthermore, the same allegation was made about another Eisenhower Court appointee: When Justice William Brennan resigned from the Supreme Court, the media reported that Eisenhower "is said to have said" that Brennan's appointment to the Court was one of the worst political mistakes he had ever made. No published basis whatsoever exists for that report so far as I know,[5] and it heightens my belief that the stories are apocryphal or at least do not represent Eisenhower's overall assessment.

It is certainly true that Eisenhower did not approve of a number of the decisions of the Warren Court, and after he left the White House he undoubtedly expressed this disapproval from time to time in private conversations. For example, he told me that he disapproved of some of the Warren Court's decisions that in his view made it difficult to prosecute criminals. He was also irritated by published statements from Chief Justice Warren that Ike's administration was slow or unresponsive in the enforcement of *Brown v. Board of Education*. Eisenhower believed, as I did, that the Supreme Court in its second *Brown* decision in 1955 had made it difficult (by laying down the vague principle that desegregation was to be adopted "with all deliberate speed," without providing as we had recommended in our brief that desegregation plans had to be filed within ninety days) for the executive branch to enforce the decision until such time—often years later—as the lower federal courts acted upon specific plans for desegregation.

Other irritants in the Eisenhower-Warren relationship also existed. When Eisenhower was considering (because of his heart attack) whether to run for reelection in early 1956, the press speculated whether the chief justice might be a presidential candidate. Warren was silent. The polls showed that if Ike didn't run, Warren was first choice for the Republican nomination. When Eisenhower was asked about this, he commented that he agreed with Warren's earlier statement that "the Supreme Court and politics should not be mixed." This seemed to imply that Warren should have made a flat statement that he was not a candidate for president. I believe that Warren had not given up the idea that he might be president. In 1944, 1948, and 1952 he had been an open candidate for the Republican nomination. Afterward Warren told Jim Hagerty, the president's press secretary, that he resented the president's comment.

Ike's feelings were also piqued when Warren stated that at a private stag dinner at the White House the president had made a remark to him that he interpreted as an attempt to influence his later decision in the *Brown* desegregation case. As best as I can reconstruct the scene at the dinner, Ike had expressed his personal sympathy for the mothers of young white children in the South who had been reared in a segregated society and feared the unknown—the arrival of a time when the public schools would be desegregated. This incident angered the chief justice, and he interpreted it as an unwarranted attempt to influence his decision in the pending case of *Brown v. Board of Education*. Eisenhower, for his part, was irritated at Warren because the president had strong feelings that conversations at his stag dinners were completely "off the record."

My own conclusion is that both men were strong leaders with separate responsibilities as president and as chief justice and that this occasionally and inevitably caused tensions. Their styles of governance, too, were different. Eisenhower, with his military training, kept his personal views and feelings separate and compartmentalized from his official views while he was in office. Warren, with his political background and temperament, spoke freely about his personal opinions. But that said, each man maintained his independence and basically respected the other's integrity and obligations as the respective leaders of two of the three branches of the federal government.

NOTES

1. In 1968 Lyndon Johnson did nominate Associate Justice Abe Fortas to the position of chief justice following Chief Justice Warren's decision to retire from the Court. Fortas, however, was not able to survive Senate scrutiny, thus leaving the appointment of a new chief justice to President Nixon. The Fortas rejection by the Senate involved a question of the propriety of receiving outside income while sitting on the Court—in this particular instance receiving it in exchange for legal advice to an individual. The propriety of a Supreme Court justice receiving gifts from friends even where no quid pro quo is involved has been commented upon adversely in instances involving Justices William O. Douglas and William Brennan.

2. In the period between the November election and this date, Lucius Clay and I had consulted with Governor Warren several times about his thoughts on some of the individuals we were considering for the cabinet. We did not, to my knowledge, offer him the position of secretary of the interior, as some individuals have reported. The controversial dispute between California and Arizona over water rights to the Colorado River would have probably precluded a nominee from either state.

3. Associate Justice Harold Burton was also initially considered, but he was not in the best of health.

4. These comments on Warren are from various sources, and I have kept them in my private papers.

5. One researcher of the subject, who concluded that no evidence existed to back up the alleged statements by Eisenhower, noted that the stories "mirrored a long-running joke used by other presidents in the past" (statement of Alyssa Sepinwall, *Sunday Star Ledger*, August 26, 1990, sec. I, p. 28). In Merle Miller's biography of President Truman, *Plain Speaking: An Oral Biography of Harry S. Truman* (New York: Berkley, 1973), he recounts that Truman once said, "When you ask me what my biggest mistake was, that's it. Putting Tom Clark on the Supreme Court of the United States" (pp. 225–26).

10

Further Reshaping of the

Federal Judiciary

❖ ❖ ❖ ❖ ❖ ❖ ❖ ❖ ❖ ❖ ❖ ❖ ❖ ❖ ❖

Former President Herbert Hoover once told me, in his retirement suite at the Waldorf Astoria Hotel in New York City, that one of the great satisfactions of the presidency was the opportunity to appoint federal judges. They have lifetime tenure and, consequently, a long-lasting role to play in interpreting the Constitution.

Hoover and Eisenhower approached the task of appointing federal judges in a similar way. With respect to members of the Supreme Court, both presidents believed that the justices should represent not only professional excellence but a diversity of ideology and political affiliation. Hoover's outstanding appointments to the Supreme Court were Chief Justice Charles E. Hughes and Associate Justices Owen J. Roberts and Benjamin N. Cardozo. Throughout his term, Hoover subordinated partisan considerations to judicial ability. By a quirk of fate both presidents considered the same individual for appointment to the high court—John J. Parker of North Carolina. Parker was actually nominated by Hoover but rejected by the Senate. Years later, Parker was on Eisenhower's short list for appointment to the Court when Chief Justice Vinson died.

President Eisenhower, like Hoover, took an unusual personal interest in judicial appointments. Until his heart attack, Ike made it a point to meet in the Oval Office with every judicial nominee who came to Washington for the confirmation hearings. Unlike some of his successors in office, he did not rely on the White House staff to screen potential nominees and to interview them about their judicial philosophy and legal views. Instead, the attorney general was the president's chief adviser on these matters. As a result, professional qualifications were given more consideration than has been the case in recent years.

Eisenhower's thinking about the qualifications of his nominees evolved over time. Gradually, based on experience in making early judicial appointments, the president developed a set of criteria for my guidance in making recommendations to him. They were communicated to me piecemeal and were mutually agreed upon.

The first controversy over an appointment arose in Ohio and involved Sen. Robert A. Taft. The man recommended by Taft for the Federal Court of Appeals (with jurisdiction in Ohio) was a distinguished leader of the bar in his community. He was sixty-two years old, only three years short of retirement, and this would have been his first appointment to the bench. I called the matter of the individual's age to the president's attention, and he immediately established a guideline that sixty-two was too old for a first appointment to the federal bench.

Taft was greatly disappointed and remained silent for a long time as to a second recommendation. Finally he came to my office one Saturday morning and stated, "I have a recommendation for that judgeship. He's young enough to satisfy even you." He presented the name of Potter Stewart, whose father was chief judge of the Ohio State Supreme Court. Young Stewart was then in his thirties. Eisenhower appointed him to the court of appeals and later, on the basis of his record there and his high professional standing, elevated him to the Supreme Court.

The criteria, other than age, that we developed for filling judicial vacancies included approval by the American Bar Association (ABA) Committee on Judicial Appointments, approval of the local bar association in the locale of the appointment, and a favorable background character check by the FBI. I adopted an informal system of conferring with the ABA on prospective appointments to the lower federal courts, a system instituted in the previous administration by Deputy Attorney General Ross Malone who himself had been president of the ABA. I extended it to include persons being considered for the Supreme Court, and I found it especially helpful in settling disputes in cases where persons recommended by senators or by personal friends did not appear to be professionally qualified. (Recently, the media have reported that certain senators are trying to eliminate this review by the ABA and any report from a local bar association as factors in judicial appointments. In my opinion this would be a great mistake.)

In his diary for February 5, 1957, Eisenhower further elaborated on the principles underlying his judicial appointments:

> Almost four years ago, the attorney general and I agreed that, except for the position of chief justice, we would confine our selections for the Supreme Court to people who had served on either minor federal benches or on the supreme courts of the various states.

But judicial competence, integrity, and experience were not Eisenhower's sole concerns. He also was attentive to the contribution the prospective appointee would make to the Court as a whole. In his diary, Eisenhower goes on to note his view that

> so far as possible, we would try to get a balance on the court between Democrats and Republicans (the court was eight-to-one Democratic when I was first inaugurated), I have (to date) two Republicans and one Democrat.[1]

I further elaborated this facet of Eisenhower's thinking in testimony I gave before the Senate Judiciary Committee years later on the confirmation of Judge Robert Bork:

> President Eisenhower believed and acted upon the belief that the Court's membership should represent diverse ideological points of view.
>
> In order to maintain public confidence in the Court which is an unelected body, it seems to me it is of great importance to have diverse points of view represented. If the Senate should confirm only nominees with an ideology that conforms to the Senate's prevailing ideology, it would be a signal that the Senate wanted the Court to decide constitutional issues not on an independent judicial basis but on a political ideological basis.
>
> Such action by the Senate, if carried to a logical conclusion, would, in my opinion, violate the separation of powers doctrine embedded in the Constitution. Your predecessors on this committee led the nation in rejecting the court packing plan of yesteryear which was aimed at requiring ideological conformity on the Court. Well, I believe, that the committee should not now do indirectly what it then refused to do directly.

During his presidency, Eisenhower had the opportunity to make five appointments to the Supreme Court. In addition to Earl Warren and Potter Stewart, the other appointees were John Marshall Harlan, William Brennan (a Democrat), and Charles Whittaker. In each case, he sought individuals who would embody the judicial competence and integrity he thought necessary for a position on the Court as well as persons who would contribute to the broader diversity of the Court itself.

Justice John Harlan had been a longtime personal friend of mine. He was my senior by a few years in the Elihu Root law office where I started my law practice. A brilliant trial lawyer, he was trained by Emory Buckner there. He was the grandson and namesake of the Justice Harlan who had written the oft-quoted dissent in *Plessy v. Ferguson* (the case later overturned by *Brown v. Board of Education*) in which he had offered the simple but elegant dicta that the Constitution "is color blind." Earlier, I had persuaded Harlan to leave private practice to become a judge of the Federal Court of Appeals, Second Circuit, and privately hoped for his later advancement to the Supreme Court. At the time he was defending the DuPont Company in a huge antitrust suit brought by the Justice Department. The president of DuPont once told me facetiously that his company lost the suit because I had deprived it of such a good lawyer.

A delay occurred in scheduling the confirmation hearings after Harlan's nomination to the Supreme Court was made public. The chairman of the Senate Judiciary Committee told me that opposition had developed to his confirmation. When the hearings were finally held, Harlan was faced with his accuser, who said that Harlan had Communist sympathies. It turned out that the committee investigator had been investigating the wrong John Harlan—an unknown gentleman from Baltimore—whom I never had the pleasure of meeting. The investigation, however, masked covert opposition to Harlan. Eleven southern senators voted against his confirmation, quite clearly evidencing their conviction that Harlan would follow his grandfather's (in their view improper) interpretation of the Fourteenth Amendment. In my opinion Harlan was an ideal Supreme Court justice during his active years. If he had not later lost his eyesight I am convinced he would have been seriously considered for chief justice.

The background of the appointment of Justice William Brennan also should be told. Even before the vacancy occurred that Brennan would eventually fill, Eisenhower had told me that he would like to appoint a Democrat to the Court should the opportunity arise. His previous nominees had been Republicans, and he wanted to demonstrate to the public that partisan politics was not the major consideration in his judicial appointments. I kept this in mind, therefore, in preparing the informal list that I kept of persons who might be recommended to the president in the event of the next Supreme Court vacancy.

Prior to that time I had convened a National Conference on Delays and Congestion in the Courts. I had asked Chief Justice Arthur Vanderbilt of the New Jersey Supreme Court, a preeminent scholar in the field of court administration, to be the chief speaker. But at the last minute he was detained and sent as a replacement Judge William Brennan, a fellow member of his court. Brennan delivered an address that made our conference a success. He and I struck up a friendship at that time.

When a vacancy in the Supreme Court occurred shortly afterward, Brennan's name was among those submitted to the president for consideration. In a talk with Eisenhower about filling the vacancy, he told me of two groups that had contacted the White House about future Supreme Court appointments. The Conference of Chief Justices of the State Courts claimed that the existing Court was weakened because none of the sitting justices had had experience on a state court. As a result, they pointed out, proper recognition of the position of the states in determining federal-state relationships was missing from the Court. The other group was the Conference of Catholic Bishops, who noted that no one of the Catholic faith was on the Supreme Court, although traditionally there had been.

Before Brennan's name was submitted to the president I had read all his published opinions, and although they did not deal with federal questions since he sat on a state court, I found them well reasoned and well written. I was also aware of Brennan's membership on the faculty of the prestigious Appellate Judges Seminar at New York University. I called Chief Judge Vanderbilt (Arthur Williams, later director of the American Judicature Society, happened to be in Vanderbilt's office), and he highly recommended Brennan, his fellow judge. The ABA report on Brennan was favorable as was the FBI's investigation. Appointment by the president followed shortly thereafter, and there was no controversy at the confirmation hearings.

By the time another vacancy on the Supreme Court occurred, the president had added another criterion for us in the Justice Department to keep in mind. He decided not to appoint anyone to the Supreme Court who had not had prior judicial experience. He believed such experience would demonstrate whether the person actually had judicial temperament, judicial craftsmanship, and the willingness to sacrifice income for public service.

In this instance, Eisenhower's guidelines led me to Charles Evans Whittaker. Eisenhower had earlier appointed Whittaker to the federal court of appeals in the Missouri district, and he had served for a short time on that court. He had been enthusiastically recommended to me by Roy Roberts of the *Kansas City Star* and by leaders of the bar in that area. Undoubtedly, too, geographical considerations were involved in filling this vacancy: the Middle West was underrepresented on the Court at the time.

Eisenhower had met Whittaker personally when appointing him to the court of appeals. He had been a successful practicing lawyer whose legal philosophy was more conservative than most of the other Eisenhower judicial appointees. It turned out, however, that he did not like the pressures involved in sitting on the Supreme Court. Nor did he enjoy good health during this period, and after a brief tenure he retired for reasons of health. His work on the Supreme Court was praised by Chief Justice Warren and others at the memorial services held at the Supreme Court after his death.

When a vacancy in the Supreme Court occurs, the name of the incumbent attorney general is always mentioned for the post in speculative press stories. I was no exception. President Eisenhower offered to nominate me for membership on the United States Court of Appeals, Second Circuit, in February 1957, noting in his diary, "I think that on balance he prefers to go back to private practice some day and earn some money for himself and family." Later, when I was leaving as attorney general, he again proposed that I go on the Second Circuit Court of Appeals. In both instances, he said he would plan thereafter to nominate me to the next occurring vacancy on the Supreme Court (which turned out to be the one filled by Potter Stewart). When that vacancy occurred, after I had left Washington, he wrote to Attorney General Rogers, my successor:

> With respect to Brownell, in my opinion he has every qualification for a Court member. I believe he is a strong character and a man of high principle. The single thing that could be argued against him would be by Southern extremists who would point out that he was attorney general when the Supreme Court's integration orders conforming to the decision of 1954 were promulgated.

Years after the president returned to private life, he generously acknowledged my role in recommending judicial appointees.[2] I was deeply touched when, from his deathbed in the hospital—as related to me by Nixon—he wrote a letter to Nixon suggesting me as successor to Chief Justice Earl Warren.

Among the many controversies over appointment to the lower federal courts, the most noteworthy were those from southern states after the *Brown* decision. Ordinarily the recommendation of a senator from the federal district involved was an important factor. But candidates recommended by southern senators during this period almost always had a public record of having been opposed to desegregation. As a result, we often made recommendations to the president for judicial positions in the southern states without senatorial endorsement. The difficulties of Senate confirmation were obvious if we hadn't selected persons of outstanding quality. Four such persons were known to me personally, so I could vouch for them. They had no record of opposing desegregation and could approach this problem with an open mind.

One was Frank Johnson of Alabama. Eisenhower had appointed him as a U.S. attorney shortly after his first inauguration. I had known Johnson and his father earlier in Republican circles. Another was Elbert Tuttle of Georgia, also a friend from my political days and at the time assistant secretary of the treasury. The third was John Minor Wisdom of Louisiana, a distinguished New Orleans attorney. The Wisdom appointment was especially significant in signaling the administration's commitment to enforcing desegregation: We selected Wisdom over Gov. Robert Kennan of Louisiana, a Democrat who had backed Eisenhower but who remained a staunch segregationist. The fourth notable appointment was that of John Brown, a native of Nebraska who was then practicing in Texas. All four were confirmed and bore the brunt of judicial enforcement of the *Brown* decision in the southern states, suffering social snubs and bitter attacks in the local media as a result. Recently I was delighted to see them honored by bench and bar at the joint conference in New Orleans in 1989 of the Fifth and Eleventh (southern) Circuits.

Deputy Attorney General William P. Rogers and his assistant Robert W. Minor were major players in obtaining high-quality federal judges and in shepherding their confirmations through the Senate. They received recommendations for appointments from U.S. senators and others and followed up these recommendations with endless personal conferences.

They instituted checks by the FBI. They canvassed local judges and lawyers to obtain their opinions of the professional qualifications of the candidates, working with the ABA's Committee on the Judiciary. At the appropriate stage they would consult me, and together we would make recommendations to the president.

Eisenhower realized the importance, after *Brown*, of appointing federal judges who would uphold the Constitution and who had not publicly opposed the desegregation decision. This is most clearly shown in the case of his nomination of Solicitor General Simon Sobeloff (who argued for desegregation in *Brown II*) to be a judge of the Federal Circuit Court of Appeals, Fourth Circuit. The Sobeloff nomination was vigorously opposed by southern senators but insisted upon by the president. Eisenhower also strongly backed our other choices—Judge Harlen H. Grooms of Alabama was one of these—despite the strong lobbying of southern senators. I was usually the go-between in dealing with members of Congress dissatisfied with the president's judicial nominees. On occasion, they appealed directly to Eisenhower and were willing to offer legislative support if we would alter our suggested choices to candidates who were unsupportive of civil rights. Eisenhower, however, resisted political temptation and supported our recommendations 100 percent.

I was reminded of the importance of Eisenhower's support some years later when I returned to Washington during my tenure as president of the Bar Association of New York City to testify at the confirmation hearings of one of President Kennedy's appointees to the federal court in the New York district. After I finished testifying, Sen. James Eastland of Mississippi, an archsegregationist and chairman of the Judiciary Committee, called me into his office to have a drink and reminisce about the old days. "Well, Jim," I asked him, "how are you getting along on the appointment of federal judges?" "Everything is fine now," he replied with a twinkle in his eye, "it's much better than when you were here!"

The high caliber of Eisenhower's judicial appointments is almost unanimously acknowledged. By the end of his second term he had, among other accomplishments, restored an approximate fifty-fifty balance between Republicans and Democrats on the federal bench, thus furthering his goal of subordinating partisan considerations in selection of judges. Most important, with our assistance he had established a beachhead in the southern states for the enforcement of the Supreme Court's civil rights decisions; without it we would have faced a repeat of the Reconstruction period during which the courts played a major role in undoing the promise of the Fourteenth Amendment. As a student of that period in history, I recognized the critical role the courts could play in advancing or retarding the cause of political equality for all Americans. I was determined not to repeal past mistakes.

NOTES

1. Diary entry for February 5, 1957, in Robert Ferrell, ed., *The Eisenhower Diaries* (New York: Norton, 1981), p. 342.

2. Eisenhower wrote:

Gettysburg, Pennsylvania
September 30, 1965

Dear Sirs:

Having learned that in the history of your law firm you intend to include a life story of my friend Herbert Brownell, I am sending you the following as possibly of some value in your project.

Due to the high opinion I had formed, during the 1952 Campaign, of Herbert Brownell's character, professional ability, and sound judgment, I had early decided to offer him the post of Attorney General. I was delighted when he accepted.

From the time of the inauguration I placed great emphasis on the work of the National Security Council, attending all of its meetings whenever I was in the city. Quickly recognizing that this work often involved legal advice I arranged for the Attorney General to attend all sessions. His counsel was invaluable.

In preparing the Administration's recommendations on civil rights and in crushing the efforts of the Governor of Arkansas to defy orders by a Federal court, Mr. Brownell took a firm and important position; in other less dramatic incidents he was equally helpful.

To another point we gave close attention. The Attorney General agreed with me that we should not use Federal Judgeships as matters of political patronage. We felt duty-bound to seek out for appointment to the Federal Judiciary individuals of the highest possible standing. I was well aware that this had not been a policy of some of my predecessors.

As guidelines for such selection we established, between us, certain criteria for the appointment of all Federal judges.

The age of any at the time of appointment could not exceed 62 and they would have to be in good health. No prospective appointee would be selected until his qualifications had been reported as satisfactory by both local and national echelons of the American Bar Association.

Before final appointment, the F.B.I. was directed to make a confidential check to determine that there was nothing in the prospect's past record that would make an appointment unwise. Later we added another: except in unusual circumstances no one would be appointed to the Supreme or Appellate Courts unless he had experience in a lower Federal court or in a State Supreme Court.

These are but a few points of our long and close association; over the years he seems to have found a thousand ways to be helpful, for which I shall never cease to be grateful to him.

With best wishes,

Sincerely,

/s/ Dwight D. Eisenhower

Lord, Day & Lord
25 Broadway
New York, New York, 10004

11

Building the Foundations of Equality

❖ ❖ ❖ ❖ ❖ ❖ ❖ ❖ ❖ ❖ ❖ ❖ ❖ ❖ ❖

On President Eisenhower's inauguration day, racial segregation prevailed in all aspects of public accommodations in the District of Columbia, the nation's capital. No black citizens could get rooms in Washington's first-class hotels nor could they eat in the city's restaurants. Parks, playgrounds, swimming pools, theaters, and bowling alleys were segregated.

For years, promises were offered by national political leaders about civil rights in the nation's capital. Their fine words were not translated into deeds, even though segregation in public facilities in Washington, D.C., was an issue wholly within the jurisdiction of the federal government. Eisenhower had promised in his 1952 presidential campaign to bring about desegregation in the capital city. In his inaugural prayer, which he himself composed for the ceremony, he had invoked, "Especially we pray that our concern shall be for all the people, regardless of station, race or calling." He now proceeded to make good on that call to the Almighty by desegregating Washington.

Segregation in public facilities in the city (except for public schools) was actually illegal under a District of Columbia ordinance passed during Reconstruction days after the Civil War. But government of the District (before home rule was instituted by Congress) was controlled by congressional committees that were dominated by Democratic members from the southern states who were opposed to desegregation. District officials, bent on preserving segregation, claimed that since the ordinance had not been enforced for so many years, it had become "lost" in the official records and could not now be enforced. This claim was opposed by private citizens in a pending court case, and the president asked me for an opinion on the validity of the claim. When I advised him that the claim was invalid, he directed me to take over from the District's Corporation Counsel the management of the test case then pending. In June 1953 the Supreme Court rejected the claim and upheld the enforceability of the "lost" statute, which was a major step forward.

The president then called together the civic leaders of the District as well as others such as Hollywood studio executives who could exert influence on local theater operators. They promptly responded to his leadership, and all public facilities in Washington, D.C., covered by the statute were forthwith desegregated. Frederic Morrow, the first black citizen on the White House staff, Max Rabb of the White House staff (later ambassador to Italy), and Eisenhower's first appointee to the District Board of Commissioners, Samuel Spencer, were effective in implementing the program, which was completed during the first year of Eisenhower's presidency.

But these achievements, though historic, were soon to be overshadowed by the action of the Supreme Court in the case of *Brown v. Board of Education*. My participation in this case, in the enforcement of the Court's decision at Little Rock, and in the development and passage of the first federal Civil Rights Act since Reconstruction proved to be the high points of my term as attorney general. All the resources from my early training, my New York State legislative experience, my political activity, and my legal practice were marshaled to meet the emerging constitutional crisis.

The *Brown* case provided the opening volley in the battle. It had been argued orally in the Supreme Court during December 1952, and its resolution by the Court was pending when Eisenhower was inaugurated. *Brown* was the outgrowth of five cases, which had been brought in various states and the District of Columbia by black schoolchildren and their parents against the local boards of education of segregated school districts. As part of the strategy of the NAACP, which led the nationwide effort to obtain a Supreme Court ruling on the constitutionality of forced segregation in the public schools, the cases had been consolidated. The case highlighted the facts about Linda Brown and her parents and the Board of Education of Topeka, Kansas. The federal government was not a party in any of the cases.

It is difficult now, almost forty years since the *Brown* decision, to recall the rampant practices of segregation that prevailed even in locations such as Topeka, Kansas, and that were regarded by the courts as "the law of the land." Generations of Americans had been reared under social conditions that the Supreme Court itself had condoned in its infamous *Plessy v. Ferguson* decision, handed down in 1896. The majority of the Court in *Plessy* strictly interpreted the due process and equal protection of the law clauses of the Fourteenth Amendment so as to allow segregation of the races. Speaking for the majority of the Court, Justice Brown stated:

> The object of the [Fourteenth] Amendment . . . in the nature of things could not have been intended to abolish distinctions based upon color, or to enforce social, as distinguished from political equality, or a commingling of the two races unsatisfactory to either.[1]

As to Plessy's claim that segregation of the races in railroad passenger cars in the state of Louisiana stamped him with a "badge of inferiority," the Court ruled that the Louisiana statute mandating segregation "is a reasonable regulation." Further, the Court held, if Plessy found that such segregation stamped him as inferior, "It is not by reason of anything found in the act, but solely because the colored race chooses to put that construction upon it." "If one race be inferior to the other socially," the Court continued, "the Constitution of the United States cannot put them upon the same plane."

That the creation of separate public facilities, such as schools, reflected the decisions of political bodies about the character of equality among its citizens and thus was not simply a matter of personal choice or social practice did not trouble the Court. Nor did it occur to the Court that one of the races might find such "commingling" a bit less unsatisfactory, to say the least, than the other. Illogic notwithstanding, "separate but equal" became the law of the land for the next sixty years.[2]

Separate public facilities, of course, were rarely if ever equal. Thus in the period before *Brown*, it had been the goal of the NAACP and other civil rights groups to force state and local governments to provide the equality that even *Plessy* had promised. This generated some measure of success; federal courts and on occasion the Supreme Court handed down decisions requiring states to establish professional schools for its black citizens, to provide a better measure of equal funding for segregated facilities, and even to integrate some institutions, such as graduate programs in a few select universities, where integration was now thought to be essential to the equal provision of a service by the state.

But "separate" still stood as sound constitutional interpretation. It was this barrier that the *Brown* case sought finally to remove by getting the Court to acknowledge that "separate was inherently unequal." Our first intimation about the status of the *Brown* case in the Supreme Court came a few days after Eisenhower was inaugurated. A ceremony was held at the Justice Department for the swearing in, by Chief Justice Vinson, of three of my assistants. After the ceremony, the chief justice remained to visit informally about a number of matters affecting the judiciary on which the previous attorney general had been asked to take action. I had to leave the room for a telephone call, and the chief justice continued in my absence to speak to the new assistant attorney general, Warren E. Burger, who had just been sworn into office. As Burger reported to me later, the chief justice said that the Supreme Court would be interested in the views of the Eisenhower administration on the pending case of *Brown v. Board of Education*.

The significance of this seemingly off-hand remark did not sink in at the moment. In retrospect, it appears that the Court was not so uniformly in favor of school desegregation as it would later be. It strikes me as plausible that Vinson was soliciting the new administration's legal views to tip the balance, either by encouraging the waverers on the Court to overturn *Plessy* if the Eisenhower administration was on that side of the issue or to dodge the question until public and political support were greater and the Court would not have to risk its prestige in such a controversial area. Furthermore, if a stronger majority, or even unanimity among all nine justices could be attained, the country might accept such a drastic change more willingly. This, of course, is informed speculation on my part; and it is also entirely within the realm of reason—although I think less plausible— that Vinson might have anticipated a negative response from the administration, which in turn might have turned the Court the other way.

Several months later, near the end of the Supreme Court term in June, instead of handing down a decision, the Court issued an order setting the *Brown* case for reargument in October of that year. It requested the attorney general to appear for oral argument as amicus curiae and to respond to five specific questions listed by the Court (see appendix B).

The gist of the questions indicated that the Court wanted a new and in-depth look from the participating attorneys on the constitutional issues raised in the case, especially the history of the Fourteenth Amendment to the Constitution—the amendment passed during the Civil War period, which introduced the concepts of due process and equal protection to add to the protections of citizens under the original Bill of Rights. What did these concepts mean as applied to practices in the public schools? If they barred segregation in the schools, how could this fundamental change in American life be brought about?

I immediately notified the president of the Court's request and met with him to discuss the whole problem the Court had raised. I knew that the matter posed a dilemma for Eisenhower, and because I very much wanted the Justice Department to support desegregation I knew I had my work cut out for me. My conversation with him in Paris before he became a candidate for president helped me in crafting my approach. I knew that he was a strong supporter of states' rights, and although certainly not opposed to the cause of civil rights, he did not intend to be a crusader on its behalf. But I also knew his strong views on the necessity of enforcing the law and his deep respect for the Constitution, its separation of powers, and the duties it placed on the president. My sense of where he stood proved useful in easing Eisenhower toward the position I favored.

After I had explained the Court's request, Eisenhower's first reaction was that we should decline the court's invitation since the federal government was not a party to the action. Under the Constitution's delineation of three separate branches, he cautiously reasoned, the decision was properly one for the judicial branch to make without executive interference. I, of course, was delighted by the Court's request, and given my history of supporting civil rights, I thought it important for the Eisenhower administration to go on record that we thought segregation was unconstitutional.

In my discussion with the president, however, I knew I would not be persuasive if I made the argument on this basis. Instead, I took a position that might resonate more favorably with Eisenhower's deep commitment to the importance of constitutional and professional duty—thus I told him that since I was an "officer of the court" as a practicing attorney, it would be most difficult for me to reject the invitation to advise the Court. I also knew that Eisenhower would generally defer to my advice and trust my opinions on matters of the law and the legal process, an area in which he did not have extensive knowledge and experience, so I emphasized that the relationship between the Supreme Court and the Justice Department (which was the most frequent litigant before the Court) would be strained if we refused the invitation. By the end of our talk, the president accepted my position, as I suspected he would.

I sought to stress those aspects of the issue that were congruent to his own deeply held beliefs. Although his political views pulled him one way, he also needed to know the legal and constitutional facets of the issue, which I brought to his attention. And I knew he would fare poorly in history if he took the position that *Brown* was merely a matter for the Court to decide.

This approach to dealing with the president in matters of serious controversy was an avenue that I would use on other occasions. Ironically, given my background in party politics, I refrained from emphasizing the political considerations at stake and focused my arguments not on politics but on law. If I could convince him that as a matter of constitutional law he had a duty—an especially important concern for him—to undertake some action or position, he would do so. I pointed out this duty in the administration's dealings with Sen. Joseph McCarthy when he sought to subpoena officials from the executive branch to appear before his subcommittee. On that occasion I stressed that Congress was stepping over the line of its constitutional powers and that Eisenhower would go down in history as a weak president unless he protected the executive branch's legitimate powers and domain. So too in *Brown*: The case was a proper one for the Court to decide, and the Justice Department had a role to play if called upon by the Court for advice. As the case progressed, I would again resort to these themes of constitutional duty and duty to the law when the question arose during oral argument before the Supreme Court as to the government's position on the constitutional issues raised in *Brown*.

Following my successful discussion with the president, the department launched into an intensive four-month study of the history of the Fourteenth Amendment, and we began preparation of our brief on the constitutional questions raised in the case. Since no new solicitor general had yet been appointed, I designated J. Lee Rankin, my assistant attorney general, to prepare the brief and the historical supplement to answer the Court's queries in what surely must be considered one of the most if not the most important constitutional question of our time. In addition to my meetings with the president, I personally read extensively the pertinent legal materials and met many times with Rankin and his staff. When the brief was in final form I signed it and submitted it to the Court along with a detailed historical analysis of the Fourteenth Amendment.

One of the career attorneys in the Justice Department, a holdover from the Truman administration, was Philip Elman. He has since written articles stating that for weeks after the Supreme Court issued its invitation, the department did nothing to comply. The explanation for this misstatement tells an "inside Washington" tale. It appeared that Elman had written a brief representing the Justice Department's views in the *Brown* case during the preceding administration. It also appeared that he had close ties of friendship with Justice Felix Frankfurter. In fact he often mentioned his meetings and friendship with Frankfurter and in later years wrote a law-journal article stressing those ties. We thought that such a connection between a staff attorney and a justice of the Court, while it was considering the *Brown* case, made Elman ineligible to represent the department before the Court in the case. Accordingly, we excluded Elman from our policy strategy meetings, and he was unaware of our activity for some period of time. He was, however, of help later to Rankin, who was in charge of the actual writing of our brief, because of his knowledge of the prior history of the case. Although I did not instruct Elman to desist from any contact with Frankfurter about the case during this period, I think he finally caught on to the reasons for keeping him initially in the dark.

I could well understand Elman's predicament; it was Frankfurter's practice to cultivate members of the executive branch and other Washington notables—he had also tried it with me. Shortly after I became attorney general, he had invited me over to his house and with great flourish and ceremony told me I was sitting in the seat that Oliver Wendell Holmes had once sat in and engaged in other blatant flatteries. I was aware of his tactics, however, and that I wasn't the first to be given the "Frankfurter treatment." I decided right from the beginning to maintain a strictly professional relationship with him.

The policy group organized to handle the case consisted of the department's best and brightest: Rankin, Deputy Attorney General Rogers, and Assistant Attorneys General Burger and Olney. We were of the opinion that the Court's decision to have the case reargued showed that the justices must be seriously divided and concluded that they needed an in-depth historical presentation as well as a more thorough analysis of legal precedents before handing down a decision. For the historical study we found a veritable gold mine of information in the microfilm collection of early state-government records, which had been gathered by Prof. W. S. Jenkins of the University of North Carolina. From these records we concluded that the history of the Fourteenth Amendment was inconclusive on the question of whether desegregated schools were covered in its scope. We did emphasize in the brief, however, that the Fourteenth Amendment created "a broad constitutional principle of full and complete equality of all persons under the law, and . . . forbade all legal distinctions based on race or color," thus giving the Court an opening for a more expansive interpretation of the amendment that could be applied—if the Court chose—to public schools.

Yet we had to face the fact that the same Congress that had initiated the Fourteenth Amendment had also appropriated funds for segregated public schools in the District of Columbia, and thus, arguably, Congress had not intended to ban school segregation when it submitted the amendment to the states for ratification. Later, on reargument of the *Brown* case, John W. Davis (a prominent New York attorney who had once been solicitor general and in 1924 had been the Democratic nominee for president) used this fact effectively in representing some of the defendants who favored segregated public schools—his last of many able arguments before the Supreme Court.

Now came the big decision: Where did the administration stand on the constitutionality of segregated public primary and secondary schools? I again consulted the president, whose reaction, again cautious, was that the executive branch had fulfilled its obligations by preparing answers to the five specific questions asked by the Court. The Justice Department, the president initially told me, need not take a stand in the brief on the ultimate constitutional question since the federal government was not a formal party in the case and he feared interfering with the workings of the judicial branch.

Once again I chose my words carefully, now emphasizing to Eisenhower the workings of the legal process and my professional opinion as his chief legal adviser. I pointed out that when Assistant Attorney General Rankin, representing the attorney general, made his oral argument he would undoubtedly be asked the question, "Is school segregation constitutional?" I added that it would be disastrous to our argument if we were not to answer that question forthrightly. The president then asked about my own views on the case. I answered that in my professional opinion public school segregation was unconstitutional and that the old *Plessy* case had been wrongly decided. He said if that was my professional opinion I (actually Rankin) should so state, if the Court asked the question. The Court indeed asked the question during oral argument—as I knew it would—and Rankin stated my position. His preparation and argument were first class.

The way our brief was presented to the Court may also have signaled the Justice Department's opposition to segregation. Although the written materials scrupulously followed President Eisenhower's charge that we present a "resume of legal fact and historical record" without taking a position on the constitutionality of separate schools, the brief was presented to the Court as a "supplement" to the earlier brief on the case produced by the Truman Justice Department, which Rankin and I had reviewed in detail. The earlier brief clearly took a position on the unconstitutionality of segregation, which our brief, by association as a supplement, might be interpreted to share. The Truman brief contained no argument that we wished to repudiate, and our association with it also avoided the risk that our opponents could claim that the Justice Department was making inconsistent claims or arguments.

Throughout this period the activist civil rights organizations wanted to work with the Justice Department in the preparation of our brief, and when we resisted, complained we were uncooperative. But I was under instructions from the president not to collaborate in preparation of our brief with activists on either side so that there could be no hints of bowing to political pressure or charges of vote-getting.

These instructions to proceed on our own illustrated another aspect of the differing approaches to the problem that Eisenhower and I had. He saw it as a major and divisive political problem, and he was wary of the various groups that had become involved in the issue. One reason he was willing to allow me to proceed as I did was that I agreed not to work with these groups. He felt, in particular, that if we collaborated with the NAACP it would be self-defeating: We would alienate potential supporters and would be open to charges by southern members of Congress of political opportunism in trying to curry favor with black voters. He saw the NAACP and other groups not as reform organizations but as political pressure groups and believed that association with them might be harmful in the long run in our efforts to gain public support for civil rights, especially from more moderate white southerners. And although he never told me this outright, I suspect that he felt that ultimately the struggle for civil rights would generate great social change; if because of his position the southerners thought he was fanatically against them, once the time came he would not be able successfully to take the kinds of decisive actions that history sometimes forces presidents to take. That action, of course, occurred in Little Rock in 1957, and he was able to garner the support of the American public at large and of many white southerners, especially some of the moderate state governors, and to isolate the extremist segregationists.

Interestingly, Eisenhower's concerns here reveal greater political sensitivity than was attributed to him at the time; he was trying to move forward by staking out a moderate position, grounded in the government's constitutional duty in the case and not in political advantage, that would draw public support and not force the country to choose sides. There were, however, some political costs. Unlike Presidents Kennedy and Johnson, who closely collaborated with civil rights groups and garnered maximum political benefit, the Eisenhower administration did not receive much recognition by the civil rights advocates for what we were doing.

Moreover, we were chided by some members of the civil rights community for involving the government in the case. Thurgood Marshall, later a Supreme Court justice, was principal counsel and strategist over an extended period of time for the parents of the black schoolchildren who were seeking integration. He told our group preparing the government's brief that he considered the government an interloper in the case even if the Supreme Court had asked us to participate. He feared that if the Court were presented with several—potentially confusing—lines of argument, we might well undermine his legal strategy in making his case.

The Supreme Court handed down its decision outlawing segregation in the public schools on May 17, 1954, near the end of its 1954 term. I sat in the Court chamber in the seat reserved for the attorney general and was surprised, as were many others, that the decision was unanimous.

The newly appointed chief justice, Earl Warren, wrote the Court's historic opinion, which has been criticized as lacking in scholarly constitutional analysis. This is explainable, I have always thought, as a tactic deemed necessary by the justices to get agreement on an opinion that would be acceptable to all nine members of the Court.[3]

One of the remaining mysteries in the history of the *Brown* decision is how and when the belief developed within the Court that unanimity was essential for public acceptance if this basic change in American life was to be obtained. Chief Justice Warren is usually credited with swaying the other members of the Court to realize the importance of getting all nine votes for a single opinion and subordinating their differences to the reasoning presented in the decision. It is my view, however, that Chief Justice Vinson may also have been cognizant of this need. Vinson was politically aware and adept, and his request for the views of the new administration may have been an effort to garner votes among the wavering members of the Court and to tip the balance strongly to one side or the other.

I also believe that the Court's view of the importance of unanimity—or something close to it—supplied the underlying motive for leaving open for decision the all-important matter of how to enforce the ruling, which it delayed until the Court's next term in 1955. The enforcement of *Brown* was thus in limbo for a whole year until the Court ruled on the second *Brown* case.

We prepared another brief and another oral argument for *Brown II* on methods of enforcement. This time our presentation was to be made by Simon Sobeloff, newly appointed solicitor general. He had been active in Maryland in advising Gov. Theodore R. McKeldin to promote civil rights legislation. We again consulted the president on the policies to be advocated in the brief.

The president was bombarded during this period by southern friends who sought to have the federal government refuse to participate in *Brown II*. Gov. James Byrnes of South Carolina, a great Eisenhower supporter in the 1952 election and Truman's secretary of state for a time, was especially active in this effort. Others who had politically supported Eisenhower in the South during the 1952 presidential campaign, such as Governors Allan Shivers of Texas and Robert Kennon of Louisiana, both Democrats, wrote the president in the same vein. They predicted a complete shutdown of public education in the South if segregation was outlawed. Primarily under the auspices of his brother Milton, the president also met with educators who gave their professional views on the administrative complexities that would result from desegregation of the public schools. The president contributed suggestions for the department's brief to emphasize these complexities, especially about the use of language that would give local school districts and local federal courts time to prepare for desegregation and to work out plans that would take into account the particular circumstances and difficulties before them.

On the basic issue of enforcement, we pointed out in our brief that among the problems would be the necessity of shifting school district lines and of building new school facilities, of training and hiring new teachers, and a myriad of other administrative tasks. These difficulties made instant compliance with *Brown I* impractical. On the other hand, we emphasized, if enforcement was indefinitely delayed, a generation of schoolchildren would not receive the benefits of desegregation.

We favored a plan to require each school district to submit a desegregation plan to the local federal district court for approval. The plans might differ from school district to school district to meet local needs. But we also urged a second point in our briefs—that school districts should be required to submit a plan within a period of ninety days. Thereby the executive branch would be empowered to step in as soon as a court approved the plan to enforce desegregation.

The Supreme Court adopted our first suggestion but rejected our second one when it handed down its decision, again unanimous, in *Brown II* in 1955. Power of enforcement was given to federal district courts but with no timetable for presentation of plans or for their completion. Desegregation was to take place "with all deliberate speed." Although the intent of this phrase may have been otherwise for members of the Court, it was interpreted by political leaders in the South as being so ambiguous as to mean "at some indefinite date in the future." No direct enforcement powers existed for the executive branch because no federal statute conferred such power and no congressional appropriation was available for enforcement. There was one bright spot, however: President Eisenhower immediately called for and obtained desegregation of the public schools in the District of Columbia. The president was also relieved that *Brown II* did not require the federal government to step in and immediately take over the question of enforcement.

Chief Justice Warren later publicly criticized the president for his lack of public statements from the Oval Office urging compliance outside Washington, D.C., with the *Brown* decisions, thus disregarding the fact that the Court's decision in *Brown II* was a major source of the enforcement problem for the executive branch. I have often wondered how the chief justice would have reacted if the president had turned the tables and publicly criticized how the Supreme Court handled problems—surely such wrangling would diminish the people's confidence in their government.

An interesting aftermath of the *Brown* decisions occurred when the Republican convention met in San Francisco to renominate President Eisenhower in 1956. The platform committee had drafted a plank crediting Eisenhower for *Brown*. The president, from Washington, wired that this proposed plank must be removed before he would accept the platform as he had not taken any public stand on the case. Decisions of the Supreme Court, he pointed out, were not actions of his administration.[4] He obviously was not ready at this point to state an opinion as to whether *Brown* had been correctly decided, although years later in his published reminiscences he said he believed that it was rightly decided.[5]

Some thoughts from my experience during and after the *Brown* decisions come to my mind. I believe our constitutional system functions best when each branch of government—executive, legislative, and judicial—bears in mind how its actions will affect the final result to be obtained. The doctrine of separation of powers among the branches is important, but the purpose of the doctrine should also be remembered—to check unbridled power by any individual official or branch of government. Its aim is not to stymie or stall orderly government. As Justice Jackson noted in the *Youngstown* case:

> While the Constitution diffuses power the better to secure liberty, it also contemplates that practice will integrate the dispersed powers into a workable government. It enjoins upon its branches separateness but interdependence, autonomy but reciprocity.[6]

As this applies to *Brown II*, I believe the Court could well have set a timetable for enforcement once it decided the constitutional issue, as it does sometimes by pronouncing whether a decision is to be applied retroactively or prospectively. Violation of the timetable would have enabled enforcement officials to act. As it was, *Brown II* created uncertainty among local educational and political officials. It unwittingly sowed the seeds for the violence that ensued at Little Rock and during the administrations of Presidents Kennedy and Johnson. It was not until many years had passed when, in 1969, Justice Hugo Black conceded that "'All deliberate speed' has turned out to be only a soft euphemism for delay."[7]

I am often asked about the personal relationship that existed between the president and me in the area of civil rights, since our positions seemed at odds if one were to judge on the basis of media reports or from attacks by the partisan opposition. Reared in communities in the Middle West where segregation in public schools did not exist, neither of us had personal experience with the local problems that flow from school segregation. Eisenhower first confronted racial segregation in the army. As commander-in-chief, he exercised certain discretion as to the role of black soldiers, subject of course to the overall policies of the president and the army's chief of staff. He ensured evenhanded treatment of black troops and sent black replacements into previous all-white units. When he ran for president he approved a plank in the Republican platform to outlaw segregation in all public facilities in the federally controlled District of Columbia, and he carried out that pledge.

For my part, I first encountered the scourge of segregation when I became a member of the New York legislature, representing a New York City district. Under Governor Dewey's leadership, I advocated a compulsory Fair Employment Practices Act. And the moderate wing of the Republican party, of which I was an adherent, was pro–civil rights during the Dewey campaigns in the 1940s.

When Eisenhower was elected president, federal enforcement of civil rights laws—to the extent that power to enforce then existed—was already lodged primarily in the Justice Department. In other words, the president didn't "assign" the area to me; I inherited it as part of being the chief law-enforcement officer of the government. Furthermore, Eisenhower's method of government was to rely on his cabinet members to initiate action on all matters within their jurisdiction, and he generally gave them great autonomy.

In the wake of the *Brown* decision, I turned my attention to the enforcement of civil rights. I soon concluded that federal laws and appropriations were completely inadequate for effecting the civil rights promises of equal protection under the Fourteenth Amendment. Nor were the rather limited proposals that had been sent to Congress by the Truman administration adequate to the task. To obtain new legislation and to develop an effective strategy to counter Senate filibusters on civil rights legislation, a new solution would have to be found.

I originated and developed a plan for new legislation and presented it to the president. He allowed me to test it before Congress, and later he endorsed the plan during his 1956 campaign for reelection. When he thought a legislative compromise weakening the bill was required in the Senate to get the legislation passed, he made the decision. When the Little Rock crisis arose, I advised him on all legal aspects, and he followed my legal advice; on policy matters, he made the decisions.

I was throughout an advocate for a strong civil rights program. Some of the legislators on Capitol Hill thought I was acting beyond the appropriate role of my office by advocating such legislative reforms. I remember Sen.

Walter George of Georgia telling a reporter that I was a "peculiar" attorney general to believe I could play a role in the legislative process. But I felt that the promises of the Constitution—of due process and equal protection—could not be realized without new legislation, especially in the field of voting rights.

Eisenhower's role, of course, was different. As head of state, he governed a nation made up of people and of geographical regions with fiercely opposing views on segregation. The southern rhetoric about the race problem was as strident as in the pre–Civil War debates over slavery. The president endeavored to keep the trust of both sides so that when he acted he would be supported by the public. He also recognized that discrimination was deeply ingrained; changes in the law may be part of the process in moving the nation to full equality, but change in the hearts and minds of many white Americans was also required, change that would not come immediately or by legal fiat. Thus, although his caution on the matter was frustrating to some civil rights advocates, it may have been ultimately more productive since it recognized that the problem was social, not merely political or legal, and that it was not amenable to quick remedy. Truman, by contrast, was more outspoken on civil rights; yet Eisenhower, for all his caution, made greater—albeit not wholly complete or immediate—progress.

Of course for Eisenhower, his duty, first and foremost, was to see that the Constitution, and by implication the Supreme Court's interpretation of it, was upheld. Politics and caution therefore played no part for him in confronting the challenge of the Southern Manifesto[8] and of the White Citizens Councils, which sprang up throughout the South to support the manifesto and to oppose desegregation and civil rights. The manifesto was especially threatening since it was a public declaration by 101 southern senators and congressmen advocating the use of all legal means to oppose implementation of the *Brown* decision.

Thus, although we sometimes differed on matters of timing and circumstance—a question of political prudence that our respective responsibilities may have led us to judge differently—we both shared the common goal of ensuring the equal exercise of civil rights by all Americans. Furthermore, when the times and circumstances required, as they would at Little Rock in 1957, we were of common mind on the need to meet the challenge before us.

NOTES

1. 163 U.S. 537 (1896), at p. 544.

2. The lone voice of dissent was by Mr. Justice Harlan. In his memorable words: "But in the view of the Constitution, in the eyes of the law, there is in this country no superior, dominant ruling class of citizens. There is no caste here. Our Constitution is color blind" (163 U.S. 537 [1896], at p. 599).

3. I have sometimes wondered whether unanimity at the price of more clarity and better constitutional reasoning was worth the price. There is some speculation among observers of the Court, for example, that if Justice Jackson's more scholarly reasoning in support of desegregation had been incorporated in the Court's final opinion, public acceptance of the decision would have been more universal—even if that had resulted in a dissenting opinion on the part of one of the other justices (see Jeffrey D. Hockett, "Justice Robert H. Jackson and Segregation," *Yearbook of the Supreme Court Historical Society* [December 1989]).

4. The platform committee complied, and the wording was changed to indicate that the Republican party "accepted" the Court's rulings in *Brown*.

5. Eisenhower, *Waging Peace* (Garden City, N.Y.: Doubleday, 1965), p. 150.

6. Youngstown Sheet & Tube v. Sawyer, 343 U.S. 579 (1952), at pp. 634–35.

7. Alexander v. Holmes County Board of Education, 396 U.S. 1219 (1969). In this case the Court held that continued operation of racially segregated schools under the standard of "all deliberate speed" was no longer constitutionally permissible.

8. See appendix C.

12

Enforcing Equality

❖ ❖ ❖ ❖ ❖ ❖ ❖ ❖ ❖ ❖ ❖ ❖ ❖ ❖ ❖ ❖

In the Department of Justice, our efforts to enforce the Supreme Court's decree in the *Brown* case outlawing segregation in the public schools were two-pronged.

First, we responded affirmatively to calls for assistance from the federal courts, which had been given primary jurisdiction over enforcement by the Supreme Court. The Little Rock crisis of 1957 was the prime example of this policy.

Second, we drafted and succeeded in getting passed the Civil Rights Act of 1957, which became the first civil rights measure enacted into law since the Reconstruction era. This act, as originally presented by us to Congress, would for the first time have given the attorney general direct power to sue in federal courts whenever there was a violation of any civil right that had been declared by the Supreme Court to be a constitutional right. The draft of the act thus empowered the attorney general, without further congressional action, to enforce the constitutional promise of equal protection for all citizens when such violations occurred. Its scope was broad enough to give the attorney general the power to enforce not only voting rights but also any federal district court decree that approved a local plan to desegregate the public schools. And it would have released moneys appropriated for general law-enforcement purposes to be used for these specific purposes.

The act was controversial. It would have broken the one-hundred-year impasse in Congress on civil rights. Leading senators from the South, such as Georgia's Richard Russell and Mississippi's James Eastland denounced the bill as making the attorney general a czar. This charge was true only to the extent that Congress, through filibusters, would no longer be able to stop the Justice Department from implementing the equal-protection promises of the Constitution through ways and means approved by the courts.

To understand the need for this two-pronged program to enforce the *Brown II* decision, a look at the conditions that faced us is in order. After a brief period of calm, the strategy of the southern segregationist forces became clear. One-hundred-one members of Congress issued a Southern Manifesto encouraging massive resistance to *Brown*: "We pledge ourselves to use all lawful means to bring about a reversal of this decision which is contrary to the Constitution and to prevent the use of force in its implementation." (Because of its historic importance, the entire manifesto, with some background, is set forth in appendix C.) The Southern Manifesto spawned the formation throughout the South of White Citizens Councils seeking to nullify the *Brown* decision, which in many cases condoned and even encouraged rioting to resist desegregation of the public schools.

I attempted to counteract the manifesto by appealing to the attorneys general of the southern states as fellow law-enforcement officers. I had been invited to their conferences each year as a speaker, and at this point their convention was to be held in Phoenix, Arizona. After my speech I asked the attorneys general from the states in the Deep South to meet with me at an off-the-record session at midnight. I asked their professional help in eliminating segregation in the schools and in interstate bus and railroad transportation now that *Brown* had been decided. I had just filed a brief with the Interstate Commerce Commission opposing segregation in interstate transportation. Some of the southerners expressed sympathy with my enforcement problem but told me every state attorney general was a potential candidate for a governorship of his state and that it would be political suicide to make any move favoring integration. Without rancor they said the federal government should not expect any help from them.

There were some bitter-enders in the group. I remember at one meeting of the American Bar Association, my wife and I were attending a reception given by Smythe Gambrell of Georgia, a distinguished attorney who was president of the ABA. Among the guests were the attorney general of Georgia, Eugene Cook, and his wife. When we were introduced to Mrs. Cook, she murmured "nigger lovers" and refused to shake hands. And my children once in a while received similar treatment in school groups. But such occasions were rare.

Next came the Emmett Till murder. A black youth from Chicago visiting in Mississippi was killed by white vigilantes for the "crime" of whistling at a white woman. The FBI investigation indicated that the killing was racially motivated, but there was no evidence that the perpetrators had crossed state lines afterward. Our hands were thus tied since intrastate murders did not come under federal criminal jurisdiction. Our proposed Civil Rights Act of 1957 would have changed that. Meanwhile we had to turn down requests for federal prosecution of the Till case because we lacked jurisdiction.

Sporadically, cases of rioting began to occur when local school board officials attempted to comply with the *Brown* decisions. In one case in Clinton, Tennessee, a man named John Kasper led a tumultuous mob that blocked the entry of black students into the local high school; the governor was forced to send in the National Guard to restore order. The federal district court ordered Kasper to desist from obstructing integration, but Kasper persisted in his actions and the court began contempt proceedings against him. The Justice Department then stepped in and assisted the school board and the federal district court, at its request, in obtaining contempt-of-court proceedings against Kasper, who was sent to jail.[1]

The tension caused by the Southern Manifesto and these incidents was further heightened when Gov. Allan Shivers of Texas used the Texas Rangers to prevent black children from entering an all-white public school in Mansfield, Texas. We were powerless to intervene, however: The local school board did not initiate an effort in the federal court that might have led to circumstances in which the Justice Department could be called in to enforce the federal court's decision (as had occurred in the Kasper case).

Commentators often miss the distinction between the Mansfield situation and the later episode in Little Rock. They forget that the second *Brown* decision gave enforcement power to implement school desegregation to the federal district courts. President Eisenhower or the Justice Department could not simply order a local school district to desegregate "or else." Enforcement had to await the submission of a plan for desegregation to the district court, the approval of the plan, the defiance of the court-approved plan, and a request from the district court to the executive branch of the federal government to enter the proceedings and exercise its vast resources for enforcement. Quite clearly, the Supreme Court deliberately decided on this procedure as preferable to having the president use military force or carpet-bagger agents directly against recalcitrant school boards or state governors.

Some observers at the time, including some of the members of the department's Civil Rights Section, thought we should take more of the initiative and test the federal government's powers in cases such as Mansfield. However, it was my view then—and still—that had we decided to intervene in the Mansfield case or cases like it and attempted to enforce desegregation we might have lost the case at the federal appeals court level (the court might have reasoned that we were exceeding our authority under *Brown II* or that we had abridged the judicial process of remedy). Such an outcome, in turn, would have meant a grave setback to our civil rights efforts and encouraged greater resistance. We could not under any circumstances lose in court in any of these early cases. Even if the Supreme Court were eventually to uphold such enforcement, significant time would have passed and the cause of desegregation would suffer. Thus we needed to make sure at all times that our efforts were strictly and indisputably in line with *Brown II* and that we were acting at the request of the federal courts in obtaining compliance with its orders, as would be the case in Little Rock.

Violence also came close to home. Shortly after the Kasper affair, unknown persons burned fiery crosses in front of the Washington residences of a number of Supreme Court justices. The following Sunday, early in the morning, I heard a commotion outside my own home and turned on a master light switch. I found that kerosene had been dumped on the ground under the bedrooms where my children slept, but the intruders were nowhere to be seen. Thereafter the FBI provided protection for a time for my residence and accompanied the children to school and to their social engagements.

At this point the date arrived on which Eisenhower and I had agreed (some months before) that I would leave government, for financial reasons, to return to private practice. I had decided that I would leave the Justice Department whenever my savings were nearly used up as I did not want my official actions to be influenced, even unconsciously, or appear to be influenced by any financial obligation to others. I went to the White House to remind the president and to make my recommendation for a successor. The president seemed surprised but acknowledged our previous agreement. "Charlie Wilson is resigning," he told me; "that gives me a problem, but come back to see me the first of the week and we'll work it out."

My timing could not have been worse. The school board of Little Rock, Arkansas, was taking steps at that point to integrate Central High School. Despite the board's willingness to comply with the *Brown* decisions, the governor of the state, Orval Faubus, decided to make political capital out of the incident by blocking the entry of black students into the high school, first by legal means and later by force. It precipitated a constitutional crisis between the state of Arkansas and the federal government of national—and even international—proportion.

When I returned to the Oval Office the Little Rock situation was in full swing. The president quickly said, "Well, of course you can't leave now. It would look as though you and I disagreed on the course of action at Little Rock." The president's firm endorsement of the positions and actions I had taken as attorney general had been of the utmost importance whenever I had to deal with others in the administration who were unsympathetic to my position, so I postponed my resignation until the Little Rock crisis had cooled.

A crisis of the magnitude that the situation in Little Rock was to become had been expected by the administration. Over a period of months we had increasingly realized that a clash of historic importance was inevitable between the president, who was required by the Constitution to enforce the law of the land, and political leaders in the South, who had announced their plan to resist the enforcement of the *Brown* decisions.

At the Justice Department we engaged in "contingency planning" in order not to be caught unprepared. Assistant Attorney General Warren Olney enlisted the full-time services of Prof. St. John Barrett of the University of California to plan a program to meet the massive changes and expanded enforcement program that were needed in the wake of *Brown* and our newly proposed civil rights legislation. The FBI undertook a survey of the southern states to determine whether local law-enforcement officials were encountering difficulties with the White Citizens Councils and whether sporadic rioting was being centrally directed. President Eisenhower arranged to have J. Edgar Hoover appear before a cabinet meeting to disclose the findings of the survey. Hoover's report indicated that although some compliance with *Brown* had occurred in the year following the decision, opposition to desegregation was mounting. I found this information helpful since it demonstrated the difficulty of our enforcement problem and the possible eruption of a serious constitutional crisis if state and local officials refused to comply with the Supreme Court's orders. Most important, we began to plan our response to such a grave crisis. By the time that Little Rock had reached a crisis, we had completed our studies of the legal precedents with respect to the president's power to intervene in localities where rioting went beyond the ability of local officials to control a violation of the Constitution.

The Little Rock crisis began in late August 1957, when a group of white parents brought suit in the state's chancery court to block the school board's desegregation plan and appealed to the governor for intervention. Based on evidence Governor Faubus provided about increased gun sales in the Little Rock area, the state chancery court issued an injunction against the plan. The school board then took its case to federal court, and the federal judge, Ronald N. Davies, ruled that the state chancery court had no jurisdiction and ordered desegregation to proceed as planned. On September 2, the day before school was to open, Faubus ordered the Arkansas National Guard to surround the high school in order to protect the nine black students, or so he announced. The school board then returned to federal court for further instructions.

On September 3 Judge Davies again repeated his earlier order, but the next day Faubus again used the National Guard to turn the black students away from the school. Judge Davies then ordered the Justice Department to investigate Faubus's claims that the imminent threat to public order, within his police powers as governor, justified his attempts to thwart integration.

I immediately dispatched FBI agents on a fact-finding mission to Little Rock at the court's request. Several days later they reported that evidence revealed that Faubus's instructions to the National Guard were not just to protect the black schoolchildren but to prevent them from entering the school building. They also noted that there had been no unusual increase in the sale of guns as Faubus had originally claimed.

By this time, Faubus was clearly in danger of a contempt citation from the judge, perhaps even arrest. I closely monitored the situation and had discussed with my associates a number of actions that the Department of Justice and the federal government might take. Prior to September 4 it was still unclear whether Faubus had explicitly violated an order of the federal court. But following Judge Davies's injunction enjoining "all persons" from interfering with desegregation and given the reports we had received from the FBI that Faubus had sent in the guard to prevent desegregation, we obviously faced a grave constitutional crisis. The governor's actions represented an attempt to nullify the Constitution and the laws of the United States and to disregard the orders of the federal court.

I had been in continual contact with President Eisenhower as these events unfolded. I briefed him on the contents of the FBI report and told him that the federal court would most likely issue an injunction against Faubus, thus making federal involvement imminent. The president was aware of the gravity of the situation and hoped that a way could be found for Faubus to make "an orderly retreat." Although the Justice Department would not directly negotiate with Faubus, we received several proposals from numerous intermediaries but none proved satisfactory.

Following the procedures we had developed in the other desegregation cases, we now needed only a request from the federal court to intervene. On September 9 that request came: Judge Davies called on the Justice Department to enter the case and file a preliminary injunction and supporting brief against the governor, who was ordered to appear before the court on September 20. I accepted the federal court's request and sent attorneys to work with the school board attorneys. I also prepared plans, including executive orders and presidential proclamations, based on the various alternative courses of action Faubus might take: defying the court, closing the schools in Little Rock, or complying with the desegregation order.

It developed that Judge Davies, the federal judge hearing the Faubus case, was from North Dakota and was only temporarily assigned to the Little Rock bench. Governor Faubus claimed we had rigged the temporary transfer to get a "favorable" judge. We showed, however, that the assignment had been made before the Little Rock case had arisen and had been undertaken by the senior circuit court judge with jurisdiction over federal judicial appeals from Arkansas.

Many appeals for help in Little Rock were being made directly to the White House in order to resolve the impasse between Faubus and the federal court. Sherman Adams, the White House chief of staff, undertook to mediate by searching for some sort of compromise. Adams was a moderate on civil rights and recognized the importance of enforcing *Brown*, but I think he had political concerns about the tactics that the Justice Department had been forced to use in this instance. Although I certainly had a different view of the matter and thought compromise impossible, I remained in daily contact with Adams and kept him informed of activities on the legal front.

Adams was approached by an old friend of his from congressional days, Congressman Brooks Hays of Arkansas, who believed that it was possible to settle with Governor Faubus (Hays's role in the matter would cost him reelection). Adams and Hays consulted with a group of southern governors, with the avowed intention of persuading Faubus to withdraw the National Guard (as I recall these were the governors of Florida, Tennessee, and North Carolina). Adams then asked the president to meet with Governor Faubus personally in a last attempt to achieve a peaceful settlement. The president asked my political opinion. I reminded him that mediation with Governor Faubus had failed a number of times in the past. Furthermore, Faubus was running for reelection in November, I told him, and it was my view that Faubus undoubtedly realized he could not allow the black children into the high school without being defeated at the polls. Therefore I predicted that the president could not persuade Faubus to reverse his position.

Eisenhower decided to hold the meeting anyway. They met on September 14, at Newport, Rhode Island, where the president was enjoying a late-summer vacation. Contrary to the usual procedures, the two men met alone with no one to take notes; accordingly, no firsthand account of their conversation exists. Faubus recounted later that he told Ike at some length of his experiences with General Patton's army in France during World War II. He described the progress being made in Arkansas in the field of civil rights, including his appointment of two black citizens to the Democratic State Central Committee. He also said he asked the president for "breathing room"—a delay of ten days to try to resolve the problem peaceably— and he suggested that federal marshals be sent in to assist his efforts.

According to President Eisenhower's version of their meeting, which he recounted in an October 8, 1957, diary entry dictated to his secretary, Ann Whitman, Eisenhower proposed that Faubus leave the troops in place but simply change their orders to allow them to escort the black children into the school building while continuing to preserve public order. If Faubus followed this course promptly, Eisenhower continued, he would instruct the Justice Department to appear in federal court and ask that the governor not be cited for contempt. Eisenhower assured Faubus that he did not desire "a trial of strength" between the president and the governor. But he had warned, "Where the federal government had assumed jurisdiction and this was upheld by the Supreme Court, there could be only one out-come—that is, the state would lose, and [he] did not want to see any governor humiliated." Faubus "seemed to be very appreciative of this attitude," Eisenhower recounted, "and I got definitely the understanding that he was going back to Arkansas to act within a matter of hours to revoke his orders to the guard to prevent reentry of the Negro children into the school."[2]

The meeting, as I recall it, was held in the president's small office at the Newport naval base, and the atmosphere was strictly businesslike. Both Eisenhower and Faubus were courteous to each other, but their assistants (including myself) were tense, realizing the significance of the outcome. Journalists were on the scene, scouting for background information and scraps of news.

At the conclusion of their session together, several of us joined them, and the president told us in the presence of Faubus that they had agreed that the black children would be admitted to the high school. Faubus said nothing to dispute the president's statement. Everyone was relieved over the apparent agreement. I knew Eisenhower was a persuasive person, but I was incredulous at Faubus's ostensible capitulation and the seemingly abrupt end of a constitutional crisis of such import. I offered my congratulations and departed to attend a reunion of some of my Yale Law School classmates in Connecticut, en route back to Washington.

Faubus returned to Arkansas and consulted with his close political advisers. As a result, he still barred entry of the black children and issued inflammatory statements clearly defying the president's position. When the president heard this, he telephoned me in Washington. "You were right," he said, "Faubus broke his word." I could tell he was furious. His voice was tense. He was acting as a military commander-in-chief, dealing with Faubus as a subordinate who had let him down in the midst of battle. Eisenhower was reluctant to use military force to resolve the situation, fearing that Faubus would simply shut down the school system and that such a strategy of noncompliance might be used by other governors in the South, yet I knew the president had no other choice.

Faubus, for his part, played this high-stakes game shrewdly if unwisely. On September 20 he failed to appear in federal court, and his legal representatives sought to have the federal judge disqualified from ruling on the matter. The judge threw out their request and ordered the governor to comply with his previous rulings to desist from interference. That evening, Faubus appeared on statewide television and announced he was removing the National Guard.

In the meantime, members of the White Citizens Councils and other rabble-rousers began arriving in Little Rock from other states, and the situation was getting out of hand. The imminent violence that Faubus had earlier used as a justification for his actions had now developed—but as a result of Faubus's own recalcitrance. Little Rock's small police force was unable to handle the large crowds that had gathered, and they refused to escort the black children into the school building. At one point, several children were able to enter the building, but they were quickly surrounded by an angry mob. In the opinion of Mayor Woodrow W. Mann of Little Rock who wired us and also telephoned, lives were endangered and federal troops were needed to quell the mounting violence. The FBI agents on the scene agreed. I presented our opinion to the president that in this state of affairs, where the Constitution as interpreted in the *Brown* cases was being defied by the governor and rioting was increasing, he had the constitutional power and duty to enforce the law (see appendix D).

Only one effective method remained to enforce the law: use of federal troops. Secretary of the Army Wilbur Brucker was alerted. "In my career I learned," the president told me over the phone from Newport, "that if you have to use force, use overwhelming force and save lives thereby." He ordered the 101st Airborne Division, which he knew had crowd-control experience, to go to Little Rock. "Meet me at the White House," the president added, "I am going to address the nation on TV." I believe, but have no firsthand knowledge, that Ike's confidante, Gen. Al Gruenther, was influential in assisting the president to make this decision speedily.

The first inkling that the public and Governor Faubus had of the president's decisive action was the appearance of the 101st Airborne Division in battle array, with bayonets, marching up the main street of Little Rock under the command of Gen. Edwin Walker. Simultaneously, the president nationalized the Arkansas National Guard, thus destroying further authority of Governor Faubus over them. The deadlock was broken, and the black children entered the high school. Television screens around the country dramatized the event. The education reporter of the *New York Times* wrote graphic day-by-day accounts, reprinted all over the world.

The black children, who must have been frightened, behaved magnificently then and throughout the ensuing weeks when the classroom atmosphere was charged with emotion. No wonder, when one considers that the white children had been brought up to believe that segregation was not only legal (as it had been only three years earlier) but justifiable and "natural." I met with four of the nine black students some thirty years later (Governor Faubus spoke on the same program) and learned the details of their constant harassment by some of the white students and their parents. Through the ensuing years, the nation watched, sympathetically and with pride, the progress of those beleaguered black schoolchildren in their mature years.

The U.S. armed forces on the spot performed with restraint and common sense in carrying out their unpleasant duty. There was no loss of life. The mayor of Little Rock, the school board, and especially the superintendent and many of the schoolteachers deserve great credit for their actions. They were a law-abiding and progressive group who accepted the Supreme Court decision in *Brown* as binding on all public officials, even though their own governor defied the Court's interpretation of the Constitution. I believe the mayor and a majority of the members of the school board also felt that desegregation of public schools was morally right and educationally advisable.

The president performed admirably in dealing with the crisis, whatever his earlier views had been about school integration. He realized the constitutional import of the crisis and sought to rally the nation behind the orders of the Court and the cause of school integration by taking to the airwaves to explain the situation and his actions to the American people. I went over the draft of his speech with him, and we made some changes to meet legal requirements. In his televised address to the nation, the president was firm in his intent to resolve the crisis at Little Rock in order to maintain the rule of law and to enforce the orders of the court. But he also struck a conciliatory tone toward "the overwhelming majority of people" in the South, who "are of good will, united in their efforts to preserve and respect the law even when they disagree with it."

As soon as the speech was delivered, southern members of Congress reacted vehemently. Majority Leader Lyndon B. Johnson made a public statement on the floor of the Senate attacking Eisenhower's action at Little Rock: "There should be no troops from either side patrolling our school campuses." Sen. Richard Russell of Georgia compared Eisenhower's tactics to Hitler's. A second Reconstruction period with carpet-bagger government of the South was predicted by some southern officials and newspapers. One of the outspoken critics of using military force at Little Rock was Sen. John F. Kennedy. In 1962 Kennedy, as president, faced a similar situation of mob violence against desegregation efforts at the University of Mississippi. After there had been loss of life when the U.S. marshals attempted to control the crowd of segregationists, he too was forced to call in the army.

I became a major target in the storm of protest. The segregationist press in the South was particularly vitriolic in its personal attacks on me—an easier target than the popular Eisenhower. And they hailed my resignation at the close of the Little Rock crisis a month later as the best news of the year.

Even after the troops were sent to Little Rock, Faubus continued to oppose integration in court and in his public statements, but the president persisted in his efforts at conciliation. He met with a group of southern governors called together by Brooks Hays and Sherman Adams, and they in turn endeavored to get Faubus to end his hostile acts. The governors at one point thought they had an agreement with Faubus, but again he reneged.

When word of this reached Eisenhower, he and I were attending a formal birthday dinner in the home of Secretary of State and Mrs. Dulles. The president immediately asked me to return to the White House with him to try to salvage the situation. Such was the personal attention he gave—and continued to give for more than a year—until he was able to withdraw the last troops from Little Rock. Today integrated public schools flourish peaceably in Little Rock and throughout the South.

Looking back at the turbulent events, I can only conclude that Eisenhower's decisive action at Little Rock crushed the forces behind the Southern Manifesto. Eventual enforcement of *Brown* was ensured. I was particularly happy that, when the Little Rock lawsuit reached the Supreme Court, it unanimously upheld the constitutionality of the president's actions.

Eisenhower's intervention at Little Rock, though clothed in terms of "law enforcement," dramatically showed that the federal government was supreme in enforcing the Constitution. The lesson was not lost on the White Citizens Councils nor on the country at large. Still, resistance to desegregation lasted for almost another ten years.

Many observers have criticized the efforts of the Eisenhower administration in enforcing desegregation as being too weak and legalistic precisely because it took so long to finally end segregation. But that assessment misses the constraints under which we operated and fails to take into account the divisive political climate of the time. First, full-scale and immediate enforcement by the federal government was impossible because it was on constitutionally questionable grounds: The Supreme Court had not embraced that position in *Brown II*, which required instead that school districts develop plans that would then be approved by the federal courts. Where federal courts were not involved or where they did not call upon the federal government to enforce their orders, as in the Mansfield, Texas, incident, the Justice Department's hands were tied.[3] Furthermore, the steps the Supreme Court specified in *Brown II*, I knew, were procedures that President Eisenhower found especially appealing; he had taken a personal interest in the Justice Department's brief in the case and had gone over it carefully, and he strongly favored giving local school districts and the local federal court time to work out an acceptable plan for integration.

Second, in the general area of civil rights enforcement, it must be remembered that existing statutes provided only very limited powers for the Justice Department to intervene (a condition I sought to remedy—unsuccessfully—in the original provisions of what would become the Civil Rights Act of 1957). Moreover, Congress had authorized and budgeted for only a very small staff of lawyers in the department's Civil Rights Section (another condition I sought to remedy—this time successfully—in the Civil Rights Act of 1957 through the transformation of the section into a larger Civil Rights Division). As a practical matter, therefore, we simply did not have the personnel or the budget to pursue an ambitious enforcement effort. Also, the Supreme Court had not yet acted to strike down other types of segregation, such as in public transportation that the Rosa Parks case raised.[4]

Third, full-scale and immediate enforcement by the Justice Department acting on its own was politically impossible. Leading segregationists controlled powerful positions in Congress and in state governments in the southern states. And public opinion in the South, perhaps even elsewhere in the country, had not yet been won over. Immediate desegregation would have plunged the country into its gravest political crisis since the civil war.

By adhering more or less strictly to the procedures that the Supreme Court had laid out, the Justice Department was able to wrap its efforts in the cloak of the Constitution and to carry out the enforcement of the law.

This approach enabled us to build political support for civil rights, especially among those individuals of more moderate opinions; it made the matter one of constitutional and legal right rather than simply a policy matter of favoring civil rights.

This method was also useful in gaining the support of the president. From my conversation with him in 1952, I knew that Eisenhower favored desegregation in the District of Columbia, but he was not going to take the initiative on civil rights. Because the federal government's efforts involved enforcing the Court's interpretation of the Constitution in ways that the Court had set out, I was able to bring Eisenhower along on the issue. Civil rights was not simply a matter of personal preference or policy view, it was a matter of constitutional duty. In the end, I was able to establish everything a lawyer could do and I obtained Eisenhower's support each step of the way: the role of the Justice Department in advising the Court on *Brown*, our view in oral argument before the Court that segregation of public schools was unconstitutional, our powers to assist local federal courts in enforcing *Brown*, and, ultimately in Little Rock, the fact that the federal government was supreme in interpreting and enforcing the Constitution. Thus, before I left office, everything had been done that legally could be done to establish *Brown v. Board of Education* as the law of the land.

The Supreme Court's decision in *Brown II* meant, of course, that we could not simply go in and order a school district to desegregate. But as I have thought about that decision in recent years, as well as the subsequent history of the civil rights struggle, it may actually have had a beneficial, if unintended, effect. By requiring local authorities to come up with desegregation plans and then submit them to the federal courts, which they often failed to do, it alerted black leaders and civil rights advocates that they must act on their own to commence and stimulate action by local school boards and other local officials to end segregation. Although the federal government could offer some help, as it did at Little Rock, the battle for civil rights would be fought and won by political action at the local level. It was only at this level, in one's home and community, that the plight of America's black citizens—living in a segregated society, lacking political rights, and facing hostility and sometimes even personal violence—could be vividly demonstrated, thereby winning greater public and political support for civil rights. By the 1960s massive citizens' protests and movements brought about the change.

The Little Rock story made the headlines again thirty years later. The Little Rock school district had sought to recover damages from the state resulting from the official actions taken by Faubus in the state's name. At the close of 1989 a federal judge approved a $129 million settlement for these damages, and the Arkansas state legislature then agreed to make such funds available to enhance desegregation programs. Thus, Governor Faubus's defiance of the Constitution cost Arkansas dearly, financially as well as morally.

During the turmoil of summer 1957 our efforts to pass a civil rights bill through Congress were also coming to a head. The need for new legislation to implement the constitutional promise of equal rights for all citizens was pressing. A valiant effort had been made after the Civil War by "radical" Republicans to implement the Thirteenth, Fourteenth, and Fifteenth Amendments to the Constitution, but the Supreme Court had declared most of their legislation unconstitutional.

The only federal civil rights laws on the statute books when Eisenhower was elected were three limited laws passed during the post–Civil War period that had escaped being held unconstitutional by the Supreme Court. One law made it a felony to conspire to deprive a citizen of any right or privilege granted by law. But try to get a southern jury to convict under that criminal law! The second statute forbade deprivation of any federal rights "under color of law." At best this was ambiguous, and it only covered the actions of state and local officials who "willfully" sought to deprive a person of a federal right. Third was a law prohibiting racial discrimination in selecting jurors. Theoretically an action could be brought in a state court to enforce this right, but no black person dared to start such an action. Clearly a new and different approach was needed.

Time after time, efforts had been made to pass new civil rights laws—thirteen times during the New Deal alone. But again time after time these bills were killed by filibuster in the Senate. This frustration resulted from the so-called "southern strategy" of the major political parties—the southern Democrats traded votes with some Republicans to ensure that the filibusters succeeded.

In pressing the need for new civil rights legislation, no doubt I was motivated partly by my study of the origins of the Republican party in 1856 and the presidency of Abraham Lincoln. A large shelf in my library consisted of Civil War books—and I was steeped in early Republican party history from having been Republican national chairman. I wanted to help direct the party toward fulfilling its original purpose in adding to the Constitution the so-called Civil War amendments, which abolished slavery and instituted due process and equal protection under the law for all citizens.

In 1954, in the aftermath of the first *Brown* decision, I became convinced that the time was ripe for new civil rights legislation. The Supreme Court was moving ahead on the constitutional front, and the Eisenhower administration needed to demonstrate its commitment to civil rights to counter pro–civil rights Democrats in Congress who were criticizing it for failing to take a stand.

Although I felt that the Justice Department's efforts to enforce *Brown* had first priority, I began to study the issue closely and to develop a new civil rights proposal. I received very pedestrian responses from the staff, however, in the department's then small Civil Rights Section. Most of their ideas were simply rewarmed versions of proposals that had been kicking around for years and had been unsuccessful in the past. It took quite a bit of effort to resist the pressure to rush in with these familiar solutions, and in internal conferences in the department I told my associates that I was completely dissatisfied with what we had come up with so far. Antilynching legislation, I said, was a dead issue, and technical changes in the criminal provisions were picayune. Although they would help a bit, nothing was appealing about these proposals, and we would be slaughtered up on the Hill.

I told them we needed a different approach and proposed voting rights as a new area for attention. I then said we needed a civil approach in addition to the limited criminal remedies then in the statutes: Civil actions would enable the department to force injunctive remedies before civil rights violations took place (unlike a criminal procedure, which takes place after a violation has been committed). Injunctive remedy would be especially useful, I knew, for enforcing voting rights. Enforcement power under civil law would also weaken the power of white juries in the South to let violators off the hook. Under the then-existing criminal procedures, the FBI was also hampered in its efforts because it required the cooperation of local authorities in the South, who were distrusted by potential witnesses and in some instances were the very officials the FBI was investigating. Despite our efforts to increase the number of cases that could be brought to trial under these statutes, only a handful had been successfully prosecuted.

I initially concentrated almost exclusively on voting rights, and at one point I was ready to send a bill to Congress that basically encompassed only voting rights. Then I began thinking about all the equal-protection matters that might come up during my testimony before Congress, and I decided that a more ambitious bill was necessary. So I created on my own, almost out of whole cloth, a set of proposals that would give the attorney general unprecedented power to enforce civil rights; these proposals would become the controversial but important section three of the eventual bill. This part of the bill would not only broaden the attorney general's statutory powers of enforcement in some legal sense but would also put Congress on record as authorizing civil rights enforcement, which was important as a practical matter in getting the support and money from Congress for that effort to be successful.

The initiative thus rested on my shoulders. I could have responded to the political pressure on the administration to propose new civil rights legislation with a weak bill that offered a lot of pious words about racial equality and simply brought forward again the orthodox solutions previously proposed. But I decided to create a more affirmative and a broader program, one that I could defend philosophically as well as politically.

In December 1955 I presented to the president our Department of Justice proposal for new civil rights legislation, which entailed:

1. creation of a presidentially appointed bipartisan Civil Rights Commission to hold hearings with subpoena power and to recommend additional civil rights legislation;

2. creation of a new Civil Rights Division in the Justice Department, headed by an assistant attorney general, to replace the three-man section in the Criminal Division, which had practically no congressional appropriation on which to function;[5]

3. empowerment of the attorney general to sue to redress all civil rights violations in cases where the Supreme Court had defined the civil right as one protected by the Constitution. Section three broadened the definition of conspiracy to deprive civil rights to encompass the actions of individuals, gave the attorney general the power—through civil suit—to seek injunctive relief against the obstruction of civil rights, and increased the penalties when such obstruction resulted in the loss of life. This part of our proposal was especially im-

portant since it sought to implement the promise of equal protection under the laws made in the Fourteenth Amendment to the Constitution. It was also the one most bitterly opposed because it not only could be applied to voting rights but it also gave the attorney general direct authority to enforce Court orders to desegregate public schools and to enter cases such as the Emmett Till murder;

4. establishment of enforcement machinery—including injunctive relief by the attorney general and federal court jurisdiction—to guarantee the right to vote in federal elections for black citizens who had been denied systematically that right by state laws and practices that existed throughout most of the South. We believed that once black citizens had the right to vote, along with equal access to the public-education system, they would have a "level playing field" and the same opportunity to achieve their political goals as all other citizens.

The president directed me to submit the proposal for discussion in the cabinet. He knew it was controversial and obviously wanted to hear all points of view. Secretary of State Dulles generally supported our proposal, citing the difficulties encountered by the State Department in dealing with foreign governments because of our domestic condonation of segregation. Considerable opposition, however, developed in the cabinet to sections three and four. Treasury Secretary Humphrey was particularly outspoken in his criticism of the bill, and Defense Secretary Wilson and HEW Secretary Marion Folsom had reservations about some of its provisions.

After the meeting I was told by the secretary of the cabinet that the president had decided not to support the third section of the proposed bill, which dealt with the attorney general's enforcement powers. But I was allowed by the president, who cautioned me not to act like "another Charles Sumner" when I testified,[6] to send the bill to Congress as a Department of Justice proposal, and I did so.

When I testified before the House Judiciary Committee in support of the bill, I was needled by some of the Democrats on the committee because it wasn't an administration bill, which ordinarily would have been submitted directly by the White House. I was fortunate, however, in having some strong allies on the committee: Congressman (later senator) Kenneth Keating of New York, an old friend, played an especially critical role both in supporting the measure and in strengthening its provisions.

Keating was disappointed that the White House had dropped section three, and he had asked me even before the hearing if I could bring the proposed legislation on section three before his committee so that he could amend the bill. Thus, at one of the committee's hearings, he asked me whether the Justice Department had prepared any legislation dealing with the attorney general's powers to enforce civil rights and, if so, whether I could make it available to the committee. As a result of Keating's request, the Justice Department sent over to the committee the third section of the bill. In July, the bill, all four parts now included, passed the House, and I had faithfully carried out Eisenhower's instructions.

The testimony to Congress of the many instances of widespread deprivation of the right to vote encountered by black citizens was dramatic. We showed that even some members of the faculty of Tuskegee Institute, a highly respected black educational institution, had been barred as "illiterates." Despite our success in the House, the bill remained buried for the rest of the 1956 session in the Senate Judiciary Committee just as other civil rights measures, such as antilynching bills, had been over the years. There was, however, one bright light: Sen. Paul Douglas of Illinois managed to extract a promise from Majority Leader Lyndon B. Johnson that civil rights legislation would be considered by the Senate early enough in the next year to allow a full-blown attempt to defeat a filibuster.

In his 1956 campaign for reelection, President Eisenhower endorsed our four-part bill. He did not consult me before making his campaign declaration of support. His open endorsement of the bill gave us a big advantage in the 1957 session. The bill quickly passed the House, with a boost from House Judiciary Committee chairman Emanuel Celler of New York.

Then came the crisis. In a spectacular parliamentary move by Vice-president Nixon (presiding officer of the Senate) and the Republican leader, Sen. William Knowland of California, the bill was rushed over to the vice-president's desk. Nixon, following a motion by Knowland that exploited an arcane rule of the Senate, immediately referred the bill to the floor of the Senate, not to the traditional graveyard of civil rights legislation, the Senate Judiciary Committee, then headed by Senator Eastland of Mississippi, a notorious segregationist.[7]

Nixon, Knowland, my deputy Bill Rogers, and I had devised this parliamentary strategy after extensive discussion in the previous weeks. Although I cannot remember who came up with the idea of exploiting this

Senate rule and having the vice-president use his seldom-exercised powers as presiding officer of the Senate to save the bill from falling into Eastland's hands, it worked. We planned our strategy without consulting the White House, especially the president's staff members for legislative liaison, Jack Martin and Wilton Persons, who were close to many of the southern senators and unsupportive of our civil rights efforts. Had word of our planned move leaked out, it would have gone straight to Richard Russell, the leader of the southern forces in the Senate; forewarned, Russell could have stopped it.[8]

As though a bomb had exploded, the southern senators headed by Johnson reacted immediately and forcefully. They filled the pages of the *Congressional Record*, denouncing the vice-president's parliamentary move as a deplorable breach of the Senate's hoary rules. Sen. John F. Kennedy of Massachusetts sided with Lyndon Johnson. The practical effect of their position would have been to kill the bill in the Senate Judiciary Committee or have it reported in emasculated form too late in the session, when it would be killed by filibuster. That had been the fate of all civil rights bills proposed since Reconstruction.

The bill proceeded to the whole Senate, although the Senate Judiciary Committee called upon me to testify on the bill before the floor debate. The questioning was led by Sen. Sam Ervin of North Carolina. He had been selected by the southern opponents of the bill to represent their point of view, and he was a bitter interrogator, quite unlike the affable image of the cracker-barrel country lawyer he presented during his chairmanship of the Watergate hearings. When he attacked President Eisenhower personally for his support of the bill, I walked out of the hearings. Summarizing his segregationist views at the conclusion of my testimony, Ervin stated that the bill

> offends the basic American concepts that ours is a government of law—rather than a government of men, . . .
>
> is deliberately designed to vest in the attorney general the autocratic and despotic power to nullify state laws—and to rob the State and local officials—of these basic and invaluable safeguards created by the Founding Fathers, . . .
>
> is deliberately designed to empower the attorney general to institute and prosecute at public expense lawsuits as numberless as the sand for the avowed benefit of any alien, citizen or private corporation.

I attempted to take some of the force out of Ervin's criticisms by indicating that I had no intention of becoming a run-away attorney general or some kind of civil rights czar, as many critics charged. I emphasized in my testimony that the Justice Department intended to follow its existing procedures in the school-integration cases, and I submitted to the committee a list of twenty or so Supreme Court decisions that would be enforceable under section three; but my efforts fell on deaf ears.

Senator Ervin was a shrewd strategist. He realized that the central objective of the segregationist senators was to prevent the president from enforcing the *Brown* decisions. That was the stated goal of the Southern Manifesto. A major part of Ervin's strategy was to incorporate in the legislation a repeal of an existing federal statute that authorized the president to employ the armed forces to aid in the execution of the judicial process in certain cases. Ervin evidently overlooked other statutes that gave the president authority to use troops to enforce the Constitution in cases such as the one at Little Rock. Accordingly we did not object to the repeal of the one statute. At the time—this was before the Little Rock crisis—there was no thought in the mind of President Eisenhower to use troops to enforce school desegregation. In fact, the idea was abhorrent to him although he did not then envision a defiance of the Constitution by a state governor. In any event we were convinced that sufficient presidential authority existed in other statutes if such defiance occurred, and if public order broke down and made a mockery of the president's powers in Article II, the president had the authority and the duty to enforce the Constitution.[9] But Senator Ervin and his like-minded colleagues were convinced that they had accomplished their goal.

When direct attack on the bill appeared to be failing, indirect attacks followed. An attempt was made to trade votes against the bill for votes to favor construction of a power dam in the Northwest. Sen. Barry Goldwater of Arizona proposed an emasculating rider to establish a federal right-to-work law that was anathema to organized labor.

But the shrewdest political maneuver was the motion, approved by Majority Leader Johnson, to attach an amendment to the proposed act that said no person could be held and punished, without trial by jury, for being in contempt of court after he had been convicted for violating the act and had refused to obey the contempt order. Traditionally, contempt of court has been punishable by the judge alone without a trial by jury; this was the mechanism we had also laid out in the bill. The only exemption from this rule is in labor-injunction cases. Organized labor, however, feared that their exemption might be jeopardized in some way by our department's bill and urged the Senate to support a jury-trial amendment. This amendment would have crippled civil rights prosecutions in the southern states since no southern jury would have supported a civil rights conviction for contempt of court. Even Sen. Hubert Humphrey of Minnesota, a staunch civil rights advocate on other occasions, favored the amendment, presumably because of the stand of organized labor. The amendment passed the Senate, 51–42.

The jury-trial amendment, however, was substantially modified later in debate. President Eisenhower and Deputy Attorney General William P. Rogers were effective in obtaining acceptable changes. In the final version of the act, federal judges were given the power to decide whether a defendant would receive a jury trial. If there was no jury trial, the judge could impose a sentence of up to forty-five days in jail and a fine of $300; if there was a jury trial, the maximum sentence was six months and a fine could be imposed up to $1,000.

The other sticking point in the bill was section three. Here, Lyndon Johnson went directly to the Oval Office to confer with President Eisenhower. It should be remembered that Senator Johnson, until this point in his career, had always voted against civil rights legislation in the Congress. And he had risen to power as Senate majority leader with the active support of the ruling clique of southern Senators who kept their power because of their seniority. It was only after the passage of the 1957 Civil Rights Act ensuring federal enforcement of voting rights for black citizens and, especially, after he became president that he modified his position and embraced the cause of civil rights.

Johnson, of course, was a shrewd political operator and had unprecedented power over the Senate. My own previous contacts with him had prepared me for his tactics. When I first went to Washington, he received me cordially, and my Texas-born wife and I accepted his invitations to attend Texas barbecues. Our official relations soon deteriorated. Johnson invited me to breakfast, during which he asked me to stop an investigation then under way in the Justice Department of a prominent Texan. This request was, of course, entirely out of line, with the result that we dealt thereafter at arms' length. Our relations were further strained when the Department of Justice successfully prosecuted George Parr, the Democratic boss of Duval County, Texas, who had been the central figure in the scandals involved in the fraudulent nomination victory of "Landslide Lyndon" in his race for the senatorial nomination against Coke Stevenson in 1948.[10] Johnson had been instrumental in getting President Truman to pardon Parr for a 1932 income-tax conviction. In addition to our disagreements over civil rights, he also opposed our program to staunch the flow of illegal immigrants across the Mexican border—immigrants who were useful to farm employers in Texas and along the border because they worked for substandard wages.

One day a story appeared in the press that Senator Johnson had appointed himself chairman of a Senate subcommittee to look into our budget in the Justice Department. This seemed inexplicable because our budget was minuscule. Then I was tipped off by a newspaper reporter that the majority leader was going to "get me" because of our frequent disagreements and that he intended to show publicly that I, as the person charged with responsibility for immigration-law enforcement, employed an illegal Mexican domestic in my home.

I bided my time until the majority leader transferred our budget hearings (usually unnoticed in the media because of their small size) to the largest hearing room in the Capitol, with television cameras trained on the witness. After I had completed my account of our law-enforcement program along the border, as if by prearrangement the cameras flashed on. Senator Johnson complimented me on our immigration program and then asked, "I understand you have a Mexican immigrant in your domestic service at home—I don't suppose by any chance she entered the country illegally, did she?" My answer was ready. "No, Senator, I have her entry visa here in my pocket," and I displayed it. The lights flashed off, and that was the last time the senator presided over our budget hearings. Thus, our strained relations had snapped by the time our civil rights legislation came to the Senate; I feel sure that was the reason Johnson went to the president directly even though I was representing the administration in handling the bill.

In any event, Johnson told Ike that the entire bill would be defeated on the Senate floor if section three—which empowered the attorney general to seek injunctive relief through civil suits on a broad range of civil rights, not just exclusively voting-rights violations—was included. He said he had the votes to do this. The president was convinced and agreed that this provision be dropped. The Senate, after the president had withdrawn his support, then voted 52 to 38 to strike section three from the bill.

Eisenhower made this decision without consulting with me, and we did not talk to one another about it then. He knew by that time that I was leaving the cabinet and returning to my private legal practice. It came as a blow to our efforts to strengthen the march toward enforcement of equal opportunity for all citizens, as promised in the Constitution, but it was a political decision. Eisenhower was dealing with a hostile Democratic majority in the Senate—future Presidents Lyndon Johnson and John Kennedy were among those senators against section three—and the fate of much of the administration's legislative program in the Senate hung in the balance. Majority Leader Johnson made that clear to the president. It was a highly practical decision.

I had favored going to the mat over section three, with full presidential support. If it was defeated on the floor of the Senate I felt confidant that the other sections of the bill—notably the voting-rights provisions—would still be salvaged, even though Johnson warned the president that this was not the case. Thus it turned out that comprehensive civil rights legislation would have to wait for another time. But voting rights had been advanced, and the way had been opened to defeat Senate filibuster as a device to kill civil rights legislation—a tactic that had thwarted passage for almost 100 years. And although section three failed to pass, its presence in the original bill had signaled to the public and to the civil rights community the kind of legislation that was needed to empower the attorney general to enforce civil rights.

Years later when I discussed the bill with Ike by phone from his retirement office in Gettysburg, he said he had concluded that this political compromise was a necessary price to pay to salvage the other provisions of the legislation and to get other badly needed administration bills through Congress before the end of its session. Eisenhower may also have had some reservations (unexpressed to me) about granting power in such broad terms to the attorney general to prosecute civil rights violations, other than voting rights, without having standards or guidelines laid down by Congress. Eisenhower was especially sensitive to the impact that school desegregation would have on the South, and I suspect that he was worried that the Justice Department—and by implication his administration—would involve itself in a myriad of school-desegregation cases that would prove to be politically divisive. I had tried to assure the president otherwise, but Senators Richard Russell and Lyndon Johnson undoubtedly pressed this point in their conversations with him during this period.

These changes made, the bill finally passed, with Sen. Lyndon Johnson claiming credit for its passage despite the legislative history I have described. Although some of our original provisions in the bill were watered-down or otherwise removed, its effects were still significant:

- The right of black citizens to enforce their constitutional right to vote in an effective manner began to become a reality. It took the ensuing Civil Rights Act of 1960 and further legislation in the 1960s to perfect the machinery. But starting with the 1957 act, the government could move in federal courts in civil actions to prevent wholesale deprivation of the right to vote in federal elections.
- Passage of the act paved the way for further change. Once black citizens obtained the enforceable power of the ballot in the South, the views of a number of senators, who had never before had to face the wrath of these voters, began to change on other civil rights legislation. Passage of the 1957 act and the 1960 Civil Rights Act opened the door, I am convinced, to the enactment of the comprehensive civil rights acts of the mid-1960s.
- The Senate's power to filibuster—used thirteen times in the New Deal years alone to kill civil rights bills—was destroyed as a major weapon. The 1957 battle demonstrated that a filibuster on civil rights legislation could be broken.
- The controversial section three, although removed from the final bill by Lyndon Johnson and the southern bloc, served as an important reminder of the kind of enforcement tool needed in future legislation. It later reappeared in different form and became law in the 1960s.
- The Justice Department obtained personnel and funds for an ongoing adequate civil rights enforcement program.

The passage of the first civil rights act of the twentieth century was the climax of my years at the Justice Department. It was time to go. I resigned and enjoyed the farewell social events. One of the perquisites of the office of attorney general was that the Society of the Cincinnati turns over to him its handsome quarters on Massachusetts Avenue for entertaining. There, too, was the location of the farewell party given to us by Bill and Adele Rogers when he succeeded me as attorney general. The other spot for official entertaining in those days was the F Street Club, where Vice-president and Mrs. Nixon gave us a farewell party, with President and

Mrs. Eisenhower and the cabinet attending. The president wrote a most generous letter in response to my letter of resignation. And we headed back to New York City.

The year 1957 was nearing a dramatic close for me. Little Rock had created headlines around the world. The passage of the first civil rights act since Reconstruction days was equally newsworthy. The decisions during the Suez crisis had involved the cabinet in strenuous sessions with far-reaching consequences. As I left Washington to return to private law practice, I somehow expected that the world outside Washington had been following all my official activities. I was brought down to earth immediately. When I walked into my old office at 25 Broadway, the first person to greet me was the elevator operator. "Hello, Mr. Brownell," he said with real enthusiasm, "glad to see you. Haven't seen you for a long time. We've missed you. Where have you been?" My Potomac fever dropped to subnormal. I was back to real life.

I was greeted by a new secretary at my office. She took the calls from Washington on leftover items, with great excitement. "The president is calling," she would announce breathlessly, or, "The attorney general is calling." Then one day she rushed in and said in a tremulous voice, "Queen Elizabeth is on the phone!" She stayed to listen to that conversation, which turned out to be a ship-to-shore phone call from an old client who was sailing on the liner, the *Queen Elizabeth*.

Transition to private life was a slowing-down process. To assist in working off my excess nervous energy I took piano lessons from Ernest Ulmer of the Manhattan School of Music. I plunged into my private law practice. I did not return phone calls from reporters or appear on any talk shows; I was out of Washington life by choice.

I should add, however, that my career as attorney general had not gone entirely unnoticed in the media. My picture had appeared once on the front page of the *New York Times*—that is, a picture of part of me. The occasion was my appearance before a congressional committee to discuss a rather fine point in the field of antitrust law. My remarks appeared to interest the photographers who are ever-present at such events on Capitol Hill. As I neared the end of my presentation the cameras moved in closer and began to flash. I looked in the papers the next morning to see the results. Sure enough, on the front page of the *Times* the story was told in a picture: The photographers had spotted that the shoes I was wearing were mismatched, and they recorded their momentous discovery for history. I told them I thought they overplayed the event because I had another pair of shoes at home just like the one in the picture.

NOTES

1. A similar chain of events led the Department of Justice to file an amicus curiae brief before the Eighth Circuit Court of Appeals supporting the orders of the federal district court against those persons who were blocking the desegregation efforts of the school board in Hoxie, Arkansas.

2. Eisenhower diary entry, October 8, 1957, Ann Whitman Files, Ann Whitman Diary Series, Eisenhower Library, Abilene, Kans.

3. In addition to the Mansfield case, our inability to act because we lacked the power to do so hampered us in the case of Autherine Lucy. Lucy had been admitted to the University of Alabama in February of 1956, but shortly thereafter demonstrations on the Alabama campus erupted. The Board of Trustees of the university, allegedly to protect her personal safety, barred her from attending classes "until further notice" and later expelled her from the university, an action that the federal court was forced to uphold on a technicality. We monitored the situation closely, but the federal court's action left us no avenue to force Lucy's readmission to the university.

An interesting historical footnote to the case: In 1988 the University of Alabama overturned Lucy's expulsion. As a sixty-two-year-old high school teacher in Birmingham, she reenrolled at the University of Alabama, and in 1992 she successfully completed the degree she had set out to achieve in 1956.

4. The Supreme Court began to move slowly into these other areas of segregation during my last year in office, and it would take many years before the constitutional questions at stake were settled by the Court.

5. These first two provisions had been developed by President Truman's Civil Rights Commission. I thought they were worthwhile and would garner wide congressional support, so I included them in the bill.

6. Senator Sumner was a fiery abolitionist. Sumner used such provocative and intemperate language in defending the rights of blacks that it resulted in a violent physical attack by Congressman Preston Brooks on the floor of the House.

7. The Senate rule in question raised a number of parliamentary complexities, but for our purposes it essentially provided that if a bill had been read in its entirety twice before the Senate it would be referred to committee unless a senator objected. Knowland moved to raise an objection, thus requiring the bill to be considered on the floor of the Senate. Sen. Richard Russell, caught by surprise, raised a point of order that this was not the proper intent of the Senate rule in question (and Russell was probably right in light of past precedent). Vice-president Nixon, the presiding officer, then ruled that the intent

of the rule in question admitted of a number of interpretations and Knowland's motion was proper. The Senate then upheld Nixon's ruling 45–39.

8. Had Russell known about our strategy, he and the other southerners could have prevented the outcome by not having the bill read in its entirety a second time but only by having its title read before the Senate. Majority leader Lyndon Johnson might also have had more time to round up enough votes to overrule Nixon's interpretation of the Senate rule.

9. Our reasoning and authorities to support it are set forth in my Little Rock opinion in appendix D.

10. See Robert Caro, *Means of Ascent* (New York: Knopf, 1990), p. 191.

13

Dealing with the Dilemma

of Internal Security

❖ ❖ ❖ ❖ ❖ ❖ ❖ ❖ ❖ ❖ ❖ ❖ ❖ ❖ ❖ ❖

One of the most difficult and controversial problems that I faced as attorney general arose from the threats to our national security at the height of the cold war. With the recent disintegration of the Soviet Union and the political changes in Eastern Europe, it is hard to appreciate fully the situation the American government faced in those years. But when I took office Stalin was still in power, and the Soviet Union was waging a significant counterespionage war against the United States within our own borders. Although many people at the time disbelieved the considerable evidence that had been revealed about these activities, protection of the internal security of the United States was a matter that could not be ignored.

The challenge we faced was to draw an appropriate line between the needs of national security, one of the principal objectives of forming our federal government under the Constitution, and the rights of the individual as set forth in the Bill of Rights. The bounds of both concepts—national security and individual liberty—are imprecise when one attempts to think about them in the abstract. They are even more difficult to define in practical application, especially since they have been given differing interpretations in wartime and in peacetime over the years.[1] We faced an added complication: Where should the line be drawn in time of cold war?

There can be little doubt now, based on recent disclosures in Nikita Khrushchev's memoirs about the Rosenbergs and evidence that has been uncovered in the archives of the former Soviet Union, that Soviet actions during the cold war involved serious dangers to our nation's internal security. Soviet agents had recruited a number of American citizens, some even at the highest levels of the federal government, to further their cause, and the USSR financially subsidized and otherwise directed the subversive activities of the Communist party in the United States,[2] so much so that President Truman instituted an employee-loyalty program under which employees of the federal government had to undergo administrative hearings to test their loyalty. Controversy ensued. President Eisenhower changed the program to test whether an employee was a security risk, and his program was drawn up in the Department of Justice. Controversy continued. Enforcement of the program was contaminated by the concurrent actions of the Senate Investigative Subcommittee headed by Sen. Joseph McCarthy, who hurled baseless charges of subversive activities—without proof—against various governmental employees, notably in the State Department and in the army.

The Department of Justice and the FBI were central participants in the investigations and the subsequent legal actions that arose out of these internal-security matters. But I quickly found on taking office that many of the legal and constitutional issues bearing on these cases were either unclear or had not been resolved by the courts or by Congress. As a result, part of my efforts as attorney general involved actions that would encourage the Supreme Court to rule on some of the constitutional questions involved, prod Congress to provide greater legislative guidance, and, within my own sphere of authority, lead to directives that would limit practices and procedures that had proven unreliable in the past

One problem concerned the information that could be made available to persons under investigation. The administrative hearings conducted as part of the employee-security program often relied for evidence on the investigations undertaken by the FBI. In a few cases, the source of the evidence—usually the name of the accuser—was not revealed in the FBI report. The accused was thus unable to cross-examine the "faceless accuser" or otherwise to challenge the reliability of the accusation, based on its source. In the minds of many people this could lead to unfair results.

An opportunity to test the constitutionality of these procedures arose when a Dr. Peters was removed from his position as a special consultant to a federal agency under the old Truman loyalty program. Peters challenged his removal in federal court. The case was ripe for Supreme Court review.

The government, in the lower court, had sought to test the constitutionality of the procedures used in the removal on the basis of a prior Supreme Court decision, the *Williams* case, in which the majority opinion was delivered by Justice Hugo Black. Black's ruling held that a criminal defendant and his lawyer could not have access to a probation report, which was the basis upon which he might be sentenced to prison or even death, and thus that they could not know the names of the accusers in the report or other sources of the information contained in it.

Simon Sobeloff, the solicitor general, reviewed the case and advised me that he could not conscientiously uphold the government's line of argument before the Supreme Court; he favored confessing error and dropping the appeal. I told him that I thought that the overriding consideration was to get a flat ruling from the Supreme Court on where to draw the line between national security and individual rights in employee-security cases. I asked Warren Burger, one of the assistant attorneys general, to substitute for the solicitor general in making the government's argument before the Supreme Court. He did so on short notice and with professional competence. His opponent in argument was former judge Thurman Arnold, at that time a well-known Washington attorney.

Despite the efforts of both sides, the Supreme Court chose to evade the larger constitutional issue and decided the case on more narrow, procedural grounds.[3] But there was a strong dissent, and the government thereafter no longer defended the "faceless informer" doctrine. Federal courts also quietly dropped the *Williams* case procedure and allowed a defendant to see his probation report in a criminal case.

An interesting sidelight to the Peters case: Justice Black and I happened to attend the same White House function when the case was before the Supreme Court—I believe it was the president's annual reception for members of the Supreme Court. Black took me aside and told me it was outrageous that we were bringing the Peters case before the Court. I rather lightheartedly replied, "Well, you know, one of the reasons we're doing so is your old opinion in the *Williams* case, which gave great latitude to the court in determining what information the defense could see." He said that the *Williams* case was an entirely different matter and lost his temper. He then stalked off.

Another problem concerned the methods used to obtain information and evidence in internal-security cases. Until the late 1960s the Supreme Court was relatively lenient in establishing prohibitions against various means of electronic surveillance. In 1928, in the landmark case of *Olmstead v. United States*, the Supreme Court had determined that neither the Fourth or the Fifth Amendments of the Constitution could be used to control wiretapping: The Court ruled that the Fourth Amendment was limited to physical intrusions of "seized" material objects, not intangible conversations and that such conversations did not constitute a form of self-incrimination prohibited under the Fifth Amendment. In 1937 the Court hedged a bit by ruling that the Communications Act of 1934 could be used to limit the public divulgence—such as to a jury in a criminal procedure—of information obtained by the wiretapping activities of federal law-enforcement officers.[4] The Justice Department, however, interpreted the 1934 act and the 1937 Court decision as exempting wiretapping for national-security purposes.

The problem was compounded by the broad intelligence-gathering activities that had been granted to the FBI by President Roosevelt at the start of World War II. Roosevelt's executive order of May 21, 1940, not only confirmed the Justice Department's interpretation of the 1934 act, but it specifically empowered the FBI to engage in domestic intelligence gathering for national-security purposes, subject to approval of the attorney general. Roosevelt's order was not rescinded after the war, and J. Edgar Hoover and the FBI continued to pursue their intelligence-gathering efforts with vigor, using the latest technologies of electronic eavesdropping. There was a perceived need to use these means in intelligence gathering against certain foreign embassies in Washington and later against the Communist party in the United States since the party was receiving cash subsidies from the USSR. The Court did not challenge the permissibility of wiretapping so long as the information obtained by this technique was not disclosed publicly, nor did it issue any rulings that had significant effect on bugging—the use of listening devices that did not involve tapping telephone lines.

As attorney general I supported legislation to prohibit wiretapping without obtaining a court order. But, in line with the Supreme Court's rulings, I would have allowed wiretapping without court supervision in national-security cases; such electronic surveillance had proven critical in obtaining information in a number of intelligence investigations. I also favored the admissibility of evidence obtained from wiretaps in criminal cases, but I was willing to forgo its use in court if that was necessary so that electronic surveillance in intelligence cases could continue. Congress thought otherwise about my proposals, however, and refused to legislate in this controversial area. It was not until the late 1960s that Congress finally passed legislation on electronic eavesdropping (wiretapping in national-security cases without a court order was also outlawed then).

The situation regarding bugging was different. It had been practiced in law enforcement for many years. On one occasion, I received a request from the FBI to determine whether a recent court decision should be interpreted as limiting its bugging activities in any way. I ruled that the Court had not restricted the use of this technique in ways that the bureau was then authorized to employ it. I had in mind that the use of this technique was limited, as it was as a matter of Justice Department policy, to investigation of Communist activities in the United States and other national-security violations.

The FBI, during my tenure as attorney general, was authorized to confine its wiretapping and bugging activities only to persons who were thought to be engaged in espionage and other subversive activities against the United States. But years later Sen. Frank Church's Senate Investigating Committee disclosed that this policy had been changed in the 1960s to widen the area to cases that were not related to investigation of Communist activities or other attempts to protect national security, for instance, the electronic surveillance of newspaper reporters and political figures such as Dr. Martin Luther King. When called to account for the use of bugging in these areas, the FBI justified its actions by referring to my opinion rendered in the 1950s, which was not my intent. Such are the hazards of operating in the field of national security.

Evidence has also recently come to light, based on J. Edgar Hoover's "secret" office files, that the FBI was conducting wiretapping and other forms of electronic surveillance without the authorization of the attorney general, as required by President Roosevelt's executive order. Although I have not seen any evidence that this abuse of power occurred during the Eisenhower presidency, Hoover apparently ordered—entirely on his own authority—that FBI wiretaps be placed on at least fifteen persons, both in and out of government, from 1940 through the Truman presidency.[5]

During my term as attorney general I was successful in setting some limits as to which individuals and groups could be subject to internal-security investigations by the FBI. Thus I made it departmental policy to restrict internal-security investigations to members of the Communist party and to other individuals who were clearly and directly suspected of threatening national security. But I opposed legislation sponsored by Congressman Martin Dies that would have outlawed membership in the Communist party. I worried that equating party membership with a conspiracy to overthrow the government might violate due process of law, and I believed that making simple membership in the party illegal would fail to separate those people who might have unknowingly or unwittingly joined the party from the real culprits: committed party members who were engaged in subversive activities. Outlawing the Communist party was politically tempting, but it would have driven the party further underground and made investigation of its subversive activities even harder to carry out.

On other occasions, too, I felt that the FBI needed to be hemmed in, and I was forced to "order" Hoover to change his procedures. In one case I was told that the bureau was sending raw and confidential file material on the suspected Communist activities of teachers to local school boards throughout the country. These boards generally were incapable of separating the facts from the rumors and unproved allegations that were frequently contained in these files; as a result, a number of persons were unjustly accused and their careers tarnished. I stopped this practice. The other case in which I intervened also involved the files in subversive-activities cases. The bureau, in its investigative activities, would advise prosecutors that certain prospective witnesses were "reliable," without giving the prosecutors all the background information allowing them to make an independent judgment. Thus we discovered we were sometimes erroneously vouching to the courts about the character of some of our witnesses. Changes were made to prevent a repetition of such errors.

These difficulties notwithstanding, the need for such investigations and for an employee-security program was clear. The Alger Hiss case had been disturbing to the public, and this fear had been heightened further when the FBI had disclosed the existence and operation of two spy rings among federal employees, both of which were engaged in delivering classified national-security documents to the USSR. Canada, too, uncovered an espionage ring operating out of the Soviet embassy in Ottawa. And even the U.S. Justice Department had been touched by the subversive activities of one of its attorneys, Judith Coplon. I thus concurred in the need for an employee-security program in the Eisenhower administration, supporting it against charges that no real danger existed on this front of Stalin's cold war against the United States. One matter now arose that dramatized the issue.

The case stemmed from efforts on my part to draw greater public and congressional attention to the real dangers to national security posed by disloyal and subversive individuals in the employ of the government. Americans working as spies and espionage agents for the Soviet Union were not, at that period of time, fictions created by overactive and suspicious imaginations, nor were they "red herrings," as President Truman had regarded them, posing little danger and reeking only of the odor of partisan politics.

This particular matter involved one Harry Dexter White, a high-level Treasury Department official and later an executive director of the International Monetary Fund, and it created national headlines early in the new administration. During the Truman administration charges had been made before a congressional committee that White had secretly passed classified government documents to Russian emissaries before and during World War II and that he had arranged employment for and subsequently sheltered other Soviet agents in the Treasury Department. In 1948 White had testified before a federal grand jury (in secret, of course), but he was not indicted. Later that year, he testified before the House Un-American Activities Committee. A few days after that he suddenly died. No legal actions in the matter were pending when I came to the Justice Department.

But, by chance, we came upon some hitherto undisclosed facts about White. In the first few weeks after I arrived, as part of my reorganization of administrative procedures in the Justice Department, I ordered that all loose files should be retrieved from desktops, cubby-holes, and closets and sent to central files. Among the documents turned in were a large number dealing with Harry Dexter White; most of these had never been made public. Warren Olney, the new head of the Criminal Division, found the papers pertaining to White—sitting of all places on a windowsill, as I recall—and he brought them to my attention.

I read them over and realized the papers had a significant bearing on whether classified documents were or had been transmitted to agents of the USSR. I immediately went to President Eisenhower about it and told him that we had found these papers, that they were shocking, and that I intended to make them public. He said that if I had the facts it was advisable to do so.

I thought that if I did not make them public I could be accused of a cover-up and be just as culpable as Truman had been for not dealing with the allegations against White, especially since they had been discovered in the files of the Justice Department. I further believed that the public had a right to know about past espionage activities (when they could be revealed without damaging current investigations) since many individuals tended to dismiss the whole issue as simply witch hunting.

I also sought to make the allegations about White public since Congress was considering legislation to tighten laws relating to internal security, especially the administration's proposed program to eliminate persons who were security risks from the ranks of government employees. Two rings of Soviet agents within the government had been exposed—the Silvermaster ring (to which it turned out White was connected) being the most notorious. The opposition to our program said that there was no need for an employee-security program and relied on President Truman's oft-quoted statement that the outcry against government infiltration by Communists was only "a red herring" and without substance. To my mind, these documents on White's activities powerfully proved otherwise.

Revelation of the documented facts against White was also useful for another reason: It provided an important contrast to the kind of slap-dash investigations of Communist infiltration that members of Congress such as Senators Joe McCarthy and William Jenner and Congressman Harold Velde were conducting. We thought it would help to show that we were serious about removing any Communists in government but that we were doing so in a more responsible, fact-based manner. The timing of my speech revealing the facts on White, I should add, was not connected to any particular set of events such as the upcoming 1954 midterm elections or Senator McCarthy's investigations into Communist infiltration at Fort Monmouth, New Jersey, as some historians have mistakenly argued. Rather, as the record shows, as soon as we found the information about White, we exposed it immediately.

One document implicating White had been disclosed previously in the course of the congressional investigation of the Alger Hiss–Whittaker Chambers controversy in 1948. In defending his allegations against Hiss, Chambers had produced the "Pumpkin Papers," which he alleged had been transmitted by him to Soviet agents. They contained classified information. One of the documents was a handwritten letter from Harry Dexter White in the Treasury Department. But such was the furor over the Alger Hiss case that little or no notice was given to the significance of the White letter. The case against White was further strengthened in separate allegations by Whittaker Chambers and one Elizabeth Bentley that they had transmitted classified information they had received from White to Soviet agents.

The information on the White case that I was now prepared to make public at a speech I was to deliver before the Executives Club of Chicago on November 6, 1953, included the Chambers and the Bentley allegations. But the bombshell was another set of documents we had discovered on that windowsill: FBI reports about White's espionage activities—including additional evidence not present in Chambers's and Bentley's later allegations—that had been forwarded to the Truman White House before White's appointment to the International Monetary Fund, information that had not been made public especially to the Senate committee that was considering White's nomination.

In my speech I stated that the files showed clearly that White had been a spy by becoming involved in transmission of classified information surreptitiously to espionage agents of Stalin's USSR. Further, the files showed that White's activities had been reported by the FBI to Truman's military aide in the White House, Gen. Harry Vaughn, in early December 1945. Vaughn was the usual channel for such reports from the FBI, and as I learned later, copies had been sent to Attorney General Tom Clark, Secretary of State James Byrnes, Navy Secretary James Forrestal, and Assistant Secretary of State Spruille Braden. In late January 1946, President Truman, although possessing this report, nominated White, who was then assistant secretary of the treasury, to be executive director of the International Monetary Fund. This was a position of importance (and one which carried a much higher and tax-free salary). Moreover, because of the special status and immunities conferred on international organizations and their officials, any further FBI investigation or surveillance of White would be seriously or totally curtailed.

In January 1946, when Truman's nomination of White became public, the FBI prepared a second special and more detailed report on White's espionage activities, stating: "This information has been received from various confidential sources whose reliability has been established either by inquiry or long established observation and evaluation. In no instance is any event or transaction related where the reliability of the source of information is questionable." This new summary of White's activity was handed to Vaughn for delivery to the president on February 4, 1946. The report had a covering letter from J. Edgar Hoover, marked "Top Secret":

> As of interest to the President and you, I am attaching a detailed memorandum hereto concerning Harry Dexter White. . . . In view of . . . the seriousness of the charges against White in the attachment, I have made every effort in preparing this memorandum, to cover all possible ramifications. As will be observed, information has come to the attention of this Bureau charging White as being a valuable adjunct to an underground Soviet espionage organization operating in Washington, D.C.

President Truman, as I later learned, discussed the report on White with a number of top-level officials who were privy to its contents but decided to proceed with White's nomination, which was then before the Senate. The Senate, however, was not told about the information and was allowed to recommend White's appointment as U.S. representative to the International Monetary Fund in ignorance of the FBI reports.

My speech in 1953 aroused a storm of controversy. At first, Truman denied to the press that White was a suspected Communist and that he had seen the FBI reports. Later he admitted he had received them, after it had been disclosed that a duplicate of the damaging second FBI report had been sent to James F. Byrnes, secretary of state, on the same day and that Byrnes had written Truman on February 5, 1946, "I deem [the FBI reports] of such importance I think you should read them." Then Truman said publicly he had fired White as soon as he discovered he was disloyal.

Quite soon, facts emerged in the press showing that Truman's account—accounts really, since he changed his story three times—was at odds with reality. White had remained for eleven months at the International Monetary Fund and then suddenly resigned without explanation, trucking away papers and effects from his office. During his tenure, however, he had appointed as his assistant one Frank Coe, who had been part of a spy ring in the federal government previously uncovered by the FBI, and Coe had remained in the IMF until December 1952.

After my speech Truman went on the air to call me a liar, in his best give-'em-hell manner, and stated he had appointed White to the International Monetary Fund with approval of the FBI to keep watch over his suspicious activities. His final position was completely contradicted by J. Edgar Hoover, director of the FBI, in sworn testimony (never since disputed), that White's appointment was never discussed with the FBI and, further, that the appointment removed White from the danger of additional investigation because officials of international organizations (such as persons in the International Monetary Fund) were essentially immune from FBI investigations.

When White resigned from his post at the IMF in April 1947, Truman wrote him a letter stating he accepted his resignation "with sincere regret and considerable reluctance." The letter praised White for his "unfaltering efforts" that had been "a source of great pride to us."

Some critics in the media denounced me for attacking a dead man. But I have never been able to find a historian who didn't approve of the use of newly discovered evidence about a public official relating to his actions in office even though the evidence came to light after the official's death.

As a result of the controversy I was asked to testify on the matter under oath before the Subcommittee to Investigate the Administration of the Internal Security Laws of the Senate Judiciary Committee. I pointed out that I had not at any time accused Truman of disloyalty, although he and his followers had made this claim. Indeed I repeated the explanation for Truman's action that I had made in my speech, i.e., the unwillingness of non-Communists in responsible positions in government to accept facts and to abandon a persistent delusion that the charge that there were Communists in the government of the United States was only a red herring.

In the original speech I had also said that "the manner in which the established facts concerning White's disloyalty were disregarded is typical of the blindness which afflicted the former administration on this matter." This statement aroused charges of partisanship in its implication that almost everyone in the Truman administration was at least soft on communism. I should have let the facts speak for themselves and not have diverted attention by providing ammunition for a charge of partisanship. The sentence was unnecessary to make my point and detracted from the main purpose of the speech. The basic charge in the speech—that clear evidence existed that White had engaged in espionage and that President Truman had failed to disclose the evidence to the Senate and the public when he nominated White to the International Monetary Fund—withstood challenge.

Truman's attack on me and on the administration unfortunately blunted the point I was trying to make in my speech on White. I had presented a factually documented case on espionage by a highly-placed governmental official that illustrated the need to take matters of internal security seriously. Now there were charges of partisanship, especially after McCarthy, Jenner, and Velde entered the picture to try to capitalize on the controversy, thus thwarting another of my aims: showing that concern for Communist infiltration could be pursued in a responsible manner and based on facts, not on wild charges. In fact, as the controversy unfolded, it was only after Congressman Velde issued a subpoena for Truman to appear before his House Un-American Activities Committee and McCarthy publicly called the former president "a liar" that Truman went on the offensive in a television broadcast.

Eisenhower publicly stated that he thought Truman should not be subpoenaed by the congressional committee. This was interpreted in the press as a withdrawal of his support for my charges and left me out on a limb, public relationswise, even though the president had said that I had made him aware of the charges and evidence against White before I made the speech.

Historians who in subsequent years have examined the evidence more dispassionately than those involved have confirmed the allegations against White.[6] New evidence of the validity of the charges against White appeared in 1977 in an article by a Canadian historian.[7] This documented account tells about the defection of a cipher clerk in the Soviet embassy in Ottawa in the 1940s. The documents smuggled out of the embassy by the clerk were turned over to Prime Minister Mackenzie King of Canada, who, upon learning that the documents disclosed, among other things, spy activities by high-level officials in the government of the United States, flew to Washington on September 29, 1945. The account then states that in the course of his meeting with President Truman and Undersecretary of State Dean Acheson, who had been briefed about the matter beforehand by Canadian officials, King told them that an assistant secretary in the State Department was among those individuals implicated. Truman "turned to Acheson," King recounted in his diary, and said, "It would not be surprising."[8] King met again with Truman on November 10, but his diaries for this period have never been found. In a diary entry for February 5, King recorded a conversation with Norman Robertson, his undersecretary for external affairs, who was in charge of the spy case and who told King that

suspicions are directed right up to the top of the treasury [in the United States], naming the person; also that it is directed against another person who was very close to Stettinius at San Francisco and who took a prominent part in matters there.

King then notes, in reference to the State Department official, that "I was not personally surprised. I confess I was surprised when I saw the particular person he mentioned filling the position he did."[9]

King did not enter into his diary the names of the individuals implicated by the documents the Soviet spy had produced. The author concludes that the individuals were Harry Dexter White and Alger Hiss.[10] He points out that shortly after the first conference with King, President Truman issued orders to Ernest Gross in the State Department not to route classified information to Alger Hiss; soon thereafter Hiss left the State Department to go to the Carnegie Endowment. Harry Dexter White, of course, left the Treasury Department and was appointed by Truman as U.S. representative on the International Monetary Fund.

This account not only validates my original charges, but it offers a most interesting theory as to Truman's motives in the Hiss and White affairs: namely, that Truman did in fact know of Hiss's and White's activities but rather than dismiss them outright and order an investigation, he shunted them to new positions—in the Carnegie Endowment and at the IMF—where they would be relatively insulated from national-security matters and FBI scrutiny. Truman, under this theory, prevented a public scandal, and he protected his "red herring" policy. One hopes that more light will be shed on the matter when the Canadian documents are made public and the missing Mackenzie King diaries are located.

I have been asked many times why I think a person who had such a prominent position in our government would actually pass classified documents to the Soviet Union. I would only say that a large number of Americans in the 1930s and 1940s, although not card-carrying members of the American Communist party, were convinced that Soviet Russia represented a new and promising phenomenon in liberal government, that its socialist educational system and its system of child care were superior to our own, and that its views on disarmament were more enlightened than Western thought. They believed that Communist Russia was the hope of the world. They either disregarded or were ignorant of Stalinist atrocities—they forgave some excesses because Russia had been our ally against Hitler (at least at the end). The reasoning of one such highly educated person is revealed in the autobiography of Michael Straight (then editor of the *New Republic*) and is illuminating.[11] Of course neither he nor most fellow travelers engaged in espionage, but they often sympathized with and defended those individuals who had already been shown to have been engaged in it. They also were opposed to our government's internal-security programs. In a few cases, persons who had such beliefs convinced themselves that violating our laws against espionage was less important than helping Stalin's Russia.

Sometimes individuals were simply naive and thought national security was unimportant or at best secondary to other, greater interests. In a case referred to me by the president, I had firsthand experience with one such individual: an atomic scientist who had helped with the production of the atomic bomb and was a member of the United States team to negotiate an arms-reduction treaty with the USSR. On one occasion he took an overnight sleeping car on a train to Washington and reported that he had left his briefcase, containing highly classified information, in the berth and couldn't locate the case when he left the train the next morning. The FBI was called in and ransacked the berth but could find no trace of the briefcase or its contents. Not long after, the same scientist, as a member of our negotiating team, went to Geneva for a session with the Russian negotiators. Again he reported that when he left the meeting he had forgotten his briefcase, containing classified information on our negotiating strategy. When he went back to retrieve it, it had disappeared. Our security people were called in but could find no trace. The security people knew this was a second serious loss caused by the same person and reported the incidents to President Eisenhower. He asked me to interview the scientist to develop an opinion on whether he was merely careless or a sinister figure.

During the interview the scientist denied he had lost the briefcases on purpose on either occasion. But he was defiant and said I had no right to cross-examine him because he was seeking "the truth" for the benefit of mankind. He compared himself to Galileo and me to Galileo's inquisitors who were willing to subordinate the truth to what they falsely deemed were greater interests (in our case, those of national security). His analogy plainly implied that even if the USSR gained information about our military secrets, it was better to have the knowledge spread throughout the world's scientific community than to protect our national security. I concluded he sincerely believed what he said but that no successful prosecution was possible. We ended the scientist's career as a government official and his access to classified information.

The occurrence of several serious leaks of security information disturbed the president to such an extent that he asked me to study the strict standards of the British Official Secrets Act. I asked Robert U. Brown, president and editor of *Editor and Publisher*, to advise me on the practical problems that would be involved if the British act were made law here. At the end of my study Mr. Brown and I went to the Oval Office to report to the president. Eisenhower decided, however, that the proposed cure for security leaks posed dangers that outweighed the benefits and dropped the idea.

The Rosenberg spy trial, which had occurred during the Truman administration, was another facet of the internal-security problem that had repercussions after Eisenhower was elected. The jury at the trial decided that Julius and Ethel Rosenberg, who were American citizens and members of the American Communist party, had transmitted to the USSR data on the location, security measures, and names of leading scientists at the Los Alamos atomic experimental station; they had also transmitted a sketch of a lens mold used in the atomic experiment and a sketch of the cross section of the atomic bomb and a ten-page exposition of it. After conviction, they had been sentenced to death.

Twice they appealed to Eisenhower for clemency, without success. We in the Justice Department furnished information about the legal proceedings to the president for use in his consideration of the clemency applications, including the fact that fifteen judges at various times had reviewed the case on appeal and had affirmed the conviction without a dissent. When the date for execution approached, Justice William Douglas of the Supreme Court granted a stay of execution on a point of law not theretofore raised. He did this shortly after the Court had adjourned for the summer and without consulting the other justices. I thereupon instructed the Justice Department to petition Chief Justice Vinson to call an unprecedented special meeting of the Court to review the stay. He granted the petition, and the Court met and reversed Justice Douglas's action.

In dismissing the petition for clemency, Justice Tom Clark (with five other justices concurring) noted:

Seven times now have the defendants been before this court. In addition, the Chief Justice, as well as individual Justices, has considered applications by the defendants. The Court of Appeals and the District Court have likewise given careful consideration to even more numerous applications than has this Court. . . . Our liberty is maintained only so long as Justice is secure. To permit our judicial processes to be used to obstruct the course of justice destroys our freedom. . . . Though the penalty is great and our responsibility heavy, our duty is clear.[12]

I then sent the director of federal prisons, James V. Bennett, to Sing Sing prison to notify the Rosenbergs that I was available to listen to any statement they wished to make that might bear on clemency. They told him they had no statement to make, and the execution proceeded on schedule. The Rosenberg attorney afterwards publicly stated that my action was, in effect, an effort to extort a confession. The writings of recent years seem almost unanimous in their conclusion that the Rosenbergs were guilty as charged. Nikita Khrushchev, in his memoirs, removes any lingering doubt about it.[13]

The prosecution of the leaders of the American Communist party resulted in convictions and jail sentences for many important policymakers in the party. They were indicted under the Smith Act, which had been passed by Congress and upheld by the Supreme Court before the Eisenhower administration took office. This act made it a felony to conspire to overthrow the government of the United States by force and violence. The first prosecution had been tried before Judge Harold Medina and affirmed during the Truman administration. This conviction and our subsequent prosecutions greatly weakened the American Communist party, by public admission of the party's own officials. Recent disclosures of previously classified information have revealed that the American Communist party was then being regularly subsidized with cash payments from the USSR, evidence which I knew about at the time but could not use. Although helpful to our prosecution, the information could not have been revealed during the trials without jeopardizing valuable security techniques and sources. A sufficient variety of other evidence was available, however, to enable us to proceed with prosecution, and most of the major figures involved were convicted.

Another spectacular spy trial further highlighted the internal-security problem. It was prepared and successfully prosecuted by Assistant Attorney General William F. Tompkins, an experienced trial lawyer who organized and headed our newly established Internal Security Division. The spy went under the name of Rudolf Ivanovich Abel, and he held the rank of colonel in the KGB. Abel was sent to the United States by the Soviet Union to engage in espionage operations. He immediately assumed the name of an artist who in fact had died in 1903. The chief government witness was a major in the Soviet Security Service, an expert in photography with special expertise in making "microdots," who was sent here under a false passport to act as Abel's assistant. He was assigned a personal code for use in exchanging messages with officials in Moscow. He was also trained in the manner of secreting messages in containers fashioned by hollowing out various objects such as coins, bolts, screws, matchbooks, and magazines, training he used in carrying out written instructions from Vitale G. Pavlov in the Kremlin, the assistant chief of the section that directed Soviet espionage in the United States. He was given money to establish himself in some sort of business as a cover for his espionage operations.

Abel's assistant used three drops in New York City. One was located in a wall on Jerome Avenue in the Bronx, one was under a lamp in Central Park, and the third under a lamppost in Fort Tryon Park. At the trial, extensive evidence, which had been painstakingly gathered by the FBI in New York, showed that Abel and his assistant had transmitted much classified information to the USSR. At one point they had paid cash to Helen Sobell, wife of convicted Soviet atomic spy Morton Sobell, and were frequently engaged in delivering messages received by shortwave radio to other Soviet agents in this country.

As reported in the media at the time, Abel was undoubtedly "the cleverest, most formidable foreign agent ever caught by U.S. counterespionage. . . . the first example Americans have ever seen of the trained Russian professional who successfully slipped himself into the stream of American life in order to spy on and steal its most precious secrets."[14] His assistant defected to the U.S. embassy in Paris and contributed to Abel's downfall. But the professional skill of Assistant Attorney General Tompkins completed Abel's defeat and educated the public to the seriousness of Stalin's espionage apparatus in the United States. Several years after his conviction, Abel was again in the news: He was traded back to the Soviets in exchange for Gary Powers, the U.S. pilot of the U-2 plane that had been shot down over Russia.

From the beginning, President Eisenhower felt a special need to reassure the public that steps were being taken so that there would be no recurrence of the notorious cases of transmission of classified information to Soviet spies by U.S. government officials as there had been in the past. The problem of internal security had been a major theme in his 1952 campaign, and he had stressed its importance in his meetings with the cabinet-designates, held before his inauguration at the Commodore Hotel, and in his first meetings as president with the congressional leadership.

When Eisenhower came into the presidency, the Truman administration's so-called loyalty program was under attack, and Eisenhower thought that a new approach was needed. In place of loyalty, the administration adopted, at Eisenhower's own suggestion, the test of whether employees were security risks—by reason of personal habits or actions. This test seemed at the time more directly linked to the ends we wished to obtain, namely protecting national security from those people who might compromise it.[15] The administration's new program also sought greater protection for the legitimate rights of employees, and it created hearing advisory boards composed of persons from outside the department or agency in question and drawn from a special roster maintained by the Civil Service Commission. The latter, I thought, would especially encourage a fair hearing in these cases, since the board would not be directly responsible to the employing department or agency.

Many people at the time thought that the internal-security program had originated in the Justice Department. This is true but only in the technical sense that the department was responsible for drafting the executive orders establishing the program and filling in the details on its organization and operation. It was, rather, an area that had been of particular concern to Eisenhower during the election campaign and one in which he took a personal interest in establishing a new approach that emphasized the test of "security risk." But because of Eisenhower's leadership style, which put the cabinet member involved out on the front lines of policy debate, I became the member of the administration most closely identified with the program. I was not, however, unsympathetic to the program's ultimate aims.

The other consideration of those of us who had to deal with the question of internal security was the specter of McCarthy and the McCarthy-like attempts to deal with the issue, which was equally threatening to individual liberty. In fact, the administration's program, as it was established, enabled the president to point to his program as the best way to destroy

McCarthy and McCarthyism by taking the issue of internal security away from him and dealing with it in a responsible manner.

Several hundred employees were removed from the government payroll as a result of administrative hearings. The program should have been limited in extent to cover only those employees who actually handled classified information in the course of their duties. Furthermore, the program lacked central coordination and oversight; individual cabinet officers established security programs under the direction of a security officer in their respective departments. Effectiveness and fairness varied from department to department, and some of the security officers lacked the proper training and legal background—for example, an ability to differentiate unsubstantiated rumor from fact or a knowledge of the standards of legal evidence—to do the job as it had been envisioned. Programs in the Agriculture and State Departments were particularly problem-ridden. As it was, the program took too long to administer and created unnecessary problems in employees' morale, which could have been avoided under a more restricted program.

As I reflect on the history of the internal-security problem, it strikes me as an issue no American official would like to deal with since it involves calling into question the loyalty or trustworthiness of other Americans. It was a disagreeable task; but given the times, it was necessary. Eisenhower had made the internal-security issue part of his campaign for the presidency in 1952. He decided it was needed, and he saw the necessity for creating an internal-security program to counter the insidious efforts of Senator McCarthy, efforts that lacked reasonable standards, fair procedures, and constitutional protections. Was the program perfect? The answer must be no. It had effects on individuals who posed no threat to national security. But that is an evaluation of the program that only hindsight permits us. If such a program were to be designed today, it would undoubtedly be different in its standards and operations. Yet such a program would hardly be needed in the present world context. The atmosphere of the cold war that existed in the 1950s was quite distinct; national security was at times threatened in ways and to an extent different from today. Individual liberty and constitutional rights were also under attack by Senator McCarthy and his friends. Between those opposing forces we were obliged to operate. That we were not wholly successful in carving out some acceptable middle ground may be correct testimony to our accomplishments, but not to our intention and aims.

NOTES

1. From time to time in our history, this tension between national security and civil liberty has generated controversy: the battle between Adams and Jefferson over the Alien and Sedition laws, Lincoln's suspension of the writ of habeas corpus during the Civil War, the Sedition Act of 1917 and the subsequent raids conducted by Attorney General A. Palmer Mitchell against "subversives," and the internment of Japanese-Americans during World War II.

2. In October 1991, Alexander Drosdov, editor of *Rossiya*, reported that the newly opened Soviet archives contained evidence indicating that the USSR had provided $21 million in subsidies to the U.S. Communist party over a ten-year period. I had known this as attorney general but I could not reveal it without compromising confidential sources of information.

3. Peters v. Hobby, 349 U.S. 331 (1955).

4. Nardone v. United States, 302 U.S. 379 (1937). In 1955 the *Nardone* precedent was extended to state law-enforcement officials (Benanti v. U.S., 355 U.S. 96 [1955]).

5. See Athan Theoharis, "FBI Wiretapping: A Case Study of Bureaucratic Autonomy," *Political Science Quarterly* 107 (1992): 101–22.

6. For example, long after the 1953 controversy, a book was written about White's career by the British author, David Rees. Rees gives an impartial review of the episode, and he states that he could not dispute the correctness of my allegations against White. He outlines White's activities in the U.S. Treasury Department, including his advocacy of the Morgenthau Plan to destroy Germany's manufacturing capacity and reduce it to an agricultural economy. The author also notes that years later in his memoirs, *Mandate for Change*, President Eisenhower referred to the "incontrovertible evidence" against White. See David Rees, *Harry Dexter White: A Study in Paradox* (London: Coward, McCann and Geohegan, 1973). See also Christopher Andrew and Oleg Gordievsky, *KGB: The Inside Story* (New York: Harper-Collins, 1990). The accuracy of the latter account, however, has been questioned by some reviewers.

7. See James Barros, "Alger Hiss and Harry Dexter White: The Canadian Connection," *Orbis* 21:3 (1977): 593–605.

8. King's diaries are extensively reproduced in J. W. Pickersgill and D. F. Foster, *The Mackenzie King Record*, 4 vols. (Toronto: University of Toronto Press, 1970); quotation is from 3:41. King does not mention whether he also told Truman about Harry Dexter White.

9. Pickersgill and Foster, *The Mackenzie King Record*, 3:134.

10. King's comments about the official in the State Department at the San Francisco conference especially implicate Hiss. Hiss had been appointed as secretary-general of the conference, a surprisingly high-level position for an official who was not of the very highest rank (in fact, it had been rumored in the press that King was in line for the position).

11. Michael Straight, *After Long Silence* (New York: Norton, 1983).

12. Rosenberg v. U.S., 346 U.S. 271 (1953), at pp. 293, 296.

13. According to Khrushchev, "Let this be a worthy tribute to the memory of those people [the Rosenbergs]. Let my words serve as an expression of gratitude to those who sacrificed their lives to a great cause of the Soviet state at a time when the U.S. was using its advantage over our state to blackmail our state and undermine its proletarian cause" (quotation from the forthcoming third and final volume of *Khrushchev Remembers*, as set forth in the *New York Times*, September 25, 1990, A3). *Time* magazine (October 1, 1990, p. 75) provides another revealing quote from the memoirs: "I was part of Stalin's circle when he mentioned the Rosenbergs with warmth. I cannot specifically say what kind of help they gave us but I heard both from Stalin and Molotov, then Minister of Foreign Affairs, that the Rosenbergs provided very significant help in accelerating the production of our atomic bomb." The Rosenberg case continues to generate controversy—witness the disruptions at Judge Irving Kaufman's funeral in 1992.

14. *Life*, November 11, 1957, p. 123.

15. Of course, ideally the best standard would be to remove only those individuals who did compromise national security. This is not practical, however, since once national security is compromised the damage is done. We wanted to prevent the damage that we knew had occurred and might still be occurring—as the spy trials indicated, national security was threatened during this period—so we opted for the next best standard: removal of employees who were at risk for compromising security.

14

Protecting the Presidency

McCarthy and Bricker

❖ ❖ ❖ ❖ ❖ ❖ ❖ ❖ ❖ ❖ ❖ ❖ ❖ ❖ ❖

Throughout his two terms in office, President Eisenhower protected the presidency against attacks by Congress on his constitutional powers. Two outstanding examples involved members of the United States Senate: Joseph McCarthy of Wisconsin and John Bricker of Ohio. I played an active role in both instances.

Joe McCarthy's challenge to the presidency—if not to our political system itself—was without doubt the more dangerous of the two. Few American presidents have had to test their political mettle and skill against such an unscrupulous opponent. Elected to the Senate in 1946, McCarthy had an undistinguished record during his first years in office. He was regarded as an ill-mannered and unpredictable outsider in an institution then dominated by influential senior members of the Senate club. McCarthy's few interests in public policy reflected those concerns of powerful interests in his home state and of other individuals who offered him political and financial support. In early 1950 his political career appeared to be in decline, with little prospect for reelection in 1952. During a dinner meeting of several of his supporters at Washington's Colony Restaurant, political legend has it, McCarthy's political plight was the prime topic of conversation. A number of issues were discussed that McCarthy might espouse in order to boost his political image. Finally, a suggestion was made that Communists in government might be a good subject. Shortly thereafter, McCarthy delivered a speech to a Republican women's group in Wheeling, West Virginia, in which he claimed that he "had in his hand" a list of 205 Communist spies and sympathizers working in the State Department.

McCarthy's allegations were hardly news. His figures on the number of alleged Communists—which changed each time McCarthy talked about them—came from public documents that the State Department had provided Congress several years earlier. The allegations, however, struck a raw nerve in the Truman White House and among the Democratic leaders of Congress. A Senate committee was established to investigate McCarthy's charges, and suddenly the junior senator from Wisconsin had a national forum from which to express his views. From 1950 until 1953, McCarthy was rarely out of the public spotlight. Although conclusive evidence against even a single one of the individuals McCarthy named was never produced and no convictions for spying or espionage activities resulted from McCarthy's efforts, a host of individuals was paraded before the Senate investigating committee. He branded his opponents in the Senate as "fellow travelers" and "Soviet dupes"; few members of Congress were willing to challenge him, and several who did were defeated by the voters in the 1950 and 1952 elections. McCarthy's own popularity with the public was on the rise.

McCarthy soon broadened his target. He denounced Truman's loyalty program as ineffective and impugned the loyalty of Secretary of State Dean Acheson and Secretary of Defense George Marshall. President Truman, in turn, rose to the bait and attacked McCarthy repeatedly. Each time these attacks emanated from the White House, the McCarthy headlines in the media grew larger. The senator had great political ambitions—somewhat like Sen. Huey Long's of Louisiana in his battles with FDR—and he thrived on the publicity. The name-calling contest masked the fact that a constitutional battle between the executive and the congressional branches was in its incipiency.

Thus Senator McCarthy was already a nationally known figure when President Eisenhower was inaugurated in 1953. In private, Eisenhower was outraged by McCarthy's tactics and behavior, especially his attacks on General Marshall. But Eisenhower also recognized that the "McCarthy problem" had to be treated delicately. The Republicans controlled the Senate after the 1952 elections but by the narrowest of margins. Furthermore, many of the conservative Republican senators whose support Eisenhower needed for his legislative program backed McCarthy; some, such as Senators William Jenner of Indiana, Herman Welker of Idaho, and George ("Molly") Malone of Nevada, believed in his cause, and others saw him as a useful tool in attacking the Democrats. During 1953 Eisenhower himself also may have felt that McCarthy constituted more of a nuisance than a threat to the presidency. The disruptions that McCarthy was soon to cause the executive branch of a Republican presidency were not then anticipated.

McCarthy was passed over by the Republican leaders as head of the Internal Security Subcommittee, which would have been his natural assignment, in favor of the equally rabid but less menacing Jenner. McCarthy was assigned instead to chair the less prestigious Committee on Government Operations. But Government Operations did have a Permanent Subcommittee on Investigations, which had the power to investigate governmental activities at all levels. McCarthy assumed its chairmanship and soon had a powerful base from which to conduct his own investigations of communism in government, Eisenhower's government.

McCarthy wasted no time in carrying on his crusade. Spurred on by tips passed by informers who shared his sentiments, the undercover work of a well-oiled if at times unscrupulous staff, and "information" collected by a range of anti-Communist groups that had been awaiting a powerful voice for their sundry allegations, McCarthy launched investigations into a wide range of governmental activities and personages. Now popularly dubbed the "McCarthy Committee," his group examined Communist influence in determining the location of the aerial transmitters of the Voice of America, security leaks at the Government Printing Office, and the kinds of books stocked in International Information Agency libraries overseas. (McCarthy especially singled out, among others, the works of such alleged "fellow travelers" as the philosopher John Dewey, the secretary of state's cousin Foster Rhea Dulles, and my old faculty adviser from Yale Law School Robert Hutchins as well as such noted historians as Arthur Schlesinger, Jr., and Henry Steele Commager.) McCarthy took aim at the appointments of James Conant, the president of Harvard University, as high commissioner to Germany and of Charles Bohlen as U.S. ambassador to the Soviet Union, Conant for "shielding" Communists on the Harvard faculty and being "an innocent" about international communism and Bohlen for his association with the "Yalta give-away." McCarthy criticized the State Department for failing to pressure Greek shipowners for trading with mainland China, with McCarthy eventually "negotiating" (his term) an agreement with them not to do so, much to the consternation of John Foster Dulles and the State Department. One of McCarthy's staffers even took on Protestant clergy members, claiming they were the single largest group supporting the Communist apparatus; in the wake of the widespread protests about such an outrageous allegation, McCarthy was forced to back off from the charge and ended up firing the staffer who made it. But the incident did little to curb McCarthy's ambitions and his abusive tactics and behavior.

So long as McCarthy stayed within the bounds of authority given to his investigating committee by the full Senate and was able to control a majority of his committee, he could continue to conduct his hearings. President Eisenhower was well aware of the damage McCarthy was causing, but he thought that a name-calling contest was futile. He was determined not to build up McCarthy's charges by engaging in such a contest from the Oval Office, despite the Senator's transferring of his personal attacks from Truman to the new president. Furthermore, Eisenhower believed that under the Constitution's separation of powers among executive, legislative, and judicial branches it was the Senate's duty to curb its committee chairman. At least at the start of the administration it was the president's hope that Republican leaders in the Senate would be able to contain McCarthy. Much as he would have liked to, Eisenhower could not "fire" McCarthy.

It was rumored from time to time in the press that Eisenhower was deterred from challenging McCarthy because the senator had obtained information damaging to Eisenhower and threatened to disclose it if the president attacked him. The rumors went on to say that Eisenhower, in setting up a civilian government in Germany at the end of World War II, had okayed the appointment of certain local officials who turned out to be Russian agents. Of course, anyone familiar with the German situation would know that hundreds of German local officials preferred the Russians to the old Nazi regime, so some of them were undoubtedly pro-Russian. But the rumors that something sinister was involved have persisted to this day. I personally believe that Ike was totally uninfluenced by these rumors in his treatment—and ultimate destruction—of McCarthy.

Although it was Eisenhower's policy never "to engage in personalities" with his opponents, McCarthy included, the president did at times implicitly criticize McCarthy in thinly veiled ways as the year wore on. At Dartmouth College's commencement in 1953 the president spoke out against book burning with obvious reference to the efforts of the Mc-

Carthy committee to censor books that were in the libraries of the International Information Agency around the world. At other times during 1953 the president criticized those individuals who used "unfair methods" in fighting communism, proposing instead a policy of following "American principles in trials and investigations." Most important, Eisenhower always refused to be drawn into a personal controversy with the senator, knowing that to do so would elevate McCarthy to the president's level and give him the kind of publicity that his tactics required in order to succeed. In choosing not to attack McCarthy directly, Eisenhower was an astute observer of Truman's fruitless experience in counteracting McCarthy.

Eisenhower also began to take steps, very discreetly, to deflect McCarthy. When Conant's name was before the Senate for confirmation as high commissioner, McCarthy quietly dropped his opposition to the appointment following a telephone conversation with Ike. McCarthy's opposition to the Bohlen nomination also came to naught, but not without a bit of controversy. During the course of the hearings on Bohlen, Secretary of State Dulles told the Foreign Relations Committee that there was no derogatory information on Bohlen in the FBI's security report. In so doing, however, Dulles had overruled the judgment of his security officer, Scott McLeod, on the matter. Dulles failed to tell the committee of McLeod's view, which was based on uncorroborated and raw intelligence reports. McLeod told McCarthy of the matter and the latter demanded Senate access to the Bohlen file and that Dulles take a lie-detector test.

The matter threatened to get out of hand and provided just the kind of incident McCarthy was skilled at exploiting. But in a series of private meetings that included Majority Leader Taft, Hoover, the president, and myself, it was agreed that Taft and Sen. John Sparkman for the Democrats could "look at"—but not copy—a summary report (but not the raw material) of the Bohlen file. Although I had reservations about allowing the Senate such unprecedented access—which could be demanded again in the future—the president decided in favor of the procedure in order to bring the matter to a quick end. The president's judgment proved right: Taft reported to the Senate that he had seen no evidence of disloyalty on Bohlen's part, and Bohlen was quickly and overwhelmingly confirmed.

The new internal-security procedures the administration developed provided another device we sought to use to take some of the wind out of McCarthy's sails. Although they were established on their own merits and without reference to McCarthy's activities, they had the added benefit of demonstrating the administration's own commitment, within the bounds of reason and fair procedure, to deal with the issue of Communists in government. We even brought Senator McCarthy and others involved in the issue such as Senator Jenner and Congressman Harold Velde of the House Un-American Activities Committee to the White House, where I explained the new program to them; Jenner and Velde were impressed; McCarthy less so.

Indirect tactics in deflating McCarthy were used a bit more effectively in the Protestant clergy affair. Sensing that attacks on the clergy were unpopular if not outlandish to most Americans, McCarthy began to reconsider the appointment of the staff member who had made the allegations. Before he could do so, however, Sherman Adams, White House speech writer Emmett Hughes, and Bill Rogers from my staff met and arranged to have religious groups wire the White House in protest. Adams, Hughes, and Rogers then drafted a presidential statement deploring the allegations, quickly brought it to the president to review, and issued it over the wire services minutes before McCarthy was scheduled to meet with the press to issue his own statement firing the staffer. Nixon and Rogers even engaged in a little subterfuge in the episode: Aware of the timing of McCarthy's press conference, they delayed him in conversation so that the president's statement could appear over the wire services before the press conference. Since the president's statement came first, it appeared that McCarthy had been forced to retract the charges and fire the staffer because of Eisenhower's actions.

It was not until McCarthy began to attack the army in late 1953, however, that the full force of Eisenhower's disgust led to a concerted effort from the administration to do the senator in. McCarthy's investigations initially centered on allegations of Communist-cell activity at the army's signal corps facility at Fort Monmouth, New Jersey. As with all of McCarthy's charges, little came of the investigation; almost all of the evidence pointed to activity that had occurred during World War II. But eventually the real reason for McCarthy's attack on the army came to light: an attempt to seek favors for one of McCarthy's staffers who recently had been inducted into the army.

The staff member in question was David Schine. Schine, a wealthy hotel heir just out of college, had no known qualifications as an investigator or any recognizable expertise on matters of Communist infiltration and espionage methods. He was, however, a close friend of McCarthy's chief legal assistant, Roy Cohn, and had been hired by Cohn to serve on Mc-Carthy's staff. The two—Cohn and Schine—became inseparable. When Schine was inducted into the army in summer 1953—the peacetime draft was still in effect—Cohn through McCarthy sought to have him commissioned as an officer, then, failing in that effort, assigned a cushy job that would allow him to continue his anti-Communist work. In each case the army balked at the pressure on Schine's behalf, and eventually Cohn and McCarthy began to put pressure on Secretary of the Army Robert Stevens and his staff for special treatment of, now, Private Schine during his basic training; evidence later came to light that Schine had been relieved from KP duty, permitted telephone privileges and outside visitors, and given weekend passes that were routinely denied to other inductees. The efforts on Schine's behalf and the army's special treatment of Schine, not surprisingly, were occurring as McCarthy's investigation of the army was under way.

The connection between McCarthy's investigation at Fort Monmouth and the Schine affair was not known to us in the administration. But on January 21, 1954, in a meeting in my office at the Justice Department, the two events came together. The ostensible purpose of the meeting was to discuss Senator McCarthy's request to subpoena members of the army's loyalty and security board regarding their actions in the case of one of the individuals under investigation at Fort Monmouth. Since the issue of a subpoena involved a matter of the separation of powers and the question of protecting the confidentiality of the army's proceedings, the army correctly sought the counsel of the Justice Department.

The president asked my advice as to his constitutional powers to order the army personnel to refuse to honor the subpoenas. McCarthy had been protected as long as he stayed within the bounds of the Senate resolution under which he had acted. But no Senate resolution, the president believed, could violate the principle embedded in the Constitution of separation of powers between the two branches of government and the long-standing implicit right for the president to claim executive privilege, whereby the president's constitutional responsibility for the functioning of the executive branch empowered him to resist congressional encroachments that would compromise the carrying out of such responsibilities.

It was a new twist to a problem that had existed since George Washington's day. We gave the president a long memorandum showing all the instances in which the presidents of the past, including George Washington, had refused to honor congressional subpoenas of executive-branch personnel and records under various circumstances.

The meeting held in my office on January 21, 1954, was convened to discuss the facts underlying the confrontation. At the meeting were Chief of Staff Sherman Adams, UN Ambassador Henry Cabot Lodge, my deputy, Bill Rogers, Gerald Morgan of the White House congressional liaison staff, and the army's general legal counsel, John Adams. The presence of such a high-powered group is testimony to the seriousness with which we took McCarthy's actions at the time. I had brought to the meeting the memorandum on executive privilege, and we decided that it would be improper to respond to McCarthy's subpoena.

But in the course of the discussion, John Adams brought to our attention the matter of McCarthy's and Cohn's attempts to secure special treatment for Schine. We immediately realized the significance of this bombshell and instructed John Adams to prepare a detailed chronology of their efforts.

Following the meeting, I gave my opinion to the president that he was justified under the Constitution in resisting McCarthy's demand. The president then struck a decisive blow. He cut off access of McCarthy's committee to records of the executive branch. McCarthy, of course, railed against the president's action as an unconstitutional act, but he was supported only by a few individuals in academia; otherwise, the president's action was unchallenged. The Senate itself did not dispute the president's action.

Eisenhower continued his practice of not criticizing McCarthy by name, but privately he became more active in the efforts against McCarthy, who by now was more direct and public in his attacks on the president. Eisenhower met with Sen. Everett Dirksen, a leading member of the conservative bloc in the Senate and a member of McCarthy's committee. The president demanded, successfully, that the Republicans on the committee show some fortitude in restraining McCarthy—who had recently berated Army Secretary Stevens during one of his hearings—by requiring a majority vote of the committee on holding hearings and issuing subpoenas so that McCarthy could no longer convene unannounced closed-session, one-man hearings as he had done in the past. The president met with other Republican legislative leaders, urging them to restrain McCarthy lest his tactics undermine the administration's whole legislative program and destroy the Republican party. Eisenhower also became more direct in his comments to the press, criticizing McCarthy's methods and praising those individuals, such as Vermont's senator Ralph Flanders, who now rose to challenge McCarthy. To the cabinet, he emphasized the need to protect individuals within our departments from the kinds of attacks McCarthy was now making. Furthermore, when Adlai Stevenson in a televised address attacked the Republican party for its handling of McCarthy, Eisenhower arranged with the networks and the Federal Communications Commission that Vice-president Nixon—not McCarthy—be given free television airtime to respond.

By this time, word of the Schine affair became known in Congress and the media, and it precipitated a chain of events that would prove to be McCarthy's undoing. The army circulated the chronology of McCarthy's and Cohn's efforts in behalf of Schine to members of McCarthy's committee. McCarthy, in turn, charged that the army was trying to blackmail him in order to stop his investigation. Members of McCarthy's committee could not avoid the issue and opened an investigation—the infamous Army-McCarthy hearings—to get at the truth.

From late April 1954 through mid-June the nation watched McCarthy's performance on television. The Wisconsin senator was now placed in the unaccustomed role of witness subject to cross-examination. A distinguished Boston attorney, Joseph Welch, was retained by the army to challenge McCarthy, and Welch performed his task brilliantly. In a notable series of exchanges with McCarthy, Welch demonstrated to the American people the dangers of McCarthy and McCarthyism. The senator's abusive behavior and bullying demeanor during the hearings, day after day, proved to be his downfall. They vividly confirmed the picture of the unprincipled and dangerous McCarthy that Edward R. Murrow had revealed to the American people only weeks before in his now famous exposé of McCarthy on his "See It Now" television program.

Although the hearings were a Senate matter, behind-the-scenes efforts from the White House contributed to the situation that produced McCarthy's demise. Although McCarthy had hoped to retain his seat as a member of the investigating committee, other members of the committee, responding partly to White House pressure and Eisenhower's public comments that it was not in the American tradition to sit in judgment on one's own dispute, forced him to relinquish his position, thus placing him in the role of witness rather than of prosecutor. Furthermore, although some Senate leaders had sought to end television coverage after the first week, we in the administration recognized the damage that live coverage of the hearings was causing McCarthy and recommended their continuation. The choice of Joseph Welch as the army's counsel at the hearing can also be traced to the White House; his name had been suggested to Sherman Adams during a conversation with Tom Dewey.

Eisenhower also made sure that Congress and the press took notice of his continued support of beleaguered Army Secretary Stevens, who once again confronted a sarcastic and abusive McCarthy in the hearings, by taking him on a well-publicized trip to army bases in the South; photographs of a beaming Eisenhower shaking hands with Stevens were prominently featured in the newspapers the next day.

When McCarthy, at one point in the hearings, stated that it was the duty of all two-million federal employees to "give us any information which they have about graft, corruption, Communists, and treason," Eisenhower privately exploded with anger. The next day he drafted a response, issued in my name, stating in no uncertain terms that:

> the executive branch has sole and fundamental responsibility to enforce laws and presidential orders. . . . That responsibility cannot be usurped by any individual who may seek to set himself above the laws of our land, or override orders of the President of the United States to federal employees of the executive branch of government.

Our preparation in the aftermath of the January 21 meeting also helped matters. The army's case was greatly strengthened by John Adams's careful and organized presentation of the evidence against McCarthy in the chronology we had suggested he develop. When Adams inadvertently told the committee about the January meeting in my office, McCarthy immediately sought to have the committee subpoena the members of the administration present on that date. His efforts, however, were easily thwarted by the brief we had earlier developed and presented on executive privilege in response to the subpoenas of the army officers; the precedent having been established and accepted in the first instance, McCarthy could not claim we were simply trying to protect ourselves.

As the Army-McCarthy hearings neared their close, a group of senators led by Flanders of Vermont became so outraged at McCarthy's behavior and tactics that they succeeded in setting up a subcommittee, headed by Sen. Arthur Watkins of Utah, to determine whether Senate rules were being violated. McCarthy now faced another round of hearings. His wild charges, innuendoes, and character assassinations continued, but they fell flat before colleagues who were now bent on preserving the traditions and sanctity of the Senate. On December 2, 1954, the Senate voted by a margin of 67 to 22 to "condemn"—in effect to censure—the Wisconsin senator, the worse penalty the Senate can mete out to one of its members, short of expulsion. McCarthy's career as a powerful and threatening member of that body in effect ended at that moment.

Following the Senate vote, President Eisenhower telephoned me at the Justice Department and said he wanted to do something for Senator Watkins, who had been kicked around badly by McCarthy and some of his supporters during the Senate's proceedings. I replied that an invitation to the senator to come to the White House and have his picture taken with the president might be an appropriate gesture; it would serve as an adroit way of taking a stand without seeming to violate senatorial prerogatives. The next day as I picked up the morning paper and saw Eisenhower and Watkins on the front page, I thought to myself what a fitting postscript it was to the whole sorry but potentially dangerous episode of Joe McCarthy: the conservative but respected Watkins representing a Senate that had had enough of McCarthy's behavior and a smiling Eisenhower who had worked behind the scenes to bring McCarthy down.

The president's method of handling the McCarthy problem probably caused the most controversial domestic dispute of his presidency. Many people criticized him at the time—and have since—for failing to use his public prestige openly to attack McCarthy and what he stood for. But I think he understood better than all of us what made McCarthy so powerful and threatening and how he could be cut down to size and eventually defeated. A direct and forceful response of the sort President Truman had attempted would be futile. It would only elevate McCarthy to the president's stature if not require the president to stoop to McCarthy's level. It would further give McCarthy the kind of forum and public attention necessary for his attacks. It would demean the presidency. And it would divide the nation. Eisenhower thus recognized he would be more effective in dealing with McCarthy if he waited till he could take decisive action that would not only calm a troubled nation—one that unfortunately at times took McCarthy seriously—but that would dispose of the problem based on the senator's own self-defeating behavior. He further recognized that the Senate had broad powers to investigate the executive branch, and only when the executive branch was attacked on such a scale as to interfere with its proper functioning or in a way that endangered national security could he oppose the McCarthy committee's actions. To do otherwise would have raised the whole Senate's ire toward the president, not just McCarthy's.

Not all of Eisenhower's efforts were successful, nor (in hindsight) did Eisenhower always correctly assess how far he could go in his attempts. In the controversy over the Greek ships, for example, Mutual Security Director Harold Stassen forcefully attacked McCarthy for undermining the constitutional powers of the executive branch by conducting his own negotiations.[1] At a subsequent press conference, Eisenhower undercut the force of Stassen's position by suggesting that Stassen probably meant "infringe" rather than "undermine."

Nor was Eisenhower ever fully able to enlist the support of Republican leaders in the Senate in restraining McCarthy. Part of Army Secretary Stevens's difficulties, for example, stemmed from a luncheon he had attended with McCarthy and two leading Republicans on his committee, Everett Dirksen and Karl Mundt. Ostensibly, Dirksen and Mundt were there to arrange a satisfactory compromise between Stevens, on the army's behalf, and McCarthy. Stevens, however, not accustomed to the rough-and-tumble of Senate politics, ended up signing a statement that was later interpreted as a "surrender" to McCarthy's requests for information; neither Dirksen nor Mundt took steps to avert the damage. Nor, even in the final hours of the McCarthy controversy, could Eisenhower count on the support of the Republican leadership in the Senate: Four of the five Republican senators in leadership positions—William Knowland of California, Styles Bridges of New Hampshire, Eugene Milliken of Colorado, and Everett Dirksen of Illinois—voted against the motion to censure McCarthy; only Leverett Saltonstall of Massachusetts voted with the majority against McCarthy.

These points notwithstanding, Eisenhower's method of dealing with McCarthy did in the end prove successful in its results. Although it left Eisenhower open to criticism for not mounting the "bully pulpit" against McCarthy, it is unlikely that McCarthy would have been brought down in the manner and at the time he was had Eisenhower engaged in a shouting match. Eisenhower's style of leadership in this instance is well summed up by the Latin motto he kept on his desk in the Oval Office—*Suaviter in modo, fortiter in re* ("Gently in manner, strong in deed").

On a wider scale, the McCarthy dispute leaves unanswered the troublesome question on the extent of the doctrine of executive privilege. When may the president refuse to turn over to Congress or to the public and the media confidential documents on the grounds of national security? On the one hand, there is danger that the president could be covering up wrongdoing or embarrassing conduct and merely using the national-security label as an excuse. On the other hand, exposure of true national-security information—such as troop movements in wartime or collaboration with friendly countries to combat terrorism—may have tragic results for the country. My own opinion is that if the president's action is responsibly challenged, the national-security information should be turned over to the courts—perhaps to a special court created for the purpose—to examine the information in camera, and the court decision (after appeal) would be binding on the question of whether the information should be made public (or to the Congress). If such a rule were adopted I believe most of these questions would be settled by negotiation between the legal counsel of both branches.

Eisenhower's actions on another occasion to preserve the powers of the presidency came in the fight with the Senate over a proposal to amend the Constitution. The proposed change was named after its chief sponsor, Sen. John W. Bricker of Ohio. The Bricker amendment was introduced in the Senate as Senate Resolution No. 1 on January 7, 1953. The measure was endorsed by a two-thirds majority of the senators, the exact number needed for its approval, with forty-four of the forty-eight Republicans in the Senate announcing their support. Later, several differing versions were introduced, but all versions curbed the power of the president to negotiate international treaties, and some versions would have limited the president's power to enter into any executive and other international agreements without Senate ratification.

On its surface the amendment looked reasonable. Its language sought to limit the scope of treaties and other international agreements to those permissible under the Constitution, thus seeming to protect individual rights and other constitutional guarantees from infringement. In practice, however, such a limitation would have radically redefined the powers of the president to make certain kinds of treaties, even when ratified by the Senate. In the past, treaty-making power had been defined more broadly: In the landmark *Curtiss-Wright* case, for example, the Supreme Court had held that treaties were entered into "under the authority of the United States," not under specific powers enumerated in the Constitution, and that the powers and supremacy of the federal government in international affairs "did not depend upon the affirmative grants of the Constitution."[2] Restrictions under the amendment might also prohibit the president from negotiating worthwhile treaties dealing with matters of international commerce: Accords that granted American citizens the right to charter corporations, control property, and otherwise engage in economic activity in foreign countries (thus involving matters of individual rights generally within the powers of individual states to regulate and not part of those enumerated powers possessed by the federal government) might fall within the domain that the amendment proscribed.[3] Nor would foreign governments be likely to enter into such agreements if the rights of their own citizens, under the Ninth and Tenth Amendments, could be abrogated piecemeal by state courts and legislatures.

The amendment also aimed to curb attempts to circumvent the treaty-ratification process. The long-recognized authority of presidents to enter into executive agreements that do not require Senate ratification had sometimes been abused in the past: Some presidents had chosen to label politically unpopular accords with foreign powers as executive agreements rather than as treaties, even though their contents were indistinguishable from what normally might be regarded as a treaty, in order to escape Senate scrutiny and possible nonratification. The amendment, however, would have made all executive agreements subject to the procedures governing treaties in the Constitution, thus broadening the foreign-policy role of Congress within the Constitution's system of shared powers and eliminating in practice an important tool presidents must sometimes use in the "necessary and proper" conduct of their foreign-policy powers.

Constitutional complexities aside, the real thrust of the amendment was political. In my opinion, the proposed amendment was an outgrowth of the adverse reaction in the Senate and among the public to some of the agreements reached by FDR in his famous meeting at Yalta with Churchill and Stalin. The notion was that FDR, without consulting the Senate, had paved the way for Stalin to take over Eastern Europe—Poland, the Baltic States, and other countries—after the war. There was also the view that President Truman had done little at the Potsdam Conference to oppose Stalin's program.[4]

Proponents of the Bricker amendment also feared that the United Nations, acting under our membership in it, could impose obligations upon the United States that overrode the Constitution. Advocates of states' rights were concerned that the covenants and conventions of such international bodies were a kind of Trojan horse that could be used by the federal government to encroach upon the powers of state and local governments. Members of Congress from the South were especially fearful that the UN's Charter and its proposed Declaration of Human Rights could be used to nullify laws mandating racial segregation and thus remove the barriers to voting by black citizens that then existed. There were worries that presidents could appeal to United Nations' obligations in contravention of the Constitution or the will of Congress, as President Truman, without a declaration of war by Congress, had done only three years earlier when he had cited our United Nations membership as his authority for sending U.S. troops to Korea. Business groups also raised the charge that the UN's various provisions for human rights would turn the country into a "socialistic state."

Many of these fears, however, were groundless. Article 2(7) of the UN Charter, for example, clearly stated that

> nothing contained in the present Charter shall authorize the United Nations to intervene in matters which are essentially within the domestic jurisdiction of any state or shall require the members to submit such matters to settlement under the present Charter.

But concerns remained that federal courts might use such international agreements to overturn state and local laws that were in contravention of political, social, and economic rights that might be embraced in such documents. Such were the fears that one former president of the ABA publicly drew the outlandish conclusion that, under the UN's proposed Convention on Genocide, a white motorist who accidentally ran over a black child could be extradited for trial by an international tribunal.

President Eisenhower studied the proposed amendment and concluded that in fact it would restrict the constitutional prerogative of the president to make treaties. An American Bar Association committee, of which the president's older brother Edgar was an active member, disagreed and vigorously supported Bricker. In Eisenhower's view, however, the ABA's support of the amendment was largely political; he told his press secretary, Jim Hagerty, that the national ABA, dominated at the time by conservative lawyers, was embarked on a crusade "to save the United States from Eleanor Roosevelt."[5] Passage of the amendment, Eisenhower wrote his brother Edgar, would mean a return to isolationism and would "cripple the executive power to the point that we become hopeless in world affairs."[6] In his private diary, the president noted that in the matter of the "so-called Bricker Amendment," the "logic of the case is all against Senator Bricker," who "has gotten almost psychopathic on the subject."[7]

Secretary of State Dulles was the logical person to represent the administration in opposing this proposed intrusion into the powers of the presidency in the field of foreign affairs. But during the 1952 presidential campaign he had made a speech that appeared to support the need for an amendment to the Constitution restricting the treaty power of the president. Eisenhower therefore asked me to work with Dulles (who later made it clear that he did not approve of the Bricker text) and with the State Department in dealing with Senator Bricker. The president expressed the hope that I could arrange a compromise that would preserve essential presidential powers.

This assignment caused me some anxious moments, inasmuch as I was a close personal friend of Dulles and I was being assigned to act in his field of foreign affairs. My professional association with the secretary of state had started in my early days in law practice in New York when he—in another law firm—retained me to work on a number of matters in which he believed I had special expertise. Subsequently he became the chief adviser on foreign affairs to Gov. Thomas E. Dewey when I was managing the Dewey campaigns. When Dulles ran for the Senate I arranged with him to assign my chief political aide, Thomas E. Stephens, to manage the campaign. And in the Eisenhower presidential campaign of 1952, Dulles had been the draftsman of the all-important foreign-affairs plank in the Republican platform. In the controversy over the Bricker Amendment, however, Dulles was fully cognizant of the need for an unusual arrangement to coordinate the administration's efforts to defeat the Bricker proposal; thus no resulting personal conflict arose between us about impinging on one another's turf.

Dulles was by far the most controversial member of the Eisenhower cabinet. Even today the mention of his name evokes strong negative reactions from some people in the foreign-policy establishment of former State Department officials. The same is true among people who served in the Foreign Offices of Great Britain and France, primarily because of their differences with him in the Suez crisis. Eisenhower, on the other hand, had great confidence in Dulles, who carried out faithfully Ike's programs in foreign affairs. I believe that Dulles brought much of this controversy on himself through his personality and temperament. He was a tenacious lawyer who fought hard for his "client"—the president—and did not engage in the customary diplomatic massaging of the personal feelings of his opponent. He was a loner in many ways. He spent days in solitude on his favorite island in the St. Lawrence River, where he developed his thoughts and speeches. He did not rely heavily on those individuals around him for ideas, and they often felt ignored. He had strong religious beliefs and a solemn manner. He gave the impression of preaching to his confreres and often painted those who disagreed with him as unintelligent. Despite these characteristics, he was a skillful negotiator and had a great mental capacity and a fine analytical mind. He was a loyal friend, and with his family and close friends, he was a delightful companion. I wish he could have lived to see the democratic forces in Europe triumph over communism. He fought hard to bring those changes about in the days when the Iron Curtain seemed impregnable.

I worked throughout the Bricker fight with Herman Phleger, Dulles's legal adviser in the State Department, and with Assistant Attorney General J. Lee Rankin. We called upon outside pro bono advisers, including Gen. Lucius D. Clay, then in private life, Prof. Paul Freund and Dean Erwin Griswold of Harvard Law School, Prof. Edward Corwin of Princeton, and John W. Davis and John J. McCloy of the New York bar, all of whom strongly opposed the amendment. The Association of the Bar of the City of New York, which especially recognized the amendment's threat to American companies doing business overseas, took a stand in opposition to that of the American Bar Association committee, thus aiding our legal stance. I held many negotiating sessions with the latter committee and with Senator Bricker (who had been the vice-presidential candidate on the Dewey ticket in 1944).

At first I sought to delay Bricker, emphasizing that it was too early in the new administration to open a political fight on such a controversial issue and that to do so would detract attention and support from the president's legislative program. Bricker was understanding but would not be deterred. I then suggested to the president that we begin to mobilize against the measure by requesting that all federal departments and agencies prepare reports on the effect the amendment would have on their activities. This would enable us to begin to build a solid case against the measure, detailing its broad and adverse impact.

The president and Secretary Dulles also sought to take some of the sting out of the opposition by announcing that the administration did not intend to press for ratification of the UN Genocide Convention and was curtailing participation in the UN's efforts to develop a human rights convention. We also sought, unsuccessfully, to enlist Bricker's support in creating a Bricker Commission to study the problem (we hoped for a long and thorough time); the president would then be free to accept or reject the recommendations of a commission led by Bricker but that represented a range of opinions on the subject.

A major part of my activities on the president's behalf involved attempts to arrange a compromise. Eisenhower was vehement in his opposition to the amendment's encroachments on the president's foreign-policy powers, but he was sympathetic to the amendment's provisions that sought to curtail the past abuses of executive agreements. And, at one of the early cabinet meetings, he had expressed his own concerns about altering the Constitution through international agreements. At least early on in the fight I thought there was some room for a reasonable meeting of the minds.

Bricker, whom I personally got along with, did not help matters, however. Rather than loosening the language of the amendment and facilitating a compromise, he grew more adamant in his position. His incorporation in the amendment of the infamous "which clause"—pressed upon him by conservative states' righters in the national ABA—was especially damaging. The "which clause" stated that "a treaty shall become effective as internal law in the United States only through legislation which would be valid in the absence of the treaty." "Only through legislation . . . valid in the absence of the treaty" seems an innocuous phrase. But had it been passed, it would have limited the ability of Congress to implement treaties only to areas clearly within its enumerated powers, powers limited in a literal reading of their scope and checked by the powers reserved to the states in the Tenth Amendment. As a result, much of the Supreme Court's expansion of the federal government's powers during the twentieth century would have been negated in the area of foreign affairs. In particular, the Court's key precedent in the case of *Missouri v. Holland*,[8] which had relied on the "necessary and proper" clause rather than on enumerated powers in enlarging the national government's treaty-making abilities, would have been rendered moot.

We persisted in our efforts to reach a reasonable settlement of the issue acceptable to all parties. At one point, in June 1953, I thought we had an agreement to a compromise, which would state merely that any treaty that violated the Constitution was invalid. This language would allay fears, I hoped, that treaties could be used to limit individual rights or to deny other constitutional guarantees. But nearly everyone in the thick of the fight on second thought realized that this solution still avoided the questions that divided us. Bricker also by this point became much more enamored of the "which clause"—earlier he had had strong reservations about it—and it was a sticking point on which neither side would budge from their positions.

One unanticipated positive consequence of our failure to reach a compromise developed: At each of my meetings with the president, Eisenhower grew more firm in his opposition. The Bricker amendment became an issue on which the administration would fight. For the president, it especially threatened his long-held views, ingrained from his West Point days, about the need zealously to guard and preserve the delicate separation of powers between executive and legislative branches. Although in statements to the press Eisenhower had been somewhat equivocal (similar to his unwillingness to criticize McCarthy) in his criticisms —the president realized it had significant public and congressional support—on July 1, 1953, he announced his opposition to the amendment. But he continued to express his willingness to compromise on the issues it raised.

Negotiations continued over the next several months, and by early January 1954 it looked as if acceptable wording had been reached. Bricker agreed to drop the vexing "which clause," and we agreed that treaties could not be used to interfere with state and local matters unless they were related to foreign affairs. The next day, after meeting with his supporters in the ABA, Bricker repudiated the agreement and once again demanded the inclusion of the "which clause." He also publicly criticized Eisenhower, which strengthened Ike's resolve to defeat the amendment once and for all. By this time, too, public sentiment against the measure had begun to develop as debate began to reveal its shortcomings. Eisenhower's increasing opposition also encouraged the Eisenhower Republicans in the Senate to abandon their support of the amendment.

All hope for compromise evaporated after Sen. Walter George, Democrat from Georgia, proposed a substitute measure. Because the proposal came from a well-respected internationalist, the administration thought that George's measure might provide the compromise everyone had been seeking. It dropped the "which clause," but unfortunately it also sought to expand the Bricker proposal to cover all executive agreements in foreign affairs. Although we had been willing earlier to compromise somewhat on the executive-agreement issue, the George measure went too far. Moreover, we also felt certain that neither the Bricker nor the George proposals could muster the two-thirds of the Senate vote needed for passage. Our experts—Davis, Clay, and Corwin—emphasized the damage to the presidency that even the watered-down George provision could do. This brought Eisenhower to the end of his tether since the provision represented the kind of encroachment on the president's constitutional powers and a redefinition of the traditional separation of powers between Congress and the presidency to which he was especially sensitive.

On February 25, 1954, the Bricker amendment was considered by the Senate and rejected by the surprisingly large margin of 50 to 42. Two days later, George's substitute was up for vote. At the end of the roll call, the vote stood at 60 in favor with 30 against, exactly the two-thirds needed for passage. At that point Sen. Harley Kilgore of West Virginia entered the Senate (rumor had it that Kilgore had been roused from a nearby tavern). The clerk called Kilgore's name, and a "nay" was heard, apparently from Kilgore. The measure was thus defeated by one vote.

Although Bricker was to persist in his efforts to curb the president's treaty powers until his election defeat in 1958, the battle over the constitutional amendment ended at that point. A number of Bricker's supporters were defeated in the 1954 congressional elections, and Eisenhower's clear opposition to the amendment doomed its passage. The president's calculated strategy of openness to compromise coupled with firmness at the right moment had avoided any infringement on presidential power. As in the McCarthy episode, Eisenhower's behind-the-scenes efforts and his attempts to stay above the political fray to avoid a head-on confrontation with the Senate led him to prevail.

Protecting the office of the presidency also often requires initiative from the attorney general. One such instance occurred when Congress was considering a bill to deregulate the natural-gas industry. President Eisenhower favored the bill's objectives. But in the last stages of debate in the Senate it was disclosed that an attempt had been made (unsuccessfully) to bribe Francis Case, a Republican senator from South Dakota, to support the bill. Eisenhower also reported to me that one day while playing golf, Sen. Prescott Bush of Connecticut had said that his son—later president of the United States—had been unduly threatened with reprisals by individuals in the oil industry, where son George was then employed, who demanded that he see to it that his father voted for the bill. The whole drive for passage of the bill became tainted with suspicions that unethical and even illegal means had been employed by industry supporters of the bill, and there was danger of subsequent revelations then unknown. The Senate, however, eventually passed the bill.

When the bill came to the White House for the president's signature, Eisenhower was away from Washington at the vacation home of Secretary of the Treasury Humphrey in Georgia and thus was unaware of some of these last-minute developments, such as the Case bribery attempt. I felt that the president was taking a terrible risk in signing the bill into law. Given the revelations that had surfaced so far about the unsavory tactics of the bill's supporters, I worried about other schemes that might come to light once the bill became law. The proposal entailed a significant risk to the president's reputation and might even evolve into a latter-day Teapot Dome scandal.

I immediately got in touch with Secretary Humphrey and told him about my fears. I persuaded Humphrey that it would be too dangerous for Eisenhower to sign the bill, and together we concluded that a veto was required if the high ethical standards maintained by the president over the years were to be preserved, regardless of the merits of the legislation. Although I suspect that Eisenhower favored the bill despite the taint associated with it, in light of our opposition he accepted our advice and vetoed it.

The attorney general, I believe, has a special duty to protect the presidency. Fulfilling this obligation well not only calls for sound constitutional and legal advice but sometimes requires a certain kind of political judgment to deflect the president from situations that might injure his office. On such occasions, whether dealing with a Joe McCarthy, defeating an ill-advised constitutional amendment, or avoiding potential scandal, expertise in and familiarity with the workings of politics contribute significantly to the attorney general's performance of his duties, without turning him into a mere instrument of the president's political will.

NOTES

1. The Stassen-McCarthy fight over the Greek ships is especially revealing about McCarthy's character. In the crucial 1948 Wisconsin primary, McCarthy had been one of Stassen's chief supporters in his quest for the presidency.
2. U.S. v. Curtiss-Wright Export Corp., 299 U.S. 304 (1936).

3. This problem with the amendment became especially likely after the insertion of the "which clause" in Bricker's subsequent versions of the amendment.

4. If President Truman had followed Eisenhower's military advice at the Potsdam Conference, it seems reasonable to assume that Stalin's domination of Eastern Europe would have been lessened if not negated. Eisenhower opposed extensive dismantling of German industry. He did not think that the United States should encourage Stalin to enter the war with Japan. He wanted civilian government to replace military government in occupied Germany as soon as possible. And he favored extending U.S. government Lend-Lease arrangements with the French and the British. All of this advice was ignored by Truman. See Dwight D. Eisenhower, *Crusade in Europe* (Garden City, N.Y.: Doubleday, 1948), pp. 441–44, and Stephen Ambrose, *Eisenhower, Soldier 1890–1952* (New York: Simon and Schuster, 1983), p. 425.

5. Mrs. Roosevelt had been an American delegate to the United Nations and was instrumental in drafting its Declaration of Human Rights. Eisenhower's comments are reported by Jim Hagerty in his diary, January 11, 1954; Robert Ferrell, ed. *The Diary of James Hagerty* (Bloomington: Indiana University Press, 1983), p. 6.

6. Dwight D. Eisenhower (DDE) to Edgar Eisenhower, March 27, 1953, Diary Series, Eisenhower Library, Abilene, Kansas.

7. DDE diary entry, April 1, 1953, in Robert Ferrell, ed., *The Eisenhower Diaries* (New York: Norton, 1981), p. 233.

8. Missouri v. Holland, 252 U.S. 416 (1920).

15

Changing the Constitution

The Twenty-fifth Amendment

❖ ❖ ❖ ❖ ❖ ❖ ❖ ❖ ❖ ❖ ❖ ❖ ❖ ❖ ❖

My experience with the Bricker amendment was not the only time I found myself in the midst of an effort to change the Constitution of the United States. In that instance, my aim was to thwart the attempt; in 1955 I was on the other side of the battle as an active proponent of constitutional change. The effort—the Twenty-fifth Amendment to the Constitution—related to presidential disability and was developed as a result of Eisenhower's heart attack that year. My part in drafting and promoting the adoption of the amendment was a high point in my tenure as attorney general.[1]

When the news of Eisenhower's heart attack flashed across the country, I was on a holiday in Spain with my wife—our first vacation in over two years. We were entertained at the U.S. embassy in Madrid by Ambassador John Davis Lodge and Mrs. Lodge, and I had the interesting experience of sitting with the Supreme Court of Spain. We had just arrived at the beach near Torremolinos and changed into our bathing suits when a message from the ambassador called me from the beach to give me the bad news. He arranged for an army plane to take us to the Azores where we caught a trans-Atlantic flight. The takeoff from our beach resort was on a dirt air strip, and the attendants chased sheep off the runway as we started.

When we arrived in Washington, I organized a research team to find out what had happened in the past when a president became ill. Specifically the study was to interpret the vague provision of the Constitution as it then stood:

> In case of . . . Inability [of the president] to discharge the Powers and Duties of the said office, the Same shall devolve to the Vice-President.

Deputy Attorney General William P. Rogers, who had been acting in my absence, had immediately contacted the vice-president and met him in the Rogers home to avoid reporters. He recounted later that they had to search for a copy of the Constitution and finally located one in the *Farmers' Almanac*.

I called a meeting in my office of Secretary of State Dulles, Secretary of the Treasury Humphrey, and Secretary of Defense Wilson to consider the cabinet's course of action. Unbeknownst to us, our meeting was leaked to the columnist Drew Pearson by a receptionist, and much press speculation followed. Congress was not in session. A canvass of departments in the executive branch showed there was no business requiring immediate presidential action. Especially important were the reassuring medical reports of the heart specialist Dr. Paul Dudley White and the president's physician Dr. Howard Snyder. I gave my oral opinion to the cabinet that under these circumstances there was no need for the vice-president to act as president.

The cabinet carried on the routine affairs of the government, with the vice-president presiding. Sherman Adams, White House chief of staff, was liaison to the group at the Denver hospital where the president was confined and to Mrs. Eisenhower. The group included the president's press secretary Jim Hagerty and his appointments secretary Thomas E. Stephens. Hagerty was instructed by the ailing president to make public all medical details of his treatment in order to keep the nation informed.

After a while, the president's recovery progressed to the point that, one after another, the members of the cabinet visited him in his hospital bed. When my turn came, he greeted me with his famous grin and asked two questions, the second one facetiously. The first: "What happens under the Constitution if my illness is prolonged and emergencies arise requiring immediate action?" The second: "The doctors tell me I'm recovering, and I wonder if we should start preparing for a reelection campaign?" Obviously he was in good spirits.

In the more serious moments of our talk, he instructed me to develop an amendment to the Constitution and to make the appropriate studies to show the necessity for such action. He was well aware that the dangers of indecision in this age of nuclear weaponry required a solution. He was convinced that Congress, which had just begun one of its periodic but inconclusive studies of presidential disability, and the public would respond favorably to a well-reasoned plan. This was the setting for a ten-year battle ending in the successful passage of the amendment by Congress in 1965 and the subsequent ratification of the Twenty-Fifth Amendment by the states on February 10, 1967, some years after Eisenhower's return to private life. A look back at the history of the problem, and its critical nature, is illuminating.[2]

The first president to come face-to-face with the constitutional problem involving a life-threatening illness that caused a temporary disability was James Madison. Since Madison was one of the Founding Fathers and a leader in the original Constitutional Convention at Philadelphia, his action served as a weighty precedent. President Madison was sixty-two years old when it became known that he was suffering from a case of "bilious fever." As could be anticipated, rumors spread that the president was in a critical condition. The vice-president was Elbridge Gerry, who was himself almost seventy years old. More than three-and-a-half years remained in the presidential term. Public concern was greatly heightened by a statement of Sen. Daniel Webster that he had found the president too ill to read a congressional resolution that appeared to require presidential response. Future president James Monroe reported that there was plotting in the Senate as to what would happen if the illness were as serious as rumored. One element of the public press reported that the president was deranged. But President Madison took no action. Nor did Congress. He completely recovered and finished his term.

The most dramatic event involving the constitutional provision occurred in the administration of President Grover Cleveland. During his second term in 1893 he left the White House, ostensibly to take a pleasure cruise on a private yacht on Long Island Sound. On board and out of touch with the public, he secretly underwent an operation for removal of a cancerous growth on the roof of his mouth. While he was unconscious and strapped to a chair, propped up against the yacht's mast, a major part of the upper jaw was removed. No external incision was made. During the president's recuperation at his summer home in Massachusetts, he was fitted with an artificial jaw made of vulcanized rubber. No public announcement was made. The incident was unknown even to the vice-president, Adlai Stevenson (grandfather of the future Democratic presidential candidate). Only one cabinet officer was let in on the secret. Although an account of the surgery was leaked to the press in a few weeks, the story was not completely revealed until 1917. One of the attending physicians was quoted as saying he did more lying after the news story appeared than in all the rest of his life put together.

The case of President Woodrow Wilson's illness during his second term was characterized by secrecy and failure or refusal to reveal his medical condition. The illness started while Wilson was on a nationwide trip by rail to rally the public to support his plan for the creation of a League of Nations. He probably suffered a small stroke, which temporarily paralyzed the left side of his body. The public was told, through his physician Adm. Cary Grayson and his aide Joseph Tumulty, that the president had suffered a nervous breakdown. For weeks the medical facts were kept hidden from the Congress and the public and even from Vice-president Marshall and the cabinet. When presidential statements were required, they were relayed from the sickroom by Mrs. Wilson or Tumulty.

As can be imagined, wild rumors swept the country; some stated that Wilson had "gone mad and was kept a prisoner in the White House." A delegation of senators was dispatched to the White House to investigate the president's condition. According to one report, one of the senators told the president that the Senate was praying for him. "And which way are they praying, Senator?" was Wilson's supposed droll response.

Wilson may have been in good humor at times, but the government limped along. The secretary of state, Robert Lansing, called meetings of the cabinet and for his pains was rather summarily dismissed from office. The vice-president refused to take any action. Twenty-eight acts of Congress became laws without the president's signature. The League of Nations plan was turned down by the Senate. The House of Representatives' Judiciary Committee held hearings on the subject of presidential disability, but no action was taken. Wilson served out the balance of his term, still a very ill president.

In 1944, the last year of his third term as president, Franklin D. Roosevelt was found to have hypertensive heart disease, hardening of the arteries, and acute bronchitis; his condition was unknown to the media and the public until much later. His attending physicians, Drs. Ross McIntire and Howard Bruenn, kept their findings private and later reported that they did not discuss the medical diagnosis even with the president or his family.

Speculative news articles appeared about FDR's health during the presidential campaign. Those of us in the Dewey campaign wondered whether we should make the president's health a campaign issue: We had disturbing but uncorroborated information that Roosevelt would not survive another term. FDR's doctors, however, issued statements that he was "constitutionally sound." The war in Europe was coming to a successful end, and the president's popularity soared with each battlefield victory. The media sided with the president's physicians and did not conduct any investigative reporting of the type common today into the president's health.

In the closing days of the campaign FDR made a triumphal automobile trip through New York City and southern New England in the rain, giving the illusion of good health and vitality as he waved to immense crowds. Six months after that he died, and Harry S. Truman became president. Later it was disclosed that on inauguration day commencing his fourth term, President Roosevelt suffered severe chest pains. His physicians were not informed. The writer John Gunther, who saw him at the inauguration, wrote, "I was terrified when I saw his face. I felt certain he was going to die. All the light had gone out underneath the skin. It was like a parchment shade on a bulb that had been dimmed. [His face] was gray, gaunt and sagging."[3]

These precedents confirmed our view in 1955 that uncertainty as to who was in charge was too risky with the cold war and the threat of nuclear strikes hanging over us. My study leading to a proposal for a constitutional amendment was completed and presented to Eisenhower when he returned to the White House. I had engaged Dr. Ruth Silva, an expert in the field, to research and help develop a plan. I consulted such constitutional scholars as Prof. Edward S. Corwin of Princeton, John W. Davis, a New York City practicing lawyer, and Dean Erwin Griswold of Harvard Law School. All were agreed that when the vice-president assumed the powers of the presidency in the event of presidential disability, he should do so only as acting president and only for the duration of the disability. And it was their view that the decision whether disability existed, within the meaning of the Constitution, should be made by the president himself or within the executive branch.

The president then asked me to present the plan to the congressional leaders—Sen. Lyndon B. Johnson and Speaker Sam Rayburn—and to represent the administration in hearings before the House Judiciary Committee. In this I had the invaluable assistance of Assistant Attorney General J. Lee Rankin. But the initial response was negative. The congressional leaders told me that they rejected the plan on the grounds that in the present circumstances the people would be unnecessarily frightened by the suspicion that President Eisenhower was more seriously ill than had been disclosed and because the plan might enhance the political stature of the vice-president, Richard M. Nixon.

The House Judiciary Committee hearings went forward, however, under the chairmanship of Congressman Emanuel Celler of New York, with Congressman Kenneth Keating also of New York taking an active role. The Eisenhower-sponsored plan, which later became the nucleus of the Twenty-fifth Amendment, basically set out two provisions: (1) Whenever the president determines that he is, or is about to be, unable to discharge the powers and duties of his office, and until such time as he decides to resume them, the powers and duties of the presidency shall be discharged by the vice-president as acting president, and (2) Whenever the vice-president and a majority of the cabinet shall decide that the president is unable to discharge the powers and duties of his office, the vice-president shall immediately assume the office as acting president. If later there is disagreement as to whether the disability has terminated, Congress shall decide the issue in the manner set forth in the plan.

It should be noted that when the plan was finally approved years later by Congress, a change was made giving Congress the authority to designate "another body" in place of a majority of the cabinet to determine with the vice-president the fact of disability. This congressional authority has not been exercised to date.

In the hearings before the House Judiciary Committee and later before the Senate Subcommittee on Constitutional Amendments, various alternatives were proposed, discussed, and finally rejected. One was to act by statute rather than by constitutional amendment, but this was rejected because of uncertainty over whether the statute would be declared unconstitutional by the Supreme Court. Such uncertainty would defeat the very purpose of the plan, which was to have certainty at all times of emergency as to who was exercising the presidential powers.

Another alternative was to leave the decision on disability to Congress, but that was rejected because it seemed unwise for the legislative branch of the government to be in a position to pressure the executive branch on the question of who was to be president of the United States and at what time.

Another alternative would have given the crucial decision to a mixed commission made up of representatives of the executive, legislative, and judicial branches of the federal government, together with representatives of the medical profession and the public. But this alternative and variations of it were rejected since long hearings would be required and dissension within the commission might exacerbate the uncertainties of the situation and create confusions, even danger, to the stability of the government. At one point Chief Justice Earl Warren announced publicly that he was opposed in any event to having any member of the Supreme Court serve on any presidential commission.

With the opposition of congressional leaders, the plan died a temporary death. In view of the gravity of the problem, President Eisenhower worked out a stopgap plan, with guidance from my successor as attorney general, William P. Rogers, by exchanging letters with Vice-president Nixon setting down steps that were to be taken in the event of his disability. Subsequently, President John F. Kennedy exchanged similar letters with his vice-president, Lyndon B. Johnson, and so did President Johnson with his vice-president, Hubert Humphrey.

But the need for a constitutional amendment remained glaring. The tragedy of President Kennedy's assassination was the spark that ignited the fire. Lyndon Johnson, assuming the presidency, now supported the temporarily discarded Eisenhower plan but asked that it be coupled with a plan to fill any vacancy in the office of vice-president. Sen. Birch Bayh of Indiana was chairman of the Senate committee that held hearings on the proposed constitutional amendment and ably supported the plan. Strong support came from a special committee of the American Bar Association, of which I was chairman. Former President Eisenhower testified forcefully for the plan. The amendment was passed by Congress with the addition of a section authorizing Congress to approve a new vice-president in the event of vacancy in that office, upon nomination of a new vice-president by the president. After approval by the Congress, the presidential disability plan was ratified by the requisite number of states and became the Twenty-fifth Amendment.[4] Our special committee of the American Bar Association played an active role in encouraging states to ratify the measure.

The amendment did not, however, put to rest the difficult question of presidential disability. At the time of the attempted assassination of Ronald Reagan, his advisers rejected the need to act under the Twenty-fifth Amendment; and later, when the president underwent an operation, he turned over the office "temporarily" to Vice-president George Bush, but he expressed doubt as to whether the amendment applied.

A substantial negative public reaction about the non-use of the amendment ensued. As a result, the Miller Center for Study of the Presidency at the University of Virginia commissioned a study of the operation of the Twenty-fifth Amendment, which former Sen. Birch Bayh and I cochaired. Our report endorsed the amendment as the most feasible solution to the disability problem. We urged, further, that it be used as a routine matter when the president was unable to perform his duties; that he be given time for complete recovery before reassuming his office; that the position of presidential physician be upgraded; and finally that at the earliest possible time every new president and his advisers should be educated on the provisions of the Twenty-fifth Amendment.

President George Bush acted speedily on the problem. He appointed as his physician Dr. Burton J. Lee III and upgraded his position. This led to a meeting of the new president and his advisers in the Oval Office on April 18, 1989, to prepare for any emergency arising from presidential disability. The precedent will undoubtedly be followed by all incoming presidents.

Certainty at all times as to who is exercising the powers and duties of the presidency is of paramount importance. It is vital at home and for our dealings with foreign governments to avoid becoming a leaderless nation or even to appear as leaderless. The amendment provides a bulwark for stability under a constitutional government.

Many other proposals have been made over the years to amend the Constitution. Only twenty-six of these have been adopted in the entire 200 years since the Constitution was ratified (a Twenty-seventh Amendment dealing with Congress voting itself a pay raise may be added in the near future).

Two proposals for further amending the Constitution stand out in my mind as worthy of consideration. One would limit the presidency to a single six-year term. The other would give the president the power of veto over specific items in appropriation bills, i.e., the so-called line-item veto power.

The advisability of a single six-year term for the president has been debated repeatedly. Indeed at one point in the original Constitutional Convention at Philadelphia, a proposal for a single seven-year term for the president was tentatively adopted but later in the debate was rejected. Many presidents and congressional leaders have advocated the change.[5]

The chief purpose of the proposal for a six-year term was to strengthen the prestige of the presidency at home and abroad by making it possible for the president to speak without the suspicion that he is influenced by reelection considerations. The proposal was nonpartisan in nature and was not perceived as a ploy to gain additional power for one branch of government over another. Recently a committee was formed to encourage renewed discussion of the proposal; it is headed by former secretary of state Cyrus Vance, former attorney general Griffin Bell, and myself.

Public statements by my two cochairmen are convincing. From experience they have learned that too much of the president's attention is required to be given to reelection. Too many long-term plans are shunted aside by the short-term considerations of reelection campaigns. Too many times the public perception is that a president is overly influenced by partisan, political reelection considerations. To free the president from these restraints and enable him to speak to the people and to the world unhampered by them is the goal of the amendment.

In Mr. Vance's words:

I have come to the conclusion, after watching it over a number of Presidencies, that we cannot afford to continue the structure we now have. I have come to this conclusion rather sadly and reluctantly because I have believed for a long time that accountability is an important principle and that it was important that the President be held accountable every four years. However, after watching it and thinking about it for a number of years, I have come to the conclusion that the negatives that flow from that structure are outweighed by the positives of a single six-year term.

I do not doubt at all that the single six-year term would add important dimensions of continuity and stability to the conduct of our foreign relations. Seen from the perspective of our friends and allies, as well as from the eyes of our adversaries, we seem to be vulnerable to the vagaries of a foreign policy that is always to some degree affected by the preoccupation with Presidential reelection. The result of this is not only a lack of continuity and stability in our dealings abroad, but also affects domestically how we are perceived in conducting our foreign policy.

The practical fact is that in the last 18 months of the first four-year term, decisions are not made that should be made, and the decisions that are made are affected by the political winds of the moment, which may change at the time of any given primary. During this 18 months Presidents sadly are frightened away from saying what they really think.

Similarly, Griffin Bell has stated:

> Whether or not Horace Greeley was right when he observed that "office-seeking is our national vice," I have been persuaded by my experiences and observations that Presidents would improve their performance if we took away the temptation to seek a second term.
>
> I have devoted most of my professional life to upholding the Constitution, but I have joined in launching a movement to change the Constitution to limit Presidents to a single six-year term because I believe that our chief executive needs to devote more time to governing and less to politicking. The aim of the change is to give our Presidents more of an opportunity to do the job for which we elect them.
>
> These days, it is extremely hard for a President to do a good job; the system is heavily influenced by special interests organized to arrogate power unto themselves. But these interests are not the government, and they do not (in many cases) represent the general interest. Presidents installed to represent all the people should not have to spend substantial portions of every day thinking about these competing interests and calculating how they may affect his reelection.

The objections to the six-year term come mainly from academia: The proposal would free the president from having to listen, at four-year intervals, to the "voice of the people." Other critics argue that, in effect, if we elect a bad president we should not have to live with him for six years instead of four. Another objection is that the president would be a lame duck and unable to lead.

In my experience the pros outweigh the cons. As a firsthand participant in the political process and as a close observer of the presidency, I have been continually struck with how electoral considerations can hamper the president in carrying out the duties of his office. This is especially true today: The high costs of political campaigns make fund-raising almost a constant activity from the moment the president enters office. And the nomination process is now a lengthy one, with candidates now announcing their intentions and mounting elaborate campaigns in key primary and caucus states often several years in advance. One hopes that leaders in the Congress and the executive branch will join in placing this amendment before the people.

An allied question is whether the Constitution should be amended to limit the terms of members of Congress and federal judges. If the proposal to limit the presidency to a single six-year term is seriously considered, I favor extending the debate and research to include these other two areas—perhaps to limit terms of members of the House of Representatives and of senators to an aggregate of twelve years and the tenure of federal judges to age seventy-five. I believe Presidents Jefferson and Madison would have approved such limitations, which would increase the control of "We, the People" over our governing officials.

The second constitutional amendment I favor would give the president the power to veto individual items in an appropriation bill passed by Congress: the so-called line-item veto. Originally, Congress, having the power of the purse, separated the appropriation bills by departments and agencies and sent them to the president seriatim. The president, if he believed such an appropriation bill contained items obtained by logrolling that clearly were not in the public interest, could veto the bill without bringing the government to a halt and send the bill back to Congress for reconsideration. More important, he could dramatize to the country at large in a meaningful way the defects in the bill to which he objected. A national debate, focused on the specific controversial items, would then be possible, and Congress could decide whether to override the veto.

The practice has grown up in Congress, however, of waiting until near the end of the session and placing all the appropriations bills in one package on a "take-it-or-stop-the-government" basis. No reasoned national debate follows. Each branch blames the other, and swollen deficits continue. As a practical matter, the deficit grows and grows, and no one can be targeted as the culprit.

Some presidents have tried to solve the dilemma by impounding the funds appropriated by Congress for specific projects and have simply declined to spend the money. But this presidential action has been successfully challenged by Congress, which is jealous of its "power of the purse." I believe the conflict calls for a constitutional amendment.

Most of the states of the Union have found a solution for this problem. Although this is not a perfect analogy since many of the same state constitutions require a balanced budget, it is instructive. These states give the governor power to veto individual items in an appropriation bill. The legislature can override the veto. But the blame for any action that threatens the financial stability of the state can be pinpointed on the specific controversial items. Any judgment can finally be made at the ballot box on which point of view should prevail.

The proposal for a line-item veto would apply this same process to the federal government. Obviously the proposal needs a new name—a public-relations treatment that will arouse popular sentiment. But the stakes are high. Everyone seemingly recognizes that the continuing federal-budget deficit is our number-one national economic problem, one that handicaps the United States in a stiffly competitive world economy. Neither branch of government would lose if the proposal is adopted. Congress would maintain the power of the purse, for all practical purposes, because it would retain the power to override the president's action, but it would have to do so in light of public debate about individual, controversial items. The president would maintain his veto power, but his actions, too, would have to be taken in the knowledge that public opinion would be focused on particular items. Finally, the budget debates would be reduced to terms understandable to the public.

NOTES

1. I was not the only member of the Brownell family to sponsor a constitutional amendment. A distant relative, Susan Brownell Anthony, sponsored and effectively advocated the women's-suffrage amendment. Her efforts are described in *To Make All Laws* (Washington D.C.: GPO, 1989), the 1989 bicentennial volume of the United States Congress:

> Throughout the 1870s and 1880s [Elizabeth Cady] Stanton and Susan B. Anthony lobbied Congress. In 1878 Senator Aaron Sargent of California rewarded their persistence by introducing what became known as the Anthony Amendment to the Constitution giving women the vote . . . but nothing was accomplished until the First World War. . . . The Senate stood out against the Anthony Amendment until June, when it passed it and sent it to the States, where it was ratified as the Nineteenth Amendment on August 18, 1920. (pp. 69–70)

I only wish we had the memoirs of Susan B. Anthony. I do know she was tried and sent to jail at one point for illegally voting (because she was a woman) before the amendment was passed.

2. I am indebted for a historical description of some of the past presidential illnesses to the work by Kenneth R. Crispell and Carlos F. Gomez, *Hidden Illness in the White House* (Durham, N.C.: Duke University Press, 1988). I recounted some of these cases in an article, "Able to Serve," *Constitution* 1 (1989): 31–37. See also Robert H. Ferrell, *Ill-Advised* (Columbia: University of Missouri Press), 1992.

3. Quoted in Crispell and Gomez, *Hidden Illness in the White House*, p. 121. The authors also disclose that FDR, while president, was treated secretly for medical advice at Bethesda Naval Hospital twenty-nine times under false names.

4. The complete text of the amendment is set forth in appendix E.

5. The presidents include Andrew Jackson, Benjamin Harrison, Grover Cleveland, Rutherford B. Hayes, William H. Taft, Dwight D. Eisenhower, Lyndon B. Johnson, Richard Nixon, and Jimmy Carter. Legislative leaders who have supported the proposal have been Charles Sumner, Henry Clay, Benjamin Wade, William Jennings Bryan, Samuel Tilden, Everett Dirksen, Mike Mansfield, George Aiken, Charles Mathias, Strom Thurmond, and Lloyd Bentsen.

16

Measuring the Man

Eisenhower as President

❖ ❖ ❖ ❖ ❖ ❖ ❖ ❖ ❖ ❖ ❖ ❖ ❖ ❖ ❖

No account of my years as attorney general would be complete without some reflections on the qualities Dwight D. Eisenhower brought to the presidency and on the kind of leadership he exercised in office. They are not neatly captured in the particular episodes I have recounted so far; rather, they form a pattern that must be related as a whole in order to be appreciated.

As I look back on my experience in serving in the Eisenhower administration, I am often struck by the differences between my assessment of it and those analyses one finds in reading various accounts of the period or in discussing it with individuals who did not experience it firsthand. Some commentators held the opinion, before Ike's White House papers were made public, that it was at best an average presidency during a rather undemanding time in our history.

Nothing, in my view, could be further from the truth. The Eisenhower era covered years of great change in response to significant political challenges both in domestic politics and in foreign affairs. In 1953 and 1954, to take merely the first two years, in my own department alone we faced and responded to unprecedented developments in race relations in the aftermath of the Supreme Court's decision in *Brown*, the dilemma of dealing with the problem of internal security, the appointment of a new chief justice that would change the complexion and the direction of the Supreme Court, and the challenges presented by Senators Joe McCarthy and John

Bricker. The list would surely lengthen if one reviewed the rosters of the other cabinet officers and considered the issues they too faced. In foreign affairs, for example, those same two years saw the successful resolution of the Korean War and the arrangement of an acceptable armistice, decisions about whether to bail the French out in Indochina and about effective responses to political instability in Iran and Guatemala, and the beginnings of a new definition of American-Soviet relations in the aftermath of Stalin's death.

Although not marked by the political conflict and turmoil of the 1960s and the Watergate period or the loss in national confidence during the Carter years, the issues before us then were as momentous as any American president has faced, save perhaps for world war or the economic collapse during the Great Depression. I am thus often amused when people pine to go back to the "quiet days" of Eisenhower. At least from our perspective they were quite active.

But those years may have appeared to the public to be a quiet time because of the dignity with which Eisenhower presided over the White House and the respect accorded to him by leaders of the Western world. This seemingly average president rather ingeniously embraced a style of political leadership that made him appear to be a benign figurehead. Yet underneath the benevolent demeanor was a knowledgeable and astute political mind that worked behind the scenes to achieve his political goals and that usually ended up attaining them.

Perhaps key to his success and the style of political leadership that produced it was his recognition that the presidency places upon its occupant two unique roles: serving as a chief of state who is a symbol of national unity and aspiration while also acting as a head of government who must delve into the muddy waters of practical politics and political conflict. Few recent presidents have understood, much less reconciled, these different aspects of the presidency, but Eisenhower did.

Eisenhower had the belief, which I also came to appreciate and share, that he was most effective as president if he maintained his tremendous popularity and support with the public and did not get beaten down by day-to-day political fights. He could rise to a challenge and respond directly and forcefully when the occasion demanded. But his preferred strategy was to be more indirect: operating through others to attain his political goals, delegating authority to his cabinet officers—when he deemed they could be trusted with it—and having them serve as his political front men and lightning rods, and projecting an image of being above the political fray.[1] This approach could be frustrating to those people who might wish the president to mount his "bully pulpit" and actively and directly do political battle, as civil rights activists and critics who opposed Senator McCarthy urged Eisenhower to do and chastised him when he didn't. And it could be politically costly: It required the president at times to be evasive in press conferences and to seem a bit too accommodating to his opponents. It also undoubtedly fed the impression, then commonly held by most of the media and many political notables not in direct contact with him, of a well-meaning but inactive chief executive.

If carried off, however, this mode of exercising presidential leadership could successfully meet the conflicting roles of the office and result in political success. This Eisenhower managed to do, given his strong backing with the public: Almost no one really quarreled when he sent troops to Lebanon, nor did many people seriously question his actions in the offshore-islands crisis in Quemoy and Matsu or in Indochina. Even in the Suez crisis, the most controversial of these incidents, he was able to carry off his policies, which challenged long-standing patterns of cooperation with Britain and of support for Israel. I don't believe a president who was not so instinctively trusted and supported—as was Eisenhower—could have succeeded. It was Eisenhower's genius to understand how that trust and support could be maintained while pursuing political goals that were controversial or that could have been divisive. His technique of governing and the results obtained were thus linked together, and it was a successful linkage.

In retrospect, I notice a parallel between Eisenhower's treatment of the officers under his military command on the battlefield and his handling of cabinet members and other high officials in his administration. To some, e.g., Bradley, Patton, and Montgomery, he allowed maximum autonomy. But he was often angered when they went to the edge of insubordination in exercising that autonomy. He used their distinctive talents to achieve teamwork and success.

During his presidency, the parallel is best exemplified in his management of foreign affairs, where Eisenhower himself was commander-in-chief. Secretary of State Dulles was his chief deputy and trusted adviser. But Dulles was reined in (as Bradley, Patton, and Montgomery had been) by Gen. Bedell Smith, Harold Stassen, Henry Cabot Lodge, George Humphrey, and Arthur Burns, who also had Ike's ear and often prevailed in their specialized fields. Eisenhower would privately express his anger at the mistakes of subordinates (as with Charles Wilson's public-relations gaffes), but he held the loyalty and enthusiasm of these diverse personalities. Even Patton and Montgomery, it will be remembered, while fuming openly at Ike's "mistakes," supported him loyally; they were his comrades to the end but not his cronies. When a president retains in his administration strong-willed individuals who have conflicting views, the media too often interprets such a situation as evidencing a lack of presidential leadership. But the country benefits. Look at Abraham Lincoln's method of dealing with cabinet officers and his generals!

Other strands in Eisenhower's background also played a part in defining his view of the presidency and of ways it might be effectively carried out. He had an intense feeling for and a developed understanding of the structure of American government: a system of divided but shared powers among the three principal branches as well as a delicate balance between federal power on the one hand and the power of state and local governments on the other.

His training at West Point had a lasting influence in impressing upon him the place of the presidency within this constitutionally defined system. Although it was not the sophisticated view of the constitutional scholar, it sufficed to foster an appreciation of the domain of presidential responsibility as distinct from the provinces of the other branches of government. With the former, he would be assertive, as in his recognition of the need to enforce the decisions of the Supreme Court or in his response to foreign-policy crises in the Suez and elsewhere. With the latter, he would be more circumspect, as in the McCarthy episode, recognizing that too heavy a presidential hand would defeat his purposes and set in motion powerful forces of institutional resistance.

This view of the president's place within a constitutional system of government allowed him to understand the rightful roles that the various institutions and political actors occupy in our political system so that he did not overextend the scope of presidential interest across the whole gamut of governmental activities. Moreover, it fostered an understanding for the need to establish a sense of comity with those individuals in the other branches with whom a president must necessarily deal. This is an aspect of presidential leadership quite different from the imperial presidency some of his successors would come to embrace. And when that constitutional balance was under attack, as it was in Little Rock or by the Bricker amendment or by the tactics of Senator McCarthy, he acted. If one could dramatize to him that the constitutional balance was in jeopardy, whether it involved the powers of the presidency, the separation of powers with another branch of government, or the balance of power between the national government and state and local governments, then he would respond affirmatively.

Eisenhower also had a more thorough understanding of practical, day-to-day politics than he has generally been given credit for. At my first meeting with him at the Century Association I was struck by how much he knew about American politics, far beyond what I imagined most members of the military possessed. And this initial impression was confirmed when I met with him at his headquarters in Paris during my visit to encourage him to run for the presidency and he was able to question me in detail on the current state of partisan politics. Eisenhower also was knowledgeable and adept in understanding the folkways and nitty-gritty of congressional politics; his experiences in the military had contributed greatly to this ability. During the 1930s he had served as part of the military's liaison to Capitol Hill. He thus knew the devious ways in which Congress and congressional committees operate and what makes things click there. During his various stints in Washington, he also was in close contact with his brother Milton, who at the time was a high-ranking official in the Department of Agriculture.

Other aspects of his prior military experience served him well. His service in Washington during the 1930s included a stint as an aide to Gen. Douglas MacArthur, which undoubtedly offered important lessons in how to deal with powerful personalities. His leadership skills were apparent in the 1940s when FDR and General Marshall selected him to head the Allied command. His wartime experience added to his bank of skills in dealing with difficult individuals, such as a Montgomery or a de Gaulle. It also incorporated new abilities, such as managing the political complexities of the Allied command and developing an appreciation of the advantages of staff support and the techniques necessary to its effective operation.

His brand of political leadership may have led others mistakenly to underrate him, but Eisenhower's own sense of equanimity and his past accomplishments did not force him into a false posture of deliberately instrumental presidential activism. He knew his reelection was secure and his standing with the public high. He had already established his place in history, and his presidency merely further confirmed that place. Thus he didn't need to take frenetic steps, as have other presidents, simply in order to make his mark on history. The results were indeed important to him; the matter of who received credit less so.

The kinds of individuals whom Eisenhower selected to assist him in governing may also have contributed—ironically, since they were all by and large superb choices and able appointees—to the failure in the 1950s and through the 1960s to appreciate fully his presidency's rather considerable accomplishments. The members of the administration generally were not politicians; they were not ambitious for political advancement and had little desire for public acclaim or higher office. Therefore they did not pay attention to dramatizing their actions or consider the need to get the story of the Eisenhower presidency across to the media and the public. Nor were individuals on the White House staff prone to engage in the kind of court-historian role that was common in the Kennedy administration. Eisenhower was not interested in engaging the services of individuals who, through historical accounts of his presidency or memoirs published in its immediate aftermath, were concerned about promoting their future careers or about settling political scores. Again, we can see differences in comparing recent presidencies: Not only do books about these administrations proliferate, but they often appear while the president is still in office.

I had direct experience with some of the facets of Eisenhower's mode of governance during my tenure as attorney general, especially in the ways he was able to draw effectively on those people around him in carrying out the duties of his office. His use of the cabinet and the National Security Council (NSC) were particularly noteworthy, and they represent one of the few cases among recent administrations of a chief executive who was able to draw productively on the various resources for his decision making offered by the institutional presidency and the executive branch. These deliberative forums not only aided Eisenhower in coming to closure on the decisions before him, but they had more indirect and less obvious effects in building an administration that could work harmoniously and productively without stifling the range of information and advice necessary for sound policy judgments. They embodied lessons about staff planning and administrative management that Eisenhower had learned well before he became president, again unlike most recent occupants of the office, whose prepresidential experiences have not particularly prepared them to deal with the administrative tasks and organizational complexities that are now part of the contemporary presidency.

My experiences in participating in Eisenhower's national-security policy-making system were especially illuminating in this regard. Shortly after I became attorney general, the president invited me to sit with the National Security Council as an observer whenever my duties in the Justice Department would permit it. I already had an ancillary role in the NSC from serving on two subcommittees relating to internal security: One dealt with the domestic activities of the Federal Bureau of Investigation in counterintelligence and the other with combating Communist subversion within the United States. The president's invitation to serve as a nonstatutory member of the NSC thus enabled me to follow the development of national-defense policy from the inside.

The process itself was well-structured and organized. Reports and position papers were developed beforehand by high-level groups of interdepartmental representatives and circulated to the NSC principals. This process enabled members of the NSC to come to its weekly meetings with a solid grounding in the facts, intricacies, and potential ways of resolving the policies at hand and well prepared to discuss relevant issues.

The NSC meetings were usually opened by a report from Allen Dulles, director of the CIA and the brother of the secretary of state. He recounted the latest developments in the trouble spots and potential trouble spots of the world. A discussion of tentative or contingency plans to meet these developments would then ensue. The meetings were lively affairs, with frank and sometimes heated exchanges among the members. On occasion Eisenhower would stand back and let the debate take its course; at other times he would become an active participant. The character of the NSC meetings, however, was a far cry from the impression of them that was fostered by the media, Congress, and academic observers at the time. They did not simply ratify the views contained in the staff work that preceded them: Staff papers almost always included the presentation of opposing views, which would have made simple ratification impossible, and policies that were eventually followed were sometimes developed in the course of the NSC's own discussions. Nor did the NSC process foster a tendency toward "government by committee," as some critics then charged: Eisenhower was never bound by the group's consensus—if any in fact developed—nor did the policies that resulted tend to reflect only those common elements—"lowest common denominator" solutions—on which members agreed. Finally, there was no voting at meetings; the president usually deferred making his own decisions on matters until after the meetings had ended.

In this manner I observed the full story of the Korean armistice, the Quemoy-Matsu near war, and the Suez crisis. Probably the most important contribution I made, for which I would not have been prepared if I hadn't attended NSC meetings, was to assist in the formulation of the Formosa Resolution, which gave the president broad authority from Congress to act militarily as needed in his opinion in the dispute with China over the Quemoy-Matsu Islands. Another contribution was the formulation of my legal opinion on retention of military bases in the Philippines.

Unfortunately, the NSC machinery developed by Eisenhower was dismantled by President Kennedy. I always believed this action was responsible for the haphazard approach in the Kennedy administration to the Bay of Pigs disaster in Cuba and for the muddled, back-and-forth floundering in the Johnson administration over decisions about the Vietnam War.

Eisenhower laid great stress on national-security planning. Thus the members of his team who would be called upon to deal with international crises became accustomed to working with each other. He believed that even if the plans were not used in all particulars when the crisis arose, the very exercise of the methodology of contingency planning was worthwhile. It familiarized those individuals who might be forced to consider policy problems or crises on short notice or under great pressure with the broad strategic course the president was seeking to chart. Such planning enabled those persons involved in the policy process to draw on knowledge and information acquired earlier that would be useful in responding to any immediate and pressing crises at hand.

Like the National Security Council, the cabinet was convened for regular (generally weekly) meetings, with President Eisenhower presiding and taking the leading role. As with the NSC process, deliberation was informed by an orderly and organized set of procedures. An agenda was prepared, approved by the president beforehand, distributed to the cabinet members, and then carefully followed. Written minutes were kept and follow-up memos were sent to the participants to see that action was taken to implement the decisions. These techniques, in my opinion, constituted sound governmental administration.

At the opening of each cabinet meeting a prayer was offered by Ezra Taft Benson, secretary of agriculture, who in later years became the presiding dignitary of the Mormon church. On one particular occasion the president strode into the meeting engaged in animated conversation with Secretary of State Dulles about an international crisis that had erupted. The lively interchange continued for some time after we had all sat down. Suddenly the president stopped and burst out, "Dammit, I forgot the prayer." Even the opening procedure was meticulously followed!

Although particular cabinet meetings might on occasion seem boring or unproductive to members whose interests and responsibilities were more peripheral to the issues under consideration, the meetings—like the NSC—served a number of useful functions for the top members of the administration. They were important, for example, in building a sense of teamwork among members of the president's cabinet. They made us feel part of the president's administration and weaned us away from our natural tendency to see things only from the perspective of our own department. Eisenhower was especially emphatic about this. Time after time he would stress:

> You are not supposed to represent your department, your home state, or anything else. You are *my* advisers. I want you to speak freely and more than that, I would like to have you reflect and comment on what other members of the Cabinet say.

In all candor, I must admit that I did not always obey the letter of the president's instructions. In meetings, I kept my nose generally in Justice Department affairs. And if I had more general comments to make, I would do so privately to the president. Still, it was his preference that differences of views be aired openly. Sometimes this went a bit far, with individuals offering opinions in areas far afield from their responsibilities and especially from their competence and expertise. But for Eisenhower it was a worthwhile practice: There was always the off chance that someone with more peripheral interests might make an important point or suggestion. Cabinet meetings served another useful purpose: Cabinet officers are frequently called upon to represent the administration's point of view and program in speeches and press conferences. The discussions of the cabinet provided an important occasion for informal preparation that would later prove useful for these public presentations.

Eisenhower encouraged teamwork in the cabinet by developing strong personal bonds among us, often in settings outside our regular meetings. He made sure from the start of his presidency—even before it—that we got to know each other well. The preinaugural trip to Korea, for example, was useful not just in preparing for the problem at hand; it also provided the setting for the president to bring us together in preparing his inaugural address and in taking stock of our views on the political agenda he might pursue in the early days of his administration. The trip enabled me to get to know the other cabinet members better, especially since I hadn't worked with any of them before except John Foster Dulles.

The sense of being a part of a team discouraged the kind of political in-fighting that seems characteristic of cabinets in recent administrations. Although we often disagreed with one another, the ethos Eisenhower created among us discouraged jealousy, especially any tendency to leak damaging information about one's fellows to the press. It also encouraged us to see how complicated the problems of the day could be from the other fellow's perspective. Thus we were, I think, less prone to usurp someone else's turf in pursuit of self- or departmental interests.

Eisenhower's techniques extended to members of the White House staff. I experienced few run-ins with staff members, which is apparently not the case with cabinet officers today. Eisenhower made it known that he would support his cabinet members. The only exception was my exclusion from a meeting of some of the southern governors and members of the staff on ways to appease Governor Faubus during the Little Rock crisis. I knew about the meeting, however, and understood that my presence, because of my strong stand on civil rights, might not be productive; there was nothing sneaky about it. As it turned out, the meeting did not lead to any compromise.

My relationship to the White House staff, as a cabinet member, was somewhat unique. Two of the staff members closest to the president were Jim Hagerty, his press secretary, and Tom Stephens, his appointments secretary. I had known both of them as far back as the 1930s when I was a member of the New York State Assembly—Hagerty (and his father) represented the *New York Times* in covering Albany, and Stephens was on my legislative staff. We had worked together during the Dewey years and in Eisenhower's first campaign for the presidency. I recommended both men for staff positions when Ike returned from Europe to run for office. We called each other for news and advice regularly—especially in times of crisis such as the Little Rock affair. There never was a hint of rivalry between my department and the White House staff principally because of the president's policy of strong support for his cabinet officers. Ann Whitman, the president's personal secretary who contributed so much to Ike's presidency, was especially skilled in promotion of liaison with the cabinet and with friends of the president outside Washington.

One would be hard put to find a better example of a president who had such good relationships with his cabinet officers (and the cabinet among themselves). Eisenhower's leadership in this instance was largely unspoken because he was a man of few words; he was not a flatterer. But he had the ability to draw different types of individuals to him and to elicit their best. He could listen to an Arthur Burns as well as to a George Humphrey, to a Stassen as well as to a Dulles. He also took a paternal interest in us. When he told Nixon that he might think about becoming secretary of defense rather than running again for vice-president, it was not to get Nixon off the ticket but to further round out Nixon's political experience and eventual preparation for the presidency. He thus had almost a fatherly interest in us, his "young people," so that we would be able to lead the Republican party and the nation.

Eisenhower did more through his approach not only in getting a range of advice but also in educating members of his administration. I found this especially beneficial because I was exposed to a range of foreign policy and domestic issues that my legal experience had not encompassed. Participation in the cabinet and in NSC meetings formed a sort of school for me; I was learning all the time. I had never had much to do with foreign affairs, for example; I had never heard of contingency plans, spying activities, covert operations, discussions of strategy in dealing with foreign leaders, and so on. I was an open-eyed student of government in this situation, learned a great deal, and was appreciative that Eisenhower was giving me the opportunity to do so.

But he may not have learned too much from us. In the two-thirds of his job dealing with foreign and military affairs he knew more than all of us put together. He might learn something from Interior Secretary Douglas McKay about running the national parks or from me about the operations of the legal system. But these pieces of information were rather minor. In short, he was so completely "the Boss" that I can't help but be amused when I read or recall the criticisms from that time that he wasn't in charge of the government.

Eisenhower's style may have contributed to some of this misperception because unlike other presidents he had no need to show off or to demonstrate his knowledge and expertise. He operated more like a judge who may know the outcome of the case and his eventual decision but who would patiently listen to the evidence and the testimony in the belief that something unanticipated might come up.

He delegated a great deal to his cabinet officers: They were the ones, in his view, who were on the front lines, taking the blows. If they were successful, fine, but if they faltered, he would get someone else. I discussed this with him on a number of occasions, and he articulated this view to me. In my own case, it meant I was given responsibility and authority in a number of controversial areas such as civil rights, antitrust, and internal security, all of which were likely to be divisive. It was wise for him to appear a bit distanced from day-to-day events to maintain his public support, which I feel is necessary for a successful presidency. Of course, he exercised control behind the scenes. There was never any doubt in the Eisenhower administration about who was in charge and who made the decisions: The president did.

The Little Rock, McCarthy, and Bricker episodes highlight my experience with his techniques in delegating broad authority to his cabinet officers to use their own initiative in carrying out his basic program. If they did not bring to his attention matters that required it, he was severe. But if they "passed the buck" to the president for front-line decisions, he equally disapproved. Two additional illustrations come to mind.

One of my first reports to him in my official capacity dealt with his presidential power to grant pardons. He had delegated to me the onerous duty of reviewing and recommending the disposition of pardon applications, first from civilians who had been convicted of violations of federal law, and second from military personnel sentenced to death under military law. I prepared diligently my first list of recommendations and, in the Oval Office, started to recite the facts of each case in my best lawyerly fashion. He interrupted after ten minutes or so, saying, "What are you doing reciting these details to me? Give me your recommendations and I'll approve them." Then as I turned to leave, he added, "But remember, you and I have initiated a policy of making these pardon actions open to the public. If anything proves to be misrepresented or incomplete about these cases, it's your responsibility." I knew if I made mistakes, I was dispensable.

On another occasion, I observed that a fellow cabinet officer presented to the president a program to renovate and improve the national parks, remarking that the program should have been instituted a couple of years earlier. The president blew up at that point, saying the job to manage the park system had been delegated to the cabinet officer—that this was the first time he, the president, had been told of the need—and it was the fault of the cabinet officer that the proposed park program hadn't been brought to his attention and instituted in a timely manner.

But delegation did not mean presidential disinterest. Even the briefest account of my years at the Justice Department would be incomplete without a recital of the great interest and encouragement given to us by President Eisenhower personally. He attended the annual dinners of the "little cabinet," the group of assistant attorneys general and their wives, and always expressed appreciation for our work. He arranged for us to hold one of our annual retreats to plan for the coming year at his quarters at Camp David. He supported the professional upgrading of the caliber of our attorneys by providing increased salaries in the department. Each year the president invited a number of us in the Justice Department to the White House when he and Mrs. Eisenhower entertained the Supreme Court. He would take us through the second-floor living quarters in a most informal manner and show us the Lincoln bedroom and the room where Winston Churchill stayed. During the course of the evening he would relate many historic tidbits about the lives of his predecessors in the White House.

More substantively, he kept in touch with the important cases being handled by my assistants to the point that he could inquire about the cases when he met with them. For example, on one occasion he asked about the details of our antitrust prosecution of Eastman Kodak for monopolizing the color-photography market—not as president but as an avid photographer who wanted to be reassured that our lawsuit would not result in lowering the quality of processing color film.

These personal contacts, over and above our official relationships, were a major factor in overcoming the rigors of public life. And as every cabinet secretary and ex-cabinet secretary will testify, when the media and "official Washington" know that one has the president's endorsement and friendship, it becomes much easier to ward off attacks and to accomplish one's goals.

I am often asked whether Eisenhower wanted to replace Nixon as vice-president for his second term. Ike called me into the Oval Office just a few days before the 1956 Republican National Convention at San Francisco. He had not before, and did not then, tell me of the talks he had had with other advisers about the second-term vice-presidency since he knew from our previous discussions that I did not want to engage in political activity while I was attorney general. On this occasion, however, he solicited my advice and told me he wanted me to go out to San Francisco right away and "do for me what you did for me at the '52 convention." I asked if he had any instructions, and he replied with a question: "What shall I do about the fight between Stassen and Nixon?" I replied that I thought Nixon would be the convention's choice, unless Eisenhower was prepared to "dump" Nixon. If he accepted Nixon, he should call in Stassen for a conference as soon as he arrived in San Francisco and tell Stassen he wanted him to second Nixon's nomination for vice-president. This would eliminate the possibility of a floor fight between followers of the two contenders. Eisenhower did what I had advised him to do, and the storm over Nixon's renomination quickly blew over.

During the 1956 convention, I also acted as intermediary between the president and the Platform Committee on the civil rights plank. Otherwise I merely observed the smooth running of the convention by the Republican National Committee, which was a pleasant respite from my usual frenzied activities at conventions in the past. I also had the opportunity to address the convention on the accomplishments of the Justice Department during my tenure as attorney general. Members of my family were in the audience, and my wife and daughters, Joan and Ann, took an active part in the 1956 presidential campaign.

Another facet of Eisenhower's mode of soliciting counsel on the weighty issues of the day—apart from reliance on formal bodies like the NSC or the cabinet—was his proclivity to tap a number of outside channels in search of timely information and advice. In fact, sometimes after receiving a telephone call from the president with some request, I would often play a game with members of my staff who happened to be in my office. Each of us would try to figure out which one of his friends he had been talking to or corresponding with that had prompted his attention on the matter.

Eisenhower's contacts with a wide range of informal sources, often outside government, were even more extensive than I realized at the time. Since his papers have been opened, for example, I have discovered a number of matters affecting the Justice Department about which he corresponded with his friends and that I knew nothing about. Comments on important issues abound in his private letters. Moreover, they were beautifully written and elaborately reasoned, a far cry from the perception that then existed of a president more concerned with the finer points of his golf game than with the pressing policy issues of the day.

John McCloy, a "wise man" to a number of postwar presidents, once told me how amazed he was by the difference between Eisenhower's erudition on paper and his failure to be articulate, on occasion, in press conferences. It is my view that some of Eisenhower's inarticulateness in press conferences may have been deliberate: an attempt to muddy the media's waters with confusing syntax and jumbled logic. In person, Eisenhower was articulate in stating his views and strong and forceful in his opinions, and he could write in such a way as to get at the heart of the problem extremely well.

We have never had an example of an individual who had so little to gain by being president, including perhaps not even George Washington. Eisenhower enjoyed great fulfillment at that point in his life; a poor boy who was now well off, a popular hero in this country and abroad, he had a wide network of influential friends. I suspect that he would say from his grave that his greatest days were during World War II rather than as president because wartime had proved more challenging to him and perhaps historically was of greater consequence.

In fact, I believe that he would not even have sought the presidency if Taft had been agreeable to pursuing Eisenhower's internationalist program in foreign policy. He would have been just as happy if Taft had accepted his views and carried through with them. But when Eisenhower saw what the situation was—that if Taft became the nominee the efforts he had devoted his mature life to were in jeopardy—it became a duty for him to seek the presidency.

Eisenhower sometimes held back his real opinions on issues. He would express these views in letters to his personal friends, I later learned, but did not share them with me at the time. I think we would have had an easier working relationship if I had known where he stood on some of the more controversial issues I dealt with as attorney general. It was my sense that he felt that if he talked to me about some pressing problem he himself should have an answer, which he sometimes did not have. So he hesitated on occasion to talk individually to a cabinet member when he was uncertain.

I would have liked to discuss the McCarthy problem or civil rights with him in more detail, for example. He evidently talked over such issues with other people, such as his brother Milton, and I would have to approach Milton to find out what Ike's thinking was. Thus, at times I was left a bit in the dark about his true feelings.

Even if he was disturbed about something I was doing—and I think he was at times, especially in civil rights—his seeming distance allowed me an area of discretion, which I appreciated. It permitted me to put my skills and expertise to work for the administration. I also suspect that he knew I was soon to leave as attorney general, so I think he didn't feel a need to consult with me over his decision to scuttle section three of the Civil Rights Act.

At times, his techniques of delegation put us out on the proverbial limb. Other cabinet members and I became the point men identified with and responsible for policies that were actually the president's. As he once told Jim Hagerty, who had to face a hostile press with some bit of unwelcome news, "Better you, Jim, than me." Eisenhower's reluctance to associate himself with difficult policy decisions sometimes made it a little harder for us to do our jobs. I was, for example, a bit too vulnerable politically than I would have preferred to be in the Harry Dexter White affair and in the political battles over the Civil Rights Act of 1957.

But I also understood, as in the negotiations over the civil rights bill, his need to compromise with the Democrats on Capitol Hill, who controlled Congress during six of his eight years as president, or, in the McCarthy case, his disinclination to do direct battle with the Old Guard of the Republican party who were influential among the Senate's leadership. Had Eisenhower been more aggressive and forward in identifying himself with controversial policies, he might have weakened his ability to strike a bargain later down the road, and, especially, he might have compromised one of the high cards he could play in partisan battles: appearing to be above the political fray.

There is one interesting character trait of his that few observers, even those of recent years who have had access to his presidential papers, have noticed: Few of us who served in Eisenhower's administration became his intimate companions. He chose his circle of personal friends almost exclusively from outside government. After he left the White House, there were few occasions when we reminisced about our years in Washington together. We had a long telephone conversation about a book that appeared in the early 1960s on the Civil Rights Act of 1957, and on another occasion I traveled to Gettysburg for lunch with him. But there was little of the hashing over of old times that I suspect other former presidents, such as Truman, engaged in with their old associates in government or that I was to enjoy with Tom Dewey once I had returned to my private law practice. I was not alone in my experience: Jim Hagerty, his trusted press secretary who later became an executive with the American Broadcasting Corporation, didn't have much contact with Eisenhower in the Gettysburg years, nor did George Humphrey, who was Eisenhower's frequent host at his plantation in Georgia when he was serving as secretary of the treasury. Perhaps the parallel to his generals in World War II is again appropriate: They were comrades in arms but not cronies; the same was true for us who served his presidency.

Eisenhower was also a bit of an amateur in handling the Republican party. He could inspire it in certain ways, especially in encouraging the participation of women and young people, but he couldn't deal well with party officials, as Dewey could. Both Len Hall and Meade Alcorn, who served as the chairmen of the party during his presidency, came to me in despair. On one occasion, for example, Hall was incredulous that Eisenhower had raised the issue of whether his brother Milton might be suitable as the vice-presidential nominee in 1956.

These are minor faults, however, in a leadership style that has yet to be replicated in its success. Considering the vast responsibility of the presidency, I liked Eisenhower's technique of governing. I liked the autonomy for members of the cabinet that went with it. I liked the opportunity to turn broad policy and theories of government into solutions. I liked the challenge to use my initiative and to be an activist in the office of attorney general.

Above all, Eisenhower accomplished the goals that impelled him to run for president as he had stated them to me at our conference at his headquarters near Paris in spring 1952. He obtained a lasting bipartisan internationalist approach to world affairs. In following that course, he turned the national leadership of the Republican party away from isolationism. In Europe, he strengthened NATO and brought Chancellor Adenauer and West Germany into close collaboration with the World War II Allies. In Asia, he stopped the Korean War and protected Japan and our other Asian allies while preventing war over the Quemoy and Matsu islands. He encouraged Europeans who were oppressed by the USSR to consider the United States as favoring their eventual freedom while avoiding war. For example, in 1956 he authorized Hungarian refugees, when Soviet tanks rolled into Budapest, to enter the United States, an action that the Justice Department facilitated in a key ruling on the legality of the president's move. In his "atoms for peace" and "open skies" proposals he laid the groundwork for later international cooperation on a global scale. In his farewell address, his warning against the excesses of the military-industrial complex served as an important admonition to the nation from a president who could speak with authority and from unmatched experience.

Thus, at the conclusion as at the beginning of the Eisenhower years, "I Liked Ike," and so did a constant majority of the people of the United States.

NOTES

1. These aspects of Eisenhower's leadership style have been best captured by Fred I. Greenstein, *The Hidden-Hand Presidency: Eisenhower as Leader* (New York: Basic Books), 1982.

17

Further Serving the Presidency

Nixon, Ford, Carter, and Reagan

❖ ❖ ❖ ❖ ❖ ❖ ❖ ❖ ❖ ❖ ❖ ❖ ❖ ❖ ❖

My departure from the Department of Justice in late 1957 was not to be the end of my governmental service. Although I have not returned to Washington for any prolonged period of time, the years since then have provided a number of opportunities to serve the president and the nation, which I have willingly accepted and eagerly undertaken.

One of the strengths of our system of government is the number of possibilities that it offers for private citizens to take on such assignments. Unlike European democracies with their entrenched bureaucracies, the American policy process readily permits persons such as myself who have had governmental and other political experience, as well as those individuals who may be serving in an official capacity for the first time, to offer their competence and expertise in solving some of the difficult national issues before us. This relative permeability of our system allows new ideas and fresh perspectives to enter on-going political debate, and it provides new energy in carrying out existing policies and programs. In my own case, it enabled me to become acquainted with and to observe the political minds and skills of one former president—Herbert Hoover—and four sitting presidents—Richard Nixon, Gerald Ford, Jimmy Carter, and Ronald Reagan. In each instance, I have watched with fascination the evolution of the American presidency and the presidents who have played a major role in it.

My first opportunity to see another president besides Eisenhower in action actually occurred during my tenure as attorney general. In 1953 Eisenhower named me as one of his two appointees to the bipartisan Second Hoover Commission on the Reorganization of the Executive Branch of the Government. Other prominent members of the commission were former Ambassador Joseph P. Kennedy and former Postmaster General James Farley, both Democrats. I specialized in studies of the proper place and function of lawyers in the executive branch and of the legal safeguards for administrative hearings.

On one occasion during the commission's meetings, I told Hoover I was seeking to locate some government documents to support a claim being prosecuted by the Justice Department relating to a dispute over water rights between some of the western states and the federal government. The controversy had originated during Hoover's tenure as secretary of commerce, when he had served as chairman of the Colorado River Basin Commission. Did he have any idea where a particular set of the commission's minutes could be located? Our extensive search had proved futile, and our claim was in jeopardy as a result. "I have them in my office," he said, with a twinkle in his eye, "but I wasn't going to hand them over to a damn New Dealer—you can have them anytime." This was a flashback, I concluded, to his resentment over the personal vilification he had experienced from the New Deal leaders in his campaign for reelection in 1932 and from petty attacks on him such as the changing of the name of the Hoover Dam on the Colorado River.

Hoover handed the documents over to me, and they turned out to be of decisive importance to the federal government's position, especially in showing the intent of a compact between the states and the federal government then under consideration. As usual, Hoover had done a thorough job and anticipated from the minutes what some of the major problems of interpretation would be. He performed a major service in seeing that the compact was properly interpreted along the lines that he had originally conceived.

Hoover presided over the Hoover Commission meetings with dignity and obtained the cooperation of the Democratic members. I came to know both Kennedy and Farley rather well. On one occasion, I invited Ambassador Kennedy, who had served under FDR both as our representative at the Court of St. James's and as chairman of the newly formed Securities and Exchange Commission, to speak at a small luncheon of my assistant attorneys general at the Justice Department. We were new in Washington and anxious to hear from a veteran on the political scene. "If you want to get along in Washington," he told us, "never let the sun go down unless you have dined with a senator, a congressman and a newspaper man."

I had known Jim Farley back in the days when he was chairman of the Democratic National Committee under FDR and I was a Republican member of the New York Assembly. I had tangled with him when he marched onto the floor of the assembly (not being a member) and issued orders to the Democratic members about voting on a highly political measure that was under consideration. Years after that, he had fallen out with FDR (as had Joe Kennedy), and the political philosophy of both men at this time was much nearer that of Herbert Hoover than of Franklin D. Roosevelt.

Unlike the First Hoover Commission, which Congress had established during the Truman years and which led to a number of important and needed changes in the organization of the presidency and the executive branch, many of the recommendations of the Second Hoover Commission were focused on the substance of public policy rather than on governmental procedures. Hoover's second effort sometimes had the character of turning the clock back to the pre–New Deal days, which was clearly out of synch with the national mood as well as with President Eisenhower's own aims; but much of it was quite progressive, hardly in line with the characterization of Hoover by the media as an unreconstructed ultraconservative.

The Second Hoover Commission, however, had been somewhat forced upon the president by conservative Republicans in Congress; Eisenhower even delayed some six months in naming the administration's representatives on the commission. He preferred to rely for advice on his own, in-house President's Advisory Commission for Governmental Organization (PACGO), headed by Nelson Rockefeller and with two trusted associates—Milton Eisenhower, the president's brother, and Arthur Flemming—as its other principal members. Thus, it came as no surprise that when the reforms advocated by the Second Hoover Commission were submitted to Congress, many of them were not acted upon; after the 1954 elections, the Democrats once again controlled Congress, and the White House was not particularly receptive to some of the more conservative recommendations that a majority of the commission favored.

Hoover's personal dedication to the purpose of the commission was impressive, however. He worked long, hard hours and even begrudged every minute we took out for a sandwich and coffee in the middle of our all-day sessions because in his view we weren't getting anything constructive done. We used to joke with him a little about it, and he would laugh, but he would go right on with business during lunch. His knowledge of the workings of government was particularly impressive, and he knew as much as any of the experts we called upon to testify. He also established great rapport with the commission's members, especially Joe Kennedy and Jim Farley, who had once been his political opponents but who now generally saw eye-to-eye with him on matters of public policy and government operations.

Perhaps my most interesting international mission, at least from a lawyer's standpoint, also occurred while I was still in office as attorney general. The American Bar Association held its convention in London in 1955, and Chief Justice Earl Warren and I were invited to speak. The Warrens and the Brownells, with David Maxwell, president of the American Bar Association, and his wife, went by ship to Southampton. Our sons Tom and Jim joined friends at the Cunard pier to give us a typical New York going-away party on the huge transatlantic liner—flowers, candy, and liquor. Our speeches were delivered at Westminster Hall. Surrounding us on the speaking platform were the bewigged judges of the British courts and the representatives of the British bar. I collaborated with Assistant Attorney General Rankin on a speech on the need for the rule of law in international affairs:

> What we need is the development of the law of nations in our age which will first bind the countries of the world into solemn voluntary pacts governing their great interests on the world scene, in contrast to unilateral exploitations by the mighty. . . . We must perfect a machinery for settlement of international disputes—not now and then or occasionally but on a total basis—under a tribunal or system of tribunals which will command general confidence as to the fairness of their judgments and whose procedures will be supported by a public opinion which will not tolerate a departure from them. We must establish an era where nations as well as individuals are subject to justice under law.

After attending the Queen's Garden Party and various other delightful social events, we American lawyers turned back our rented morning coats and top hats to Moss Brothers, the famous clothiers. We attended an impressive commemorative ceremony at Runnymede, the site of Magna

Carta. Then the chief justice and I journeyed to Dublin where we received honorary degrees from the university at the hands of President Eamon DeValera, the great Irish patriot. We stayed with the president of Ireland and his wife in their mansion and were captivated by their stories of their participation in the fight for freedom of their country.

As an aftermath, when I returned to Washington Secretary of State Dulles asked me to come to his office. He was upset by the content of my speech at Westminster Hall and thought it was at variance with his policies. He thought foreign affairs should be handled by diplomats—that international courts were an inappropriate forum for settlement of international disputes. It was the only policy disagreement I had with him during the time we were in the cabinet together.[1]

On several other occasions I was appointed to represent our government at international events. When the City of Quebec celebrated in 1958 the 350th anniversary of its founding by the explorer Champlain, representatives of France, Great Britain, and the United States were invited to participate, and President Eisenhower appointed me as the U.S. representative. We were royally entertained. When the time for speech making arrived I discovered that I was the only one who would not be delivering his speech in French. But the Canadian prime minister, John Diefenbaker, comforted me by relating a story from his political past. It seems that after being successful in his election as premier of his native province, he aspired to national office. He was told that he must first learn to speak in French, so he assiduously applied himself to learning it. After considerable study, his teacher told him he was proficient enough to try out his skill at a public meeting in Quebec. His teacher accompanied him to the great event and was told to check around the audience for its reaction. Immediately after his closing remarks, Diefenbaker queried his teacher, who reported that two little old French ladies in the audience listened intently, and one said to the other, "Wasn't that awful!" The other replied, "If you think that was bad, you ought to hear him in English." I didn't risk my French, and the audience was most polite.

My next international assignment would not occur until the next Republican administration, that of Richard Nixon. My job was to represent the United States at the inauguration of Juan Peron as president of Argentina, along with the inauguration of Isabella Peron, his second wife, as vice-president (Peron's first wife, Evita, had also held the office during part of his first stint as president of Argentina from 1945 to 1955). We were housed at the U.S. embassy as guests of Ambassador and Mrs. John Davis Lodge. At the inauguration ceremonies, I was seated next to the ambassador from a Central American country who was more familiar with Argentine history than I. Juan Peron walked onto the inauguration platform, bedecked with his Argentine military decorations from the past, and received the plaudits of the crowd. My friendly neighbor leaned over to me and said, "You remember history, don't you? Juan Peron was driven from office by the military, who deprived him of his decorations. He escaped to Panama where he discovered Isabella in a Panama night club, where she was a dancer. Now that the general is back, in his old costume with Argentine medals, I wonder if his wife will appear for her inauguration in her old costume." But my irreverent friend applauded loudly when the new vice-president made her appearance in proper inaugural regalia.

The Nixon years also saw my first major substantive assignment by a president in the post-Eisenhower years. In the early 1990s, the largest water desalting plant in the world is scheduled to be opened at Yuma, Arizona. This event will be the culmination of my first venture into the slippery arena of international diplomacy. It followed from my appointment as special ambassador to Mexico by President Nixon.

My experience in the Justice Department in the field of conservation of natural resources, notably in the bitter litigation between the western states and the federal government over the water rights from the rivers in the West, was the background for this assignment. In one such lawsuit, which later culminated in the landmark case of *Arizona v. California*,[2] the federal government sought to protect the water rights of the Indian tribes and of federally sponsored recreation areas. Congressmen from some of the western states demanded of President Eisenhower that he order me to remove the attorney I had designated to uphold these rights because the attorney was too zealously guarding federal rights. The president upheld my decision, however, and eventually the Supreme Court sustained our position.

The dispute I was now called upon to settle grew out of a 1944 water treaty with Mexico. The treaty guaranteed an annual allotment to Mexico of a fixed quantity of water from the Colorado River, regardless of the amount of rainfall in the upper watershed of the Colorado River in the United States. This was of vital importance to the seven Colorado River basin states in this country. They opposed any enlargement of Mexico's allotment or any restrictions on irrigation north of the border. These seven states worked closely together, in and out of Congress, to make their voice heard by the federal government.

In June 1972 President Luis Alvarez Echeverria of Mexico had protested to President Nixon and to a joint session of the U.S. Congress that the high levels of salinity in the waters of the Colorado River delivered to Mexico under the treaty were damaging Mexico's irrigated crops. This salinity was caused by the increasing use of river waters for irrigation by American farmers upstream. The return reflows to the river from our irrigated lands carried with them the salts of the soil; the more irrigation in the United States, the more saline was the water delivered to Mexico.

Our treaty with Mexico did not mention the quality of the water to be delivered. But Mexico claimed that "water" meant water usable for agricultural purposes—not sludge. President Echeverria identified the problem as the most serious issue to come between the United States and Mexico in many years. At home he was faced with extreme dissatisfaction and electoral revolt by the farmers in the Mexicali Valley.

Even before Echeverria's protestations, President Kennedy and President Lopez Mateos had met twice in attempts to solve the dispute. They arranged to have a panel of U.S. scientists selected by the secretary of the interior to meet with a panel of Mexican scientists, but the joint panel was unable to agree on a joint report. Later in 1971, U.S. Department of State negotiators met with their counterparts from the Foreign Relations Department of Mexico, but the negotiations had broken down. Efforts by the permanent International Boundary and Water Commission of the two countries resulted in a slight reduction in salinity, but these attempts were not acceptable to Mexico.

With this impasse, the outlook for agreement was anything but encouraging. President Echeverria named Foreign Secretary Emilio Rabasa and Hydraulic Resources Secretary Leandro Rovirosa from his cabinet to meet with me to reach the "early, definitive agreement" envisioned by him and President Nixon.

Dramatizing the diverse technical and political problems involved, President Nixon set up an interagency advisory task force of representatives from the Departments of State, Interior, and Agriculture, the International Boundary Commission, the Army Corps of Engineers, the Environmental Protection Agency, the Council on Environmental Quality, the President's Office of Science and Technology, the Office of Management and Budget, and the president's Domestic Council. It was quite a cast of characters.

For several months I met weekly with the task force. By plane we examined the terrain of the Colorado River from its source in the north to the Mexican border. We stopped along the way to inspect several critical areas, such as the Wellton-Mohawk irrigation district and the Imperial Valley. We visited, too, the Mexicali Valley in Mexico with agricultural and irrigation technicians and met with the governor of Baja California and local officials in the area most directly concerned with crop devastation in irrigated lands.

It soon developed that before an agreement with Mexico was possible, we needed a united position from the United States. The western states had formed a Committee of Fourteen, two representatives from each of the seven basin states, to present their views. I met with them on a number of occasions as well as with Gov. John A. Love of Colorado and Gov. John R. Williams of Arizona. I pointed out that if no solution was found in the near future the United States would almost certainly be faced with a case brought by Mexico before an international tribunal or an international arbitration panel. The results of such a case were problematic but might be quite adverse to the status quo they sought to defend.

Testimony from witnesses at task-force meetings gave us an overview of the technical problems that we faced. The scientists gave us a picture of the various methods used around the world to combat problems of salinity as well as methods (such as solar and geophysical heating) being tested in university laboratories and industrial plants to reduce salinity resulting from irrigation.

We then journeyed to Mexico City for conferences with President Echeverria, Foreign Secretary Rabasa, and Secretary Rovirosa and in these meetings reduced the possible solutions to a small number. The State Department's representative, Sam Eaton, was a most practical and diplomatic adviser and was extremely helpful to me at every stage of the proceedings. Joseph Friedkin of the Boundary Commission also aided our efforts in a most constructive way.

Finally, I decided that the most practical conclusion was to have the United States agree to construct at its own expense a desalting plant near the border to reduce the salinity of the river waters at the international boundary to a point acceptable to Mexico. This solution would be expensive, but it would make unnecessary any new restrictions on irrigation in the United States and would result in improving the quality of the water guaranteed to Mexico so that it would be acceptable for agricultural use.

In a tense conversation with Secretary Rabasa, while he and I were together pacing up and down the grounds of the meeting hall where we had gathered for a do-or-die session, the two of us finally agreed on all remaining points at issue. The world's largest desalting plant was to be built, and, it was hoped, would become a model for desert areas in the Middle East and elsewhere faced with a salinity problem in connection with their water supplies. The Committee of Fourteen agreed to support this solution in Congress.

I flew to California to submit my final report to President Nixon. He was by that time in the midst of his Watergate problems and the pending resignation of Vice-president Spiro Agnew but gave his approval to our report. The formal agreement with Mexico shortly followed. I then testified before Congress, which authorized and directed the secretary of the interior to build the desalting plant near Yuma, Arizona, as needed to carry out the agreement.[3]

As a midwesterner born on the banks of the Missouri River, I was always intrigued by stories of the Lewis and Clark expedition. These two explorers, by appointment of President Thomas Jefferson, were sent to map and reconnoiter the great new West that had been added to the United States as a result of the Louisiana Purchase. They traveled the length of the Missouri River and kept a day-by-day diary of their adventures. Their diary is one of the great stories of the opening of the West by settlers from the East.

For many years pages from the diary covering several days of the trip were missing; a valuable historic document was thus incomplete. One day Assistant Attorney General Rankin reported to me that there was a case pending in the department involving the lost pages. It appeared that a descendant of one of the explorers had found the missing papers in the attic of her home and claimed ownership. The federal government's position was that they were official documents, being the report made by Lewis and Clark to President Jefferson at the conclusion of their journey up the Missouri and back, and therefore belonged to the government. The descendant won in court but, happily for all concerned, agreed to turn the papers over to the Minnesota State Historical Society.

This case was very much on my mind when I was asked by President Ford in 1975 to be chairman of the National Study Commission on Records and Documents of Federal Officials. The study had been authorized by Congress as a result of the dispute over the ownership of papers that President Nixon wanted to take with him when he left the White House, as his predecessors had done before him. In September 1974, shortly after leaving office, Nixon had entered into an agreement with Arthur Sampson of the General Services Administration giving Nixon the right, among others, to destroy the infamous White House tapes and to take from federal custody any papers that Nixon chose to withdraw within a period of three years.

The Nixon-Sampson agreement proved controversial when news of it became public. Congress responded almost immediately by passing the Presidential Records and Materials Preservation Act in December 1974. Title I of the act voided the Nixon-Sampson agreement; Title II authorized President Ford to establish the National Commission to investigate the issues raised by the controversy and to make appropriate recommendations. The study, moreover, was to involve not only papers originating in the executive branch but also in the legislative and judicial branches. No such study had been made before in this country although some studies had previously been made by the British government concerning its diplomatic files.

President George Washington, when he left office, took his accumulated papers to his home in Mount Vernon. Indeed, he had good reason to do so because the government did not provide a place for the papers to be stored. Subsequent presidents followed Washington's example in removing papers at the end of their term of office. Some of the early private collections were preserved; others have been scattered to the four winds. Some papers were sold and others presented as gifts to friends, autograph seekers, and, more recently, institutions. Some were deliberately destroyed, and others fell victim to chance destruction. Many were passed on by will or intestacy to family members or literary executors.

There is no evidence of the government's laying claim to the papers removed by a president until the Nixon case. Indeed in 1924, when members of the White House staff discovered additional Taft, Wilson, and Harding papers in the attic of the White House, they were sent away to be added to the collections of those presidents and were subjected to the same private control-and-access restrictions as the existing collections. Congress from time to time showed an awareness of the historical value of certain of the collections and on several occasions appropriated funds for the purchase of privately held presidential collections, including those of Washington, Jefferson, Madison, and Monroe. But there was little governmental regulation of these valuable records.

A general absence of concern over the ownership of presidential papers is in part understandable: The presidency was largely a personal office, with only a handful of secretaries and assistants, until the days of Franklin Roosevelt. The White House staff as we know it today simply did not exist in any recognizable form. Presidents often hired relatives to fill the few staff positions that did exist in the nineteenth and early twentieth centuries, with these individuals serving as personal aides rather than as the policymakers we are familiar with today. The presidency did not have an institutional capacity as did the State Department or the old War Department, and therefore it did not develop facilities or procedures for creating an ongoing record. This absence of institutional continuity inhibited the development of any clear distinctions between the purely personal and the public papers in the office of the president. It was not until 1897 that one of the biggest problems, the lack of a suitable repository owned by the government, was partially solved when the Library of Congress' manuscript division was established. Theodore Roosevelt and William Howard Taft, both avid record keepers, made arrangements to take advantage of the library's custody of presidential collections, although they placed the control of their papers in their heirs. Mrs. Wilson likewise placed Woodrow Wilson's voluminous papers in custody of the library.

Franklin D. Roosevelt was the first president to establish a presidential library, which was built with private funds in Hyde Park, New York. He arranged to deposit his presidential and personal papers in the library and appointed a private committee to screen the papers. He provided that certain categories of papers should never be made public and others were to be made public from time to time over a period according to the discretion of the committee. Every president since that time, through the use of private funds, has built a presidential library or has announced that he intends to make similar provision for his papers and records.

Under the Presidential Libraries Act of 1955, the federal government may receive gifts of presidential papers and related materials, whether public or personal, and thereafter staffs and maintains the libraries at government expense. The papers and records of the members of Congress and of the United States Supreme Court, by contrast, have uniformly been treated as their private property.

After considering the welter of conflicting rules, or absence of rules, relating to the ownership of, access to, and disposition of records and papers developed by federal officials, the commission took testimony from officeholders and former officeholders of the federal government. We also heard the views of historians, political scientists, representatives of the media, lawyers, and judges as to the desirability of establishing by law the status of these papers and records.

The commission soon reached the decision that there was no constitutional bar to legislation making the official papers and documents of all federal officials public property. It found no sufficient reason to differentiate between the three branches of government and their officials in this regard. It unanimously recommended that Congress enact a statute providing that all documentary materials made or received by federal officials in connection with their constitutional and statutory duties (other than personal papers) should be the property of the United States.

A split developed in the commission as to whether publicly owned documentary materials, for purposes of access, should be governed by the Freedom of Information Act, which presently applies only to certain agencies in the executive branch of the government. The majority of the commission—fifteen of its seventeen members—held the opinion that the public should have access to federal records and public papers but only "at the earliest feasible time." It recommended, however, that the Freedom of Information Act should not apply to "confidential communications between an official and his staff; conference notes; and various other materials found in presidential papers, the office files of members of Congress, and the chamber files of judges." It also recommended that because of the sensitive nature of these documents, access to them could be limited by the officials who accumulated them for a period not to exceed fifteen years after the end of government service, provided, however, they should not be exempt from access according to due process of law when required for purposes of the criminal or civil justice systems or for impeachment. The majority recommended that at the end of the fifteen-year period Congress establish a mechanism similar to that contained in the Freedom of Information Act to provide any citizen with the legal right of access to these papers. But it concluded that immediate application of the Freedom of Information Act to this type of document would create a substantial risk of interference with the continuing operation of government.

My view as chairman of the commission was somewhat different. I found the majority position too restrictive and, joining with Sen. Lowell Weicker of Connecticut, issued a dissenting, alternate report that took issue especially with the fifteen-year waiting period in the majority report. In my view, two principles are overriding. First, official papers are clearly governmental property and should be subject to governmental custody. Second, the public's right to know about the activities of its government must always be respected, other things being equal. As the alternate report stated:

> a government, if it is to be truly responsive to the wishes of its people, must furnish them, in detail, the information as to its activities. [The authors of the alternate report] realize that experience teaches that secrecy is the enemy of citizen participation and are satisfied that the country's ambition should be an informed citizenry. . . . By no other means can the people learn how the government is affecting them and acquire the knowledge for valid decisions in the discharge of their responsibilities as citizens.[4]

Congress has essentially adopted the commission's majority view as to presidential papers, and they are now considered public property by law. Yet the Congress has not taken action with respect to papers of the legislative and judicial branches, which the majority and minority reports of the commission also sought to bring under the purview of federal law and control.

Delays in opening government papers to the public remain to be solved. For example, the chore of declassifying documents is immense, and funds are not always available. Attitudes of public officials also require change: Many do not welcome the idea of having their files opened to the public without their permission. It has been reported, for example, that President Reagan disregarded the report of the commission when he left the White House.

I still believe that the alternate report's approach is the proper one—that public papers and documents are public property and that the Freedom of Information Act should apply to the public papers of officials as soon as they leave office. These papers should be turned over to a government depository—probably separate depositories for each of the three branches of government. Public officials and their staffs, during their term of office, should keep two sets of files. This should apply to Congress and to federal judges as well as to the executive branch. One set, which includes all documents on which they relied in making official decisions and all papers containing the sole record of official decisions or actions, constitutes public property. The other, including family correspondence, social correspondence, and private diaries, constitutes personal property. The judgment and good faith of the public official as to which papers are public and which are private should carry great weight and it should be determinative in the first instance. As in all legal matters, a body of precedent will soon develop that will decide any controversial categories, and eventually some clarifying legislation may be advisable. Most public officials will want their reputations for honesty in this regard to be paramount, and I see no reason at this time to impose sanctions for violations. In an egregious case, in which the distinction between public and private is obviously being violated—if the official carries away all his files—the courts would be available to adjudicate complaints.

There are a number of objections to this view that are raised in the majority opinion. The majority recommended a fifteen-year period after officials leave office before their public papers are turned over, reasoning that otherwise the officials would be subject to partisan attacks but not have the staff to defend themselves. But more important, they argued, it would be harmful to open up documents of the presidency that disclose remarks from close advisers who give "candid and uninhibited advice" on the expectation that it will never be made public. The president needs such uninhibited advice, they claimed, and would not get it if it is later to be made public.

In my view, the need for executive privilege and confidentiality are clearly important when a president is still in office but weaken substantially once he has left office. Unlike a monarch, the president's powers derive solely from the trust placed in him by the electorate. His official papers, when he leaves office, should be available to the public, subject to the usual exception for classified information to protect national security. National-security matters, of course, ought to remain secret when it is in the national interest to keep them so; however, national-security interests can still be protected by such laws as the Freedom of Information Act and the procedures it specifies. Above all, the "trouble," "uncertainty," and "nuisance" caused by more extensive and timely access to governmental documents were to my mind at the time (and since) very subordinate considerations, especially, as I told the commission, "compared to the real meaning of our form of government, which is that it should be as open as possible."

Another objection raised in the majority report is that historians will have a better opportunity to review public papers and comment upon them if such papers are not opened to the media and others in a piecemeal fashion. I believe the public's right to know is superior to the claim of any one group among the public for preferred treatment. Similarly, the desire of certain former officials to keep the public ignorant until such time as they themselves profit from writing a book should not override the public interest. Such officials can always publish their views on and recollections of public events even though details about the events, i.e., the underlying documents, have been disclosed.

The only time I was asked to advise the White House during a Democratic administration came when Secretary of State Cyrus Vance asked me to prepare a study for the Carter White House on a question of constitutional law involved in the president's plan to abrogate the Mutual Defense Treaty with Taiwan without action by Congress or the government of Taiwan. My previous study of the constitutional power of the president in treaty making at the time of the Bricker amendment fight was helpful in this new assignment.

The issue at hand stemmed from President Nixon's visit to the People's Republic of China in 1972. At the time the two nations agreed upon the so-called "Shanghai Communique," declaring their goal to be normalization of relations between China and the United States. China stipulated that full diplomatic recognition depended upon whether the United States would agree to cease all diplomatic and other official relations with Taiwan, withdraw its military units from Taiwan, and terminate our Mutual Defense Treaty with Taiwan.

By September 1978 the Carter administration clearly was moving toward full diplomatic recognition of China. Thereupon Congress passed a resolution including a provision that it was the sense of Congress that there should be prior consultation between Congress and the president on any proposed policy changes affecting the continuation in force of the Mutual Defense Treaty of 1954 with Taiwan. The stage was thus set for another round in the constitutional dispute between the executive and legislative branches over the extent of the president's powers with respect to treaties with foreign governments.

Could the president acting alone abrogate the Mutual Defense Treaty with Taiwan? When Secretary of State Vance asked my opinion, he noted that there was considerable sentiment within the State Department that the president had such power and should exercise it by a statement that the treaty was terminated forthwith, coincident with establishment of full diplomatic relations with the People's Republic of China.

I undertook a study of the problem in collaboration with my partner Franklin G. Hunt, on a pro bono basis. After completing our study, we had a breakfast meeting with the secretary of state and Herbert Hansell, legal adviser of the State Department, at my apartment in New York City. We pointed out that the Constitution provided that the president shall take care that the laws of the United States be faithfully executed. The Constitution also provides that the laws and treaties shall be "the supreme law of the land." We concluded that this duty of the president to enforce the laws means that he may not terminate a treaty by an action *that would violate the treaty* (the latter clause was key). In other words, the president may not, acting alone, simply declare a treaty invalid. Thus, although the Supreme Court has on occasion recognized a president's authority to exercise powers not explicitly stated in the Constitution—the so-called power of presidential prerogative—the explicit provisions in the Constitution relevant to this particular situation appeared to limit such power.

The terms of this particular treaty, which had been approved by Congress, could provide an opening for presidential termination, however. Article X of the treaty stated: "This treaty shall remain in force indefinitely. Either party may terminate it one year after notice has been given to the other party." The next question was whether the president, acting without congressional approval, could validly act for the United States in terminating the treaty one year after he gave notice that the United States was exercising its right to terminate, as provided for in Article X.

Here the constitutional issues became more clouded: The Constitution does not specifically provide a method for the president or for any other institution of our federal government to terminate a treaty, as it does for the making of a treaty. Yet the silence of the Constitution does not mean, we argued, that constitutional principles are not applicable. We concluded that the power to terminate the treaty, in light of the termination procedures established within it, falls within the general power of the president to conduct foreign affairs on behalf of the nation, a power recognized by the Supreme Court in other landmark decisions. It is fortified by the additional constitutional powers of the president, as commander-in-chief of the armed forces, to make treaties and to nominate and receive ambassadors. Thus, the "party" in Article X of the treaty that was empowered to terminate the treaty could reasonably be construed to be the president, acting without congressional approval if he so chose.

Therefore we advised the secretary of state that the president had the power to terminate the treaty in accordance with its terms. Mr. Vance concurred in this opinion and so advised President Carter. The president followed this course of action as part of his program to recognize the People's Republic of China with full diplomatic relations.

The president's action did not settle the internal dispute within our government over the president's power. Sen. Barry Goldwater and other senators brought suit in federal court to block the president's action in terminating the treaty under Article X. While the suit was pending I testified before the Senate Committee on Foreign Relations in support of the validity of the president's action. I pointed out that the president has large reserves of discretionary authority in foreign relations. He can declare to foreign governments the policies and intentions of the United States on a whole range of international issues: recognition of foreign governments; termination of diplomatic relations; recognition of the status of belligerency and insurgency; declaration of our position on questions of customary international law; claiming of new rights to territory or property; and seeking redress if another country violates our international treaty rights. He can even employ the armed forces to vindicate such international law and treaty rights. The president determines how we exercise our treaty right to cast votes at the United Nations. The president might, in exercising these powers, seek concurrence of the Senate or Congress in order to have the broadest possible public support. He has often done this, but he is not obligated to do so.

The Goldwater lawsuit reached the Supreme Court, which was severely split on the applicable legal principles to be applied.[5] The Court noted, however, that the Senate had not taken final and definitive action to challenge the president's action. The practical result was that the president's action in this case was permitted to stand. The Taiwan treaty expired at the end of the one-year notice.

A postscript to my action in this matter occurred some years later. As vice-chairman of the Bicentennial Commission on the U.S. Constitution, I was invited to participate in a symposium in Great Britain and Ireland as part of the celebration in those countries of the 200th anniversary of our Constitution—the oldest written Constitution in the free world. The symposium was held at Oxford University and repeated first at Middle Temple in London and then at the National University of Ireland in Dublin. It was cast in the form of a moot-court presentation before British and Irish judges. The case heard by these judges was on the question of whether the president of the United States had power without obtaining congressional approval to terminate a treaty. Among the other participants were Robert Clare of the New York bar and Lloyd Cutler of the Washington, D.C., bar, with former Chief Justice Warren E. Burger sitting with the British and Irish judges who heard the case. A majority upheld the president's power to terminate.

The treaty powers of the president—indeed the extent of the powers of the president in the field of foreign relations—will undoubtedly continue to be a source of controversy as long as the Constitution stands as presently written. Whether in political debate or in Court proceedings or in other forums, I trust that emphasis will always be placed upon the experience that brought our nation into existence and resulted in the adoption of the original Constitution. More than for any other reason, the Founding Fathers decided to supersede the Articles of Confederation (under which the Revolutionary War was fought) with our Constitution because of the inability of the nation to act decisively and with one voice in the field of foreign affairs under the old Articles. Each passing year and each new era in our history—now the post–cold war era of a new world order—emphasize our need for strong presidential authority in the conduct of foreign affairs. The countervailing fear of the development of dictatorship can always be met, as it has been throughout our history as a nation, at the ballot box and through the exercise of the constitutional right of free press and free speech. And ultimately, of course, the danger of presidential abuse of power can be checked by the Constitution's own provisions of presidential impeachment and removal from office.

Fittingly, my last governmental assignment involved the Constitution directly: appointment by President Reagan as a member of the commission established to prepare for the nationwide celebration of the Bicentennial of the United States Constitution. He was the fifth president—sixth if former President Hoover is counted—under whom I have served in one capacity or another. The commission was headed by my colleague from the days we spent in the Justice Department, former Chief Justice Warren E. Burger. The celebration was a five-year commemoration.

- In 1987, the nation commemorated the signing of the Constitution in Philadelphia.
- In 1988, emphasis was placed upon the struggle for ratification in the thirteen original states.
- In 1989, the inauguration of George Washington as the first president and the establishment of the executive and legislative branches of our government was marked.
- In 1990, tribute was paid to the judicial branch.
- In 1991, the commemoration celebrated the bicentennial of the passage of the original Bill of Rights, with attention also to the broadening of our civil rights and civil liberties by the passage of subsequent amendments to the Constitution.

From its inception the commission emphasized an educational program—cerebration over celebration; but celebrations there were. Two noteworthy public ceremonies were convened—one in Philadelphia and one in New York City. The first one commemorated the 200th anniversary of the actual signing of the Constitution, with a huge parade and the ringing of the Liberty Bell in Philadelphia. The second event was a celebration of the 200th anniversary of the inauguration of George Washington as our first president under the new Constitution. This took place at Federal Hall in New York City, where Washington had taken the oath of office. I was privileged to attend the speech there of President George Bush on this occasion. Fifty years earlier I had stood on the same spot to hear President Franklin D. Roosevelt commemorate the 150th anniversary of George Washington's inauguration as part of the opening ceremony of the New York World's Fair of 1939–1940, for which I was legal counsel.

In every state, the response to the Bicentennial was enormous, showing the appreciation at the grass roots for the constitutional form of government under which we live. In Philadelphia the Founding Fathers designed a government not of the Old World variety wherein governmental powers were imposed by monarchs or military dictators; rather, "We, the People" established the Constitution, which provides the means by which our federal government shall operate. All officers of government take an oath to support the Constitution rather than pledging to support any individual or group temporarily in power. The people are free at any time to amend the Constitution. "We, the People" thus became the slogan of the Bicentennial.

The Constitution has been called by the British statesman Edmund Burke "the greatest document ever struck off by the hand and mind of man." It preserved our liberties, hard won in the Revolutionary War. It gave us a central government strong enough to enable us to become the world's leading democracy. It encouraged the exercise of individual initiative. It protected us from totalitarianism by distributing governmental powers between the federal government and the states and within the federal government between the executive, legislative, and judicial branches. It established the world's first common market by removing impediments to commerce that had existed among the states. It protected individual rights and liberty, giving us freedom of speech, religion, and press.

As vice-chairman of the national commission and as head of its Finance Committee—as well as being a member of New York City's Bicentennial Commission—I have had many diverse duties. I found the greatest enjoyment in addressing college and high school audiences on the origin and significance of our Constitution. Indeed the reaction of the college and high school audiences to the constitutional problems arising in the Eisenhower years encouraged me to write these memoirs about my experiences in government. The Bicentennial Commission's educational efforts will have been well worthwhile if they result in more attention being paid in our schools to the study of American history and government. For myself, celebration and cerebration of the Constitution's 200 years served as a most fitting capstone to my public life.

NOTES

1. The London meetings had international attention. As Henry Luce, publisher of *Time* and *Life*, stated in his speech to the Indiana Bar Association at French Lick Springs, Indiana, September 20, 1957: "Somehow the speeches caught fire, oratory took on a touch of profundity. The Americans and British found—when the wounds of Suez were still smarting—what deeply united them—liberty under law. Mr. Herbert Brownell, the Attorney General of the United States said: 'We must perfect a machinery for a settlement of international disputes—not occasionally but on a total basis—under a tribunal or system of tribunals which will command general confidence.' Also at that meet-

ing there rose up Sir Winston Churchill himself and he said: 'We have now reached the point where nations must contrive a system and practice to resolve their disputes and settle them peacefully.' Thus the chief law officer of the United States and the ranking statesman of the West took the lead, among many others, in saying that our chief business now must be to expand and vitalize the rule of law" (John K. Jessup, ed., *The Ideas of Henry Luce* [New York: Atheneum, 1949], pp. 174–76).

2. 373 U.S. 546 (1963).

3. For my efforts, I was later given the Conservation Award of the Department of Interior for outstanding achievement in the field of conservation of natural resources.

4. *Final Report of the National Study Commission on Records and Documents of Federal Officials*, March 31, 1977, p. 65.

5. Goldwater et al. v. Carter, 444 U.S. 996 (1979).

18

Practicing Law

❖ ❖ ❖ ❖ ❖ ❖ ❖ ❖ ❖ ❖ ❖ ❖ ❖ ❖ ❖

Although my political and governmental activities involved me in many of the weighty issues of the day and brought me into contact and association with many leading political figures, I have always considered the practice of law to be the foundation and continuing touchstone of my career. It has permitted me the freedom to enter public service when called upon to do so, but it has also offered the means to return to private pursuits when the time was right.

The flexibility to move between the public and private spheres is an especially healthy feature of our form of government. It can prevent persons from having their official actions constrained by the prospect of political advancement, thereby protecting the independence of thought and action that is vital to effective government. And it can open the way for citizens with energy and new ideas to enter political life, which is critical to the volunteer ethic and citizen participation necessary in a democracy.

In my case, the freedom of pursuit that a legal career permits was accentuated by the generosity of my partners and associates who cooperated in making it possible for me to be of service to an ever-widening list of clients and to maintain a commitment to public service.

The law has also been a source of intrinsic interest to me because of the variety of legal problems it can offer. My private practice has followed many different courses over the years, beginning with securities work and corporate finance, then moving into hotel law and a broader range of corporate law, and after my service in Washington, delving into the interesting and varied realm of private international law. Each phase of my legal career has brought new aspects of the law to my attention and continually captured my interest and imagination. Many of my cases brought me into contact with unique figures in business, the arts, sports, and national and international politics and constantly broadened and enriched my own knowledge and interests in these areas. I have chosen some vignettes and anecdotes from my law practice that do not reveal professional confidences but that may provide a glimpse into the fascination and variety involved in a long life at the bar.

Early in my law practice I decided to join the corporate department rather than the litigation, tax, or the trust and estates departments, the alternatives offered in the large New York firms to their young associates. From 1927 to 1929 I was an associate at one such firm: Root, Clark, Buckner, Howland and Ballantine. Most of my work involved legal research for the firm's senior partners and very little contact with clients. I was privileged to work directly for Elihu Root, Jr., a senior partner (whose father had been secretary of state and was spending his last years in private practice as counsel for the firm). "Sec" Root, as he was called, assigned me my first legal-research project. It was to analyze whether the estate of Ellsworth Statler, the hotel magnate, was entitled to an estate-tax exemption for a bequest establishing the Cornell University School of Hotel Management. The government claimed it was a taxable gift because the Statler Hotels might benefit from receiving better-trained hotel employees.

The first corporate job that I can remember was in connection with the Dodge-Chrysler merger. That was a big event on Wall Street in those days. And my job—I think I had been in the office about a month or so—was to telephone around the country to all the different banks that were going to be transfer agents and registrars for the stock and get the exact spelling of their corporate names. Such was my part in the Dodge-Chrysler merger!

In 1929 I moved to the smaller firm of Lord, Day & Lord. One of their senior partners who handled corporate work was leaving the firm to become an investment banker. They contacted Yale Law School for suggestions about a suitable replacement and I was recommended. I was not particularly eager to leave Root, Clark; I enjoyed excellent personal relationships with the other lawyers and had no reason to think I would not get along there. A position at Lord, Day & Lord, however, presented a unique opportunity to work directly with clients and to advance at a faster pace than at a larger firm.

My move to Lord, Day & Lord proved right: I plunged into work that was more important than I had been doing at the old firm, and I enjoyed more responsibility right from the start. The 1929 stock market crash and the ensuing depression brought a lot of bankruptcy work to the firm. The Irving Trust Company was appointed as receiver for hundreds of companies in financial difficulty, and they farmed out the legal work to a number of Wall Street firms, including Lord, Day & Lord. For a period of several years, we were working extensively in this area of the law: planning corporate reorganizations, getting companies out of bankruptcy, and distributing the assets of firms that had gone broke.

I began to carve out a niche for myself in the firm by developing expertise in the corporate-securities field. This was before the New Deal created the Securities and Exchange Commission (SEC) to regulate the securities market. The prospectuses under which securities were sold in the pre-SEC era were based on the principle, "Let the buyer beware." When SEC brought about the era of full disclosure and made the seller beware that he was responsible for misrepresentations and omissions, there was new law to be learned. I went to night school at Columbia Law School to learn the new rules under the guidance of Adolf Berle, Jr., my next-door neighbor, who had been one of the original Brain Trusters of the New Deal and who later became deputy mayor of New York City under Mayor LaGuardia.

New York real estate values as well as stock prices were dealt a heavy blow in the aftermath of the 1929 crash. I had a unique perspective, not only because my firm, where I became a partner in 1932, had an extensive real-estate practice but also because I was a member of the New York Assembly. As a member of the Judiciary Committee, the Rules Committee, and as chairman of the New York City Committee I had a comprehensive view of proposals for government aid to stricken corporations and other regulatory measures to deal with the financial crisis.

Before long I developed a specialty in hotel corporate law. I wrote a book on hotel law with my partner Charles W. Merritt and in due course became general counsel to the New York City and State Hotel Associations and to the American Hotel Association. My activities in these positions included forming the New York Visitors and Convention Bureau, which has played such an important role in New York City's economy by promoting the tourist trade.

I found hotel law fascinating because of the scope and variety of legal problems found in the industry. People are born in hotels, they get married there, they entertain there and sometimes die there. Hotels have strong relationships with the local community and have to comply with a myriad of municipal, state, and federal laws. They deal primarily with people and the social customs of the time and get into just about every aspect of the law you can think of; they are a kind of fascinating miniature of a community.

This was a period of great change in the hotel industry, a shift from essentially individually owned and operated hotels to the formation of large national and international chains. Most of the city's hotels had been bankrupted in the Great Depression and bought for nominal sums by individual entrepreneurs. They were rugged individualists, willing to flirt with bankruptcy when the rate of occupancy in the city's hotels was at an all-time low and when government rent-control laws became popular and were first instituted. The roster of names of New York City hotel managers at the time contained prominent personalities who became instrumental in building the great hotel chains that dominate the industry today. To name but a few: Oscar of the Waldorf, David Mulligan, Robert Christenberry, Martin Sweeney, Thomas Green, Fred Muschenheim, Lucius Boomer, David Knott, and Frank Andrews. These men formed the nucleus of an organization known as the Tavern Club. I was chosen as the first nonhotelman member, and through the years I have enjoyed their hospitality and that of their successors. When I went to Washington my hotel friends presented me with a huge cake with elaborate icing depicting the Department of Justice building at Tenth and Constitution Streets.

I had occasion after I became attorney general to recall the uncomplicated and pleasant relationships I had with these bon vivants over the years when federal tax officials turned up a case involving the alleged failure of the banquet manager and waiters at the Waldorf Astoria Hotel in New York to pay taxes on banquet tips. Unbeknownst to me, my old friend the banquet manager was indicted. Shortly thereafter I was called upon to speak at a large banquet at the Waldorf. Between courses (especially before the soup course), I noticed the waiters would whisper in my ear that the tax indictment should be dropped. Their sotto voce comments made me a bit nervous, but I must report that the soup was pure and uncontaminated, and there were no adverse consequences.

My law practice also brought me into contact with many interesting public figures. Mike Todd, the theatrical producer, became a client after the New York World's Fair of 1939–1940 came to a close. At the time he was married to Elizabeth Taylor, the famous actress, and Mike, Elizabeth Taylor, and Mike, Jr., formed a company to produce a movie about Don Quixote to be filmed in Spain. Mike called a luncheon meeting of the Board of Directors to consider the problems; the board consisted of the three of them. Mike insisted on great formality from his "Counsellor," as he called me, and we prepared an elaborate agenda. The meeting was suddenly interrupted when Elizabeth objected to the menu for the lunch. We recessed our meeting to send out for a hot pastrami sandwich. Mike then submitted the name of the actor whom he proposed to engage to play the part of Don Quixote. Elizabeth objected to the proposed selection, and Mike, Jr., sided with her. Mike summarily announced that the motion to engage the actor had been carried. "Counsellor," he said, "make a note of it." He then turned to Mike, Jr., as treasurer, and handed him a proposed budget for the production. Mike, Jr., said he objected because it was too extravagant. Elizabeth sided with Mike, Jr. Mike then pronounced that the motion to approve the budget had carried. "Counsellor," he said, "make a note of it." And so it went, and I had a full day of on-the-job training on how corporate law can be practiced in the theatrical world. Incidentally, the proposed screen version of Don Quixote never was produced.

Dan Topping, who with Del Webb owned the New York Yankees baseball club, was also a client in those years, bringing me near the world of sports until Topping sold out his interest in the Yankees. My family became great Yankee fans and heartily approved this client and the chance to meet famous athletes. I remember I was able to untangle enough governmental red tape to get Billy Martin, the famous second baseman, out of the marines in time to play in the World Series. Topping even wanted to propose my name for baseball commissioner at one point, and he and George Weiss, the general manager, and Hank Greenburg urged me to change careers—but instead I remained a Yankee rooter from our family box at Yankee Stadium.

In late 1957 I returned to New York to resume my practice. Under the law then in force I could not take any case for two years that involved a matter that had been under investigation by the Justice Department during my term of office. The facts of these matters under investigation usually had been completely unknown to me personally; even so I was barred (and I think, in the interests of ethics in government, quite rightly). Furthermore, if I joined a firm, that firm would for two years similarly be prohibited from opposing the government, for example, in antitrust or tax matters. So I set up an individual practice for two years. Even after the two-year limit expired, my old firm (which I then rejoined) and I were barred from acting against the government in any lawsuit involving a matter in which I had personally participated during my governmental service.

In 1966 I was appointed special master by the local federal court to hear testimony and to assess damages in the antitrust litigation between Howard Hughes and Trans World Airlines. Hughes had refused to appear personally as a witness and as a result had defaulted; his lawyers had to defend his interests on the question of damages in his absence. Many unique questions of evidence and procedure popped up during the months of the hearings. It was my first experience as a quasi-judicial official. Finally, at the close of the hearings, I submitted my report—over 300 printed pages—assessing heavy damages. My report was twice confirmed in the federal courts but later became moot when the Supreme Court rejected the basis on which the suit had originally been brought; but the battle for assessment of damages continued in a state court.

Following the Hughes-TWA suit, word spread that I was available to sit as an arbitrator of disputes, even though I continued in private practice. I was also on the roster of American lawyers appointed as members of the International Court of Arbitration based at The Hague in the Netherlands. One such quasi-judicial assignment that lasted for several years resulted from an experiment by the "Big Three" automobile companies to endeavor to settle disputes with their dealers through mediation rather than by court litigation. I was selected by Chrysler to umpire its disputes with dealers by conducting hearings and recommending settlements on the basis of facts developed at the hearings. Charles E. Whittaker, retired justice of the United States Supreme Court, was acting for another one of the Big Three automobile companies in a similar capacity.

One significant and interesting case in private practice grew out of the publication in the *New York Times*, a longtime Lord, Day & Lord client, of an advertisement setting forth the anti–civil rights actions of Police Chief "Bull" Connors of Birmingham, Alabama. Connors sued the *Times* for libel. In each of the first two cases tried in Alabama, the *Times* had been assessed damages of $500,000. It seemed quite clear that a free press could hardly be expected to continue under such circumstances.

The *Times* appealed the decision, and the case was carried to the United States Supreme Court. I participated in writing our client's brief for the Supreme Court, and I was part of the discussion that had led us to enlist the services of Prof. Herbert Wechsler to argue the case before the Court. Wechsler did a brilliant job, and the Supreme Court found in favor of the *Times*. The case, *New York Times v. Sullivan*, established limitations on the liability of the press in libel actions brought by public personages.[1] The Court developed the new doctrine that damages in a libel case could not be awarded to a public official unless he or she proved that the falsity of the libel was either intentional or reckless. The *Times* was adjudged innocent of intentional or reckless conduct. We were all surprised that the Supreme Court went as far as it did in protecting freedom of the press, and the case still stands as a landmark First Amendment decision.

In 1971 I became involved in further litigation against the *New York Times* that would also prove to be of great constitutional importance: the famous Pentagon Papers case.[2] The case involved a classified Defense Department study of the steps American policymakers had taken to involve the United States in the Vietnam War. Daniel Ellsberg, a one-time governmental official who had access to the study (dubbed the Pentagon Papers), passed a copy to the *Times* for publication. The federal government got wind of Ellsberg's plans and sued the *Times* to prevent publication. The case had an interesting twist to it, not only because it raised important issues about the freedom of the press and disclosure of classified information but because it had bearing on my prior actions as attorney general and the rules governing conflict of interest of former governmental officials.

My firm had represented the *New York Times* for quite a few years through its partner Louis Loeb. When the Pentagon Papers matter arose, I learned from Loeb that he had advised the *Times* that if it published the Pentagon Papers the *Times* could be subject to criminal prosecution. Up to that point I had not been consulted about the matter. And then on Sunday, June 13, 1971, I got a call from John Mitchell, who was the attorney general of the United States at the time. He said that the Justice Department was planning to prosecute the *Times* for violation of the criminal law if they published the Pentagon Papers. He wanted me to know that their case was based on President Eisenhower's executive order 10501, which was the executive order defining which classified papers could not be made public without governmental approval.

When I was attorney general I had drafted that executive order and sent it to the president and told him that I thought it was constitutional. Mitchell said that if the prosecution of the *Times* went forward and Lord, Day & Lord represented the paper in court, we would be in a conflict-of-interest position, and he wanted to notify me of that. In effect, if not in words, he said that the government would move to disqualify us as attorneys in the matter if we represented the *Times*.

I immediately telephoned Louis Loeb and told him about this call; we discussed it at length and decided that if the government went ahead with the prosecution, the firm would probably be disqualified from acting further in the case by the court. That would be most embarrassing to the *Times*, so either that day or early that week, Loeb notified our client that it would not be in the best interests of the *Times* for us to continue and that we therefore felt it ought to get other counsel in the matter.

It wasn't until the actual court papers were filed that we found out that the government was not only going to prosecute under the criminal statute that Mitchell had told me about but was also going to ask for an injunction to prevent the publication in the first instance. This claim by the government of power to prevent publication (prior restraint) was a novel claim—one that we had never confronted and as to which we had never given advice to our client. But the government's complaint and the supporting affidavits were explicitly based on Executive Order 10501. This fact made it necessary, from an ethical point of view, for us to withdraw from the case. I think that some of the top officials of the *Times* felt that we had "abandoned them on the courthouse steps," but given Mitchell's threat there was little else we or the *Times* could do. Fortunately our firm's long-standing professional relationship with the *Times* continued.

The government's course of action in seeking prior restraint of publication left undecided the question of whether the *Times* would have been liable after publishing the papers under the criminal statute relating to national security. As to this question, undecided to this date, Justice Byron White in his concurring opinion, noted:

> Congress has addressed itself to the problems of protecting the security of the country and the national defense from unauthorized disclosure of potentially damaging information [citation omitted]. It has not, however, authorized the injunctive remedy against threatened publication. It has apparently been satisfied to rely on criminal sanctions and their deterrent effect on the responsible as well as the irresponsible press. I am not, of course, saying that either of these newspapers has yet committed a crime or that either would commit a crime if it published all the material now in its possession. That mat-

ter must await resolution in the context of a criminal proceeding if one is instituted by the United States. In that event, the issue of guilt or innocence would be determined by procedures and standards quite different from those that have purported to govern these injunctive proceedings.[3]

At the time of the financial crisis and the threatened bankruptcy of the City of New York in the 1970s, the city government came under considerable pressure from the State Control Board and the underwriters of city bonds to reform its methods of marketing its securities. The mayor, the comptroller and members of the Board of Estimate decided to retain a special securities counsel. At the time I carried on an active securities law practice. I had also been a public member of the Board of Governors of the American Stock Exchange and then became its regular outside counsel. I was chosen as the city's special securities counsel and in that capacity developed a novel "complete disclosure" prospectus to be used in marketing city securities and to replace the incomplete letters of intent that had been used up to that time. The new type of municipal prospectus was a significant factor in the improvement of the city's financial practices under Mayor Ed Koch and Comptroller Harrison Goldin. It has been widely used as a model by other cities.

After my return from Washington, much of my law practice was in the field of private international law. A number of these matters, which involved unusual personal experiences, stand out in my memory.

Legal work for the shipping industry constituted one area of this interesting work. The U.S. Navy had arrangements with private American shipowners of oil tankers whereby the ships would be turned over to the United States government for transportation of oil in the event of a national emergency even though the ships were registered under foreign flags. Liberia, Panama, and Honduras were countries that allowed such arrangements. The shipowners saved on wages and taxes by registering their ships under the foreign flags. The shipowners wanted to organize an association to look after their needs. As one of my first retainers after leaving government, Erling Naess, of Norwegian shipping background, asked me to be counsel for the group, the American Committee for Flags of Necessity. My legal work entailed trips with Mr. Naess to negotiate with British labor leaders and trips to Liberia and Panama to discuss shipping matters with the governments there.

One of the powerful shipowners in the association with whom I became acquainted was Daniel K. Ludwig. He attracted media attention as the "richest man in the world," but he abhorred personal publicity. He retained me as his principal legal counsel, an association that lasted for the remainder of my professional career. Much overseas travel was involved— to Asia, Australia, North and South America, Europe, Africa, and the West Indies. Shipping and shipbuilding, insurance, hotels, citrus fruit, mining, oil and gas, cattle ranching, coal, iron ore, heavy construction, real estate, and merchant banking were among the units of his far-flung empire.

D.K., as he was known to his friends, was a unique person. He made an indelible impression on everyone he met: a quick and inquiring mind, a rough-and-ready humor and a flashing temper on occasion, singleness of purpose in pursuing everything he undertook, a believer in and practitioner of the virtues of hard work, a Midas touch, a man of high business standards, a rugged individualist, and a benefactor of mankind who devoted his great fortune to a study of the cause and cure of cancer.

He used to say, "I did not graduate from Harvard Business School, but I wasn't a high school drop-out. I was a grade school drop-out." Indeed, he did go to work after the eighth grade. "I was weak in mathematics," he said, "so I went through a correspondence-school course and ended up with a marine engineer certificate." Whether in Washington State, Texas, the Great Lakes, operating a tug-and-barge service in New York Harbor with his own ships, or in shipyards in Virginia or Japan, he was never far from the water.

The first ship that he built was a large tanker in 1940, the SS *Virginia*, named after his wife. He has been described by his great friend and business associate, Frank Joyce, as an "intuitive engineer." His ability to convert ships and ship machinery to other uses, foresee new uses for them, envision new markets, and plan for new construction methods plus his driving force earned him a reputation as a shipping genius.

He had an absorbing interest in geography, especially the study of the sea-lanes and harbors of the world. Between marathon telephone calls around the world, he would pore over the huge world globe that always stood behind his desk. He translated these studies into visions of new types of vessels that could be built to accommodate these lanes and the sea harbors.

Perhaps Ludwig's reputation as a shipping genius is traceable largely to his development of the giant oil tanker. He first went to the big international oil companies and persuaded them to agree to a long-term charter of an oil tanker to commence when he later built the tanker. Then he went to a bank to obtain a building loan for the vessels, using the long-term charter as collateral. The huge tankers, containing new features he had developed as a result of his experience in the operation of carriers-by-water, transformed the methods of transporting the world's oil supply.

Known, too, throughout the world was his yacht, the *Danginn* (a combination of Dan and Ginger, his wife's name). In later years he constructed a luxury barge to travel up and down the canals and rivers of France. His business and personal entertainment of friends also extended to his luxury hotels, notably the Acapulco Princess. The opening of this hotel was a lavish and colorful event, ending with a performance of the Mexican Ballet Company.

D.K.'s last mammoth business adventure was in Brazil, on the Jari River, a tributary of the Amazon. He bought a tract of jungle land, larger than the state of Connecticut, and developed on it a forestation project to supply a huge papermaking mill. The mill was constructed in Japan and floated across the oceans to be installed at Jari. The magnitude of the project, with side enterprises of rice cultivation and kaolin mining, was breathtaking, but he never realized the profits he had envisioned and sold out to a Brazilian syndicate. By recent accounts, the project is now profitable, and methods have been perfected to preserve the ecology of the jungle.[4]

In the 1960s Ludwig decided to give to charity the bulk of his foreign holdings, including his remaining interest in Jari. He set up a giant nonprofit corporation, based in Zurich and with the Swiss government as a participant, devoted exclusively to cancer research. The gift was by far the largest from an individual benefactor for studying the causes, treatment, and cure of cancer. The corporation is called the Ludwig Institute for Cancer Research. Today it has branches in Switzerland, Belgium, Sweden, Britain, Australia, and Brazil and in Canada and New York City where the research is carried on by groups of scientists in association with hospitals that treat cancer patients.

Dr. Hugh Butt of the Mayo Clinic was the first medical director. His successor is Dr. Lloyd Old, formerly of the Sloan-Kettering Memorial Hospital in New York City. The institute has faithfully carried out the wishes of the founder: not to spend money on "bricks and mortar" and not to construct costly headquarters or memorial buildings that would divert funds from research and equipment. Ludwig also desired to set up small research centers just adequate in size to allow young doctors of great promise and a small staff to carry on their research. In other words, the research facilities would go to the researcher, not the researcher to a giant, bureaucratic headquarters. This plan allows maximum incentive for the researchers in the various parts of the world that have indigenous cancer problems. The electronic age in which they operate, with the most modern equipment, allows cross-fertilization of ideas and cooperative use of discoveries to be carried on by the far-flung branches. I became a director and legal counsel for the institute at an early date and have continued an association with it and with underlying companies whose profits furnish its resources. This association involved quarterly travel to Zurich, Switzerland, through the years. I have made it a point to take a short holiday after many of these trips—to London, Paris, Berlin, Leningrad, Rome, and Prague and to the Lascaux caves—to add to the spice of life.

Another client with international interests was William Wood Prince of Chicago, who asked me to work with J. B. "Jock" Lawrence, a noted public-relations expert, to set up a program to import Charolais cattle from the West Indies to the United States to comply with our severe agricultural-import regulations. In the course of a trip for Mr. Prince I became acquainted with Harold Christie, a real-estate tycoon on the islands of Nassau and Eleuthera and the leader of the Conservative party in the Parliament in Nassau. Christie was present by chance as a guest in the home of Sir Harry Oakes on the night that Oakes was mysteriously murdered. The murder trial was sensational. Some years later the Canadian Broadcasting System, owned by the Canadian government, broadcast a story of the Oakes case implying that Harold Christie was involved in the murder. I was retained by Christie to clear his name. After extensive negotiations I obtained an appropriate retraction and damages. And I was delighted afterward when Queen Elizabeth knighted my client as Sir Harold for his public-service career. We celebrated on the Ludwig yacht in the harbor off Lyford Key—he came aboard fresh from a session of Parliament, dressed in his morning coat and high hat—the first ever seen on the *Danginn*.

Another international case in private practice took me to Iraq in 1958 to negotiate a concession from the Iraqi government for one of my clients. This was in the days when the government was friendly to the United States. I was successful in my mission and obtained the appropriate signatures. On the way home, over Beirut, the news came on the air that there had been a revolution in Baghdad. Everyone from the government who had signed our agreement, it turned out, had been beheaded and the bodies dragged through the streets. The new revolutionary government never did recognize the existence of the contract.

One day I received an overseas call from Madrid from my good friend John Davis Lodge, a former governor of Connecticut and at the time U.S. ambassador to Spain. He told me that a few months earlier a U.S. Air Force plane, after a collision with another plane off the Spanish seacoast, had dropped a hydrogen bomb into the ocean. For nearly three months the U.S. Navy had frantically searched the sea bottom to recover the missile. The international and domestic political repercussions from the incident, he commented, might have been horrendous if the missile had not been recovered intact because of speculation that the lives of Spaniards were being endangered.

Lodge recounted that a Spanish fisherman, Francisco Simo Orts, had guided the navy to the spot where he thought the missile had been lost, and from his detailed knowledge of the terrain, he had predicted where the missile probably lay on the ocean floor. The navy, which had already spent millions of dollars on the unsuccessful recovery search, finally decided to listen to the fisherman even though officially discounting his story. He led them to the exact spot that he insisted was the logical location of the lost missile; sure enough, he was right, and the missile was recovered intact. The crisis was avoided. The fisherman had the satisfaction of being an international celebrity for the moment.

Ambassador Lodge then explained that the fisherman wanted a reward from the U.S. government and that he, Lodge, thought that the fisherman deserved one, but he had been turned down. The upshot was that the fisherman retained me along with Spanish lawyers to represent him. I sought a substantial recovery from the government but was unable to get any high governmental official to support our claim. Finally I reached an agreement on a token, $10,000 settlement (and some expenses). The government had previously presented the fisherman with an embossed scroll and a medallion with a picture of President Lyndon Johnson. I called upon my friend and client, George Sorondo, formerly of the Argentine Diplomatic Corps, who was then living in Spain, and upon my law partner Jack Jefferies to arrange an appropriate ceremony in my client's fishing-village hometown. They presented him with the check at the local bank (not at his home) because he wanted to cash it right away. By the standard of living in the village the check was large, though inadequate in my view in the light of his services. My client was the local hero of the day. He is still around—sometimes on television—complaining about his treatment by our government.

On another occasion a consortium of Texas oilmen retained me to try to obtain a concession to build a gas pipeline across the Ural Mountains in Russia, in the days before Gorbachev. After a day in Paris we arrived in Moscow. I had cautioned my clients on the pitfalls they would undoubtedly encounter at the Moscow airport. They went sailing through, but I was asked to step aside. After a long wait, the reason was revealed. In New York I had bought a supply of rubles; I made it a practice to carry some local currency on trips abroad for taxi fare and incidentals. I had duly declared my rubles to the airport officials, only to discover that the USSR considered rubles acquired outside Russia as contraband, and they were confiscated. You can imagine the hilarity with which the legal adviser, caught in the toils of the law, was greeted at the hotel by his Texas friends who were in the midst of their vodka and caviar. Every time I sought to give them legal advice, they of course reminded me of my airport experience.

On still another occasion I represented a museum that had come upon a valuable set of frescoes, obviously from an ancient Christian church in the Middle East; the museum wished to buy them. The European seller wanted a handsome price indeed but couldn't furnish a credible provenance for the frescoes. I advised the client to write to all the governments in the Middle East where the frescoes might have originated: Syria, Lebanon, Israel, Turkey, Greece, and Cyprus, for example, enclosing a photo of the frescoes and asking whether they could identify them. In due course we received replies. The letter from Cyprus exactly identified the frescoes as coming from an ancient Christian church in Turkish-occupied northern Cyprus. My client and I traveled to Nicosia upon receipt of this information and consulted with high authorities of the Cypriot government and of the Orthodox church. They verified their ownership from old records and satisfied us of the valuable nature of the frescoes. After a tour of the great archeological museum in Nicosia we began to discuss means to acquire the frescoes before they were cut up on the black market and separately sold, as everyone concerned feared might happen. A second trip to Cyprus was needed before we reached agreement. My client acknowledged the title of the Church of Cyprus to the frescoes and agreed to purchase them at her expense in return for a long-term loan of the frescoes to display them in Houston, Texas; she generously agreed to build a chapel, consecrated by the Church of Cyprus, to exhibit the frescoes. The client took the frescoes first to London, where in a specially designed workshop, the intricate craft of restoring and preserving the glorious work of art was achieved over a period of time.

The Cyprus adventure led to my introduction to the DeMenil family, headed by a remarkable woman, Dominique DeMenil, the creator of the Menil Art Collection in Houston. She had engineered the recovery of the Cypriot frescoes. She asked me to join the Board of Directors of Dia Art Foundation in New York, which gave me my introduction to modern abstract art. At about this time I was married to Marion (Riki) Taylor of New York, a beautiful and talented modern abstract-art painter who, until our later separation, continued my education in the art world. In recent years, one of the principal aims of the Dia Foundation has been its attempt to make art more accessible to the public by sponsoring the creation of smaller galleries in various cities; presently the foundation is cosponsor of the Andy Warhol Museum, which is scheduled to open soon in Pittsburgh.

For the Metropolitan Museum of Art in New York, of which I was "outside counsel," a number of international transactions enlivened my practice. One involved the great painting by Velasquez, *Juan du Pareja*. The museum had acquired the masterpiece at auction in London, but strict British governmental regulations relating to the export of such valuable works had to be followed. An administrative hearing was called. Our British solicitor, with whom I worked, wanted to prove that there would be left remaining in England a representative piece of each period of Velasquez's paintings, which meant we had to travel around Britain to inspect and verify the location of such paintings. Expert witnesses of course were required. And the museum had to wait to find out whether British bidders could match the Metropolitan's bid. If they could, the painting would be required to stay in England. Our case was capably tried by the British attorneys, and I later had the enjoyable experience of attending the unveiling of the painting at the Met.

To argue an appeal of a Netherlands citizen who had been convicted of diamond smuggling, I made one of my trips to Monrovia, the capital of Liberia in western Africa. I started off swimmingly: When I awoke in the hotel the first morning and stepped out of bed, I discovered that a leaky air-conditioning system had deposited water a couple of inches deep over the floor. I paddled down to the lobby where I met a reporter from *Time* magazine similarly stranded. He was in Monrovia to cover the presidential election and was having a hard time locating the candidate opposing the incumbent president, William Tubman. Tubman had dominated the government scene in Liberia completely for many years and still did so, as I was about to find out.

I soon proceeded to the high court to argue my appeal. It was the first day of the opening session, and lawyers were required to wear formal morning coats on this occasion even though the temperature was 110 degrees in the shade. Custom also required that all lawyers who expected to appear before the court during that term must attend on that day and be sworn in. That took hours in the sweltering heat.

Because my case was number one on the calendar I then got up to argue, but the judge intervened and announced to the people in the courtroom, "There is a distinguished visitor from overseas present today, and we would be pleased to hear his comments on the state of the world today." My imprisoned Dutch client would have to wait for a while.

After I concluded my impromptu speech, I again picked up my papers to argue the appeal. But the judge, it was now quite clear, had been stalling for time; he whispered to me that President Tubman would like to speak to me at his presidential palace before I argued. Mystified, I arrived at the palace where the president received me in style, and to make a long story short, we settled my case. I never had to make my argument; my client was freed. And that evening President Tubman graciously gave a dinner and awarded me the Star of Africa in honor of my civil rights activities in the United States. En route home I visited the newly independent country of Ghana, which was then dominated by its new ruler Nkrumah, and the international industrial diamond market in Amsterdam.

One more tale of international cases in the course of my private law practice: A client wanted to marry an American woman who had previously been married to a maharajah in India. On the breakup of that marriage she had been given valuable Indian jewelry but had never been allowed to take the jewelry out of India. She wanted it in the United States before she married my client, so I was retained to get possession of the jewelry, which was lodged in a vault in New Delhi under the supervision of the Indian government. There was plenty of time for me to sightsee after my arrival in New Delhi because I found that a large number of governmental agencies had to be contacted and their approval obtained. That meant day after day of getting in line and waiting my turn—often only to be told to return the next day—to see and negotiate with the officials. Finally the red tape was unwound, and I received possession of the beautiful red and green jewels. I had expected to ship them to New York but was warned by the depository bank not to do so. Thus I carried them with me on the long plane trip home and was afraid to sleep while the package remained under the seat. I delivered the jewels safely to the bride.

When Volkswagen of Germany decided to start manufacturing operations in the United States I was asked to represent their legal interests here. In the course of negotiating with officials of the state of Pennsylvania on incentives to be offered to my client, I had an opportunity to learn the fascinating history of the company's rise to success, literally out of the rubble of postwar Germany. Before the war Volkswagen had developed and sold the immensely popular "people's car." Then the Nazis took over the plant for war production. After the war the returning German soldiers could not find employment. Those people formerly employed in the Volkswagen plant found that it had been so heavily bombed by the Allies as to be completely out of commission. With immense energy they succeeded in repairing the plant to the extent of being able to produce cars by hand—no assembly line. The only prospective customers with money were the soldiers of the occupying military forces, who eagerly snapped up the bargains. The enterprise grew by leaps and bounds. But because the Nazi government was no longer in existence, nobody owned the Volkswagen Company. Finally the banks arranged financing for expanded operations, and a plan was devised so that the postwar company would be owned by the new government, the lending banks, and—appropriately—the enterprising employees who had created the miracle.

As I look back on my career at the bar, I would urge lawyers to volunteer from time to time to serve the government and the community. I have found that such service pays rich dividends in attracting clients, friendships, and new outlooks and interests in life so that it is far from being a burden. When you get through, too, you've done something besides make money. My friend the late John J. McCloy was outstanding in his zeal to combine private law practice and service to the public. He once gave a lecture that expressed my views as well, "The Extra-Curricular Lawyer":

The lawyerly arts are only potentials. They represent challenges, not certainties. You can well be proud of the great avenues in public service, in business, in the practice of law itself that your profession opens to you; but you should refrain from taking pride in the mere fact that you are a member of the legal profession unless you have brought heavily to bear on your work the fullest expression of your own inherent character and ability.

This point of view about public service is often challenged as out-of-date by many people, especially younger people who formerly would have willingly served in governmental positions. Objections are raised that public service is no longer attractive because first, it entails a complete loss of privacy and second, it can compromise one's beliefs in a particular cause to which one is dedicated.

It is true, especially since the Watergate scandals during the Nixon administration, that the media has subjected public figures to a barrage of personal criticism, formerly considered off-limits, in an attempt to portray a candidate's character or to uncover fully the facts in a news story. All aspects of one's private life, family life, personal finances, and associations are exhibited for public consumption. Mistakes of judgment in office are labeled or implied to be sinister. At times gossipy stories appear in print primarily for the media's financial profit, and only incidentally are they of legitimate public concern. As a result, citizens hesitate to enter public service, and employers in private life frown upon such service. One hopes the media will someday act more responsibly, preserving its watchdog role while striving to minimize needless invasions of privacy. But in the interim, citizens must accept the burden because of the overriding need for their entry into public service. Our system of government will fail without them.

The second objection to entering public service is that participation in politics and government entails compromise of principle. A citizen can serve the public weal, it is said, more effectively by supporting a particular cause such as women's rights or protection of the environment. This is an appealing position on the surface. It eases the conscience by allowing one to avoid situations where compromises must be made to obtain any action and where choices are not often easy. But it fails to recognize that in a diverse nation such as ours a myriad of interests, views, and even principles must be brought together and reconciled for the public good. Two hundred years ago, many worthy citizens opposed ratification of the U.S. Constitution because they sincerely believed that it compromised sectional, economic, or political interests they held dear. Patrick Henry was one such "single-issue" figure of the day. His eloquence notwithstanding, Henry was wrong because establishment of the Constitution was of paramount importance.

These two objections to public service are potent. But there is an overriding need for voluntary citizen participation in government to preserve our liberties and our political system. Their preservation depends on maintaining a constitutional government "of the people, by the people, and for the people." Benjamin Franklin, when asked about the Constitution produced at Philadelphia, said, "It's a republic, if you can keep it." We are that "you." The president, the members of Congress, the judiciary, and the media are ultimately subordinate to "We, the people" and the constitutional system we have established. Citizens of goodwill who are willing to take part in our politics play a vital role in maintaining the ordered liberty that has been and remains so central to its continuation.

Just as important as entering public service is leaving public service when one has accomplished one's goals. The so-called "Wise Men" (the small group of former public officials who gave advice to FDR, Truman, and Eisenhower in the post–World War II era) lived, by and large, outside Washington. They did not acquire Potomac fever. Too often I have seen governmental officials stay in Washington and become paid lobbyists to try to cash in on their governmental experience; in my view at least that is not the kind of public service that brings lasting satisfaction or contributes to the public good. The model of the old Roman magistrates who retired to their farms at the end of their service and gave advice on a pro bono basis from time to time is still a good one.

My law school, Yale, recently announced that it was awarding me its highest honor. The occasion brings to mind that time in my legal education when we were told that "the law is a jealous mistress, demanding great attention but giving great pleasure." I have always found it so. The jealous mistress has commanded my constant attention for six decades but has left me still a happy suitor.

NOTES

1. New York Times v. Sullivan, 376 U.S. 254 (1964).
2. New York Times v. U.S., 403 U.S. 713 (1971).
3. New York Times v. U.S., 403 U.S. 713 (1971) at p. 740.
4. *Financial Times*, Nov. 4, 1992.

19

Bar Association Activity

❖　❖　❖　❖　❖　❖　❖　❖　❖　❖　❖　❖　❖　❖　❖

Another important facet of my legal career has been my involvement in various bar associations and other groups concerned with the integrity and reform of the legal system and with broader political and social issues. I joined the Association of the Bar of the City of New York early in my career and have maintained an active interest in its affairs for over sixty years. Later in the course of my law practice I became its president, and also served as president of the American Judicature Society and chairman of the board of the Institute for Court Management.

I joined the Association of the Bar of the City of New York in 1931 as a young lawyer. At the time I was just entering into my first campaign for a seat in the state assembly on an anti-Tammany platform, and I admired the role of the association in the civic-reform movement of that era. The association was actively inspiring the series of investigations that came to be known as the Seabury Committee, Judge Samuel Seabury being the counsel.

The main plank in my platform that year was my support of Seabury's work. Seabury had uncovered massive corruption in the administration of Mayor Jimmy Walker. In his testimony before the committee, Walker was glib—at times even entertaining—in his answers, but he could not provide any credible explanation for the payments he had received from various groups interested in doing business with the city or for the vast sums—over $1 million—that Seabury's investigators had uncovered in brokerage accounts under the mayor's name.

Seabury then sent the committee's report to Gov. Franklin D. Roosevelt, who delayed acting on it until after the Democratic convention of 1932, where FDR was nominated for president. Finally, Roosevelt conducted his own investigation of the charges, and Walker resigned as mayor. FDR thereupon declared the inquiry completed; Walker fled to Europe, a free man with his ill-gotten fortune still intact.[1]

The bar association had been instrumental in supporting Seabury's work and in bringing Walker's actions under scrutiny. Roosevelt's handling of Walker, moreover, strengthened my view that the association's role as a watchdog against corruption was of vital importance; its independence prevented the intrusion of political calculations that even FDR succumbed to.

I was also interested in the bar association because the members of my law firm had been active in the association from the beginning, and one of them had been a founder of it. The first president of the association was former U.S. Attorney General and Secretary of State William M. Evarts, a close friend of Lord, Day & Lord's founder. The *Centennial History of the Bar Association* described these men:

> Evarts arrived [from Harvard Law School in 1840] with a letter of introduction to Chancellor Kent which led him eventually to Daniel Lord, Jr.—one of the city's leading lawyers who had John Jacob Astor among his clients. Within a year Evarts had opened his own office, largely on clients sent to him by Lord. A few years later, in 1845, Daniel Lord formed the partnership of Lord, Day & Lord. This firm, which still continues, is said to be, and probably is, the oldest firm in the city retaining its original name. The Lords, father and son, were distinguished socially as well as legally and, in the opinion of some, took themselves rather too seriously. Once when [Charles] O'Conor was attending the Court of Appeals, he identified the lawyer who was speaking by growling in response to an inquiry: "That is Daniel Lord, Jr.—he adds Jr. to his name to distinguish him from the Lord Almighty."

My first assignment as a committee member in the association was to write a brief supporting the proposition that the office of attorney general of New York State should be changed from an elective office to one appointed by the governor. Then, too, as a member of the assembly I acted as a sort of liaison between the assembly committees that were considering bills affecting New York City and the association's Committee on State Legislation.

When I became U.S. attorney general in 1953, I was called upon by a delegation from the association headed by Whitney North Seymour, Jr., and Bethuel Webster, as a result of which the association took an active role in assisting the attorney general in investigating the qualifications of persons being considered for federal judgeships from the New York area. And I requested help from the association in defeating the Bricker amendment and in formulating proper standards for the internal-security regulations of the federal government.

Against this background I was greatly honored, when I returned from Washington to private practice in New York, to be chosen as president of the bar association. The association was at the time undergoing a transition from its earlier days when it was considered (by legislators, among others) as a sort of elitist organization into its current status as a widely representative professional society taking an active interest in all significant legal and social problems of the day. Some of the old rules still prevailed when I assumed my duties: The president-elect was presented to the membership at a formal white-tie reception with an interminable receiving line—shades of Washington, D.C.!

The leading spirits in transforming the society to an informal and warm-hearted professional association were a former president of the association, Harrison Tweed, and the long-time executive secretary, Paul DeWitt. They had energized the work of dozens of committees, which met regularly to research and report upon the current problems in the field of law. Emphasis was on improving standards of the bar and the judiciary. The output of the committees was recognized throughout the country as first-class. As a result, the office of president of the association during my two-year stint was both stimulating and professionally rewarding.

Presidency of the association in 1962 and 1963 gave me an opportunity to continue some aspects of the civil rights activities in which I had been engaged as attorney general. I created a Civil Rights Committee and appointed as its chairman Frank Rivers, a black judge who had been originally appointed to the bench by Governor Dewey. His committee worked constructively with the Senate and House committees in Washington that were considering civil rights legislation.

At the time, legal assistance for the poor was grossly underfinanced, and the Legal Aid Society was desperately in need of additional funding. The bar association advocated the use of substantial public funds for this purpose, and I was privileged to work with Mayor Robert F. Wagner, Jr., of New York, who made city funds available for this work in sizable amounts.

My chief effort as president was in the field of protecting the interest of forgotten victims of crime. I summarized my efforts to obtain justice for these victims when I delivered the Thirty-second Annual Benjamin N. Cardozo Lecture at the Association of the Bar on March 4, 1976, and quoted an excerpt from one of Cardozo's opinions: "Justice, though due to the accused, is due to the accuser also. The concept of fairness must not be strained till it is narrowed to a filament. We are to keep the balance true." I painted a rather drab picture of the neglect in our criminal-justice system for the innocent victim of crime. I described how badly we treat the victim when we ask him to help prosecute the criminal:

> Several times he will be made to wait tedious, unconscionably long intervals of time in dingy courthouse corridors or in other grim surroundings. Several times he will suffer the discomfort of being ignored by busy officials and the bewilderment and painful anxiety of not knowing what is going on around him or what is going to happen to him. On most of these occasions he will never be asked to testify or to give anyone any information, often because of the last-minute adjournment granted in a huddled conference at the judge's bench. He will miss many hours from work (or school) and consequently will lose many hours of wages. In most jurisdictions he will receive at best only token payment in the form of ridiculously low witness fees for his time and trouble. In many metropolitan areas he will, in fact, receive no recompense at all because he will be told neither that he is entitled to fees nor how to get them. Through long months of waiting for the end of a criminal case, he must remain ever on call, reminded of his continuing attachment to the court by sporadic subpoenas. For some, each subpoena and each appearance at court is accompanied by tension and terror prompted by fear of the lawyers, fear of the defendant or his friends, and fear of the unknown. In sum, the experience is dreary, time-wasting, depressing, exhausting, confusing, frustrating, numbing and seemingly endless.

I am glad to say that the New York courts are attempting to cure this problem and have established a witness-aid services unit to respond to the needs of crime victims and witnesses, including the creation of a witness-intimidation program, which aids crime victims who have been harassed either verbally or physically by the defendant or his associates.

One of my first assignments as president was to represent the association at a hearing before the Senate Judiciary Committee to oppose the confirmation of an attorney who had been nominated as a federal district court judge. I was seated next to the candidate as I recited all the reasons that our association's Judiciary Committee gave for its opinion that he was unqualified. Not long after, as luck would have it, I had to argue an antitrust motion in federal court, and who should be sitting but the newly appointed judge who had been confirmed by the U.S. Senate over our association's opposition. There was a happy ending for me, however, when the judge granted my motion.

The association at one point selected Chief Justice Earl Warren as one of the very few persons to be chosen as an honorary member of the association. When he arrived in New York to accept the honor and to deliver an address, he came to my apartment for dinner and of course we reminisced. When we arrived in the vicinity of the bar association headquarters the street was completely blocked by a crowd waving banners proclaiming "Impeach Earl Warren." It was impossible to get to the front door but we found our way through a back entrance. The chief justice was greeted warmly by one of the largest crowds in the association's long history.

At the time the association was designated by the state courts to hear and to make recommendations in disciplinary matters involving members of the bar. (Since then the system has been changed so that the court directly handles such matters.) One of the saddest cases to come before the association involved a distinguished member of the bar, former Dean James Landis of Harvard Law School. With no apparent excuse he failed to file his income-tax returns and was convicted for it. This conviction, under the law, required almost automatically that he be disbarred. He was well and favorably known to the members of the association, but we had to perform that disagreeable task. The story had a tragic ending when Landis committed suicide.

Other aspects of the bar association presidency were more appealing. They involved travels abroad (mostly after the term of my presidency expired) to attend international conferences of lawyers. On one of these trips, I encountered the "Night of Long Knives," the name attached to the great shake-up in the British cabinet by Prime Minister Harold Macmillan in summer 1962. It was memorialized by Jeremy Thorpe's wisecrack:

"Greater love hath no man than he lay down his friends for his life." My wife and I had planned to have lunch with Lord Chancellor David Kilmuir and his wife (the sister of Rex Harrison of *My Fair Lady* fame) together with Attorney General Reginald Manningham-Buller and Lady Mary on the following day. But in the shake-up Macmillan had replaced the lord chancellor with the attorney general quite unceremoniously, so we hastily arranged separate lunches with our friends in the House of Lords dining room. After witnessing the elaborate ceremony of the investiture of the new lord chancellor we attended a meeting of the International Bar Association in Edinburgh. Between sessions devoted mostly to international aspects of antitrust laws, we gave a reception for the lawyers from all over the English-speaking world and their wives at Prestonfield House. We entertained as a special guest the widow of a former mayor of Edinburgh, Peter Given, who had made an international reputation after World War II by pioneering in municipal low-cost housing for the poor. The widow was distinguished in her own right in the field of social service, but to us she was Aunt Maggie, my wife's aunt who had entertained us some years before when we were on our honeymoon in Scotland.

As a former president of the City Bar Association, I was designated as a delegate to a meeting of the International Commission of Jurists in New Delhi, my first trip to India. The Jurists Commission has done yeoman work in exposing violations of human rights of citizens by governmental action in various parts of the world. A highlight of the meeting was the opening address by Prime Minister Jawaharlal Nehru, who humorously recounted his experiences in enforcing the rule of law as a governmental official after his years of activity in leading passive resistance to British rule in India. As a sidelight, I learned that most of the attorneys from the Indian delegation were members of the Parsi religion, and in the course of their hospitality we had an unusual opportunity to learn about their history and customs.

Two other meetings of lawyers in an international setting involved the Inter-American Bar Association, a group of attorneys from various South and Central American countries with which our bar association had a working relationship. At one of these meetings in Puerto Rico in 1965, Chief Justice Warren and I were guests of the local bar association and helped dedicate two of their handsome new buildings—a bar association headquarters and a new courthouse. An amusing incident occurred when the president of the American Bar Association arrived by plane very late and was hustled into the meeting hall without time to get his bearings before he was called upon to speak: He solemnly dedicated the wrong building. The other goodwill visit to an Inter-American Bar Association meeting was to Paraguay. I must say the social events on that occasion were more interesting than the legal presentations—they included fascinating sidetrips to the Isazu Falls and to Buenos Aires.

I was followed as president of the association by Judge Samuel Rosenman. During our transition talks, as can well be imagined, he and I and our wives conversed as much about our Washington experiences as about the work of the bar association. Rosenman was FDR's special counsel and chief speech writer, continuing in that capacity for a while under Harry S. Truman. As such, he was the creator of some of the most vigorous attacks by these two Democrats against Thomas E. Dewey. I had to concede that his bosses' oratory was more effective in the political arena than ours. But we agreed on the importance of the activities of the bar association and worked harmoniously there.

Another professional association in which I have maintained an active interest is the American Judicature Society, a nationwide association of lawyers, judges, and laymen interested in improving our court systems. It is best known for its advocacy of a merit plan for the selection of judges. Many states choose their judges by popular election. This practice throws the process into partisan politics and often minimizes the emphasis that should be put on professional qualifications. Even where judges are appointed rather than elected, especially in areas ruled by well-entrenched political machines, politics is a major factor. These procedures, of course, cast suspicion on the impartiality of the bench. In my opinion, too often the system results in mediocrity and in a few instances corruption.

I expressed this view one time in a national magazine and flatly asserted that some corruption was involved in the selection of New York City judges. Straightaway I received a letter from the chief judge of the state court system, who had disciplinary power over the members of the bar of the state. He asked me for proof of my assertions and indicated that if I didn't produce it, he would order a disciplinary proceeding. If corroboration was needed, like manna from heaven came to my hands a recently published book of reminiscences written by a well-known former political leader of the city, citing chapter and verse of instances where judgeships had been purchased. I sent the book, with a few added comments, to the chief judge. That was the end of our correspondence.

In any event, I was eager to further the work of the Judicature Society to introduce the merit system in as many states as possible. The system calls for appointment by the governor or mayor of a nonpartisan commission of citizens, composed of lawyers and laypersons, to interview candidates for judgeships. The commission would choose the three or five names of persons it deemed most qualified. The governor or mayor would then be limited to choosing one of those names on the commission's list. Many jurisdictions have adopted the merit plan. Although it is not a perfect system, it has improved the quality of the judiciary where the plan is in effect. And in quite a number of places, elected officials have expressed relief at being freed from the pressure from political parties or special interests since they are forced to follow the requirements of the merit system.

During my term at the Judicature Society we also set up training lessons for the members of the Judicial Selection Commissions to acquaint them—especially the lay members—with the qualities desirable in a judge: integrity, standing in the community, professional experience and competence, and judicial temperament, among others.

Still another pro bono professional assignment was my appointment by Chief Justice Warren E. Burger as the first chairman of the Board of the Institute for Court Management. Burger excelled in his encouragement of movements to improve the federal judicial system. Delays in the administration of justice, he noted in a report to the public, resulted in part from the failure to apply modern business-management techniques in handling court work. Judges who tried to manage the overloaded court calendars were untrained in that area and usually were unsuccessful. He caused an Institute for Court Management to be established, a training school for laypersons to learn to apply business-management techniques to the work of the courts. Today graduates of the training courses of the institute have been appointed to administer the business side of the work of the federal courts in most if not all the districts throughout the country.

Finally, the professional association of lawyers in bar associations and other groups concerned with reforms in the law and the professional conduct of members form a vital part in the ability of the legal profession to perform its proper role in the legal system, regulate its members, and otherwise aid the rule of law, fair legal procedure, and the enforcement of constitutional rights. The Association of the Bar of New York City was formed precisely for these reasons, and over the years it not only has nobly guarded the integrity of the legal community but has been at the forefront of constructive reform in the city, state, and nation.

NOTES

1. George Martin, *Causes and Conflicts: Centennial History of the Association of the Bar of the City of New York* (Boston: Houghton Mifflin, 1970), p. 235.

20

Winding Down

❖ ❖ ❖ ❖ ❖ ❖ ❖ ❖ ❖ ❖ ❖ ❖ ❖ ❖ ❖

During the post-Washington years that I have described, our family lived at Sixty-sixth and Park Avenue across the street from the Armory, a New York landmark. It was a most pleasant mode of living, with neighbors in the building such as Walter and Jane Pickens Hoving, Mrs. Harriett Pratt, Mr. and Mrs. Thornton Bradshaw, and other well-known New Yorkers. In 1979, however, Doris died after a courageous fight against cancer. Several years later I suffered a heart attack, which slowed down my activities. As my law practice wound down, I turned to service on the boards of directors of various nonprofit corporations. These included the Bicentennial Commission on the U.S. Constitution, the Ludwig Institute for Cancer Research, the Dia Center for the Arts, and the Miller Center for Study of the Presidency at the University of Virginia.

Eventually I retired, after sixty-two years at the bar. I am blessed with recovery from the heart attack and, at this writing, receive unbounded pleasure from my children, grandchildren, and great-grandchildren.

In a symbolic way, I wrapped up my public and political career at events in 1990 marking the centenary of Dwight D. Eisenhower's birth. The first was a Joint Session of Congress, followed by a White House luncheon. At the joint session in the House of Representatives, the army and the West Point choir played and sang the two patriotic songs that always "get me"— "West Point" and "America the Beautiful." John Eisenhower and Sen. Robert Dole gave great tributes to Ike. Walter Cronkite, the embodiment of a free press in America, was magnificent in his remarks, and Winston Churchill III thrilled the audience with recollections of his grandfather and Ike in World War II. The British, French, and Russian ambassadors were in the audience to further remind us of the war and the cold-war years. At the White House, President and Mrs. Bush spoke of Ike and Mamie eloquently.

I was the sole survivor there of Ike's first cabinet, but two former assistants from my old team at the Justice Department were there, adding to my pleasure—former chief justice Warren E. Burger and former secretary of state and attorney general William P. Rogers. I was seated between Betsy Cronkite, a friend and an avid Eisenhower fan, and Sen. James Exon from my native state of Nebraska. Clark Clifford was across the table, reminding me of the Truman-Dewey campaign of 1948 when we had played campaign-manager roles opposite each other. Just about every facet of my public life was encompassed in those few hours.

Then, in June of Ike's centennial year, there was a meeting of the survivors of the Little Rock desegregation crisis. It was held at the Eisenhower Library in Abilene, Kansas, in connection with a symposium, Civil Rights in the Eisenhower Presidency. Former Governor Orval Faubus of Arkansas attended and spoke, restating his original views opposing school desegregation. Four of the original nine black students who were barred from attending high school in 1957 by Governor Faubus were there and retold their stories of the crisis. The widow and family of Oliver Brown, who was the first-named plaintiff in *Brown v. Board of Education*, were also on hand. The lawyer for the state of Kansas in the *Brown* case, Paul Wilson, was there, as was Hugh Spear, the key witness for the schoolchildren in that case. Ambassador Maxwell Rabb, who assisted Eisenhower at the desegregation of Washington, D.C., attended, as did Rocco Siciliano, who had arranged a historic meeting between Eisenhower and Martin Luther King. Arthur Fletcher, currently chairman of the U.S. Civil Rights Commission established under the Civil Rights Act of 1957, delivered a stirring address. And I was there to keynote the event and to review Ike's actions in desegregating the nation's capital, intervening in the *Brown* case then before the Supreme Court, enforcing the *Brown* decision by sending troops to Little Rock to enable the black students to enter the high school, and advancing the cause of civil rights by sponsoring successfully the Civil Rights Act of 1957, the first such legislation in almost 100 years. It was a dramatic retelling of one of the high points in my public life.

Appendix A

Eisenhower's Letter to Brownell, March 18, 1952

❖ ❖ ❖ ❖ ❖ ❖ ❖

Supreme Headquarters
Allied Powers Europe
18 March 1952

Dear Mr. Brownell:

I understand that there is a prospect of my seeing you over here very soon. This note is just to assure you of a warm welcome. I have just been visiting with General Clay, who tells me how much of your time and effort you have been devoting in the affairs of the National Committee that is dedicated to the purpose of drafting me into the Republican nomination. I have a profound sense of distinction in the knowledge that so many outstanding American citizens—including yourself—are giving expression to their conviction that I could serve the country well in the highest political post.

As you and your associates study the New Hampshire election, I know that you must feel gratified that the first visible results of your long and hard work are beginning to show up. To everyone who has sent me a congratulatory message on the New Hampshire Primary, I have replied to the effect that the credit belongs to the workers in the cause. Among all these, the first is obviously the group comprising the National Committee. I sent a note to Governor Adams of which he apparently approved. At least, he published it in New Hampshire.

With personal regard and best wishes.

Very sincerely,

/s/ Dwight D. Eisenhower
18 March

Mr. Herbert Brownell, Jr.
25 Broadway
New York 4, New York

Appendix B

United States Supreme Court Order in

Brown v. Board of Education

In their briefs and on oral argument [on reargument] counsel are requested to discuss particularly the following questions insofar as they are relevant to the respective cases:

1. What evidence is there that the Congress which submitted and the State legislatures and conventions which ratified the Fourteenth Amendment contemplated or did not contemplate, understood or did not understand, that it would abolish segregation in public schools?

2. If neither the Congress in submitting nor the States in ratifying the Fourteenth Amendment understood that compliance with it would require the immediate abolition of segregation in public schools, was it nevertheless the understanding of the framers of the Amendment

(a) that future Congresses might, in the exercise of their power under section 5 of the Amendment, abolish such segregation, or

(b) that it would be within the judicial power, in light of future conditions, to construe the Amendment as abolishing such segregation of its own force?

3. On the assumption that the answers to questions 2(a) and (b) do not dispose of the issue, is it within the judicial power, in construing the Amendment, to abolish segregation in public schools?

4. Assuming it is decided that segregation in public schools violates the Fourteenth Amendment

(a) would a decree necessarily follow providing that, within the limits set by normal geographic school districting, Negro children should forth-with be admitted to schools of their choice, or

(b) may this Court, in the exercise of its equity powers permit an effective gradual adjustment to be brought about from existing segregated systems to a system not based on color distinctions?

5. On the assumption on which questions 4(a) and (b) are based, and assuming further that this Court will exercise its equity powers to the end described in question 4(b),

(a) should this Court formulate detailed decrees in these cases;

(b) if so, what specific issues should the decrees reach;

(c) should this Court appoint a special master to hear evidence with a view to recommending specific terms for such decrees;

(d) should this Court remand to the courts of first instance with directions to frame decrees in these cases, and if so what general directions should the decrees of this Court include and what procedures should the courts of first instance follow in arriving at the specific terms of more detailed decrees?

The attorney general of the United States is invited to take part in the oral argument and to file an additional brief if he so desires.

Appendix C

Southern Manifesto

❖ ❖ ❖ ❖ ❖ ❖ ❖

The unwarranted decision of the Supreme Court in the public school cases is now bearing the fruit always produced when men substitute naked power to established law.

The Founding Fathers gave us a Constitution of checks and balances because they realized the inescapable lesson of history that no man or group of men can be safely entrusted with unlimited power. They framed this Constitution with its provisions for change by amendment in order to secure the fundamentals of government against the dangers of temporary popular passion or the personal predilections of public office holders.

We regard the decision of the Supreme Court in the school cases as a clear abuse of judicial power. It climaxes a trend in the federal judiciary undertaking to legislate, in derogation of the authority of Congress, and to encroach upon the reserved rights of the States and the people.

The original Constitution does not mention education. Neither does the Fourteenth Amendment nor any other Amendment. The debates preceding the submission of the Fourteenth Amendment clearly show that there was no intent that it should affect the systems of education maintained by the States.

The very Congress which proposed the amendment subsequently provided for segregated schools in the District of Columbia.

When the Amendment was adopted in 1865, there were 37 States in the Union. Every one of the 26 States that had any substantial racial differences among its people either approved the operation of the segregated schools already in existence or subsequently established such schools by action of the same law-making body which considered the Fourteenth Amendment.

As admitted by the Supreme Court in the public school case (Brown v. Board of Education) the doctrine of separate but equal schools "apparently originated in Roberts v. City of Boston . . . (1849), upholding school segregation against attack as being violative of a State constitutional guarantee of equality." The constitutional doctrine began in the North—not in the South, and it was followed not only in Massachusetts, but in Connecticut, New York, Illinois, Indiana, Michigan, Minnesota, New Jersey, Ohio, Pennsylvania, and other northern States until they, exercising their rights as states through the constitutional processes of local self-government, changed their school systems.

In the case of Plessy v. Ferguson in 1896 the Supreme Court expressly declared that under the Fourteenth Amendment no person was denied any of his rights if the states provided separate but equal public facilities. This decision has been followed in many other cases. It is notable that the Supreme Court, speaking through Chief Justice Taft, a former President of the United States, unanimously declared in 1927 in Lum v. Rice that "separate but equal" principle is . . . "within the discretion of the State in regulating its public schools and does not conflict with the Fourteenth Amendment."

This interpretation, restated time and again, became a part of the life of the people of many of the States and confirmed their habits, customs, traditions, and way of life. It is founded on elemental humanity and common sense, for parents should not be deprived by government of the right to direct the lives and education of their own children.

Though there has been no constitutional amendment or Act of Congress changing this established legal principle almost a century old, the Supreme Court of the United States, with no legal basis for such action, undertook to exercise their naked judicial power and substituted their personal political and social ideas for the established law of the land.

This unwarranted exercise of power by the Court, contrary to the Constitution, is creating chaos and confusion in the States principally affected. It is destroying the amicable relations between the white and Negro races that have been created through 90 years of patient effort by the good people of both races. It has planted hatred and suspicion where there has been heretofore friendship and understanding.

Without regard to the consent of the governed, outside agitators are threatening immediate and revolutionary changes in our public school systems. If done, this is certain to destroy the system of public education in some of the States.

With the greatest concern for the explosive and dangerous condition created by this decision and inflamed by outside meddlers:

We reaffirm our reliance on the Constitution as the fundamental law of the land.

We decry the Supreme Court's encroachments on rights reserved to the States and to the people, contrary to established law and to the Constitution.

We commend the motives of those States which have declared the intention to resist forced integration by any lawful means.

We appeal to the States and people who are not directly affected by these decisions to consider the constitutional principles involved against the time when they too, on issues vital to them, may be victims of judicial encroachment.

Even though we constitute a minority in the present Congress, we have full faith that a majority of the American people believe in the dual system of government which has enabled us to achieve our greatness and will in time demand that the reserved rights of the States and of the people be made secure against judicial usurpation.

We pledge ourselves to use all lawful means to bring about a reversal of this decision which is contrary to the Constitution and to prevent the use of force in its implementation.

In this trying period, as we all seek to right this wrong, we appeal to our people not to be provoked by the agitators and troublemakers invading our States and to scrupulously refrain from disorder and lawless acts.

Signed by (all are Democrats unless otherwise noted):

Alabama
Senators:
Lister Hill
John Sparkman

Reps:
George Andrews
Frank Boyden
Carl Elliott
George Grant

George Huddleston, Jr.
Robert Jones
Albert Rains
Kenneth Roberts
Armistead Selden, Jr.

Arkansas
Senators:
J. W. Fulbright
John McClellan

Reps:
E. C. Gathings
Oren Harris
Brooks Hays
Wilbur Mills
W. F. Norrell
James Trimble

Florida
Senators:
Spessard Holland
George Smathers

Reps:
Charles Bennett
William Cramer (R)
James Haley
A. S. Herlong, Jr.
D. R. Matthews
Paul Rogers
Robert Sikes

Georgia
Senators:
Walter George
Richard Russell

Reps:
Iris Blitch
Paul Brown
James Davis
John James Flynt, Jr.
E. L. Forrester
Phil Landrum
Henderson Lanham
John Pilcher
Prince Preston
Carl Vinson

Louisiana
Senators:
Allen Ellender
Russell Long

Reps:
Hale Boggs
Overton Brooks
F. Edward Hebert
George Long
James Morrison
Otto Passman
T. Ashton Thompson
Edwin Willis

Mississippi
Senators:
James Eastland
John Stennis

Reps:
Thomas Abernethy
William Colmer
Frank Smith
Jamie Whitten
John Bell Williams
Arthur Winstead

North Carolina
Senators:
Sam Ervin, Jr.
W. Kerr Scott

Reps:
Hugh Alexander
Graham Barden
Herbert Bonner
F. Ertel Carlyle
Carl Durham
L. H. Fountain

Charles Raper Jonas (R)
Woodrow Jones
George Shuford

South Carolina
Senators:
Olin Johnston
Strom Thurmond

Reps:
Robert Ashmore
W. J. Bryan Dorn
John McMillan
James Richards
John Riley
L. Mendel Rivers

Tennessee
Senators:
none

Reps:
Ross Bass
Jere Cooper
Clifford Davis
Joe Evins
James Frazier, Jr.
Tom Murray

Texas
Senators:
Price Daniel

Reps:
Martin Dies
John Dowdy
O. C. Fisher
Wright Patman
Walter Rogers

Virginia
Senators:
Harry F. Byrd
A. Willis Robertson

Reps:
Watkins Abbitt
Joel Broyhill (R)
J. Vaughan Gary
Porter Hardy, Jr.
Burr Harrison
W. Pat Jennings
Richard Poff (R)
Edward Robeson, Jr.
Howard Smith
William Tuck

Neither Speaker of the House Sam
Rayburn nor Senate Majority Leader
Lyndon Johnson, both from Texas,
was asked to sign the manifesto.
Other Southern legislators who did
not sign: Senate—Albert Gore and
Estes Kefauver, both of Tenn.;
House—Florida, Dante Fascell;
North Carolina, Thurmond
Chatham, Harold Cooley, Charles
Deane; Tenn., Howard Baker (R),
J. Percy Priest, B. Carroll Reece (R);
Texas, Bruce Alger (R), John Bell,
Jack Brooks, Omar Burleson, Brady
Gentry, Frank Ikard, Paul Kilday, Joe
Kilgore, George Mahon, W. R.
Poage, J. T. Rutherford, Olin Teague,
Albert Thomas, Clark Thompson,
Homer Thornberry, James Wright,
Jr.

Appendix D

Brownell Opinion to Eisenhower

on Little Rock School Desegregation

[Letterhead of]
Office of the Attorney General
Washington, D.C.

The President
  The White House
My dear Mr. President:

I am formally submitting to you in this opinion the legal advice which I have given you on separate recent occasions on certain questions arising in the school desegregation case in Little Rock, Arkansas, between September 3, 1957, and October 1, 1957. Because of the grave constitutional issues involved, and the direct bearing of those issues upon the action taken by you as President of the United States, I believe it advisable that this advice should be made into a permanent record.

On May 24, 1955, the School Board of Little Rock School district formulated a plan for a transition to a system of racially desegregated schools in several successive stages. Desegregation at the senior high school level was to take place in the fall of 1957, at the junior high school level in 1959 or 1960, and at the elementary school level in 1962 or 1963. There was no Federal participation in the development of the plan.

Litigation involving this plan began with an action on behalf of certain Negro children who complained that the period of time proposed for desegregation was too long. The United States did not participate in this litigation. The United States District Court, E.D. Arkansas (Judge Miller) found the plan of the School Board to be adequate and, accordingly, denied the prayer for a declaratory judgment and injunctive relief. The Court retained jurisdiction "for the entry of such other and further orders as may be necessary to obtain the effectuation of the plan as contemplated and set forth herein" (*Aaron v. Cooper*, 143 F. Supp. 855, 866, decree dated August 28, 1956). The Court of Appeals for the Eighth Circuit, affirming the action of the lower court, stated:

> Jurisdiction of this case shall be retained by the District Court to insure full opportunity for further showing in the event compliance at the "earliest practicable date" ceases to be the objective. The prayer for a declaratory judgment and injunctive relief was properly denied. (243 F.2d 36, 364, April 26, 1957)

Some four months later, upon the basis of an action instituted in the Arkansas State courts (Pulaski Chancery Court, First Division), following testimony by Governor Orval E. Faubus that desegregation at the Central High School, if carried out, might lead to violence, that Court on August 29, 1957, entered a restraining order to prevent the desegregation plan from taking effect (*Thomason v. Cooper*). The following day, August 30, 1957, upon petition of the School Board, the United States District Court, Eastern District of Arkansas, Western Division (Judge Davies), issued an order enjoining the plaintiff in the Chancery Court action "and the Class she represents, and all others" from (a) using the Chancery Court order "as a means of preventing or interfering with the opening of the integrated high schools in Little Rock School District, on September 3, 1957, in accordance with the Decree of this Court entered on August 15, 1956,[1] (b) taking steps to cause the School Board members to be punished for contempt in failing to obey the Chancery Court order; and (c) "in any manner, directly and indirectly, interfering with or hindering the actions of the petitioners in carrying out the Decree of this Court entered herein on August 15, 1956" (*Aaron v. Cooper*). In other words, Judge Davies acted to prevent obstruction of the court order issued by Judge Miller over a year prior thereto, which order of Judge Miller had been upheld on appeal by the Eighth Circuit Court of Appeals.

On September 2, 1957, units of the National Guard were stationed at the Little Rock Central High School, upon order of the Governor, for the announced reason to "preserve the peace and good order." Upon direction of the Governor, the Arkansas State Police was mobilized "to act as an arm of the State Militia in maintaining or restoring the peace and order of the community and to act in every way possible to protect the lives and property of the citizens of Pulaski County." According to the Governor's statement:

Units of the National Guard have been or are now being mobilized with the mission to maintain or restore the peace and good order of this community. Advance units are already on duty on the grounds of Central High School.

The mission of the State Militia is to maintain or restore order and to protect the lives and property of citizens. They will act not as segregationists or integrationists, but as soldiers called to active duty to carry out their assigned tasks.

But, I must state here in all sincerity that it is my opinion—yes, even a conviction, that it will not be possible to restore or to maintain order and protect the lives and property of the citizens if forcible integration is carried out tomorrow in the schools of this community. The inevitable conclusion therefore must be that the schools in Pulaski County, for the time being, must be operated on the same basis as they have been operated in the past.

Later in the day, on September 2, the School Board issued the following statement:

Although the Federal Court has ordered integration to proceed, Governor Faubus has said that schools should continue as they have in the past and has stationed troops at Central High School to maintain order.

In view of this situation, we ask that no Negro students attempt to attend Central or any white high school until this dilemma is legally resolved.

In a petition filed with the District Court on September 3, the School Board described its attempt to proceed in conformity with the announced and approved plan of desegregation; the action of the Governor in placing members of the Arkansas National Guard around Central High School; and the statement of the School Board requesting Negro students not to attempt to attend any white high school. The School Board then asked "that this Court exempt them from any charge of contempt and instruct them as to whether they should recall the request" that no Negro students should attend Central or any white high school.

On the same day, September 3, Judge Davies ordered:

> The evidence presented to this Court reveals no reason why the original plan of integration approved by this Court cannot be carried out forthwith.
>
> It is concluded that the defendants should be directed and ordered to integrate in the Little Rock school district, the senior high schools, immediately and without delay, and thereafter to pursue the plan heretofore approved by this Court.
>
> It is, therefore, by the Court ordered that the defendants, and each of them, as the Little Rock School Board and as Superintendent of Little Rock Public Schools, integrate, in accordance with the plan approved by this Court, the senior high school grades in the Little Rock school district forthwith.
>
> The injunction entered by this Court on August 30, 1957, upon application of these defendants shall remain valid and in full force and effect.

Notwithstanding the order of the Federal Court directing that the school plan proceed, the National Guard, under orders of the Governor, turned away the Negro students who attempted to enter the school. It later developed that the Governor's order to General Sherman T. Clinger, Adjutant General, read: "You are directed to place off limits to white students those schools for colored students and to place off limits to colored students those schools heretofore operated and recently set up for white students. This order will remain in effect until the demobilization of the Guard or until further orders." This action was in direct derogation of the orders of the Federal Court and effectively frustrated those orders.

The first issue on which you requested my opinion was whether the United States courts possessed the power to review the action of the Governor in preventing execution of the Federal Court's orders through the use by the Governor of military force, and, if that power existed, the manner of its exercise and the factors upon which its decision to review the Governor's action would hinge.

I then advised you, and do again advise you, that the United States courts have jurisdiction to determine the legality of the action of a State governor which contravenes an order of a Federal Court. This power exists although the Governor seeks to justify his action as required to maintain peace and order within the State, and announces his considered judgment that domestic order could not be maintained unless the action in question were taken. The law in such cases is that the Federal courts are vested with power to review the judgment of the Governor of the necessity for his action and to determine the validity of the justification he asserts.

This principle is unequivocally set forth in *Sterling v. Constantin*, 287 U.S. 370 (1932).

The *Sterling* case arose out of attempts by the authorities of Texas to limit oil production. The producers had obtained an order from the United States District Court restraining the enforcement of limitations set by the State Commission. The Governor declared the oil producing area concerned to be in "a state of insurrection, tumult, riot, and a breach of the peace," declared martial law in the area, and directed the commanders of the National Guard to enforce the production limitations. The Governor and the Adjutant General of the National Guard were made parties to the proceedings and, after hearing, an injunction was issued against them. The Supreme Court of the United States affirmed the judgment. The Court, in an opinion by Chief Justice Hughes, stated that it was "obviously untenable" to accept the conclusion that "the Governor's order had the quality of a supreme and unchallengeable edict, overriding all conflicting rights of property and unreviewable through the judicial power of the Federal Government" (p. 397). The Court added that:

> When there is a substantial showing that the exertion of state power has overridden private rights secured by that Constitution, the subject is necessarily one for judicial inquiry in an appropriate proceeding directed against the individuals charged with the transgression. To such a case the federal judicial power extends (Art. III, Sec. 2) and, so extending, the court has all the authority appropriate to its exercise. Accordingly, it has been decided in a great variety of circumstances that when questions of law and fact are so intermingled as to make it necessary, in order to pass upon the federal question, the court may, and should, analyze the facts. (p. 398)

It is further my opinion, as I have advised you, that the mere existence of a threat of domestic violence would be insufficient to justify the Governor in taking action to nullify the order of the Federal Court by the use of force. The United States Supreme Court stated the well-recognized rule that the executive is necessarily vested with discretion to determine whether an exigency requiring military aid to suppress disorder has arisen. But this rule is subject to the reservation that the courts may determine whether the limits of allowable discretion have been overstepped (*Sterling v. Constantin*, supra):

> It does not follow from the fact that the Executive has this range of discretion, deemed to be a necessary incident of his power to suppress disorder, that every sort of action the Governor may take, no matter how unjustified by the exigency or subversive of private right and the jurisdiction of the courts, otherwise available, is conclusively supported by mere executive fiat. The contrary is well established. What are the allowable limits of military discretion, and whether or not they have been overstepped in a particular case, are judicial questions. (pp. 400–401)

It is clear from the Court's opinion that the Governor's duty and responsibility in using military force is to support the law, not to subvert it, and to remove any domestic disorder that would prevent compliance with the Court's decrees. Said the Court:

> Fundamentally, the question here is not of the power of the Governor to proclaim that a state of insurrection, or tumult, or riot, or breach of the peace exists, and that it is necessary to call military force to the aid of the civil power. Nor does the question relate to the quelling of disturbances and the overcoming of unlawful resistance to civil authority. The question before us is simply with respect to the Governor's attempt to regulate by executive order the lawful use of complainants' properties in the production of oil. *Instead of affording them protection in the lawful exercise of their rights as determined by the courts, he sought, by his executive orders, to make that exercise impossible."* (pp. 401–2; emphasis added)

Continuing, the Court added:

> In the present case, the findings of fact made by the District Court are fully supported by the evidence. They leave no room for doubt that there was no military necessity which, from any point of view, could be taken to justify the action of the Governor in attempting to limit

complainants' oil production, otherwise lawful. . . . There was no exigency which justified the Governor in attempting to enforce by executive or military order the restriction which the District Judge had restrained pending proper judicial inquiry. If it be assumed that the Governor was entitled to declare a state of insurrection and to bring military force to the aid of civil authority, the proper use of that power in this instance was to maintain the federal court in the exercise of its jurisdiction and not to attempt to override it; to aid in making its process effective and not to nullify it; to remove, and not to create, obstructions to the exercise by the complainants of their rights as judicially declared. (pp. 403–4)

The principles expressed in *Sterling v. Constantin* have been reaffirmed in a number of later decisions.[2] Of particular significance is the language of the Court in *Strutwear Knitting Co. v. Olson*, 33 Fed. supp. 364 (D.C. Minn. 1936). The Governor of Minnesota has used National Guard troops to close a factory to prevent probable loss of life and property from the acts of a mob objecting to its operation. Holding that such use of force by the Governor was not permissible the Court stated:

It is certain that while the state government is functioning, it cannot suppress disorders the object of which is to deprive citizens of their lawful rights, by using its forces to assist in carrying out the unlawful purposes of those who create the disorders, or by suppressing rights which it is the duty of the state to defend. The use of troops or police for such purposes would breed violence. It would constitute an assurance to those who resort to violence to attain their ends that, if they gathered in sufficient numbers to constitute a menace to life, the forces of law would not only not oppose them, but would actually assist them in accomplishing their objective. There could be but one final result, namely, a complete breakdown of government and a resort to force both by the law-abiding and the lawless. (p. 391)

To summarize: the action of a State Governor in using troops to invade rights protected by the Federal Constitution, and, in particular, to frustrate by direct action the order of a federal court, is reviewable by the Federal judicial process. The mere existence or threat of domestic violence, disorder, or riot cannot serve as justification for such invasion of rights or frustration of a court order; where domestic violence arises, it is the overriding duty of the State authorities to use its forces to protect such rights against invasion and such court orders against obstruction.[3]

In the Little Rock matter, no effort whatever had been made by the Governor of Arkansas to use his powers to uphold the jurisdiction of the federal court and to aid, rather than subvert, the execution of its orders. On the contrary, his purpose seemed clearly directed toward a nullification of the court's mandate. I advised you that the propriety of his action should be judicially determined.

The wise counsel and cautionary expressions of Chief Justice Taney, speaking for the Court in *Ableman v. Booth* and *United States v. Booth*, 21 How. 62 (U.S.) 506 (1856) compelled this course:

> controversies as to the respective powers of the United States and the States, instead of being determined by military and physical force, are heard, investigated, and finally settled, with the calmness and deliberation of judicial inquiry. And no one can fail to see, that if such an arbiter had not been provided, in our complicated system of government, internal tranquillity could not have been preserved; and if such controversies were left in arbitration of physical force, our government, State and National, would soon cease to be Governments of laws, and revolutions by force of arms would take the place of courts of justice and judicial decisions. (pp. 520–21)

I further advised you that review of the Governor's action should be submitted to the District Court, rather than to a three-judge Federal Court. This advice was based particularly upon the decision of the Supreme Court in *Phillips v. United States*, 312 U.S. 246 (1961), wherein it was held that a three-judge court is not the proper forum unless the challenged action of the State Governor was taken under State legislation, the constitutionality of which is attacked. The court declared that where the Governor's action in using the National Guard is attacked, his claim that a State statute authorizes him to call out the National Guard when he deems it necessary does not make the suit one to challenge the statute:

> Some constitutional or statutory provision is the ultimate source of all actions by state officials. But an attack on lawless exercise of authority in a particular case is not an attack upon the constitutionality of the statute conferring the authority even though a misreading of the statute is invoked as justification. (p. 252)

On September 4th, the Federal Court instituted an inquiry to enable it to find out whether additional persons not already parties to the case appeared to be obstructing the court's orders so that they could be joined as defendants in the case. They would then be given an opportunity to appear in court and would have the right to attempt to justify their actions or deny that they were obstructing the court's orders. The court requested the local United States Attorney to undertake such an inquiry and report to the court. Such an investigation was undertaken by the Federal Bureau of Investigation, representing the Department of Justice, and the report was made to the court.

On September 9th, the court requested the United States to enter the case as *amicus curiae* and to file a petition for an injunction against the Governor of Arkansas.[4] I advised you that the court had the power to make this request. In *Universal Oil Co. v. Root Refining Co.*, 328 U.S. 575 (1946) the Supreme Court held that "a federal court can always call on law officers of the United States to serve as *amici*" (p. 561). The Court fixed September 30th as the date of hearing on the issue of the legality of the action of the Governor of Arkansas. The Department of Justice, in compliance with the request of the Court, engaged in preparing for the hearing.

While we were preparing for the hearing, it became increasingly evident that the normal judicial procedure might be inadequate to prevent obstruction of the orders of the Court. The activities of agitators which had commenced after the Governor had placed the National Guard at the school presented a threat of concerted obstruction.

You accordingly asked for advice as to your power and duty as President to aid in the execution of the Court's orders if obstruction should continue after the September 30th hearing and further action by the Court. Between the dates of September 10th and September 24th I gave you the advice which I am now setting forth.

Whenever interference and obstruction to enforcement of law exists, and domestic violence is interposed to frustrate the judicial process, it is the primary and mandatory duty of the authorities of the State to suppress the violence and to remove any obstruction to the orderly enforcement of law. This same duty fully exists where the domestic violence is interposed in opposition to the enforcement of Federal law rather than to the local law of the state. Under Article VI, clause 2 of the Constitution, it is declared:

This Constitution, and the laws of the United States which shall be made in Pursuance thereof; . . . shall be the supreme Law of the Land.

This principle has been recognized as essential to the survival of the Union since the days of Chief Justice Marshall. He stated in *Cohens v. Virginia*, 6 Wheat. 264, 361, that that clause:

is the authoritative language of the American people; and, if gentlemen please, of the American states. It marks, with lines too strong to be mistaken, the characteristic distinction between the government of the Union, and those of the states. The general government, though limited as to its objects, is supreme with respect to those objects. This principle is a part of the Constution; and if there be any who deny its necessity, none can deny its authority.

The supremacy of Federal law is ensured by clause 3 of Article VI providing that:

the Members of the several State Legislatures, and all executive and judicial Officers, both of the United States and of the several States, shall be bound by Oath or Affirmation, to support this constitution.

In discussing this provision Alexander Hamilton stated, in No. 27 of the Federalist:

Thus the legislatures, courts, and magistrates, of the respective members, will be incorporated into the operations of the national government *as far as its just and constitutional authority extends*; and it will be rendered auxiliary to the endorsement of its laws.

In compliance with Article VI, clause 3, the Constitution of Arkansas, like other State constitutions, requires all its judicial and executive officers, both civil and military, to "support the Constitution of the United States." Ark. Const. Art. 19, Sec. 20.

The supremacy of Federal law and the obligation of State officials to support the Federal Constitution find expression in the rule that State courts cannot decline to enforce Federal laws on the theory that they are laws "emanating from a foreign sovereign." *Testa v. Katt*, 330 U.S. 386, 391. The same principle is recognized by State courts in holding that "it is the duty of all officials, whether legislative, judicial, executive, administrative, or ministerial to so perform every official act as not to violate the [Federal] constitutional provisions." *Montgomery v. State*, 55 Fla. 97, 103 (1908). Evidence of recognition of this principle is demonstrated by the further rule that state officers in performing their duties will be presumed to do so in accord with the mandates of Federal supremacy. *Neal v. Delaware*, 103 U.S. 370, 389–90; *Brewer v. Moxie School District*, 236 F.2d 91, 95 (C.A. 8, 1956); *Commonwealth v. Johnson*, 36 Ky, 509, 511 (1880); *Montgomery v. State*, supra, at 107.

The obligation which the Federal Constitution imposes upon State officers to uphold Federal law is in accord with their primary responsibility to maintain order within the State. Acts of violent or forcible resistance to Federal law disrupt peace and order in the State and violate State law. It is the duty of State officers in such circumstances to suppress the disorders in a manner which will not nullify and will permit the effectuation of State and federal law.

When State officers refuse or fail to discharge their duty in this respect, it becomes the responsibility of the national government, through the Chief Executive, to dispel any such forcible resistance to Federal law. Otherwise, lawlessness would be permitted to exist for lack of any counteracting force.

Shortly before the hearings on September 30, the attorneys for Governor Faubus and his codefendants filed an affidavit of bias and prejudice seeking to disqualify Judge Davies. They also filed motions to dismiss the pleadings filed by the United States as *amicus curiae* on the grounds of lack of jurisdiction and failure to convene a three-judge Court, as well as a motion to quash the service of the subpoenas which had been served on the commanding officers of the Arkansas National Guard. At the hearing on September 20, the court heard argument on these motions and denied them. At that point, the attorneys for Governor Faubus and his codefendants announced their petition that the Governor could not be questioned in a United States Court "or anywhere" as to the exercise of his judgment in the performance of a duty under the Constitution and laws of a State. They then requested permission to leave the hearing. They were excused by the court with the explanation that the hearing would proceed notwithstanding their withdrawal.

The Department of Justice then placed witnesses on the stand, including the Mayor of Little Rock, the Chief of Police, and local school authorities. These witnesses gave unchallenged testimony of local peaceful relations among the races in Little Rock for a quarter of a century, including the removal of seating restrictions based upon race in local buses in January 1957, and the absence of any indication that violence or disorder would be present upon the opening of the school term.[5] The attorneys for the Governor and his codefendants remained absent during the taking of the testimony by the court and chose not to take advantage of their right to crossexamine the witnesses, to present evidence on their behalf, and to assist the court in its functions.

After hearing the witnesses, the court announced:

> It is very clear to this Court from the evidence and the testimony adduced upon the hearing today that the plan of integration adopted by the Little Rock School Board and approved by this Court and the Court of Appeals for the Eighth Circuit has been thwarted by the Governor of Arkansas by the use of National Guard troops.
>
> It is equally demonstrable from the testimony here today that there would have been no violence in carrying out the plan of integration and that there has been no violence.

Late on September 20, the Court handed down its decree enjoining the Governor of Arkansas and his National Guard commanders from further interference with the orders of that Court. The Governor thereupon announced that he was withdrawing the National Guard from the school. No stay of enforcements of the Court's order was sought by the Governor or others.

The local authorities of Little Rock announced their intention of maintaining order in support of the decrees of the Court. The test of the ability of these authorities to control the situation came on September 23d. At the opening of the school, a mob of about 1,000 persons assembled. When the Negro children who were entitled to admission to the school arrived, violence broke out. After three hours of riot and tumult, the Negro children were removed from the school by orders of the Mayor and local officials. Mob force had successfully frustrated the carrying out of the orders of the court and had demonstrably overpowered such police forces as could be mustered by local officials. The Governor did not use his power to support the local authorities.

I thereupon advised you that you then had the undoubted power, under the Constitution and laws of the United States, to call the National Guard into service and to use those forces, together with such of the armed forces as you considered necessary, to suppress the domestic violence, obstruction, and resistance of law then and there existing.

I further advised you, and do again advise you, that your power so to act rested upon both your powers as President under the Constitution and the powers vested in you, by the Congress under federal law, particularly as reflected by sections 332 and 333 of Title 10 of the United States Code.

The Supreme Court has recognized the Constitutional power and responsibility which reposes in the national government to compel obedience to law and order. (*Ex parte Siebold*, 100 U.S. 371, 395 [1879]):

> We hold it to be an incontrovertible principle, that the government of the United States may, by means of physical force, exercised through its official agents, execute on every foot of American soil the powers and functions that belong to it. This necessarily involves the power to command obedience to its laws, and hence the power to keep the peace to that extent.

To similar effect was the declaration by the Court in a later case (*In Re Debs*, 158 U.S. 564, 582 [1894]):

> The entire strength of the nation may be used to enforce in any part of the land the full and free exercise of all national powers and the security of all rights entrusted by the Constitution in its care. . . . If the emergency arises, the army of the Nation, and all its militia, are at the service of the Nation to compel obedience to its laws.

In addition to the Constitutional power in the President in such matters, a series of statutes of broad sweep enable the President to deal effectively with civil disturbances within a state when compelling circumstances are present.

By Section 331 of Title 10 of the United States Code, the President may use the State militia and the armed forces of the United States, upon call of the State legislature or of its Governor if the legislature cannot be convened, to put down any insurrection against a State government. This authority was not appropriate for use and was not used in Little Rock.

Under Section 332 of Title 10, the President is vested with similar authority as to the militia and armed forces when, in his judgment, unlawful obstructions, combinations, or assemblages, or rebellion against the authority of the United States make it impracticable to enforce the laws of the United States in any State by the ordinary course of judicial proceedings. A third statute, Section 333 of Title 10, gives the President like powers to suppress in a State any insurrection, domestic violence, unlawful combination, or conspiracy which so hinders the execution of the laws of the State and of the United States that any class of its people is deprived of a right, privilege, immunity, or protection named in the Constitution and secured by law, and the constituted authorities of the State are unable, fail, or refuse to protect the right, privilege, or immunity or to give that protection, or which opposes or obstructs the execution of the laws of the United States or impedes the course of justice under those laws. Congress declared in this statute that when the execution of the laws are so hindered, without State protection, the State shall be considered to have denied the equal protection of the laws secured by the Constitution.

In order that the authority of either of these two sections of the Code may be invoked, it is required that the President first issue a proclamation, as set forth in Section 334 of Title 10. You issued an appropriate proclamation prior to the issuance of Executive Order No. 10730 of September 24, 1957. This Executive order cited, as a basis for the authorized use of federal forces, the Constitution and statutes of the United States, including particularly the above-noted Sections 332 and 333 of Title 10.

As applied to the Little Rock events, I advised you that unlawful obstructions, combinations, or assemblages made it impracticable to enforce the laws of the United States in Little Rock by the ordinary course of judicial proceedings (Sec. 332, Title 10). The facts upon which these conclusions were based were reported to you as they occurred, and included an account of the determined group of hundreds of men and women bent upon overpowering the local peace officers, the several incidents of violence with their very real and discernible trend toward a larger-scale inflammatory assault, the action of the Mayor and local authorities in ordering the withdrawal of the Negro students so as to appease the unruly mob, the admission of local authorities that such peace officers as they could command were unable to cope with the disorderly assemblage, and the indifference or refusal of the Governor of the State to supply a sufficient force to quell the lawless movement.

I also advised you that the local strength of the United States Marshal was insufficient to achieve enforcement of the order of the United States District Court, and that, because of the local situation and the need for timely action, it would not have been reasonable, or effective in the circumstances, to attempt to have the Marshal enlist the support of the citizenry to carry out the court order. In accordance with the salutary policy that the agents of the Federal Bureau of Investigation shall not be used as a national police, you rejected suggestions originating outside the Federal Government that such agents be called upon to enforce the Court's orders.

These facts were still present on the day after issuance of the proclamation. The street mobs reassembled. The Mayor of Little Rock wired you as follows:

THE IMMEDIATE NEED FOR FEDERAL TROOPS IS URGENT. THE MOB IS MUCH LARGER IN NUMBERS AT 8AM THAN AT ANY TIME YESTERDAY PEOPLE ARE CONVERGING ON THE SCENE FROM ALL DIRECTIONS MOB IS ARMED AND ENGAGING IN FISTICUFFS AND OTHER ACTS OF VIOLENCE. SITUATION IS OUT OF CONTROL AND POLICE CANNOT DISPERSE THE MOB I AM PLEADING TO YOU AS PRESIDENT OF THE UNITED STATES IN THE INTEREST OF HUMANITY LAW AND ORDER AND THE CAUSE OF DEMOCRACY WORLD WIDE TO PROVIDE THE NECESSARY FEDERAL TROOPS WITHIN SEVERAL HOURS. ACTION BY YOU WILL RESTORE PEACE AND ORDER AND COMPLIANCE WITH YOUR PROCLAMATION.

Thereupon you ordered the use of United States troops and the federalization of the Arkansas National Guard.

This, in sum, was in my view—and I so advised you—a situation which compelled action by the Chief Executive under provisions of law designed to uphold the strength of law enforcement and the standing and authority of the courts.

I also advised you that the execution of the laws of Arkansas and of the United States within the State of Arkansas was being hindered by unlawful combinations so as to deprive people in that State of a right, privilege, immunity, or protection named in the Constitution and secured by law, and that the appropriate State authorities were unable, unwilling, or failed to protect that right, privilege, immunity, or to give that protection. The requisites of law were met. (Sec. 333, Title 10)

During the course of consideration relative to the use of federal troops, attention also was given to the Posse Comitatus Act (18 U.S.C. Sec. 1385).

In its present form, that Act provides:

Whoever, except in cases and under circumstances expressly authorized by the Constitution or Act of Congress, willfully uses any part of the Army or the Air Force as a posse comitatus or otherwise to execute the laws shall be fined not more than $10,000 or imprisoned not more than two years, or both. This section does not apply in Alaska.

I pointed out to you that the Act, by its specific terms, excepts from its prohibition the use of the Army or Air Force as a posse comitatus or otherwise to execute the law "in cases and under circumstances expressly authorized by the Constitution or Act of Congress." I advised you that your authority to dispatch federal troops to Little Rock would be predicated upon express statutory right (10 U.S.C. Secs. 332, 333) and, therefore, would be within the exception contained in the Posse Comitatus Act.

Although there has been no judicial decision on this question, the advice given you has support in a long line of opinions of past Attorneys General and in executive action.[6] The legislative history surrounding this Act fully supports this view. In brief, it discloses that, at the time the Posse Comitatus Act was enacted, the predecessors to 10 U.S.C. Secs. 332 and 333 were in force and the Congress did not intend or interpret the Act as impairing whatever powers the President had under these statutes. The sponsors of the Posse Comitatus Act expressly so stated during the course of the debates.[7] This was also the view of President Hayes who approved the Posse Comitatus Act. In his diary entry for July 30, 1878, President Hayes wrote:

> The whiskey cases in the South call for wise and firm conduct. No doubt the Government is a good deal crippled in its means of enforcing the laws by the proviso attached to the Army Appropriation Bill which prohibits the use of the army as a posse comitatus to aid United States officers in the execution of process. The states may and do employ state military force to support as a posse comitatus the state civil authorities. If a conflict of jurisdiction occurs between the State and the United States on any question, the United States is thus placed at a great disadvantage. But in the last resort, I am confident that the laws give the Executive ample power to enforce obedience to United States process. The machinery is cumbersome and its exercise will tend to give undue importance to petty attempts to resist or evade the laws. But I must use such machinery as the laws give.
>
> Without passion or haste, the enforcement of the laws must go on. If the sheriffs or other state officers resist the laws, and by the aid of state militia do it successfully, that is a case of rebellion to be dealt with under the laws framed to enable the Executive to subdue combi-

nations or conspiracies too powerful to be suppressed by the ordinary civil officers of the United States. This involves proclamations, the movement of United States land and naval forces, and possibly the calling out of volunteers, and this looks like war. It is like the Whiskey Rebellion in the time of Washington. That precedent, if the case demands it, will be followed. Good citizens who wish to avoid such a result must see to it that neither their State Governments nor mobs undertake to prevent United States officers from enforcing the laws. My duty is plain. The laws must be enforced.[8]

There are in any event grave doubts as to the authority of the Congress to limit the constitutional powers of the President to enforce the laws and preserve the peace under circumstances which he deems appropriate. However, that consideration was not reached because of the express congressional authority for the action taken.

Finally, much of what the Supreme Court said in the *Debs* case has special and peculiar relevance to the Little Rock situation. There a Federal District Court issued a sweeping order enjoining strikers in the Pullman company riots at Chicago in 1894. When the mobs continued their lawless course, Federal troops, both regular and National Guardsmen, were dispatched to the city and actively intervened to restore order. In reviewing this situation, the Supreme Court pointed out that what had happened at Chicago transcended municipal boundaries (158 U.S. 592):

> That the bill filed in this case alleged special facts calling for the exercise of all the powers of the court is not open to question. The picture drawn in it of the vast interests involved, not merely of the city of Chicago and the State of Illinois, but of all the States, and the general confusion into which the interstate commerce of the country was thrown; the forcible intervention with that commerce; the attempted exercise by individuals of powers belonging only to government, and the threatened continuance of such invasions of public right, presented a condition of affairs which called for the fullest exercise of all the powers of the courts. If ever there was a special exigency, one which demanded that the court should do all that courts can do, it was disclosed by this bill, and we need not turn to the public history of the day, which only reaffirms with clearest emphasis all its allegations.

In Little Rock, the "vast interests involved" also reached beyond the confines of that one city and, as publicly stated by you and the Secretary of State, vitally affected our country's international relations. When an unruly mob arrogates to itself the power to nullify a constitutionally-assured right, a statutory prescription, and a court order, it may reasonably be assumed that the danger of a fast-moving, destructive volcanic force is immediately present. Success of the unlawful assemblage in Little Rock inevitably would have led to mob rule, and a probable breakdown of law and order in an ever-increasing area. When a local and State government is unable or unwilling to meet such a threat, the Federal Government is not impotent.

The foregoing reflects the more significant aspects of my advice on the legal aspects of the events at Little Rock. I call your attention to the fact that a proceeding is presently pending before the United States Court of Appeals for the Eighth Circuit which may embrace consideration of some of the matters here presented.

Respectfully,

/s/ Herbert Brownell, Jr.
Attorney General

NOTES

1. Quite aside from this litigation and because of accumulating backlog of cases and without knowledge of the Justice Department, Chief Judge Archibald K. Gardner of the Eighth Circuit had assigned Federal Judge Davies to sit in the Little Rock district; and Judge Miller who had handled the desegregation litigation up to this point requested Chief Judge Gardner to transfer it to Judge Davies. Chief Judge Gardner granted this request. Although the date "August 15, 1956," the date of the trial, is specified in the above-described court order, the decree and judgment of the court filed on April 28, 1956, is dated August 28, 1956.

2. Powers Mercantile Co. v. Olson, 7 Fed. Supp. 865 (D.C. Minn. 1934); Strutwear Knitting Co. v. Olson, 13 Fed. 384 (D.C. Minn. 1936); United States v. Phillips, 33 Fed. Supp. 261 (D.C. N.D. Okla. 1940), rev. on other grounds *sub nom.* Phillips v. United States, 312 U.S. 246 (1941).

3. The only case in which a Governor's action in restricting private rights to restore order was upheld was one in which the military forces of the State had endeavored to suppress riots and violence arising out of strikes of truck drivers. These forces were so employed intermittently over a period of more than two months, during which four men were killed and many wounded, and

food became scarce. The Governor ultimately placed an embargo on movement of the trucks owned by the plaintiffs. An injunction against the Governor was denied by the court in this instance. Powers Mercantile Co. v. Olson, 7 Fed. Supp. 865 (D.C. Minn. 1934).

4. The court also requested that such injunction petition name the Governor of Arkansas, the Adjutant General of the State, and the Unit Commander of the Arkansas National Guard as parties to the case, and requested the United States to give the court the benefit of its views and recommendations, and, under direction of the court, to initiate such further proceedings as might be appropriate.

5. The President of the Little Rock School Board and the Superintendent of Schools explained the considerable effort made to explain the proposed school plan, after its formulation in May 1955, and the community willingness to accept it. The Mayor and the Chief of Police testified to their planning for any eventuality of violence which might develop upon the opening of Central High School; that they did not anticipate violence, based upon many years of experience in viewing local race relationships; that the Governor at no time asked for a report from the police as to the local situation; and that the local plans for maintaining peace and order were, in their judgment, reasonable and calculated to dispel any disturbances which might arise. These plans included a possible request to the Governor for use of the National Guard if need arose, but no such request was ever made by any civil authority of Little Rock.

6. 16 Op. A.G. 162, 164 (1878); 17 Op. A.G. 242 (1881); 17 Op. A.G. 333, 335 (1882); 19 Op. A.G. 293, 296 (1889); 19 Op. A.G. 570, 571 (1890). An account of the action of President Cleveland in reference to the Pullman strike in 1894 and that of President Wilson in connection with unlawful assemblages in Arkansas in 1914 is set forth in *Federal Aid in Domestic Disturbances*, Sen Doc. No. 263, 67th Cong., 2d Sess., pp. 197, 321; Sen. Exec. Doc. No. 7, 53d Cong., 3d Sess., p. xx.

7. The predecessors of 10 U.S.C. 332 and 333 were part of Title 69 of the Revised Statutes of 1873 when the Posse Comitatus Act was enacted. The sponsors of the legislation were aware of Title 69 and stated that the new legislation would not affect the powers contained in that Title. 7 Cong. Rec. 3646, 4243. Congressman Knott, who introduced the provision, said:

This amendment expressly excepts those cases and those circumstances in which troops are now authorized by any act of Congress to be employed in the enforcement of said law. (ibid., 3847)

There are, as I have already remarked, particular cases in which Congress has provided that the Army may be used, which this bill does not militate against, such as the case of the enforcement of the neutrality laws, the enforcement of the collection of customs duties and of the civil-rights bill, and one or two other instances. But this amendment is designed to put a stop to the practice, which has become fearfully common, of military officers of every grade answering the call of every marshal and deputy marshal to aid in the enforcement of the laws. (ibid., 3649)

Senator Beck, a supporter of the provision, stated with respect to the use of troops to enforce the laws: "Wherever the law authorizes it, it is admitted to be right."

8. *Diary and Letters of Rutherford Birchard Hayes* (1929), 3:492-93.

Appendix E

Twenty-fifth Amendment to the

Constitution of the United States

❖   ❖   ❖   ❖   ❖   ❖   ❖

SECTION 1. In case of the removal of the President from office or of his death or resignation, the Vice President shall become President.

SECTION 2. Whenever there is a vacancy in the office of the Vice President, the President shall nominate a Vice President who shall take office upon confirmation by a majority vote of both houses of Congress.

SECTION 3. Whenever the President transmits to the President pro tempore of the Senate and the Speaker of the House of Representatives his written declaration that he is unable to discharge the powers and duties of his office, and until he transmits to them a written declaration to the contrary, such powers and duties shall be discharged by the Vice President as Acting President.

SECTION 4. Whenever the Vice President and a majority of either the principal officers of the executive departments or of such other body as Congress may by law provide, transmit to the President pro tempore of the Senate and the Speaker of the House of Representatives their written declaration that the President is unable to discharge the powers and duties of his office, the Vice President shall immediately assume the powers and duties of the office as Acting President.

Thereafter, when the President transmits to the President pro tempore of the Senate and the Speaker of the House of Representatives his written declaration that no inability exists, he shall resume the powers and duties of his office unless the Vice President and a majority of either the principal officers of the executive department or of such other body as Congress may by law provide, transmit within four days to the President pro tempore of the Senate and the Speaker of the House of Representatives their written declaration that the President is unable to discharge the powers and duties of his office. Thereupon Congress shall decide the issue, assembling within forty-eight hours for that purpose if not in session. If the Congress within twenty-one days after receipt of the latter written declaration, or, if Congress is not in session within twenty-one days after Congress is required to assemble, determines by two-thirds vote of both houses that the President is unable to discharge the powers and duties of his office, the Vice President shall continue to discharge the same as Acting President; otherwise, the President shall resume the powers and duties of his office.

Note: Ratification completed February 10, 1967.

Index